COMPUTER BOOK SERIES FROM IDG

Delphi™ 3 For Dummies®

Cheat

G000078367

A Field Guide to Delphi Component Properties

Property Type	Symbol before Name	Symbol after Value	Example Property	Example Value
Exploding Object	+	···	TForm.Font	(TFont)
List		▼	TForm.Cursor	crDefault
Numeric			TForm.Left	123
Object		···	TForm.Icon	(TIcon)
Set	+		TForm.BorderIcons	[biSystemMenu]
String-list		···	TMemo.Lines	(TStrings)
True/False		▼	TForm.Enabled	True
"Anything goes"			TForm.Caption	Whatever!

Amazing Secret Editor Keys

Key Combination	Effect
Ctrl+O, C	Enter column-marking mode
Ctrl+O, K	Leave column-marking mode
Alt+Shift+Arrow	Mark a rectangular column of text
Ctrl+K, I	Indent marked block
Ctrl+K, U	Un-indent marked block
Ctrl+K, N	Convert marked block to uppercase
Ctrl+K, O	Convert marked block to lowercase
Ctrl+O, U	Toggle marked block's case; e.g. *Up* becomes *uP*
Ctrl+K, F	Convert word at cursor to uppercase
Ctrl+K, E	Convert word at cursor to lowercase
Ctrl+E	Start incremental text search
Alt+[	Search for the closing parenthesis, bracket, or brace matching the opening parenthesis, bracket, or brace at the cursor (forward search)
Alt+]	Search for the opening parenthesis, bracket, or brace matching the closing parenthesis, bracket, or brace at the cursor (backward search)

...For Dummies: #1 Computer Book Series for Beginners

...FOR DUMMIES
COMPUTER
BOOK SERIES
FROM IDG

Delphi™ 3 For Dummies®

Cheat Sheet

Essential Data Types

Type	Data Represented
LongInt	A whole number (no fractional part)
Extended	A number that may have a fractional part
Boolean	A True or False value
Char	One character, such as *A*
String	A string of characters, such as *'Delphi'*
PChar	A character string for use with a Windows API function

Essential System Events for Forms

Event	Occasion	Usual Response
OnActivate	The form has just become the program's active window	Update any information displayed in the form
OnClose	OnCloseQuery already happened, and the form is being shut down	Last chance to refuse to shut down
OnCloseQuery	Windows asks the form whether it's willing to shut down	Prompt the user to save changed data, or *refuse* to shut down
OnCreate	The form is created	Perform any necessary initialization
OnDeactivate	The form has just stopped being the program's active window	Undo any actions taken in the OnActivate event handler
OnDestroy	The form is about to disappear for good	Clean up any resources the program allocated
OnPaint	The form needs to be redisplayed	Draw lines or other simple graphics directly on the form
OnResize	The form has been resized	Adjust the size or position of components

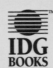

...For Dummies: #1 Computer Book Series for Beginners

References for the Rest of Us!®

COMPUTER BOOK SERIES FROM IDG

Are you intimidated and confused by computers? Do you find that traditional manuals are overloaded with technical details you'll never use? Do your friends and family always call you to fix simple problems on their PCs? Then the *...For Dummies*® computer book series from IDG Books Worldwide is for you.

...For Dummies books are written for those frustrated computer users who know they aren't really dumb but find that PC hardware, software, and indeed the unique vocabulary of computing make them feel helpless. *...For Dummies* books use a lighthearted approach, a down-to-earth style, and even cartoons and humorous icons to diffuse computer novices' fears and build their confidence. Lighthearted but not lightweight, these books are a perfect survival guide for anyone forced to use a computer.

"I like my copy so much I told friends; now they bought copies."

Irene C., Orwell, Ohio

"Quick, concise, nontechnical, and humorous."

Jay A., Elburn, Illinois

"Thanks, I needed this book. Now I can sleep at night."

Robin F., British Columbia, Canada

Already, hundreds of thousands of satisfied readers agree. They have made *...For Dummies* books the #1 introductory level computer book series and have written asking for more. So, if you're looking for the most fun and easy way to learn about computers, look to *...For Dummies* books to give you a helping hand.

IDG BOOKS WORLDWIDE™

7/96r

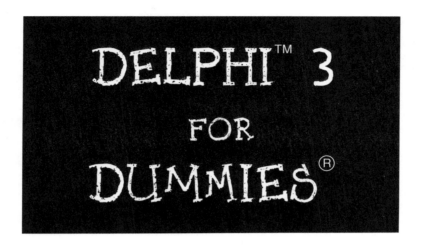

by Neil J. Rubenking

IDG Books Worldwide, Inc.
An International Data Group Company

Foster City, CA ♦ Chicago, IL ♦ Indianapolis, IN ♦ Southlake, TX

Delphi™ 3 For Dummies®

Published by
IDG Books Worldwide, Inc.
An International Data Group Company
919 E. Hillsdale Blvd.
Suite 400
Foster City, CA 94404
http://www.idgbooks.com (IDG Books Worldwide Web site)
http://www.dummies.com (Dummies Press Web site)

Library of Congress Catalog Card No.: 97-70740

ISBN: 0-7645-0179-8

Printed in the United States of America

10 9 8 7 6 5 4 3 2 1

1E/SS/QV/ZX/IN

Distributed in the United States by IDG Books Worldwide, Inc.

Distributed by Macmillan Canada for Canada; by Transworld Publishers Limited in the United Kingdom and Europe; by WoodsLane Pty. Ltd. for Australia; by WoodsLane Enterprises Ltd. for New Zealand; by Longman Singapore Publishers Ltd. for Singapore, Malaysia, Thailand, and Indonesia; by Simron Pty. Ltd. for South Africa; by Toppan Company Ltd. for Japan; by Distribuidora Cuspide for Argentina; by Livraria Cultura for Brazil; by Ediciencia S.A. for Ecuador; by Addison-Wesley Publishing Company for Korea; by Ediciones ZETA S.C.R. Ltda. for Peru; by WS Computer Publishing Company, Inc., for the Philippines; by Unalis Corporation for Taiwan; by Contemporanea de Ediciones for Venezuela. Authorized Sales Agent: Anthony Rudkin Associates for the Middle East and North Africa.

For general information on IDG Books Worldwide's books in the U.S., please call our Consumer Customer Service department at 800-762-2974. For reseller information, including discounts and premium sales, please call our Reseller Customer Service department at 800-434-3422.

For information on where to purchase IDG Books Worldwide's books outside the U.S., please contact our International Sales department at 415-655-3023 or fax 415-655-3299.

For information on foreign language translations, please contact our Foreign & Subsidiary Rights department at 415-655-3021 or fax 415-655-3281.

For sales inquiries and special prices for bulk quantities, please contact our Sales department at 415-655-3200 or write to the address above.

For information on using IDG Books Worldwide's books in the classroom or for ordering examination copies, please contact our Educational Sales department at 800-434-2086 or fax 817-251-8174.

For press review copies, author interviews, or other publicity information, please contact our Public Relations department at 415-655-3000 or fax 415-655-3299.

For authorization to photocopy items for corporate, personal, or educational use, please contact Copyright Clearance Center, 222 Rosewood Drive, Danvers, MA 01923, or fax 508-750-4470.

is a trademark under exclusive license to IDG Books Worldwide, Inc., from International Data Group, Inc.

About the Author

Neil Rubenking came to California to seek enlightenment, but got distracted along the way. Someone had to placate the tutelary deities of the Zen Master's brand-new IBM PC. Because he was too slow running from the office, he served as vice president and president of the San Francisco PC User Group for three years.

In 1986, *PC Magazine* brought Neil on board to handle the torrent of Turbo Pascal tips submitted by readers. By 1990, he had become *PC Magazine's* technical editor and a coast-to-coast telecommuter. His "User-to-User" column showcases tips from readers on using DOS and Windows. Between editing articles and writing *PC Magazine* utilities in Pascal, Visual Basic, and Delphi, Neil has found time to write *Delphi Programming Problem Solver* (a book of solutions for problems in Delphi 1.0 and 2.0) and five other books covering Turbo Pascal, Windows, and DOS. (Batch files rule!)

In his occasional free moments, Neil likes to play with his children and read cheap fiction.

ABOUT IDG BOOKS WORLDWIDE

Welcome to the world of IDG Books Worldwide.

IDG Books Worldwide, Inc., is a subsidiary of International Data Group, the world's largest publisher of computer-related information and the leading global provider of information services on information technology. IDG was founded more than 25 years ago and now employs more than 8,500 people worldwide. IDG publishes more than 275 computer publications in over 75 countries (see listing below). More than 60 million people read one or more IDG publications each month.

Launched in 1990, IDG Books Worldwide is today the #1 publisher of best-selling computer books in the United States. We are proud to have received eight awards from the Computer Press Association in recognition of editorial excellence and three from *Computer Currents'* First Annual Readers' Choice Awards. Our best-selling *...For Dummies®* series has more than 30 million copies in print with translations in 30 languages. IDG Books Worldwide, through a joint venture with IDG's Hi-Tech Beijing, became the first U.S. publisher to publish a computer book in the People's Republic of China. In record time, IDG Books Worldwide has become the first choice for millions of readers around the world who want to learn how to better manage their businesses.

Our mission is simple: Every one of our books is designed to bring extra value and skill-building instructions to the reader. Our books are written by experts who understand and care about our readers. The knowledge base of our editorial staff comes from years of experience in publishing, education, and journalism — experience we use to produce books for the '90s. In short, we care about books, so we attract the best people. We devote special attention to details such as audience, interior design, use of icons, and illustrations. And because we use an efficient process of authoring, editing, and desktop publishing our books electronically, we can spend more time ensuring superior content and spend less time on the technicalities of making books.

You can count on our commitment to deliver high-quality books at competitive prices on topics you want to read about. At IDG Books Worldwide, we continue in the IDG tradition of delivering quality for more than 25 years. You'll find no better book on a subject than one from IDG Books Worldwide.

John Kilcullen
CEO
IDG Books Worldwide, Inc.

Steven Berkowitz
President and Publisher
IDG Books Worldwide, Inc.

Eighth Annual Computer Press Awards ≥1992

Ninth Annual Computer Press Awards ≥1993

Tenth Annual Computer Press Awards ≥1994

Eleventh Annual Computer Press Awards ≥1995

IDG Books Worldwide, Inc., is a subsidiary of International Data Group, the world's largest publisher of computer-related information and the leading global provider of information services on information technology. International Data Group publishes over 275 computer publications in over 75 countries. Sixty million people read one or more International Data Group publications each month. International Data Group's publications include: **ARGENTINA:** Buyer's Guide, Computerworld Argentina, PC World Argentina; **AUSTRALIA:** Australian Macworld, Australian PC World, Australian Reseller News, Computerworld, IT Casebook, Network World, Publish, Webmaster; **AUSTRIA:** Computerwelt Osterreich, Networks Austria, PC Tip Austria; **BANGLADESH:** PC World Bangladesh; **BELARUS:** PC World Belarus; **BELGIUM:** Data News; **BRAZIL:** Annuário de Informática, Computerworld, Connections, Macworld, PC Player, PC World, Publish, Reseller News, Supergamepower; **BULGARIA:** Computerworld Bulgaria, Network World Bulgaria, PC & MacWorld Bulgaria; **CANADA:** CIO Canada, Client/Server World, ComputerWorld Canada, InfoWorld Canada, NetworkWorld Canada, WebWorld; **CHILE:** Computerworld Chile, PC World Chile; **COLOMBIA:** Computerworld Colombia, PC World Colombia; **COSTA RICA:** PC World Centro America; **THE CZECH AND SLOVAK REPUBLICS:** Computerworld Czechoslovakia, Macworld Czech Republic, PC World Czechoslovakia; **DENMARK:** Communications World Danmark, Computerworld Danmark, Macworld Danmark, PC World Danmark, Techworld Denmark; **DOMINICAN REPUBLIC:** PC World Republica Dominicana; **ECUADOR:** PC World Ecuador; **EGYPT:** Computerworld Middle East, PC World Middle East; **EL SALVADOR:** PC World Centro America; **FINLAND:** MikroPC, Tietoverkko, Tietoviikko; **FRANCE:** Distributique, Hebdo, Info PC, Le Monde Informatique, Macworld, Reseaux & Telecoms, WebMaster France; **GERMANY:** Computer Partner, Computerwoche, Computerwoche Extra, Computerwoche FOCUS, Global Online, Macwelt, PC Welt; **GREECE:** Amiga Computing, GamePro Greece, Multimedia World; **GUATEMALA:** PC World Centro America; **HONDURAS:** PC World Centro America; **HONG KONG:** Computerworld Hong Kong, PC World Hong Kong, Publish in Asia; **HUNGARY:** ABCD CD-ROM, Computerworld Szamitastechnika, Internetto online Magazine, PC World Hungary, PC-X Magazin Hungary; **ICELAND:** Tolvuheimur PC World Island; **INDIA:** Information Communications World, Information Systems Computerworld, PC World India, Publish in Asia; **INDONESIA:** InfoKomputer PC World, Komputek Computerworld, Publish in Asia; **IRELAND:** ComputerScope, PC Live!; **ISRAEL:** Macworld Israel, People & Computers/Computerworld; **ITALY:** Computerworld Italia, Macworld Italia, Networking Italia, PC World Italia; **JAPAN:** DTP World, Macworld Japan, Nikkei Personal Computing, OS/2 World Japan, SunWorld Japan, Windows NT World, Windows World Japan; **KENYA:** PC World East African; **KOREA:** Hi-Tech Information, Macworld Korea, PC World Korea; **MACEDONIA:** PC World Macedonia; **MALAYSIA:** Computerworld Malaysia, PC World Malaysia, Publish in Asia; **MALTA:** PC World Malta; **MEXICO:** Computerworld Mexico, PC World Mexico; **MYANMAR:** PC World Myanmar; **NETHERLANDS:** Computer! Totaal, LAN Internetworking Magazine, LAN World Buyers Guide, Macworld Netherlands, Net, WebWereld; **NEW ZEALAND:** Absolute Beginners Guide and Plain & Simple Series, Computer Buyer, Computer Industry Directory, Computerworld New Zealand, MTB, Network World, PC World New Zealand; **NICARAGUA:** PC World Centro America; **NORWAY:** Computerworld Norge, CW Rapport, Datamagasinet, Financial Rapport, Kursguide Norge, Macworld Norge, Multimediaworld Norge, PC World Ekspress Norge, PC World Nettverk, PC World Norge, PC World ProduktGuide Norge; **PAKISTAN:** Computerworld Pakistan; **PANAMA:** PC World Panama; **PEOPLE'S REPUBLIC OF CHINA:** China Computer Users, China Computerworld, China InfoWorld, China Telecom World Weekly, Computer & Communication, Electronic Design China, Electronics Today, Electronics Weekly, Game Software, PC World China, Popular Computer Week, Software Weekly, Software World, Telecom World; **PERU:** Computerworld Peru, PC World Profesional Peru, PC World SoHo Peru; **PHILIPPINES:** Click!, Computerworld Philippines, PC World Philippines, Publish in Asia; **POLAND:** Computerworld Poland, Computerworld Special Report Poland, Cyber, Macworld Poland, Networld Poland, PC World Komputer; **PORTUGAL:** Cerebro/PC World, Computerworld/Correio Informático, Dealer World Portugal, Mac*In/PC*In Portugal, Multimedia World; **PUERTO RICO:** PC World Puerto Rico; **ROMANIA:** Computerworld Romania, PC World Romania, Telecom Romania; **RUSSIA:** Computerworld Russia, Mir PK, Publish, Seti; **SINGAPORE:** Computerworld Singapore, PC World Singapore, Publish in Asia; **SLOVENIA:** Monitor; **SOUTH AFRICA:** Computing SA, Network World SA, Software World SA; **SPAIN:** Comunicaciones World España, Computerworld España, Dealer World España, Macworld España, PC World España; **SRI LANKA:** Infolink PC World; **SWEDEN:** CAP&Design, Computer Sweden, Corporate Computing Sweden, Internetworld Sweden, it.branschen, Macworld Sweden, MaxiData Sweden, MikroDatorn, Nätverk & Kommunikation, PC World Sweden, PCaktiv, Windows World Sweden; **SWITZERLAND:** Computerworld Schweiz, Macworld Schweiz, PCtip; **TAIWAN:** Computerworld Taiwan, Macworld Taiwan, NEW VISION/Publish, PC World Taiwan, Windows World Taiwan; **THAILAND:** Publish in Asia, Thai Computerworld; **TURKEY:** Computerworld Turkiye, Macworld Turkiye, Network World Turkiye, PC World Turkiye; **UKRAINE:** Computerworld Kiev, Multimedia World Ukraine, PC World Ukraine; **UNITED KINGDOM:** Acorn User UK, Amiga Action UK, Amiga Computing UK, Apple Talk UK, Computing, Macworld, Parents and Computers UK, PC Advisor, PC Home, PSX Pro, The WEB; **UNITED STATES:** Cable in the Classroom, CIO Magazine, Computerworld, DOS World, Federal Computer Week, GamePro Magazine, InfoWorld, I-Way, Macworld, Network World, PC Games, PC World, Publish, Video Event, THE WEB Magazine, and WebMaster; online webzines: JavaWorld, NetscapeWorld, and SunWorld Online; **URUGUAY:** InfoWorld Uruguay; **VENEZUELA:** Computerworld Venezuela, PC World Venezuela; and **VIETNAM:** PC World Vietnam.
3/24/97

Dedication

To my family — you all helped!

Acknowledgments

During the writing of this book's first edition, Borland's Delphi development team put up with a lot of bother from me. Each time a new field-test version appeared, I revised the growing book and plagued the team with old and new questions. I'd like to thank the entire team — and especially Danny Thorpe — who gave the first edition of this book a most thorough technical review.

Janet, my wife, deserves a medal for never once complaining about how this book and our son were due to be "born" at almost precisely the same time. A medal? Make it a halo! My daughter Sophie and stepdaughter Katherine showed admirable restraint, leaving me free to work even when I wished for an interruption — thanks, kids!

Incidentally, baby John, the youngster who shares his birthday with Delphi's, is walking, talking, running, climbing bookcases, and programming in Delphi. Well, perhaps he's not programming *yet,* but he will be soon. And that's not just fatherly pride. Honest!

Major kudos to Namir Shammas for his efforts in revising this book for the third edition. Namir's texts on Delphi's uses on the Web (Chapter 16) and Delphi and ActiveX (Chapter 17) were wonderful additions to this book. Thanks so much, Namir. Your work is greatly appreciated.

Special thanks go to Trudy Neuhaus, my old friend and editor, for convincing me to write this book. Writing a book, even an enjoyable book such as this one, is a painful process; my appreciation to all the folks at IDG for easing the pain.

And of course, thanks to all of you who bought the first and/or second editions of this book. I'm especially grateful to those of you who sent me e-mail with your questions and problems. Cogitating on those conundrums inspired me to write *Delphi Programming Problem Solver,* which is also published by IDG Books Worldwide, Inc. Thanks!

Publisher's Acknowledgments

We're proud of this book; please send us your comments about it by using the Reader Response Card at the back of the book or by e-mailing us at feedback/dummies@idgbooks.com. Some of the people who helped bring this book to market include the following:

Acquisitions, Development, and Editorial

Project Editor: Robert H. Wallace

Acquisitions Editor: Michael Kelly

Product Development Director: Mary Bednarek

Associate Permissions Editor: Heather H. Dismore

Copy Editors: Suzanne Packer, Clark Sheffy, William A. Barton

Technical Editor: Jeff Bankston

Editorial Manager: Leah P. Cameron

Editorial Assistants: Chris H. Collins and Michael D. Sullivan

Production

Project Coordinator: Debbie Stailey

Layout and Graphics: Brett Black, Cameron Booker, Angela F. Hunckler, Todd Klemme, Brent Savage, Kate Snell

Proofreaders: Christine D. Berman, Joel K. Draper, Rachel Garvey, Robert Springer, Karen York

Indexer: Richard S. Shrout

Special Help: Joe Jansen, Senior Copy Editor; Joyce Pepple, Media Development Manager; Richard Graves, Editorial Executive Assistant

General and Administrative

IDG Books Worldwide, Inc.: John Kilcullen, CEO; Steven Berkowitz, President and Publisher

IDG Books Technology Publishing: Brenda McLaughlin, Senior Vice President and Group Publisher

Dummies Technology Press and Dummies Editorial: Diane Graves Steele, Vice President and Associate Publisher; Judith A. Taylor, Brand Manager; Kristin A. Cocks, Editorial Director

Dummies Trade Press: Kathleen A. Welton, Vice President and Publisher; Stacy S. Collins, Brand Manager

IDG Books Production for Dummies Press: Beth Jenkins, Production Director; Cindy L. Phipps, Supervisor of Project Coordination, Production Proofreading, and Indexing; Kathie S. Schutte, Supervisor of Page Layout; Shelley Lea, Supervisor of Graphics and Design; Debbie J. Gates, Production Systems Specialist; Tony Augsburger, Supervisor of Reprints and Bluelines; Leslie Popplewell, Media Archive Coordinator

Dummies Packaging and Book Design: Patti Sandez, Packaging Specialist; Lance Kayser, Packaging Assistant; Kavish + Kavish, Cover Design

◆

The publisher would like to give special thanks to Patrick J. McGovern, without whom this book would not have been possible.

◆

Contents at a Glance

Introduction **1**

Part I: Getting Started **7**
Chapter 1: Meet Delphi 9
Chapter 2: Programming in Good Form 25

Part II: Programming with Components **45**
Chapter 3: Hooking Up Components 47
Chapter 4: Standard Components 67
Chapter 5: A Dialog with Windows 89
Chapter 6: What's on the Menu? 109

Part III: More Components **125**
Chapter 7: Look-and-Feel Components 127
Chapter 8: Additional Components 149
Chapter 9: Advanced Additional Components 173
Chapter 10: File Components 203
Chapter 11: Database Components 221

Part IV: Real Programming **253**
Chapter 12: Windows 95 Components 255
Chapter 13: Learn Programming from the Master 285
Chapter 14: Elements of Programming 301
Chapter 15: Debugging 329
Chapter 16: Working with Internet Components 343
Chapter 17: Handling RadioActive(X) Materials 353

Part V: The Part of Tens **365**
Chapter 18: Ten Common Mistakes 367
Chapter 19: Ten Windows API Functions 381
Chapter 20: Ten Fabulous Function Families 399

Index **411**

IDG Books Worldwide Registration Card .... *Back of Book*

Cartoons at a Glance

By Rich Tennant • Fax: 508-546-7747 • E-mail: the5wave@tiac.net

page 125

page 365

page 253

page 45

page 7

Table of Contents

Introduction *1*

   About This Book 1
   Who Are You? 1
   Why Delphi? 2
   How to Use This Book 3
   What Not to Read 4
   How This Book Is Organized 4
      Part I: Getting Started 5
      Part II: Programming with Components 5
      Part III: More Components 5
      Part IV: Real Programming 6
      Part V: The Part of Tens 6
   Icons Used in This Book 6
   Where to Go from Here 6

Part I: Getting Started *7*

Chapter 1: Meet Delphi **9**

   Installing Delphi 9
   Which Delphi? 10
   Don't Program without a Safety Net! 10
      Setting compiler options for safety 10
      Setting preferences for safety 14
   Delphi All Over the Screen 15
      It's all happening at the Form window 16
      Detailing with the Object Inspector window 16
      Instant program — the Code Editor 17
      Take action with the Main window 18
         Selecting from the menu 19
         SpeedBar buttons 19
         The Component palette 20
   Your First Program RIGHT NOW! 21
   An Embarrassment of Windows 23

Chapter 2: Programming in Good Form 25

Blueprint for a Program 25
Making a FORMal Inspection 26
  Tweaking visible properties 27
  That's about the size of it 30
  Delayed gratification 31
  Form families—the Multiple Document Interface 34
A Field Guide to Properties 36
The Main Events 37
  Mouse events 38
  Keyboard events 40
  System events 41

Part II: Programming with Components *45*

Chapter 3: Hooking Up Components 47

The Component Palette 47
Placing Components 49
  Placing, moving, and resizing a single component 49
  Nonvisible components 50
  Scientists announce cloning breakthrough! 50
  Selecting multiple components 51
  One size fits all 52
  Putting your ducks in a row 53
  Enforcing component conformity 54
Common Component Properties 55
  A rose by any other caption 55
  Color me beautiful 56
  That's about the size of it 57
  Behind the scenes 57
Common Events 60
  Mouse events 61
  Drag-and-drop events 61
  Keyboard events 63
  System events 63
  Special events 64
Entering the Fourth Dimension 64

Chapter 4: Standard Components 67

Choosing Standard Components 68
You're Pushing My Buttons! 69
  Properties 69
  Events 70

Join the In Group 71
Punching Radio Buttons 72
    Properties 72
    Events 73
Checking Off Your Options 74
Pinning Labels on Components 74
Fill in the Blank in an Edit Box 75
    Properties 76
    Events 77
Take a Memo 80
I've Got a Little List 81
    Properties 81
    Events 84
A Two-Player Combo (Box) 85
Belly Up to the (Scroll) Bar 86
    Properties 86
    Events 87

Chapter 5: A Dialog with Windows **89**
Common Habits of Common Dialogs 89
Opening Data Files 90
    Properties 90
    Options that affect the display 92
    Options that affect what you can do 92
    Other options 93
Brother, Is Your Data Saved? 94
    Properties 94
    Build a simple text editor 94
Taking Advantage of Windows Fonts 97
    Properties 97
    Options that affect screen elements 98
    Options that affect which fonts are available 98
    Events 99
A Rainbow of Color Dialog 100
Calling on Windows to Configure Printers 102
Preparing to Print 103
Searching for Text in All the Right Places 105
    Properties 105
    Events 106
Making Replacements 106

Chapter 6: What's on the Menu? **109**
Preparing a Tasty Menu 109
    The main menu component 109
    Menu item components 110

Standard Menu Templates 114
    File menu 115
    Edit menu 115
    Help menu 116
    Beautify the simple text editor 117
Pop-Up Menus 119
Caution: Merging Menus 122
    On-again off-again merging 123
    Multiple-choice merging 123

Part III: More Components 125

Chapter 7: Look-and-Feel Components 127

Choosing Look-and-Feel Components 127
Get into Shape by Using Shapes 128
    Properties 128
    Events 129
Paint Any Shape You Like 133
Color Control with Color Grid 137
    Properties 137
    Events 137
Image Is Everything 138
    Properties 138
    Events 139
Gauging Your Progress 140
Introducing Our Panel 142
    Properties 142
    Events 144
    Status symbols 145
    A template with status 146
    Bumpy and dippy forms 147
Controlling Scrolling 148

Chapter 8: Additional Components 149

Choosing Additional Components 149
Wake Up with a Timer Component 150
    Properties and events 151
    Locks again 152
Putting the Best Spin on Things 153
    Properties 153
    Events 154
    Delphi as artiste 154
    Organizing the vertically challenged 156
Who Was That Masked Edit Box? 157

Compositions in a Tabbed Notebook 159
Gluing Tabs on a Notebook 161
    Properties 161
    Events 162
Using Your Header 164
    Properties 164
    Events 165
Brighten Forms with Bitmap Buttons 166
Get Up to Speed with Speed Buttons 168
    Properties 168
    Events 171

Chapter 9: Advanced Additional Components 173
Choosing Additional Components 173
The Media Player Is the Message 174
    Properties 174
    Events 175
    Join the audio-visual club 175
    Turn your PC into a boom box 178
Let Me Outline My Plan. 181
    Properties 181
    Sneak a peek at INI files 182
    Events 185
Cookin' with the Draw Grid(dle) 186
    Properties 186
    Events 187
Super Lists in a String Grid 189
    Properties and events 189
    Here I go gathering icons in May 190
I'll Check My Calendar 194
¡OLE! ¡OLE! ¡OLE! 196
    Rev-OLE-ution version number 2.0 197
    Saving embedded objects to disk 200

Chapter 10: File Components 203
Choosing File Components 204
Flipping through the File List 204
    Properties 204
    Events 205
Directory Assistance 209
A Combo Box with Real Drive 210
Filter Your Files with a Combo Box 213
More Directory Assistance 216
    Properties and events 216
Steal This Bitmap! 217

Chapter 11: Database Components **221**

Walk the Walk, Talk the Talk 222
Nurture Your Relationships 223
Get Help from the Expert 224
DataBasics 227
Lay your cards on the table 227
Get your data from the source 229
Instant view with a data grid 229
Control columns for gorgeous grids 231
The great navigator 234
Build a Database Editor 235
There's a Blob in Your Data 238
Awakening components to data 238
You could look it up! 241
This grid is in control 243
Getting Results 245
Information please — the query 245
Get me that report! 248
Database Guts 249

Part IV: Real Programming **253**

Chapter 12: Windows 95 Components **255**

Choosing Windows 95 Components 255
Delphi Has Its Ups and Downs 255
Properties 256
Events 257
Bar Hopping 258
Progress bar properties and events 259
Track bar properties and events 259
Status bar properties and methods 260
Visiting a few bars 261
Hot! Hot! Hotkey! 263
Properties and events 263
The Strong, Silent Image List 264
View from a Tree 266
Properties 267
Events 267
Growing a menu tree 268
Keeping Tabs on Your Pages 272
Properties 272
Events 272

Two Headers Are Better Than One 274
    Properties 274
    Events 274
The Amazing List View 276
    Properties 276
    Events 277
    A Liszt of composers 277
Get Rich (Text) Quick! 280
    Properties 281
    Events 281
    Enriching the simple editor 281

Chapter 13: Learn Programming from the Master 285

Dissecting an Empty Program 285
    What's inside an empty unit? 286
        The interface section: the inside story 287
        The implementation section: deep, dark secrets 289
        The initialization section: last-minute preparations 289
    The innards of an empty program 290
    A program by any other name 291
What a Difference a Component Makes 292
    Delphi deals with dependencies 293
    What's in a name? 294
Handling Event Handlers 295
    Easy come, easy go 295
    But are we compatible? 296
What Can You Edit in the Code? 298
    Event handler innards 298
    Adding units to the uses clause 298
    Touch not the body! 299
    My object all sublime 299
Delphi Programming Basics 299

Chapter 14: Elements of Programming 301

Datas De Way It Goes 301
    It depends on several variables. 302
        Scoping out variables 302
        What to name the new variable 303
    She's not my (data) type.. 304
        Choosing data types 304
        Whole numbers count 304
        I'll have just a fraction more 305
        That sounds logical 306
        A real character 306
        There are some strings on me 307
        Honey, I blew up the string 308

Roll your own types 309
The typecasting couch 310
Constant as the North Star 311
Arrays, records, and sets: building structured data types 312
Array of hope 312
A new world record 313
Set 'em up 313
Nailing your files 315
Let me give you a pointer 315
Putting It All Together 317
Idiomatic expressions and hot operators 317
Making a statement 319
Just a simple statement 319
Compounding statements 320
Conditional statements: decisions, decisions 320
Loops: going around in circles 322
What's my function? 323
The Object under Discussion 325
Strawberry data fields forever 325
A method to your madness 325
The Key to Understanding Programming 327

Chapter 15: Debugging **329**

Grammar Lessons 329
Can You Take a Hint? 331
I Take Exception to That! 332
Tiptoe through the Code Lines 337
Gimme a breakpoint 337
Hot on the trace 337
Step on it 338
Advanced breakpoints 338
Demystifying Data 340
Don't hesitate — evaluate 340
Watch it! 341
How'd I Get Here? 341
Bug-Repellent Programs 342

Chapter 16: Working with Internet Components **343**

Surfing The Net! (Fur Sure) 343
The guts of Go 345
Canceling that View 345
Files to Go! 347
Handling that FTP 348
Copying that file 349
Zapping that file 349

The miracle of (folder) creation 350
Oh, Yeah! Wait a Minute, Mr. Postman! 350

Chapter 17: Handling RadioActive(X) Materials 353

Creating an ActiveX Form 354
    Making an ActiveForm 354
    Adding boxes and buttons 355
Deploying the ActiveForm 356
It's about Time! 357
Web Page Animated Counter 359

Part V: The Part of Tens 365

Chapter 18: Ten Common Mistakes 367

Fencepost Errors 367
Empty Statements and Spurious Semicolons 368
The Myth of Floating-Point Equality 370
Don't Forget the Function Result 372
Home In on the Range Errors 372
Stacking Up Errors 374
Overflowing Integers 376
PChar Panic — Error Galore 377
Let Sleeping I/O Errors Lie 379

Chapter 19: Ten Windows API Functions 381

Where's the BEEP? 382
Bossing Other Programs Around 384
    A quick launch with WinExec 384
    ShellExecute eats WinExecs launch 385
    CreateProcess for control freaks 386
Lemme Outta Here! 389
    Exit, stage left 389
    Fifty ways to leave your windows 390
Where's Windo(ws)? 392
Take Your Systems Measurements 392
Free the System Resources! 395
A-Version Therapy 396
Flag Waving 396

Chapter 20: Ten Fabulous Function Families 399

A Conversion Experience 399
Some Random Thoughts 400
The Commando Line-O 402

The Secret Life of Files 402

Disk Must Be the Place 403

Casing the Strings Joint 405

PChar "Pculiarities" 407

New Math 408

Newer Math 408

Dangerous Moves 410

Index *411*

IDG Books Worldwide Registration Card .... *Back of Book*

Introduction

. . . .

Congratulations! You found *Delphi 3 For Dummies,* the book that puts *you* in control of your computer. Add your copy of Delphi 3 itself, and you have everything you need to start creating your own Windows 95 and Windows NT applications. You design programs right on the screen and let Delphi do most of the programming. Sound easy? It is!

About This Book

You need no prerequisites for reading and using this book. It isn't a text-book, and you don't need to be able to pass an entrance exam on arcane programming language syntax or Windows internal functions to understand the concepts that I discuss here. With this book and Delphi 3, you can get results right away and figure out the technical stuff later on — if you need to. No long hours of preparation and study here; you can build and run a program in Chapter 1.

You're not going to find syntax diagrams, exhaustive function lists, or dissertations on the painful technicalities of data types in this book. That stuff is all available in the Delphi manual and online help, and you can look it up if you *really* want to. Working with this book, you get personal with Delphi, discover all its features, and gain practical experience in constructing programs.

Who Are You?

You've wisely chosen to read this book, and that lets me guess a few things about you. First and foremost, you have a fair amount of experience using Windows and Windows programs. You're comfortable working in Windows, and you're ready to take a little more control of what's happening in your computer.

You may be skilled in using your primary application's macro language, but frustrated by its limitations. Chances are good that your coworkers turn to you when they need help customizing their working environment. You could make your work and theirs more efficient, but the boss won't allow it unless you can show results right away.

You're too busy to study programming in night school or spend time decoding cryptic expressions such as y–=x++. Possibly you're an accomplished DOS programmer just beginning to program in Windows. Or you may simply be interested in getting the most out of your computer. You have ideas for projects that the computer could accomplish, but you don't know how to implement them.

Possibly you're already familiar with Delphi 1.0 or 2.0 but feel you need a refresher before you switch over to using Delphi 3 under Windows 95 or Windows NT. In truth, some of your knowledge will carry over from Delphi 1.0 or 2.0 to Delphi 3.

Whatever your reasons for wanting to know more about Delphi, welcome! If you want to *do* things in Windows, you've come to the right place.

Why Delphi?

Programming has long been a practice shrouded in mystery, with practitioners protecting their secrets by using languages unintelligible to normal human beings. Some overenthusiastic programmers delete sacrificial data files by the light of the full moon while chanting "GetPrivateProfileString! WritePrivateProfileString! AbortDoc! AbortProc! Pie! Chord! Yield!" But a new breed of visual programming tool is lifting the curtain and blowing away the smoke to let ordinary humans write programs. Delphi is the latest arrival in the visual programming field; Visual Basic (VB) is its main rival.

Deep down, both Delphi and VB rely on programming languages originally designed to *teach* programming. Delphi is a descendant of Pascal; VB, of BASIC. (Pascal promoters and BASIC boosters have been feuding longer than the Hatfields and the McCoys, but at heart they're not all that different.) Both products have a handy visual interface that eliminates a lot of unnecessary effort, but Delphi has certain key advantages.

To the neophyte, the two seem very similar. However, VB users eventually run into some major limitations. VB can use the function libraries called *DLLs* (Dynamic Link Library), but it can't create new DLLs. VB can react to events that occur in Windows *only* if Microsoft preprogrammed a response to those events. Your VB programs can use Visual Basic custom controls (such as ActiveX) to add functionality, but if you want to make your own custom controls, VB won't do the job.

Delphi has none of these limitations. It can use or create DLLs, and its programs can respond to and initiate absolutely any Windows event. Delphi components are written *in* Delphi, and you don't have to leave Delphi to create new or enhanced components. You don't even have to leave Delphi to use ActiveX controls because Delphi programs can use ActiveX components! In fact, Delphi users can customize ActiveX components in ways most programmers only dream of.

In addition, Delphi does a complete job of compiling your programs into the machine code that your computer understands. VB does a halfway job, translating BASIC instructions into an intermediate language called *p-code*. When the VB program runs, it interprets the p-code into actual machine instructions. Delphi goes straight to the machine code level. What are the advantages of going straight to machine code? Speed, speed, and speed!

Want to see an example of what Delphi can do? Just look at Delphi itself. In an amazing feat of self-referential programming, Delphi was written *using* Delphi. Any design element you see in Delphi, such as a pop-up menu or a tabbed dialog box, is available to *you* for use in your own programs. You won't find another visual development tool that's written with itself! Some tools lack the necessary power or flexibility; others would just be impossibly *slow*.

How to Use This Book

Clear a space near your computer and grab something heavy to hold the book open — a brick, perhaps, or a Windows manual. That way you can try out the many exercises as you come to them. Or if you prefer, relax with the book in your easy chair, hammock, or Jacuzzi (watch those bubbles!), and then come back to the computer and try out what you've discovered. Either way, you *will* be spending time at the computer.

You'll find that later chapters build on concepts from earlier chapters, but don't be afraid to plow ahead even if you haven't quite mastered a particular chapter. Nothing is like some real-world practice to hammer home new concepts. After you've worked with Delphi a bit, you can reread any chapters that seemed tough at first.

You won't be typing interminable program listings into Delphi — Delphi isn't *about* typing. Most of the program design and layout in Delphi is accomplished by choosing and arranging components with the mouse and setting properties that describe them. A minitable like this

Property	Value
Caption	Fantastic Program

means that you should set the property called Caption to the value Fantastic Program — you find out how to do that in Chapter 1.

When you do need to type in a few lines of program code, I display them like this:

```
Edit2.Enabled := Edit1.Text = 'Delphi';
Edit3.Enabled := Edit2.Enabled;
```

All you do is type the lines precisely as shown. If you have to type in something very brief or something that's not exactly program code (like a line of text), the text that you're to type will appear in **bold type**.

What Not to Read

Hi, my name is Neil, and I'm a technoholic. . . . I know lots of boring things like what the TabTheTextOutForWimps function does, why the mysterious word "BurgerMaster" is buried deep inside Windows 95, and how to invoke the musical credits display that's hidden in Windows 95. This information isn't important or even necessary for you to know, but sometimes I can't resist talking about it anyway. Don't worry — you'll have plenty of warning so that you can skip those parts. (And no, I wasn't kidding about that function name. A *lot* of weird names are buried in Windows, including Death, Resurrection, Brute, Bunny_351, BozosLiveHere, and WinOldAppHackOMatic!)

How This Book Is Organized

This book is divided into five parts that more or less follow each other logically. You don't have to read the chapters in order, but if you skip ahead and find yourself confused, come back and work through the background material. The key concept here is understanding by *doing*. After I introduce you to Delphi in general, you can start writing programs that use each of the many components of Delphi. When the book starts giving you instructions such as "place this component, set that property," that's your cue to plunk yourself down in front of Delphi and create a brand-new program. Only *after* you have several dozen programs under your belt will you discover the programming concepts behind them. That way, you have some experience to hang those concepts on.

Occasionally, the chapters refer to Delphi 1.0 and 2.0, the first two versions that came before Delphi 3. Also the chapters may refer to Windows 3.1, the precursor to Windows 95. The reason for referring to the older Delphi and Windows versions is to trace the lineage of some features. After all, neither Delphi 3 nor Windows 95 appeared out of the blue! They evolved from earlier versions.

For the record, when I talk about Windows without a version number, I mean Windows 95. The references to Windows 3.1 always include the version number.

Part I: Getting Started

Part I tells you how to install the Delphi files on your system and how to configure it most effectively. It also introduces you to the *form,* the basic unit of visual programming, and gets you started running programs.

Part II: Programming with Components

The Delphi components have so much built-in power that the biggest task for a Delphi programmer is learning what all the components do. That's what Part II is all about. You *use* all the basic components in small but powerful programs.

Part III: More Components

The capabilities of Delphi go far beyond simply managing the standard controls built into Windows. Part III introduces you to all the rest of the Delphi components and extends the range of projects you can build. It also includes a chapter on the snazzy Windows 95 interface components!

Part IV: Real Programming

Part IV gets into programming in the old-fashioned sense — writing statements in a programming language. It introduces basic programming concepts and shows how they're implemented in Pascal (the programming language that underlies Delphi). And this part brings up the unsavory topic of debugging, or what to do when your program does what you *told* it to do instead of what you *meant* for it to do.

Part V: The Part of Tens

There's more to know about programming in Windows than just placing components and writing a few lines of code. However, you don't need to find out all this information at once. Part V introduces some of the most useful functions found in Windows and in Delphi, along with common pitfalls to avoid.

Icons Used in This Book

This book, like other *...For Dummies* books, uses icons to signal important information, to warn you about certain potential problems, or to prepare you for technical discussions. I use the following icons throughout the text:

This icon points out a dandy shortcut, a timesaving technique, or a hot tip.

This icon is a warning flag for text that talks about technical stuff. You can read the text if you want, but you don't have to. If you start to feel lightheaded, or develop an urge to break your glasses and patch them with adhesive tape, stop reading!

Watch out — here's something you should *not* do!

When you see this icon, you can say "I knew that!" You read this information earlier, and you need to remember it now.

Where to Go from Here

Get to your computer, get Delphi running, and start programming!

Part I
Getting Started

The 5th Wave — By Rich Tennant

"THE SYSTEM CAME BUNDLED WITH A GRAPHICS BOARD, A SPREADSHEET, AND THE DEVELOPER'S OUT OF WORK NEPHEW."

In this part . . .

Getting used to a new program is like familiarizing yourself with a new car. At first, you don't know which lever is the cruise control and which is the turn signal. You may squirt the windshield when you mean to turn on the heat, or open the hood when you mean to lock the doors. You make a few mistakes at first, but even if you figuratively run into a lamppost, nobody will be hurt. And of course, you learn the rules of the road and tips for safe programming. Before long you're driving Delphi like a pro.

In Part I, I help you install Delphi and set its options for safe, effective programming. I introduce the many different elements that make up Delphi, show how you can configure them to suit yourself, and point out areas you can personalize but shouldn't. You also meet the *form* — the canvas on which you lay out your Delphi programs. A form, like every Delphi component, is defined by properties and responds to events. I show you how to set properties and define events; these are skills you use every time you write a program in Delphi. And of course, you start building working programs right away!

If you already know and love Delphi 1.0 or 2.0, moving to Delphi 3 is a breeze. A few of the knobs and levers are in different places — such as choosing Options from the Project menu instead of Project from the Options menu as in version 1.0 — but the differences are surprisingly few.

Chapter 1

Meet Delphi

● ●

In This Chapter

▶ Installing Delphi on your system

▶ Setting Delphi options to ensure safe programming

▶ Discovering how to be an instant programmer

▶ Configuring Delphi's SpeedBar to suit your taste

▶ Looking through the Delphi windows

● ●

Did you already install Delphi on your system? Good! You can skip ahead to the "Don't Program Without a Safety Net!" section. If you haven't installed Delphi yet, now's the time.

Installing Delphi

Installing your copy of Delphi is a snap. Just slide the CD-ROM you purchased into the CD-ROM drive. Double-click the My Computer icon on the desktop to access the drive. Double-click the CD-ROM drive icon to open the root folder of the CD-ROM. Next, double-click the Install folder to open it. Finally, double-click the SETUP program to run the Delphi installation program. This program guides you through the various setup options.

The Delphi program is not included with this book. It must be purchased separately; the installation instructions are simply for your convenience.

When the process is complete, you'll have a few dozen new Delphi-related menu items in a new Delphi submenu of the Start menu. To start Delphi, choose Start⇨Programs, and then select Delphi from the Programs menu.

Which Delphi?

Delphi 3 comes in three flavors:

- ✔ **Delphi Desktop:** The Desktop version is a complete and fully functioning development environment, with one tiny exception — Delphi Desktop doesn't include the Multi Object Grid component (discussed in Chapter 11) or the Math unit (Chapter 20).
- ✔ **Delphi Client/Server:** The Client/Server version contains everything that's in the Desktop version, along with additional tools for advanced and networked database development. Either way, you get the whole Delphi cake; with the Client/Server version, however, you get icing.
- ✔ **Delphi Developer:** The Delphi Developer version is intended for network-based professional developers.

This book concentrates on what's common to all versions of Delphi.

Don't Program without a Safety Net!

Life is full of trade-offs. You can afford a health club membership to buff your bod *or* a beach vacation to show off your new physique — but not both. Delphi is no different. With the Delphi options, the main trade-off is between safety and speed. Your programs can be armored against error, but they'll be slower and larger. Or your programs can be svelte and speedy but more vulnerable to your programming oversights.

Setting compiler options for safety

While you're creating, editing, and testing a project, safety is the Prime Directive. After the project is tested, debugged, and ready for production, you can remove the safety net to speed up and slim down the program.

To create your safety net, select Options from the Delphi Project menu and click the Compiler tab. You'll be transported to Nerd Nirvana, a.k.a. the Compiler page in the Project Options dialog box.

Figure 1-1 shows a screenful of compiler-option choices for Delphi. Fear not; the choices may look intimidating now, but your task is actually quite simple. Use the mouse to check off all the options *except* the Complete boolean eval option. Also check off the lonely box that says Default (near the OK button), to tell Delphi that you want these options to be the default for all projects. Click OK and you're finished.

Figure 1-1:
Turn on all
but one of
the Delphi
compiler
options.

What's so bad about the Complete boolean eval option? Well, sometimes complete Boolean evaluation can even be dangerous. For example, take the expression "x is not zero and 1/x is less than 4." If x is zero, a short-circuit Boolean evaluation (which is the *opposite* of a complete Boolean evaluation) returns False right away. However, complete Boolean evaluation would try to calculate 1/0 to see whether the result is less than 4. Computers just hate it when you divide by zero, mainly because no definite numeric result exists for that operation! Complete Boolean evaluation is both wasteful and dangerous — that's why it's the one option you should leave turned off.

When a program is working perfectly and is totally bug-free . . . then pigs will fly! Let me rephrase that. When a program *seems* to be working perfectly and all *known* bugs have been corrected, you can turn off certain options to make the final version smaller and faster. To do this, choose Options⇨Project from the Delphi menu again. In the Runtime errors section, check off only I/O checking and blank out all the others. The improvement in size and speed will vary from program to program, but it can be dramatic.

Why does your program bloat and drag its feet when the Runtime errors options are turned on? Delphi adds machine code to your program to warn you when certain errors occur. For example, if you try to put ten gallons of data into a one-gallon variable, overflow checking will catch the mistake. And if you try to examine the seventh bullet in a six-shooter, range checking will stop you. But to make those things happen, every spot in your program that assigns a value to a variable needs to have overflow- and range-check-ing code added. If you call a function from within a function from within a function too many times, you'll run out of something called stack space;

stack checking will catch that error. That's why every function call has stack-checking code added. In each of these cases, the error-checking code is just a few bytes, but those bytes add up!

The Project Options dialog box actually has five pages, identified by tabs at the top or bottom of the window. You may see a lot of these multipage tabbed windows in Delphi — in fact, Delphi includes these same multipage and tab components for you to use in your own programs.

The options you've set thus far are all on the Compiler page, and they're by far the most important, but you need to know about the other options, too.

Look at the Linker options now; click the Linker tab in the Project Options dialog box to display the Linker page, as shown in Figure 1-2. In the Linker output area, the choice is between generating DCU files (Delphi's own format for compiled units) and OBJ files (a format used by other compilers). Unless you're already a programming wizard *and* have a need for multilanguage programming, leave this one set to Generate DCUs.

Figure 1-2:
Keep the
Linker
options the
way the
Delphi
install
program set
them.

After you've mastered Delphi and its built-in debugger, you may graduate to an external debugging program. At that time (not now), set the Map file option to Detailed and check off the box that says Include TDW debug info.

The Directories/Conditionals page of the Project Options dialog box tells Delphi where to find certain important files. The Delphi install program leaves these lines blank, because the files you need are in the same directory as Delphi. If you buy third-party component libraries to extend Delphi, you need to add the directory for those libraries to the Search path list on this page. To do that, just add a semicolon to the end of the existing line, followed by the new directory. For example, if the line were C:\DELPHI3\ UNITS, you might change it to C:\DELPHI3\UNITS;C:\NEWUTIL. But hey: Don't go buying add-on libraries before you've mastered the substantial collection of components built into Delphi!

The Output directory line on the Directories/Conditionals page starts out blank, and that's the way it should stay. If you put a directory name on this line, the compiled program files for all your projects will be dumped higgledy-piggledy into that directory. Leave the line blank, and the compiled files will be stored along with the source files, which is where they belong.

As Figure 1-3 shows, the Application page of the Project Options dialog box lets you specify some important attributes for the final compiled program. The value that you fill in for Title is what appears under the icon when you minimize the program, and the icon itself is displayed in the Icon field (in Project Options). You press the Load Icon button to choose an icon that suits your program's style. A modern Windows program should always have a help file; associate one with your program by filling in the Help file line.

What about the remaining page, the one labeled Forms? Well, a project can have one form or dozens, but one of them is always the boss form. The boss form is the one named in the Main form combo box, and it's always the first one in the Auto-create forms list box. This box lists forms that will be automatically created when your program starts. The other list box holds forms that are available but don't exist until your program creates them. Figure 1-4 shows how this page looks for one of the Delphi sample projects. I know, I know, I've hardly talked about forms, but don't worry. Even when you *do* build multiform projects, you rarely need to meddle with this page.

Figure 1-3:
The Application page in the Project Options dialog box controls your program's icon, title, and help file.

Figure 1-4:
The Forms page of the Project Options dialog box lets you promote a new Main form, but you rarely need to do that.

Setting preferences for safety

The computer always does what your program tells it to do, but frequently that's not what you *meant* for it to do. To put it bluntly, programs under development have bugs (whether the programs are written in Delphi, Visual Basic, or Swahili). If you have a buggy program that crashes, the fallout from the crash may blow up Delphi itself, or even bring Windows to a screeching halt. Windows 95 is somewhat less crash-prone than Windows 3.1, and Windows NT is quite skilled at avoiding fallout from exploding programs. However, you still need to program defensively and assume the worst.

When Windows crashes, you lose all unsaved data in all applications, including the latest changes in the form layout and source code for your Delphi *program*. That is, you lose this data *unless* you've set your preferences correctly. Did that get your attention? Good. Here's how to set your preferences: Choose Tools⇨Environment Options from the Delphi menu and look at the first page, titled Preferences. Make sure that both check boxes in the Autosave Options area are checked and then click OK. Now each time you run a program, Delphi automatically saves all open files, the layout of your Delphi desktop, and any options you changed. Whew! That's a relief!

You should take one more precaution, though. In the same Environment Options dialog box, click the Display tab. A check box in the top panel is titled Create backup file; make sure that this box is checked. Now each time Delphi saves a file, it will store the previous version with the extension ~*xx*, where *xx* are the first two letters of the file's extension. For example, the backup file for UNIT.PAS would be called UNIT.~PA, and UNIT1.DFM's backup would be UNIT1.~DF. Round up and delete these backup files from time to time by deleting *.~*. Having a backup can sure save your bacon.

Delphi All Over the Screen

Windows 95 and the Desktop keeps its group folders nicely corralled, and Word for Windows wouldn't think of letting a document creep outside its frame. But as Figure 1-5 shows, Delphi is much more permissive. Like Visual Basic, Delphi splatters windows all over the screen. Get used to it — this "Single Document Interface" is the latest style, recommended by Microsoft for Windows 95 and Windows NT programs.

The four primary Delphi windows are

- ✔ Form window
- ✔ Object Inspector window
- ✔ Code Editor window
- ✔ Main window

Figure 1-5:
The Delphi
Main
window
doesn't
corral its
other
windows —
they spread
out all over
the place.

Fire up Delphi and examine these windows. Move them around, stretch them, poke them a little, and see what they do. These are your new friends — you're going to get to know them *very* well!

The multitude of Delphi windows can take up a lot of space on your desktop. If your video card supports 800-by-600 resolution, go into Windows Setup and select that resolution — it gives you more space. If you have a huge monitor or *very* sharp eyes, try 1,024-by-768 resolution, which lets you fit even more on the screen.

It's all happening at the Form window

Find a window with the caption Form1 and a bad case of measles — that's the Form window. It's already loaded with default properties that define an ordinary window for your program's use. Every normal Delphi program displays a main form when it loads, and many use secondary forms to display or exchange information with the user. You design a program by dropping buttons, labels, and other components on the form, adjusting the properties of the form and components, and adding code to respond to events that occur as the user interacts with the program.

The black dots in the window aren't really measles, by the way. They define a grid that helps you line up components on the form. To change, hide, or eliminate the grid, choose Tools➪Options from the menu and click the Preferences tab. A rectangular area titled Form Designer contains check boxes that determine whether or not Delphi displays the grid and whether or not controls snap to the grid points when you size or move them. You can also set the distance between grid dots in the X (left/right) and Y (up/down) directions; however, the default distance of eight pixels usually works well. Hiding the grid can make visualizing what your form will look like easier, but don't turn the grid off entirely. Making components line up nicely in the form is tough without the grid's help.

Detailing with the Object Inspector window

After roughing out your Delphi program in the Form window, you can fine-tune your design by using the Properties page of the Object Inspector window, shown in Figure 1-6. Initially the Object Inspector exposes intimate details of the program's main and only form, named Form1 by default. Every property starts with a default value; you personalize a program by changing these properties. To change the form's caption, for example, select the Caption property in the Properties page of the Object Inspector window and type a new value. Some properties define visible aspects of a form or component, such as its color and caption. Others define run-time behavior, such as whether or not a form is resizable.

The Object Inspector window has a second page labeled Events. Flip to this page and you see that the event names have a dreary sameness — OnActivate, OnClick, OnCreate, and so *On*. Delphi forms can respond to a variety of events generated by the mouse, the keyboard, or the Windows system itself. *You* control the form's response by defining an *event handler* for a particular event; you write event handlers in the very next chapter. For now, think of an event handler as a program piece that reacts to events, such as clicking the mouse.

Instant program — the Code Editor

You'll do a lot of "programming" without ever looking at the Code Editor because Delphi itself writes the code. Even in a brand-spanking new project, the Code Editor already contains a page of program source code generated by Delphi, with the inspiring name Unit1. Choose the Code Editor to take a peek at the code on this page, but don't make any changes — not yet.

Choose Tools⇨Options from the Delphi menu and look at the tabs that name the dialog box's pages. Three of the seven tabs relate to the Code Editor — Editor, Display, and Colors. There's nothing you *need* to change on these pages, except possibly the editor font (on the Display page). The Delphi editor uses only fixed-pitch fonts, and changes to color and style are reserved for syntax highlighting. Thus the editor font option just displays the available fixed-pitch fonts and possible sizes for each. Set it to phone book-size font to cram tons of code onto one screen or choose the Large Type edition for easy reading. Experiment and choose the size you prefer.

The syntax highlighting options on the Colors page give different program elements different colors and text styles in the editor. For example, reserved words such as *begin, end,* and *procedure* are automatically displayed in boldface. Syntax highlighting is a handy feature once you get used to it — for example, if you accidentally type *procedrue* when you mean *procedure,* you'll notice the typo right away because the word won't snap into boldface. Unless you're addicted to fiddling with options, you have no need to change the details of syntax highlighting. Figure 1-7 shows what happens if you lose control while setting syntax highlighting options.

Notice that a large number of other options are for customizing the editor. You can change the keystrokes it responds to, change the colors, and so on. Here's a tip — *don't.* Customizing an editor is just an exercise in frustration. If you try working on someone else's system, your special layout won't be available, and when Delphi gets an upgrade, you may have to customize all over again. Just get accustomed to the standard keystrokes.

Figure 1-7:
With syntax highlighting, you can put comments in reverse video, give reserved words a gray background, and underline all identifiers — but you probably shouldn't.

Take action with the Main window

Stretched across the top of your screen is the big boss window, the Main window. You can tell this window's the boss because, if you close it, Delphi goes away. This is the window that keeps the other windows under control. It's divided into three parts:

✔ Main menu

✔ SpeedBar buttons

✔ Component palette

Figure 1-8 shows the Delphi Main window.

Selecting from the menu

There's just no point in droning through a lengthy list of all the Delphi menu commands. Many of the commands will be familiar to any Windows user, and many other commands are self-explanatory. This book takes the practical approach of introducing individual menu commands as they're needed.

One aspect of the Delphi menu may throw you at first. In Delphi, the standard Windows File menu shortcut keys are assigned to options that deal with the current file in the Code Editor, *not* the whole project. For example, Alt+F, S saves just the current file, and the shortcut key for Save All is Alt+F, V. Until you get used to the difference, use the mouse to select directly from the menu.

Figure 1-8:
The Delphi Main window controls all the other windows, but it doesn't contain them.

SpeedBar buttons

You live in an instant society, and fast is never fast enough. Menus were invented to save you the trouble of remembering and typing complicated commands. And SpeedBar buttons (also known as speed buttons) save you the trouble of reading and clicking menu items! The Delphi SpeedBar buttons provide fast access to several especially useful menu items.

Most large and modern Windows applications have SpeedBar buttons under one name or another (SmartIcons, ToolBar buttons, HotCrossButtons, whatever). And all suffer from the same problem — the meaning of the button icon isn't always obvious. For example, one Delphi button looks like a flea jumping into a box, and another button looks like a flea jumping over a box. Something to do with debugging, perhaps? Luckily you don't have to guess. Place the mouse cursor on a button for a second or two. A tiny help window *(flyover help)* appears to tell you what the button does.

The six buttons in the left-hand block of the SpeedBar (refer to Figure 1-8) smooth your access to common file-related actions. You recognize the standard glyphs (graphics) for open file and save to disk, which load and save individual files. Two other buttons depict a folder emerging from and re-entering a hard disk; these symbolize opening and saving a whole project. Finally, the buttons that display a folder emblazoned with a plus or minus sign let you add and remove files from your project. That sounds logical!

The next block of four buttons helps you navigate among the forms and unit files in a large project. One button shows several pieces of paper; pressing it displays a list of units to choose from. Another button depicts several forms and displays a list of forms. The lower left button takes you from the active form to the corresponding unit or vice versa. Finally, the lower right button creates and adds a shiny, new, blank form to your project.

When you have just one unit and one form in your project, these buttons don't seem terribly important. Later, though, when you have a dozen forms and as many units in one project, you find them extremely helpful.

The last four standard SpeedBar buttons handle running and debugging your programs. The two that look like the play and pause buttons on a VCR do what you'd expect — run the program and pause its execution. The flea-jumping buttons that I mention previously *are* used for debugging!

The whole point of SpeedBar buttons is so you can work more efficiently. But you're not me, and neither of us works the same way as Delphi's authors. That's why the SpeedBar is completely configurable. Just right-click the bar itself, outside the buttons, and choose Configure from the pop-up menu. You can add a button for any menu choice, or rearrange the buttons that are already there. If you never use a particular button, just drag it right *off* the SpeedBar. And when, in your excitement, you utterly scramble the SpeedBar, click the Reset Defaults button and start again, calmly this time.

The Component palette

The Delphi Component palette is like a cabinet stuffed with parts that you can use to build programs. Every item on every page of the Component palette is a functioning gadget that you can drop into your program with the click of a mouse. Push buttons and scroll bars, data grids and text editors — they're all here. A major part of this book is dedicated to explaining and demonstrating each of the Delphi components.

Here, again, the meaning of the icons that Delphi uses to represent the components may not be crystal clear to you. Just leave the mouse cursor sitting on any one of them, and in a second or two, the flyover help will show you the name Delphi uses for that type of component.

If you experiment with the Options menu choices, you eventually find the page of the Environment dialog Palette box. Don't mess with it! Yes, you can change the order of the pages in the Component palette and change the order of the components. Yes, you can rename the existing pages, add or delete pages, and add or delete components. However, you don't *need* to fiddle around with these things. Leave the components with the names they started with, and you can talk about them with other Delphi users. Keep their original positions, and you won't be confused when an update to Delphi *restores* those positions. The same is true of the Library page. The options on this page affect what happens when you rebuild the entire component library — which isn't a task for the neophyte!

Your First Program RIGHT NOW!

Windows mega-guru Charles Petzold, in his classic book *Programming Windows,* demonstrates that creating a minimal "Hello, World" Windows program in the C programming language requires writing 80 lines of code. Here's a little test: How many lines of code would you expect to write to convert a blank new Delphi form into a working program? Did you say absolutely none? You're right!

To create your first Delphi program, just click the Run button on the SpeedBar (the button with a picture of a right-pointing wedge; it looks like the Play button on a VCR). If you prefer to use menus, choose Run⇨Run from the menu, ignoring the redundancy. Or press the Run program shortcut key, F9. Delphi first compiles the program — that is, converts it into a self-contained EXE file — and then runs it.

The resulting program, stored as PROJECT1.EXE, displays a blank window with Form1 as its caption. You can maximize this window to fill the screen or shrink it down to an icon. Use the mouse to move it around and change its size, and when you get bored, double-click the system menu box at the top left corner to shut it.

This instant program doesn't do anything *useful,* but consider the implications: You never have to write code to do any of the things it does! All the basic behaviors that make up a Windows program are already in place.

The do-nothing program you just built represents a kind of lowest common denominator for Windows programs. It's utterly generic, and you have to do a bit of work to turn it into a really useful program. The Delphi object repository provides another way for you to get started on a program, and it does more of the work for you.

The Delphi object repository expands the template concept. When you create a new form based on an object from the repository, your new form retains its relationship with the original. This can be extremely handy for building company-wide standardized forms. For example, suppose the standard form style for TechnoGrub, Inc., includes a picture of the company logo. When TechnoGrub is acquired by DataSlug, a simple change to the original form in the object repository puts the *new* company logo on all forms derived from that original.

To pull a form or project from the Delphi object repository, you choose File⇨New from the menu, instead of choosing one of the more specific choices such as New Form or New Application. Delphi displays the dialog box shown in Figure 1-9, inviting you to choose an object. Notice that the project's name appears on one of the tabs — yes, you can use a form that's already in your project as a model for another form in the same project.

Figure 1-9:
The Delphi object repository makes reusing forms and other Delphi objects incredibly simple.

You won't be relying heavily on templates or objects from the repository as you do the exercises in this book; most projects are built from scratch. Unless you're instructed otherwise, choose New Application or New Form when this book tells you to open a new project or a new form.

An Embarrassment of Windows

The Main window *is* Delphi — close it and Delphi is gone. Whenever Delphi is running, the Main window will be present. The Form, Code Editor, and Object Inspector windows are so important that you'll always keep them open as well. If you think that makes for a crowded screen, wait until you see the *rest* of the Delphi windows! Delphi provides a number of other windows that you can open for a specific purpose and then close after you've finished using them.

The first section of the View menu is a list of Delphi windows. If you select a window from this menu, you open it (or you bring it into view if it's already open). The windows are

- **Project Manager:** The Project Manager window shows all the forms and units contained in your project. With it, you can add or remove files from the project or jump directly into the Form Designer or editor for a particular file. Most times, though, you leave it packed away.

- **Project Source:** Choosing Project Source adds the source code for the project file itself to the Code Editor Window. However, you rarely need to even see the project file, much less edit it!

- **Object Inspector:** You've already been introduced to the Object Inspector window (if you read the section "Detailing with the Object Inspector window"), so you can skip ahead to the next window.

- **Align:** The Alignment palette is a specialized window used for lining up components that you've already placed on a form. Open it up when you're fine-tuning component placement, and close it after you're finished. Get the lowdown on using the Alignment palette in Chapter 3.

- **Browse Objects:** The Delphi forms and components are all related, and their family tree is called the *object hierarchy*. The Browse Objects window (*browser* for short) displays the entire hierarchy or details about any particular component. The browser is truly overwhelming! For the most part, the genealogical, anatomical, and referential information supplied by the browser won't be useful to you until you know more about the Delphi overall component architecture and programming model. Go ahead and look at the browser, but don't worry if the information doesn't make sense yet. Note that the Browser window can't be opened until you've successfully compiled your project.

- **Breakpoint list:** Four of the windows deal with debugging topics. The Breakpoint list window is the first one, and it lists breakpoints (no kidding), which are lines that you've specially marked so that Delphi drops into debugging mode before executing them.

✔ **Watch List:** The Watch List window, second of the windows that deal with debugging, displays the value of specified variables as they change during a run of your program.

✔ **Call stack:** The third of the four debugging windows, the Call stack window, lists the name of the function that's currently executing, the function that called it, the function that called *it*, and so on. (I discuss variables and functions later.) You find out how to use these three windows in Chapter 15, the debugging chapter.

✔ **Thread Status:** The fourth and final debugging window, Thread Status, monitors threads that let your program develop a split personality and run multiple processes at the same time. Sound alarming? Fear not. You won't be writing any multithreaded programs in this book.

✔ **Components:** The Components list window is simply an alternate way to add components to the form. It lists all available components alphabetically, so it's handy when you don't remember where to find a particular component. The Components list lets you get at all the components using just the keyboard, for those times when you get tired of wrestling with the minimouse on your laptop.

✔ **Window List:** When the impossible mass of windows on the screen has you tearing your hair out, open the Window List window. This window just lists all the other open Delphi windows and lets you jump directly to the one you want.

All these multifarious windows have their uses, but they merely play supporting roles to the real star — the Form Designer window. The next chapter dishes the dirt on form design.

Chapter 2
Programming in Good Form

● ●

In This Chapter

▶ Finding out how properties define a form

▶ Putting a Windows 95-style help icon on Delphi 3 forms

▶ Discovering the various types of properties

▶ Making one form the "child" of another form

▶ Assigning new values to different types of properties

▶ Identifying the events that forms can respond to

▶ Creating a project template for programs with a fixed-size main form

▶ Making a form respond to mouse-clicks or keyboard input

▶ Making a program ask, "Are you sure?" before it terminates

● ●

*E*very normal Windows program communicates with the user through a rectangular area on the screen — a window. Yes, that's where Windows gets its name. In the Delphi world, windows are represented by *form* components. Everything else depends on the form, so it's the first of Delphi's many components that you'll meet.

Blueprint for a Program

Before you build a new house, you draw up a plan that shows the size, shape, and other properties of the edifice that you want to build. Markings on the plan show where various standard components will go — doors, windows, the Jacuzzi, and so on. When the design is complete, you hand it to a contractor and cross your fingers, hoping it will come out the way you want it.

A Delphi program's blueprint is the form. You design a program by setting the properties of the form and placing standard components on it. However, you don't have to wait for a contractor to build the final program to see what it will look like. Once you've worked up a design for the program, you can see immediately what it will look like. Don't like it? Change it! Redesigning is a snap when no lumber is involved, and getting the design correct before you start adding code is smart.

What if you like the house so much that you want another just like it? You have to call the contractor again (and find out that the cost of materials has gone up). Delphi 3 users can get a duplicate form simply by using *visual inheritance*. The new form is identical to the old, yet you can still add to it. Still more amazing, enhancements made to the original form appear in the copy — it's as if you could add a swimming pool to your house and have an identical pool appear in other houses built to the same plan.

Most programs you create start with a main form, and many have secondary forms as well. The form is what holds your program together — everything else relies on forms. Without a form, you don't have a program.

Making a FORMal Inspection

Suppose that you're going to meet an e-mail acquaintance at the airport — someone who's never seen you before. How do you describe yourself? You probably offer a list of *properties* — your height, hair color, tattoos, and so on. A Delphi form has properties, too; as Figure 2-1 shows, the Object Inspector window lists several dozen. For example, the form's caption, size, and on-screen position are properties. If you change a value in the Object Inspector window, the form changes accordingly. Making a form skinnier is a lot easier than reducing your own weight!

If you don't see the Object Inspector window on the screen, choose View⇨ Object Inspector from the menu. The window has two pages, with tabs labeled Properties and Events. Click the Properties tab and move the scroll bar to see all the properties for the form. Depending on your video resolution, you may be able to stretch the window's height so that all the properties are displayed at once.

The left column of the Properties page lists property names, and the right column holds the current values. You make changes by entering new values in the right column. The way you enter a new value depends on the property — the list is designed to help you enter suitable values for each property.

Component name

Component type

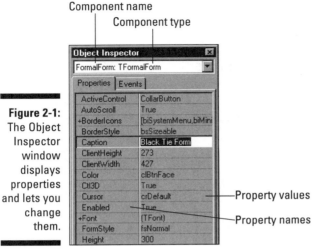

Figure 2-1:
The Object
Inspector
window
displays
properties
and lets you
change
them.

Property values

Property names

When you click various properties, you notice differences in the way their values are displayed. For some, a down arrow appears next to the value; clicking the arrow pulls down a list of possible values. Others display a button with an ellipsis (…). Pressing the button displays a dialog box for setting the property's value. Still others have a plus sign at the start of the property name. Double-clicking the name "explodes" the property into a number of subproperties. Figure 2-2 is a composite showing several different types of properties; the section "A Field Guide to Properties" (later in this chapter) sums up the possibilities. You can experiment and become familiar with the important properties.

Tweaking visible properties

The most impressive form properties are those that affect the on-screen design image of the form. When you change one of these, the effect is immediate. For example, click the Caption property and enter your name — the change shows up right away in the form's title bar. You always wanted your name in lights, didn't you?

Changing the form's Color property also makes a big difference. You can set the Color property in three ways: Choose a color by name, match the color of a Windows screen element, or choose any color of the rainbow. Click the down arrow next to the current Color value and you get a list of possible values, all starting with the letters *cl*. The first 16 items on the list — clBlack, clMaroon, clGreen, clOlive, and so on — define actual colors. Choose one and the form's color changes to match. (The exact shade may vary slightly with different video drivers.)

Figure 2-2:
This composite figure shows properties with value lists pulled down and not pulled down, exploding properties exploded and not exploded, and an ellipsis button that brings up a property-setting dialog.

Exploded property

Pulled-down value list

Value list

Exploding property

Ellipsis button

The remaining items on the list have names such as clScrollBar and clBtnHighlight rather than particular colors. Those items correspond to the colors you can set using the Color module in the Appearance page of the Display Properties dialog in Windows 95. If you choose one of these, your form's color will vary depending on the user's color scheme. Delphi trusts you to make sensible color choices. For example, setting a form's color to match the color of inactive window borders or highlighted menu items doesn't really make sense.

1. **Right-click the Windows 95 desktop.**

2. **Choose Properties from the pop-up menu.**

3. **Click the Appearance tab at the top of the dialog that appears.**

4. **Pull down the combo box labeled Items.**

   Here again you get a list of screen elements whose colors are user-defined. In addition, Windows 95 lets you tweak the font for screen elements that include text and the size of elements, such as scroll bars and window borders.

   If you don't want to match your form to the color of a standard Windows screen element and the 16 basic colors don't excite you, you can choose any color that Windows is capable of showing.

5. Double-click the current color value.

The special color-setting dialog shown in Figure 2-3 pops up.

Figure 2-3:
The Color dialog lets you select from all the possible Windows colors.

6. Choose one of the colors shown, or press the Define Custom Colors button and mix the exact color you want.

7. If you want to save the color for future use, click the Add to Custom Colors button.

8. Click OK after you have it just right.

The resulting custom color value shows up in the properties list as a hexadecimal number like $00BA0BAB.

Yes, Delphi does use those alarming hexadecimal (hex) numbers, with As and Fs mixed in with the 3s and 4s. We humans use decimals (base ten) because we have ten fingers. Computers have no fingers, and counting from zero to zero is deadly dull, so computers use binary numbers (base two). Programmers like hexadecimal numbers because one hex digit represents exactly four binary digits. Fortunately, Delphi handles converting decimal to hexadecimal and vice versa.

To convert a hexadecimal number to decimal, select Evaluate/Modify from Delphi's Run menu, type the hex number (including the dollar sign at the start) in the top line, and press Enter. To convert a decimal number to hex, type the decimal number in the top line, follow that with a comma and an *h* for hex, and then press Enter. Try it now. Bring up the Evaluate/Modify dialog and type **12648430,h** in the top (Expression) line and then press Enter. You discover what nutrient is most important to programmers!

Double-click the value of the Ctl3D property to toggle it from False to True and back. Setting it to True doesn't have any visible effect except to change the form's color to clBtnFace. When you add components to the form, however, the components take on the popular three-dimensional look. That is, the components appear to be chiseled into the surface of the form.

The colors used on the beveled edges of Ctl3D controls match the colors for the 3D Objects element. In the Windows 95 Display Properties dialog, this element controls the button face and button text colors; the shadow and highlight colors aren't exposed for meddling by the uninitiated.

That's about the size of it

Half a dozen properties define the size and position of your form on the screen. Most of the time you won't bother typing values for these properties — you just drag the form around with the mouse until it looks right. Move the form and you change the Left and Top properties. Resize it and you change the Width and Height. Resizing also changes the ClientWidth and ClientHeight properties, which are the dimensions of the inside of the form, not including the frame, caption, or menu. You can set these to particular numbers to create a form with specific interior dimensions.

Another pair of properties that relate to the form's size are HorzScrollBar and VertScrollBar. These are *exploding properties* — when you double-click the property name in the Object Inspector window, they expand to display seven subproperties. The most important subproperty is Range. Any time the form's ClientWidth is smaller than HorzScrollBar.Range, the form displays a horizontal scroll bar. Any time the ClientHeight is smaller than VertScrollBar.Range, the form displays a vertical scroll bar. If you set the ranges to 1,024 and 768, for example, you can create a form that uses the whole screen in 1,024-by-768 mode, but is fully accessible to the user when it's smaller. To do so, follow these steps:

1. **Scroll the Object Inspector window so that both Height and ClientHeight are visible.**

2. **Use the mouse to tweak the form's height.**

   Note that both properties change, but the difference between them remains the same.

3. **Set ClientHeight to a particular value and watch the form's size change.**

4. **Now set both the Left and Top properties to –32000.**

   This hides the form by pushing it way off the screen.

5. **Bring the form back into view by setting Left and Top to 0.**

Delayed gratification

Some of the properties that change the way your form looks don't seem to have any effect at design time. That's because displaying those changes could interfere with the design process. To see the result of making changes to these properties, you have to run the program.

The BorderIcons property has a plus sign in front of it, which means that double-clicking explodes it into several subproperties. The subproperties that appear control whether or not your form will have a system menu box (which has Restore, Move, Size, Minimize, Maximize, and Close command selections), a minimize button, and a maximize button. Your main form should always have a system menu box, and almost always a minimize button. If it's a resizable window, it should have a maximize button as well. Delphi is smart — if you remove the minimize or maximize button, the corresponding item in the system menu is disabled.

If you are familiar with Windows 3.1, you may remember that the system menu box in Windows 3.1 occupies the top left corner of a window and contains a picture of the Spacebar. Why the Spacebar? Because Alt+Spacebar is one way to pull up the system menu. In Windows 95, the Alt+Spacebar keystroke still works, even though the system menu box displays a reduced version of the window's icon. The minimize and maximize buttons live at the top right corner of a window and contain wedge shapes that point downward and upward.

After you finish editing the border icons, double-click the BorderIcons property name again to hide the subproperties. If you look closely at the value of BorderIcons, you see that it consists of a pair of square brackets surrounding a list of the subproperties whose values are True. If you set all the subproperty values to False, the value shrinks to [] (just the empty square brackets).

The BorderIcons property has a subproperty called biHelp. When this property is True, the form displays context-sensitive help in pop-up panels rather than calling up the full WinHelp window. If the form has a system menu but no minimize or maximize button, a special question-mark icon appears on the form. Clicking this icon adds a question-mark to the cursor; clicking a component with this help cursor is an alternate way of bringing up a context-sensitive help panel. Figure 2-4 shows an example of the help cursor in action.

The question mark icon appears *only* when the form has a system menu but no minimize or maximize button. That means the form must have a BorderStyle of bsSizeable or bsSingle because in Delphi all other BorderStyle values suppress the system menu. (What's BorderStyle? Read on!)

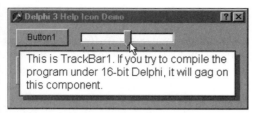

The BorderStyle property is closely related to BorderIcons. The BorderStyle property defaults to a border that you can grab with the mouse and resize, just as you can resize it at design time. Sometimes, however, resizing the form just doesn't make sense. Suppose you spend all day agonizing over the placement of dozens of components on your form. You don't want the user to shrink the form so that half the components aren't visible or expand the form to put a useless expanse of blank space around the components. To make your program's main form nonresizeable, set its BorderStyle to bsSingle. To make a secondary form nonresizeable, use bsDialog.

Don't try to use the bsDialog style on a form that has a menu! Because of a quirk in Windows itself, this combination leaves a visible (and ugly) gap around the menu. Note, too, that you don't get the minimize or maximize border icons with this style.

In addition to the preceding border styles, Delphi 3 offers the values bsToolWindow and bsSizeToolWin. The value bsToolWindow is resizable and the value bsSizeToolWin is not. A form that uses one of these styles has no system menu, maximize button, or minimize button, and its title bar is smaller than usual. Figure 2-5 shows the difference. Use one of the two tool window styles for secondary windows such as floating toolbars and palettes.

The Position property tells Delphi whether or not you consider the size and position of the form at design time to be important. By default, its value is poDesigned, which means the form will initially be displayed at precisely the size and position it had at design time. A value of poDefault lets Windows choose the size and position; poDefaultSizeOnly and poDefaultPosOnly let

Windows choose the size *or* the position, respectively. Finally, poScreenCenter retains the designed size but positions the form in the center of the screen, regardless of what screen resolution Windows is running in. Of course, if you set a form's BorderStyle to anything but bsSizeable or bsSizeToolWin, Windows can't give it a default size regardless of the value of Position.

Your program's initial appearance on the screen is determined by the WindowState property. Most of the time the default of wsNormal is correct. If you change it to wsMinimized, the program will load as an icon. If you set it to wsMaximized, it fills the whole screen.

Don't use the wsMaximized window state with a window that doesn't include a maximize button among its border icons. You end up with a window that covers the entire screen and has no restore button. (It can be restored to a smaller size only by double-clicking its caption.)

The default mouse cursor is the familiar arrow, pointing upward and just a bit to the left. If you change the form's Cursor property, the cursor will change to match, but only when it's over your form's client area. Try it. Select the different values and run the program to see the result.

Changing a form's Font property doesn't have any visible effect unless you add some components to the form. By default, components automatically display text using the font of the underlying form. You can change this property in two ways. You can click the ellipsis (. . .) button to display a standard Windows Font dialog, or you can double-click the property name to explode it into a set of subproperties. As you can see in Figure 2-6, Font is a double-bang property — its Style subproperty can also be exploded to let you set the bold, italic, underline, and strikeout styles.

Figure 2-6:
All the subproperties of a form's Font property are hidden until you "explode" them by double-clicking.

Delphi 3 uses MS Sans Serif as its default font. This isn't a TrueType font, but it comes in many different sizes, so it's a reasonable choice.

If you minimize a Delphi form, it appears as a default Delphi icon unless you set its Icon property to an icon specific to your application. Before you release any Delphi application for others to use, you definitely want to give each of its forms a distinctive icon. You can use one of the icons supplied with Delphi or draw your own using Delphi's Image Editor — just choose Tools⇨Image Editor from the menu. You also want the Windows 95 desktop to use your icon when displaying your application in a group window. For that to happen, you must set the application's icon property to be the same as the main form's icon property.

To set the icon for your application, choose Project⇨Options from the menu and click the Application tab.

Frequently, you want to store some information about a form that's just not covered by the existing properties. If the information can be stored as a number, put it in the Tag property. Every component has a Tag property, and I use this property frequently in the examples.

Form families—the Multiple Document Interface

Sometimes one big window isn't enough. The Windows Multiple Document Interface (MDI) lets the program enlist the help of other windows that live inside the main window. The main window is called the *parent,* and the helpers are called *child windows.* An MDI program acts like a miniature version of the Windows desktop; it can tile or cascade the child windows within its boundaries, or minimize them to icons at the bottom of the main window. The child windows can be either the same type (for example, they can all be text editing windows but with a different file open in each) or different types (perhaps some text editing windows and some bitmap-display windows).The Desktop is the most famous MDI program — its group windows are its children.

The FormStyle property controls whether a Delphi form is a normal window, an MDI parent window, or an MDI child window. You never define a program's main form as an MDI child.

Before starting the following set of instructions, choose File⇨New Application from the menu so that you start with a new blank form. Do this *every* time you come to a set of instructions like this from now on, unless you're specifically told to use a program created previously.

1. Choose File⇨New Form from the menu.

A second form named Form2 is added to your project.

2. Set the FormStyle property of Form2 to fsMDIChild and the FormStyle property of Form1 to fsMDIForm.

3. Run the program and try moving and resizing the secondary form.

You find that the form stays entirely within the parent MDI form. As Figure 2-7 shows, if any portion of the child form extends beyond the boundaries of the main form, the child form is cut off from view, and the main form sprouts scroll bars along the bottom, the right edge, or both, to let you bring the entire child form into view. If you minimize the child form, its icon appears at the bottom of the main form. A minimized child form turns into a tiny caption bar rather than an icon.

Figure 2-7:
This MDI form has three child forms; one is minimized and another is cut off at the edge of the main form.

An MDI form created by Delphi has the built-in capability to tile or cascade its child windows and to arrange their icons neatly across its bottom edge. Because these features are normally invoked from the program's main menu, I wait until Chapter 6 (the menu chapter) to talk about them in detail.

But wait, there's more! FormStyle has one more possible value, StayOnTop. When you choose this value, your form "floats" on top of other programs even when it's not active, like the Windows Clock utility. This can be aggravating if something is important under the floating form, so if you use the StayOnTop style, make the form as small as you can.

The WindowMenu property enables a handy feature. After creating a menu for the main form, you set this property to point to one of the top-level menu choices. Then as each child window is created, its name is added to the tail end of the specified menu, and the currently active child window has a check mark beside it. You can take a good look at this property in Chapter 6.

A Field Guide to Properties

When you go stalking the wild property, you'll be more successful if you can recognize the common types. You see quite a few of them in this chapter — I review and categorize them in this section:

- **Exploding object properties:** The value is an object name such as (TFont), the name has a plus sign in front of it, and the value has an ellipsis button. Click the button to display a dialog or double-click the name to explode a list of subproperties. Example: Font.

- **List properties:** A down arrow appears next to the property value; clicking this arrow displays a list of possible values. Double-clicking the value selects the next item on the list; if the current value is the last, the first item is selected. (The Color property looks like a list property, but it's a special case.) Examples: WindowState, Cursor, FormStyle.

- **Numeric properties:** You can type anything at all for the value, but non-numeric input will be rejected. In most cases, impossible numeric values will be converted to reasonable values. For example, a ClientHeight of –1 will be converted to 0. Examples: Left, Height, Top.

- **Object properties:** The value displayed is (None) or an object name such as (TIcon), and an ellipsis button (. . .) appears next to it. Clicking the button brings up a standard file-selection dialog. Example: Icon.

- **Set properties:** The property name has a plus sign in front of it, and the value is a list of words in brackets. If you double-click the name, the property explodes into a list of True or False subproperties. Examples: BorderIcons, HorzScrollBar, VertScrollBar.

- **String-list properties:** The value displayed is (TStrings), and an ellipsis button (. . .) appears next to it. Click the button to display a special editor that lets you enter a list of strings. The Form component doesn't include any properties of this type, but you see it in chapters to come.

- **True/False properties:** A down arrow appears next to the value; clicking this arrow displays a list containing just True and False. Double-clicking the value toggles it from True to False or False to True. Examples: Ctl3D, Enabled, Visible.

- **"Anything goes" properties:** A few properties accept *almost* anything you enter. If you type something that isn't valid, Delphi rejects it — for example, try typing Visual Basic for the Name property. Examples: Caption, Hint.

Every component has its own properties, and almost all of them fit one of these types, so you may want to review this list from time to time.

The Main Events

Raise your hand if you already learned programming under DOS. Did you raise your hand? If you *didn't,* you have an advantage. DOS programmers are accustomed to picturing a program as a sequential list of instructions: Go to the grocery, buy a dozen kumquats, IF they're on sale THEN buy two dozen — that sort of thing. DOS programmers expect the computer to execute instructions in sequence, occasionally swirling in a loop or leaping into a subroutine. If you did raise your hand, pay special attention, because Windows programming is not what you're used to.

After a Windows program loads in memory and executes any initialization code, it doesn't do anything. Nothing at all. There is no "next step." Nothing happens until an event occurs, and then the program responds to the event. Rather than a list of instructions, a Windows program has a set of contingency plans that tell it what to do for each important event.

In Delphi, these contingency plans are called *event handlers,* and they respond to a variety of different events. Figure 2-8 shows the Events page of the Object Inspector window. The Events page appears when you click the Events tab.

Figure 2-8:
The Events page of the Object Inspector window lists all the events a Delphi component responds to.

The events fall into three main categories: mouse events, keyboard events, and system events. Get your fingers warmed up, because you're going to be keying in some very simple programs that respond to events in each of these categories.

Mouse events

For starters, you build a program that changes its cursor every time you click with the mouse. If you click the Cursor property and then click the down arrow to look at its list of values, you notice that they run from crAppStart through crHelp. A little experimentation shows that for a form, crDefault is effectively the same as crArrow. Each value has a numeric equivalent ranging from –20 (crHelp) to 0 (crDefault).

To find out the numeric value of a named constant such as crVSplit, press Ctrl+F7 to display the Evaluate/Modify dialog. Type the name of the constant into the Expression line and press Enter. Note that this works only after you compile or run the project successfully.

The first step in writing an event handler is to mentally plan out exactly what you want to happen. The computer always does precisely what you tell it to, nothing more, nothing less. If what you say isn't exactly what you mean, the computer can't second-guess you. So for example, it's not enough to say that each time the user clicks with the mouse, the cursor changes to the next value in the list. You have to specify that when the cursor is on the *last* value (crDefault), it should wrap back to the first value (crHelp). Expressing this concept in broken English, you get

> IF Cursor equals crDefault THEN
>
> Set Cursor equal to crHelp
>
> OTHERWISE
>
> Set Cursor equal to the next value.

As you'll see, this translates very nicely into Delphi code.

Click the Events tab in the Object Inspector window and then double-click the event handler column next to the OnClick event. The Code Editor comes to the top, with the framework for an OnClick event handler already in place. Figure 2-9 shows the result — you just enter code between the event handler's begin and end lines.

Enter the following code at the cursor:

```
IF Cursor = crDefault THEN
Cursor := crHelp
ELSE
Cursor := Succ(Cursor);
```

Figure 2-9:
Delphi
automatically
provides
you with the
framework
for an
empty event
handler —
all you do is
fill the
inside.

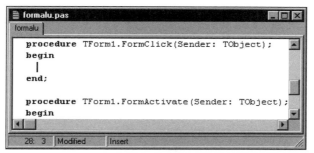

This is almost a direct translation of the pseudo-English code that I gave previously. The equal sign (=) stands for testing equality in a comparison, and the := symbol stands for the act of moving data to make one thing equal to another. Weird, but you get used to it.

The built-in function Succ returns the successor of Cursor — the next available value. And the period at the end of the sentence is replaced by a semicolon. That's not too difficult now, is it?

You can break a line of Delphi code almost anywhere except in the middle of a word or in the middle of a literal string of text (that is, text enclosed in a pair of single quotes). The sample code you just typed is on four lines, but it can just as well be on one or two:

```
IF Cursor = crDefault THEN Cursor := crHelp
ELSE Cursor := Succ(Cursor);
```

For that matter, you can put each of the 16 words and symbols on a separate line. The important thing is that the code should be easy to read and understand. When you type the code samples in this book just as they're shown, you're getting practice in a consistent and legible style.

Run the program and click the mouse on the form several times. Each time, the cursor changes to a new shape. After the cursor has taken on every shape (including the plain arrow shape *twice*), it starts over again. See? You've written a program that responds to mouse events! The other mouse events are OnDblClick, OnMouseDown, OnMouseMove, and OnMouseUp, along with OnDragOver and OnDragDrop. You use these events in later chapters.

Keyboard events

Now you can build a program window that moves around on the screen when you press the arrow keys. The program should respond to the left, right, up, and down arrows by moving eight pixels in the specified direction.

1. **Shrink the form as narrow as it will go and make it about as high as it is wide.**

2. **Set its BorderStyle to bsSingle.**

3. **Double-click the BorderIcons property and set biMaximize to False.**

4. **Enter this code for the OnKeyDown event handler:**

```
CASE Key OF
VK_LEFT  : Left := Left - 8;
VK_UP    : Top := Top - 8;
VK_RIGHT : Left := Left + 8;
VK_DOWN  : Top := Top + 8;
END;
```

To enter code for a particular event, double-click the event handler column to the right of the event's name. Delphi creates a framework for the event handler, and you enter code between the begin and end lines of the framework.

This CASE thing looks more complicated than the IF..THEN logic in the last example, but it's not. Delphi passes the event handler a variable called Key. The Key variable contains a code to identify which key was pressed, and the CASE statement compares that variable to four specific numbers.

What? You say VK_LEFT isn't a number? That's true. The four names beginning with *VK* are constants — descriptive names applied to numbers. You can replace them with 37, 38, 39, and 40. However, the bare numbers don't tell you anything about what's going on. The named constants make it clear that 37 here identifies the Virtual Key (VK) left arrow.

You can get the numeric value of a named constant using the Evaluate/Modify dialog, as long as you successfully compile or run the program. Just press Ctrl+F7, enter the name of the constant, and press Enter.

You can add one more keyboard event handler to make the program quit if you type the letter *Q*. You add this event handler to the OnKeyPress event. How is this different from OnKeyDown or OnKeyUp? The OnKeyPress event occurs after a key has been pressed (down), and the system has identified it as a simple typing key such as *A* or *!*, and not as an arrow key, a function key, an Alt+key combination, and so on.

Without starting a new project, create an OnKeyPress event handler for the form containing this single line:

```
IF UpCase(Key) = 'Q' THEN Close;
```

The UpCase function is built into Delphi. When you pass to it a letter of the alphabet, it returns the uppercase version of that letter. When you pass to it any other character, it just returns the character unchanged.

Run the program and take it for a walk. When you press the up, down, left, or right arrow key, the form obediently moves in the specified direction. Press *Q* and it quits. This is actually a weird and deviant use of the keyboard events — you can move and close a form in other ways. But this serves to give you an example of how keyboard events work.

The keyboard-driven form project that you just built is a program with a main window that retains the size you gave it at design time, resisting attempts to maximize it or tweak it with the mouse. In effect, the main form is a dialog. This style is very handy for the small programs that you create in this book — handy enough to merit its own project stored in the Delphi 3 object repository. See the information on object repository in Chapter 1.

Start a new blank project and set the form's BorderStyle to bsSingle and its BorderIcons.biMaximize property to False. Change the form's caption to Fixed-Size Form. Now choose View⇨Project Manager from the menu and right-click the Project Manager window. Select Add Project to Repository from the pop-up menu. Fill in Fixed-Size Form for the template title and enter your own description. Select Projects from the Page combo box and fill in your own name in the Author box. Use the default bitmap to represent this project and click OK.

From now on, you'll use this stored project to create fixed-size forms for the exercises in this book. Of course, Delphi supplies a variety of stored projects, but using your own gives such a feeling of power! The fixed-size form project you just built creates a program in which the main form's size is fixed.

System events

The mouse and keyboard events are triggered by things that the user does with the program. System events come straight from Windows, so their use is a little less obvious. Table 2-1 describes the most important system events.

Table 2-1	Important System Events	
Event	*Occasion*	*Usual Response*
OnActivate	The form has just become the program's active window.	Update any information.
OnClose	OnCloseQuery already happened, and the form is being shut down.	This is the program's last chance to refuse to shut down.
OnCloseQuery	Windows asks the form whether it's willing to shut down.	Prompt the user to save any changed data or refuse to shut down.
OnCreate	The form is created.	Perform any necessary initialization.
OnDeactivate	The form has just stopped being the program's active window.	Undo any actions taken in the OnActivate event handler.
OnDestroy	The form is about to disappear for good.	Clean up any resources the program allocated.
OnPaint	The form needs to be redisplayed because, for example, it has just been uncovered or restored from an icon.	Draw lines or other simple graphics directly on the form.
OnResize	The form has been resized.	Adjust the size or position of components when the form is resized.

Many Windows programs interrupt your attempt to shut them down by asking whether you're sure that's what you want to do. Your Delphi programs can ask for this kind of confirmation in the OnCloseQuery event handler.

Insert these lines in a new form's OnCloseQuery event handler:

```
CanClose := MessageDlg('Are you sure?',
  mtConfirmation,
  [mbYes, mbNo], 0) = IDYES;
```

Run the program and then double-click the system menu box to shut it down. A message dialog like the one in Figure 2-10 appears, asking for confirmation. If you choose No, the program won't terminate.

MessageDlg is a function supplied by Delphi to let programs communicate with the user. This is a more complicated function than the UpCase function that I present earlier in this chapter, and you have to pass to it four pieces of information, called *parameters* or *arguments*.

The first parameter is the message you want to display, enclosed in single quotation marks. The second parameter is a constant that determines what kind of message box this is: possible values are constants named mtWarning, mtError, mtInformation, and mtConfirmation. Each constant has a specific icon associated with it, and a specific title for the message box. In this case, the icon is a large question mark and the title is Confirm.

The third parameter is a set of constants specifying what buttons should appear in the dialog. Brackets surround the list, and your choices are mbYes, mbNo, mbOk, mbCancel, and mbHelp, mbAbort, mbRetry, mbIgnore, and mbAll. If mbHelp is among the choices and your program has a Windows help file associated with it, pressing the Help button displays the help topic associated with the number in the fourth parameter. Finally, the MessageDlg function *returns* a constant identifying which button the user pressed. If the returned value isn't IDYES, the program is not permitted to close. You use the MessageDlg function quite a bit.

A program with just a main form is like a house with no furniture. It keeps the rain off, but it's not very comfortable!

The next part of this book explains how to furnish your forms with Delphi components. You become an instant interior decorator and learn to move furniture without straining your back.

Part II
Programming with Components

The 5th Wave   By Rich Tennant

"I'LL BE WITH YOU AS SOON AS I EXECUTE A FEW MORE COMMANDS."

In this part . . .

Delphi supplies you with a huge number of prefabricated program components. Some are simple, such as push buttons, check boxes, and labels. Others incorporate amazing power, such as displaying a complex dialog box to let users choose which file to open. The biggest step in programming with Delphi is understanding how incredibly much Delphi can do for you.

In Part II, I introduce the most basic Delphi components and show off their capabilities. You gain experience in laying out Delphi forms, and you become familiar with the process of writing event handlers to tell the components what to do. Along the way, you use all the basic components in programs ranging from tiny demo projects to a text editor comparable to the Windows Notepad.

Chapter 3
Hooking Up Components

In This Chapter

▶ Designing a program by arranging components on the form

▶ Lining up groups of components

▶ Finding out which properties and events are common to most components

▶ Giving your programs a three-dimensional look

▶ Adding drag-and-drop functionality to programs

▶ Making the Tab key move between components in the order *you* choose

*F*inding out that your workbench has exactly the right screw or bolt or wing nut on hand to deal with your current project is always satisfying. Imagine the thrill of building programs with Delphi: You never have to run to the hardware store for parts! The Component palette is your multidrawer parts chest, and the only tool you need is a mouse.

The Component Palette

The Delphi basic Component palette has 12 pages as shown in this list:

✔ **Standard:** Most components on this page correspond directly to on-screen elements of Windows itself. Menus, push buttons, scroll bars — they're all here. Delphi, however, has some handy extra features built-in. See Chapter 4 to find out more about Standard components.

✔ **Additional:** This page contains more-advanced components. For example, the outline component is handy for displaying data that's organized in some kind of hierarchy, and the amazing media player component lets your programs play sounds, music, and video. This page also holds components whose main purpose is to display graphical information. The image component loads and displays bitmaps, and the shape component decorates your form with circles, squares, and so on. See Chapters 8 and 9 to read more about Additional components.

✔ **System:** Not every file-handling need can be shoehorned into the standard common dialogs, so the Delphi System page lets you mix individual elements such as drive, directory, and file lists. System also holds components that handle high-level communications between programs that support OLE (Object Linking and Embedding). And System's timer component can trigger events at preset time intervals. See Chapters 9 and 10 for more about System components.

✔ **Win32:** This page holds the components that let Delphi programs take advantage of 32-bit Windows user-interface enhancements such as the tree view, list view, and status bar used in Windows 95 Explorer, and Wordpad's rich text editor. See Chapter 12 for more about these components.

✔ **Dialogs:** Windows 3.1 introduced standardized common dialogs for file operations, font selection, color selection, and so on. However, using them in an ordinary Windows program can require lots of setup code. The Dialogs page gives Delphi programs easy access to common dialogs. See Chapter 5 for more about Dialog components.

✔ **Data Access and Data Controls:** Delphi uses the Borland Database Engine (BDE) to access database files in a variety of file formats. The components on these two pages make it easy for Delphi programs to tie into the database services provided by the BDE, such as multiuser reading, writing, indexing, and querying of dBASE and Paradox tables. It takes almost no programming at all to write a program for manipulating information in a database. See Chapter 11 for more on these components.

✔ **Win 3.1:** Components that existed in Delphi 1.0 but have since been superseded by fancy Windows 95 components get sent to Siberia, otherwise known as the Win 3.1 page.

✔ **Internet:** This page offers components for creating applications that produce HTML content directly from information databases and files, and interact with other Internet applications. Delphi 3 allows you to create Web server applications as Dynamic Link Libraries (DLL) that may contain any nonvisual component. Internet-specific components make it easy to create event handlers associated with a specific Uniform Resource Identifier (URI) and, when processing is complete, to programmatically construct HTML documents and transfer them to the client. See Chapter 2 for information about event handlers. See Chapter 16 for more about Internet components.

✔ **Samples:** This catch-all page is for components that aren't intrinsic to the Delphi package but do demonstrate the power of the component system. Online help for these components isn't built-in. Still, they're just as useful as their companion components on the other pages.

✔ **ActiveX:** This page contains sample ActiveX components (which are 32-bit OLE controls) created by third party software vendors, such as a grid, chart, and speller components.

✔ **QReport:** This page offers components that support database query report forms. It includes special versions of labels, text boxes, memos, and other visual controls that work with the query report.

The chapters that follow introduce you to components from all of these pages. This chapter provides general information about components.

Placing Components

Placing components is very simple. You just click the tab of the Component palette page you want, click the speed button for the component you want to place, and click the form. That's it! Or if you prefer, you can click the component and then drag a rectangle on the form; the component appears inside the rectangle. If the component's size is adjustable, it appears sized to match the rectangle that contains the component.

If you can't remember which page a particular component is on, choose View⟶Components List from the menu for an alphabetical listing.

Placing, moving, and resizing a single component

When you click a component in the Component palette, its button appears pushed in. When you click a different component, the first button pops out — only one component at a time can be selected. To pop all the buttons out and regain normal use of the mouse, click the selection arrow that appears at the left end of every page in the palette (see Figure 3-1).

Figure 3-1:
To return to normal use of the mouse, click the selection arrow.

Selection arrow

Flyover help window

1. **Select the Standard page on the Component palette.**

2. **Put the mouse cursor on the square that looks like an OK button.**

   After the mouse has been still for a second or two, a tiny flyover help window appears and identifies this component as a Button — you can see the flyover help window in Figure 3-1.

3. **Click the flyover help window, and then click your form.**

   An average-sized button captioned "Button1" appears.

4. **Click the button component again, but this time use the mouse to draw a big rectangle on the form.**

   Button2 can fill the rectangle. Note that the button has little square sizing handles at each corner and in the middle of each edge. Use these to resize the button using the mouse.

5. **Now click Button1 and drag it to a new position.**

Notice that when you move and resize components, they snap to the grid points on the form. Often this is a good thing — it helps avoid that snaggletoothed look. If you want to turn off this feature or change the spacing of the grid points, choose Tools⇨Options from the menu. You see the Environment Options dialog box. Click the Preferences tab of the dialog box. This first page of options relates to your preferences, and it includes the Form Designer section. The Display grid and Snap to grid check boxes control whether the grid is visible and whether it's active. You can also change the values of Grid Size X and Grid Size Y to change the size of the grid.

To get finer control over the placement and size of your components, try this: Set the grid size values to 4 instead of 8, turn off the visible grid, but leave the Snap to grid check box active.

Nonvisible components

Not every component shows up on the form at run time. For example, the menu component causes the form to have a menu, but the corresponding square icon doesn't show up on the form when the program runs. The common dialog components don't appear on the form at all at run time. A nonvisible component can't be resized — it always shows up as a simple icon.

Stash your nonvisible components in a nonbusy corner of the form, where they are easy to find.

Scientists announce cloning breakthrough!

After you have correctly sized and placed a component, with all its properties set precisely to your taste, you can clone it easily. Just click the component, press Ctrl+C to copy it to the Clipboard, and then press Ctrl+V to paste a copy into the form. The clone will be identical to the original in all properties except a few that are required to be unique, such as the component's name. So as not to hide the original, the clone is positioned a little to the right and down, as you can see in Figure 3-2.

Figure 3-2:
This form
contains
ten buttons
cloned from
the original
button in
the top-left
corner.

To see a still more amazing trick, select a component, press Ctrl+C, and then switch to the Editor window. Move to the very end of the unit, beyond the line that reads end. Now press Ctrl+V. You've just inserted a text description of the component. You can edit this description, cut or copy it to the Clipboard, and paste the edited component back into the form. You can even mutate the component from one type to another, if the two types are similar.

1. **Find the list box button in the Standard page of the Component palette and place a list box on a new form.**
2. **Press Ctrl+X to cut it to the Clipboard.**
3. **Switch to the tail end of a file in the editor.**
4. **Press Ctrl+V.**

   The first line of the text description should be object ListBox1: TListBox.

5. **Change this description to object** ComboBox1: TComboBox.
6. **Select and cut the modified text block to the Clipboard.**
7. **Switch back to the Form Designer, and press Ctrl+V.**

   The combo box will appear right where the original list box was, because its Left and Top properties are the same as those of the list box. Hey presto! You've transformed a list box into a combo box.

Selecting multiple components

It's a snap to select one component on the form — you just click it. Selecting several components at once isn't any more difficult. If you drag a rectangle that intersects all the components you're interested in, they'll all be selected. Or if you want to pick and choose, hold down the Shift key while you click each component in turn. You can even combine the two methods. If your dragnet catches more components than you want, as seems to have happened in Figure 3-3, just Shift+click the undesirables to throw them back.

Figure 3-3:
You can
select a
group of
components
all at once
and then
deselect
any that
don't
belong.

After you've selected a group of components, you can move them as a group. They remain positioned in relation to each other. So, for example, if you get the urge to place a new component at the top of the form, it's easy to select *all* the other components and drag them down to make room.

One size fits all

After a flurry of placing components, you're likely to find that they're not all the same size, or not all the size you *want* them to be. To correct this, start by setting one of the components to the desired final size. Then select all the components whose size you want to adjust, either by dragging a rectangle that encloses them or by Shift+clicking them. Choose Edit⇨Select Size from the menu and make your choices from the Size dialog, shown in Figure 3-4. To see what I mean, start a new form and follow these steps:

1. **Shift+click the button item on the Component palette.**

2. **Place six or eight standard-sized buttons on a new form.**

Figure 3-4:
With the
Size dialog,
you can
adjust the
width and
height of
several
components
at once.

3. **Click the selection arrow to stop placing buttons.**

4. **Select Button1 and shrink it so that the caption just barely fits inside.**

5. **Drag a rectangle that selects all the buttons and then choose Edit⇨Size from the menu.**

6. **Select the Shrink to smallest option in both the Width and Height areas of the Size dialog, and click OK.**

Now all the buttons are the size of the smallest one. You can also enter the width and height for all selected components directly in the Size dialog box. By doing this, however, you forfeit the advantage of using the sizing grid. As you see later, you can also use the Object Inspector window to set the width and height for a group of components. In fact, using the Object Inspector window for this task is often better because the width and height of the first component you select show up as default values.

Most of the time, the components that you're nudging into shape will be the same type, but that's not a requirement. You can adjust, for example, the width of a whole column of different type components.

Putting your ducks in a row

If you enjoy stacking alphabet blocks and solving jigsaw puzzles, you may find the process of lining up your components on the form by hand both soothing and entertaining. But if you don't have time for that, the Delphi Alignment palette, grandly displayed in Figure 3-5, will help. If the icons on the speed buttons don't make sense to you, just rest the mouse cursor on each in turn and read the flyover help.

The pictures for the buttons that align components on one of the four edges suggest that selected items will move to line up with the item that extends farthest in the direction of the arrow, but it's not so! Rather, all selected components line up with the first selected component, along the specified edge. The two buttons that align the centers of a group of selected components align them with the center of the first selected component. (You probably won't use this pair very much.)

You can center one component or a group of components in the window, horizontally or vertically. If it's a group, the components in the group stay in the same relationship to each other. Finally, the buttons that equalize the horizontal or vertical spacing of the selected components do so by adjusting the amount of space between the top or left edges of the components, *not* the actual space between them. These two buttons, therefore, work best when the selected components are all the same size.

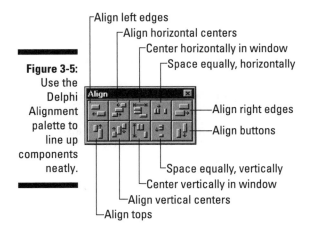

Align left edges
Align horizontal centers
Center horizontally in window
Space equally, horizontally

Align right edges
Align buttons

Space equally, vertically
Center vertically in window
Align vertical centers
Align tops

Figure 3-5:
Use the
Delphi
Alignment
palette to
line up
components
neatly.

If you have ten edit boxes in a row and accidentally align them at the top instead of the left, they'll all be stacked on top of the first edit box. Any time you slip and choose the wrong alignment option, you can end up with a group of controls all stacked up in the same place. It's always a good idea to *save* your form before performing major alignment tasks, because there's no undo for slips like this.

Enforcing component conformity

You might notice a flash from the Object Inspector window when you select more than one component. The flash occurs because the list of properties is redrawn, usually with fewer items on the list. What's going on? To find out, place two buttons on the form. Select one of them and position the cursor above the other one. While watching the properties page of the Object Inspector window, Shift+click the second button several times and watch what changes. A little experimentation shows that the Name and TabOrder properties disappear from the list when both buttons are selected.

Now, with both buttons selected, set the Width property to double its present value. Both buttons expand to the new width.

When more than one component is selected, the list of properties shrinks to include only the properties the two items have in common. Suppose that you selected a dragon component and a horse component; the resulting properties list would include legs and a tail, but not scales or a mane. Also, properties that must be unique disappear from the list. In the previous exercise, the Name property disappeared because Delphi won't let two components have the same name (how would it tell them apart?). The TabOrder property disappeared because it, too, must be different for every component on the form. Also, if a property remains on the list when more than one component is selected, it's fair game. You can set that property for all the selected components at once. That's what happened when you changed the width — both buttons got the new value.

The more different kinds of components you select, the fewer the common properties will be, and the shorter the property list will be. For example, select a check box along with the two push buttons that you selected at the beginning of this section, and the Cancel, Default, and ModalResult properties disappear. That's because these properties have no meaning for a check box. It's even possible to select a set of controls that have *no* properties in common except the ubiquitous Tag property.

Common Component Properties

If you flip through the Properties list for a number of different components, you notice certain items coming up again and again. Just about every component has Height and Width properties, for example. Many of the common properties should be familiar from the preceding chapter because the Form component has them, too. In the next chapter, I start digging into the properties specific to individual components. For now, though, look at what the components have in common.

A rose by any other caption

The most visible property of many components is the Caption property. You can enter just about anything as a value for the Caption property — a word, a phrase, a sentence, even a short poem, such as "Fleas: Adam had 'em." The kind of caption that's appropriate depends on the particular component. For example, push buttons tend to have short action words for captions, but check boxes and radio buttons sometimes have complete sentences describing the options they control.

The ampersand (&) has amazing powers when used in a component caption. It turns the next character into a hot key (mnemonic access key) for the component. If a button's caption is &Press Me, the *P* shows up underlined, and pressing Alt+P has the same effect as pressing that button.

What if you want an ampersand in a caption, as in Save & Exit, or Ham & Eggs? No problem — just use *two* ampersands in the Caption property, for example, Ham && Eggs.

Any component that displays text has a Font property, just like a form has. However, if the ParentFont property is True, the component will automatically display its text in the font that was selected for the main form, and changing the main form's font will change the font used by the component. Most of the time, you'll leave ParentFont set to True.

As Figure 3-6 shows, you can use a nontext font such as Wingdings for a component's caption, but there are a few pitfalls. The character in the font that's in the position normally occupied by the ampersand will be treated as the ampersand. That & character causes the following character to be underlined, and the access key for the component is the text-font key corresponding to that character. If you want to use the character that corresponds to the &, you have to use *two* of them, the same as with an ampersand. "&L" in the Wingdings font is an underlined unhappy face, and Alt+L triggers it. Don't use mnemonic access keys with nontext fonts!

Figure 3-6:
You can use
a symbol
font for
button
captions.

Color me beautiful

Most components have a Color property that works just like the Color property for the form itself. You can select one of 16 named colors, or match the component's color to a Windows on-screen element, or choose any custom color that Windows can display. However, unless you're writing a program for designing patchwork quilts, chances are good that you won't want to set a different color for every component on the form. The True/False ParentColor property saves you the trouble of having to do so. When this property is True (which it is by default), the component takes on the color of the form. Change the form's color and the component changes to match. If you change the Color property of a component to something different than the form's color, Delphi flips ParentColor to False.

Most components also have a Ctl3D property and the corresponding ParentCtl3D property. As you might expect, when ParentCtl3D is True, the Ctl3D property is tied to the corresponding property of the main form. You almost always want to leave ParentCtl3D set to True.

Start with a new form, and set its Ctl3D property to False. Find the group box button on the Standard page of the Component palette. Place a group box on the form. It will appear as a black rectangle with the name GroupBox1 displayed on the top line, near the left corner. Now click the form and change its Ctl3D property to True. The group box changes, too — now its border appears to be incised into the imaginary surface of the form. Figure 3-7 shows the same form with and without Ctl3D.

Figure 3-7:
A form's
Ctl3D
property
gives a 3-D
look.

Don't ever set a component's Ctl3D property to True and leave ParentCtl3D set to False. The three-dimensional look is a cooperative effort between the form and its components.

That's about the size of it

Every component that shows up on the form when the program runs has dimension and location properties — Height, Width, Left, and Top. All four properties are expressed in pixels, and the Left and Top properties are measured relative to the top left corner of the form. If you snuggle a component right up into that top left corner, its Left and Top properties are both 0.

You can control the alignment and size of a group of components by setting these properties. If you know that a particular component is already the size you want, select it first and then Shift+click the others. Now when you go to set one of the dimension or location properties for the group, the value used by that first component appears as the default.

Some components, such as list boxes and memo boxes, have a property called Align, which controls the way they grab real estate from the form. Setting Align to alTop, alBottom, alRight, or alLeft causes the component to stick to the specified edge. For example, if Align is alBottom, the component snuggles up against the bottom of the form. When the form's size changes, the component keeps its height as designed, but change its width to fill the form's width. If another component is already aligned on the same edge, the two don't overlap — they stack against that edge. Setting Align to alClient causes the component to fill the form's client area (or at least, the part of the client area that's not already occupied by components aligned on the edges). Figure 3-8 shows a form filled by components aligned in various ways.

Behind the scenes

Quite a few of the common properties have no visible effect at design time, but quite an effect at run time. If you set the Enabled property to False, for example, the component rolls over and plays dead. It acquires a gray, deathly pallor, and it doesn't respond to any events.

Figure 3-8:
The
Alignment
property for
a Delphi
component
causes it to
hug one
edge of the
form or to
fill all
unoccupied
space on
the form.

First top-aligned panel gets top position

Second top-aligned panel stacks up against first

Client-aligned panel takes all remaining space

Left- and right-aligned panels stick to the sides

Bottom-aligned panel fills form's width

If you set the Visible property to False, the component is invisible at run time. It's still present, and the program can make it visible later on. The most common reason to make components invisible is to put more than one at the same location on the form, and make just one of them visible at a time.

You may be tempted to make controls invisible when they're not available. (For example, a File Save button may be invisible when no file is loaded.) Don't do it! Components that appear and disappear confuse the user. Instead, if a component is not available, disable it (set Enabled to False).

After you've mastered programming with Delphi, you can turn your energies toward a *truly* difficult task — creating Windows help systems for your programs. With the right tools, this is an onerous task, but the tools don't come with Delphi. Assuming that you've built a help file for your program, you can link a component to a topic in the help system by assigning the topic number to the component's HelpContext property. When you do that for all the program's components, the user can just press F1 for context-sensitive help. If you enable the Windows 95 help button by setting the form's BorderIcons.biHelp property to True, the user can also get help by pressing the Help button and then clicking a component.

If you don't feel ready to attack the Windows help system, consider giving hints. Just enter a pithy phrase describing each component into that component's Hint property. To have these hints displayed as flyover help, set the main form's ShowHint property to True, and leave each component's ParentShowHint property set to True. Don't meddle with the component's own ShowHint property; if you don't want a hint for a particular component, simply leave the Hint property blank. Your program can also display a hint for the active component or menu item on its status bar (see Chapter 7).

To store information that doesn't correspond to any existing property, you can use the Tag property. This capacious property holds any number from –2,147,483,647 to 2,147,483,648! You can represent a lot of different things with 4 billion numbers to choose from.

Pop-up menus are all the rage these days. If you click an object on the screen with the right mouse button, a menu related to that object pops up. The PopupMenu property defines a Delphi component's pop-up menu, but you can't just type in a value. You have to create a pop-up menu component (you discover how to do that in Chapter 6) before you can select it as a component's PopupMenu property. If you're not familiar with this type of menu, turn to Delphi itself. Display the Code Editor and right-click it. The items in the pop-up menu are enabled or disabled depending on where you click and whether any text is selected.

The mouse is essential to using Windows, but sometimes you don't want to take your hands off the keyboard. The TabStop and TabOrder properties help make programs work efficiently without a mouse. Pressing the Tab key moves the focus to the next component that has TabStop set to True. The word *next* in this case means the component with the next higher value for TabOrder. If you enter a value for TabOrder that's already in use by another component, Delphi adjusts the TabOrder of other components to make room for your new value.

As much as possible, all your programs should be usable with or without a mouse.

The DragMode and DragCursor properties automate drag-and-drop for components. If DragMode is set to dmAutomatic, you can click the component and drag a cursor representing the object. If the component the cursor is over can accept dropped objects, the cursor displays as whatever you chose for DragCursor; otherwise it becomes the universal No symbol: ∅.

1. **Start with a new form and place a label component on it.**

   The glyph for a label is just a big letter *A*.

2. **Set the label's caption to Drag me!**

3. **Double-click the label's DragMode property to change it to dmAutomatic.**

4. **Click the form and flip to the Events page in the Object Inspector.**

5. **Double-click the OnDragOver event and insert this code:**

```
Accept := Source IS TLabel;
```

This means that the form will accept dragged components as long as the type of the component is TLabel.

6. **Double-click the OnDragDrop event line in the Object Inspector window and insert these lines:**

```
WITH Source AS TLabel DO
BEGIN
 Left := X;
 Top := Y;
END;
```

These lines move the dragged component to the coordinates the cursor is pointing at.

7. **Run this program and drag the label around.**

Note that when you first press the mouse button, the cursor changes to the no-drag (slashed-circle No) symbol. That's because it's over the label itself and you didn't tell the label to accept dragged components. As soon as the cursor moves off the label, it turns into the default drag cursor, an arrow with a rectangle attached. When you release the mouse button to drop the label on the form, the form's OnDragDrop event handler moves the label to its new location. (Try dragging the label so that it protrudes off the right edge of the form; a horizontal scroll bar appears like magic.)

Every component has a unique Name property. Initially, Delphi assigns a default name such as Form1 or Button2, choosing the first number that's not in use. You can replace this with a name of your own choice, subject to certain restrictions: The name can't already be in use by another component; it must be composed solely of letters, digits, or the underscore character; and it can't begin with a digit. You can also delete the name entirely, if your program has no need to refer to the component by name — this is often true of label components. In general, you'll find it's just as easy to stick with the default names that Delphi provides.

You can't delete the name of *every* component of a given type. If your program uses labels, for example, you need to leave a name on at least one label. Delphi needs this information to decide which of its many code modules your program depends on.

Common Events

Like forms, most components respond to mouse, keyboard, and system events. There are exceptions — for example, static text labels don't respond to the keyboard, and Timer components respond only to the OnTimer event.

Most components have a default event; double-clicking the component in the Form Designer transports you instantly to the code for the default event. The three standard default events are OnChange, OnClick, and OnCreate, in that order. The first of these that's available will be the component's default. If a component doesn't respond to any of the three, it doesn't have a default.

Mouse events

As your sore index finger knows well, the most common mouse event is clicking, specifically clicking the left button. The OnClick event is definitely the most popular mouse event. A component receives the OnClick event when the left mouse button is released while the mouse pointer is over the component. As a bonus, Delphi also sends an OnClick event to many components when they're activated from the keyboard.

Occasionally, you want the more detailed information that comes with the OnMouseDown and OnMouseUp events. These two tell you which mouse button was pressed, where the mouse cursor was positioned, and even which Shift keys were held down, if any. You can also use OnMouseUp instead of OnClick if you need to tell a mouse-click from a hot key.

Oddly enough, when mouse-clicking is *not* the primary occupation of a component, it's more likely to respond to the OnDblClick event as well as OnClick. It's important to remember that OnDblClick is always preceded by OnClick. Windows can't read your mind, so it sends an OnClick event with the first click and then sets an internal timer. If another click comes before the timer runs out, it sends an OnDblClick event.

Drag-and-drop events

Drag-and-drop events are a variety of mouse event, but they're specialized enough to deserve separate mention. As you see in the discussion of the DragMode property (in the "Behind the scenes" section), a component's OnDragOver event is triggered when the user drags another component over it. Commonly, this event responds by setting the Accept parameter to True or False, indicating whether or not it can accept the particular component. A component's OnDragDrop event occurs when the user actually drops another component on it.

OnStartDrag, on the other hand, is received by the component that's being dragged, and it's triggered when the user starts dragging. Likewise, OnEndDrag is received by the component that's being dragged, and it's triggered when the user stops dragging, whether or not the component was successfully dropped.

Place a label on a new form, change its caption to Drag Me, and set its DragMode to dmAutomatic. Place several more labels on the form, select them all, and change the caption for all of them to Target. Then flip to the Events page in the Object Inspector window and create an OnDragOver handler for the Target labels; the handler should contain just one line:

```
Accept := True;
```

Select the Drag Me! label and give it an OnDragOver event handler containing these lines:

```
WITH Sender AS TLabel DO
Caption := 'Dragging';
Accept := False;
```

Create an OnEndDrag method for it like this:

```
IF Target <> NIL THEN
WITH Target AS TLabel DO
 Caption := 'A HIT!';
WITH Sender AS TLabel DO
Caption := 'Drag Me!';
```

The WITH Sender AS TLabel DO expression takes the Sender variable (which could theoretically be any draggable component) and treats it as a TLabel. Using it is like a promise to Delphi that the sender *is* a TLabel. If it's not, Delphi will complain that you've made an invalid typecast.

Run the program and try dragging the Drag Me! label around. Its caption changes to Dragging. The form itself doesn't accept drag-drop events, so the cursor displays a slashed-circle No symbol. When the dragged label is over a Target label, the cursor changes to an arrow, indicating that the Target label will accept a drop. Drop on the target and its caption changes to A HIT! Whether you drop on a target or not, when you release the mouse button the original label changes back to Drag Me!

Keyboard events

For most components, the built-in processing of access keys is all the keyboard input you need. For components that accept text input from the keyboard, advanced Delphi users can filter or modify text input through the keyboard events, as you see in the next chapter. Here's a little project to see how the mouse and keyboard events interact.

Place a single button on an empty form. Set its caption to &Up, and set its Default property to True. Fill in its event handlers as follows:

Event Handler	Code
OnClick:	MessageBeep(0);
OnMouseDown:	Button1.Caption := '&Down';
OnMouseUp:	Button1.Caption := '&Up';
OnKeyDown:	IF Key = 32 THEN Button1.Caption := '&Down';
OnKeyUp:	IF Key = 32 THEN Button1.Caption := '&Up';

Run the program and play with the button. When you press the mouse down while pointing at the button, the caption changes to Down; after you release the mouse, the caption changes back to Up. Press the Spacebar and the caption changes to Down; release the Spacebar and the caption changes back to Up. When you release the mouse button or Spacebar, an OnClick event occurs, and you hear a beep. Press Alt+U or Enter, and the OnClick event occurs audibly, with no other key or mouse event. Nine times out of ten, the OnClick method is sufficient to handle mouse and keyboard interaction with a component. As you can see, however, the other events give you finer control.

System events

The form is a program's big boss, and it does most of the negotiating with the Windows bureaucracy. Individual components don't have the wealth of system events that a form has. For the most part, when a component gets the focus, it receives an OnEnter event; when it loses the focus, it gets an OnExit event. That's it for system events. I can show you how this works. Start the next set of steps on a new form.

1. **Shift+click the edit box icon in the Component palette.**

   Its glyph looks like a tiny edit box with the letters *ab* inside.

2. **Place five or six edit boxes on the form, select all the boxes, and set their AutoSelect property to False.**

3. **Insert these lines as the boxes' OnEnter event handler:**

```
WITH Sender AS TEdit DO
Font.Color := clRed;
```

4. **Use these lines as the boxes' OnExit event handler:**

```
WITH Sender AS TEdit DO
Font.Color := clWindowText;
```

5. **Run the program and try selecting the different edit boxes with the mouse, or press Tab repeatedly.**

The text of the active edit box always shows up in red. Remember this trick when you're writing big data entry forms with dozens of edit boxes!

Special events

For the occasional component that responds to the OnChange event, OnChange takes precedence over OnClick as the default event for that component. If you double-click an edit box in the Form Designer, for example, you get the skeleton of an OnChange event handler. For an edit box, OnChange is triggered any time the text changes, whether it's due to the user's input or a command from the program itself.

Place a label above an edit box on a new form and stretch them both to fill the width of the form. Double-click the edit box and insert this line in its OnChange event handler:

```
Label1.Caption := UpperCase(Edit1.Text);
```

Run the program and type some text in the edit box. The label's caption faithfully echoes what you type, converted to uppercase.

Entering the Fourth Dimension

The position of components on a form is determined by their Left and Top properties. These are like the X and Y dimensions you may remember from graphs in high school algebra (assuming you stayed awake). There are actually two more dimensions involved in component positioning, Tab order and Z-order. *Tab order* is the order defined by the TabOrder property of the components on your form. One component at a time has the focus; that component receives the user's keyboard input. TabOrder controls the order in which the focus moves when the user presses Tab. The Tab order usually flows logically from left to right and top to bottom. Naturally, no two components can have the same TabOrder.

Unfortunately, the normal style of building a form is to add components as you think of them — not in a logical order. Each component gets the next unused TabOrder value, so the result is a Tab order that's based solely on *when* you placed the components, not on their order within the form. Before you can call a form finished, you need to adjust the Tab order of its components. To do this, choose Edit⇨Tab Order from the menu (or from any component's local menu), and simply shove components up and down in the resulting Edit Tab Order dialog, shown in Figure 3-9, until you get them in the right order. The easiest way to do that is to select the component that ought to be first in Tab order and drag it to the top slot in the list box. Then select the component that should be second and drag *it* into place, and so on.

If you have trouble relating the list of component names in the Edit Tab Order dialog to the components on your form, you can try another method. Here's what you do. First, decide how you want the focus to move around your form — remember that left to right and top to bottom is the standard. Now click the last component in your chosen order and set its TabOrder to 0. Delphi finds the component that had a TabOrder of 0 before and changes its TabOrder to 1, and this change ripples through all the other components as necessary to avoid duplication. Click the next-to-last component and set its TabOrder to 0. Again Delphi adjusts all the other components. Continue until you reach the first component; now every item has the correct TabOrder for your chosen order.

A combination of mouse and keyboard agility makes this process easy. Click the very first component and then click TabOrder in the Object Inspector, type **0**, and press Enter. For all the rest of the components, the sequence is click, type **0**, press Enter. You don't have to go back to the Object Inspector window, because Delphi assumes you want to type a new value for the property you used most recently.

Z-order can probably best be described as a dimension. The X dimension runs left to right, the Y dimension runs top to bottom, and the Z dimension runs straight out of the screen and hits you between the eyes. Place a few components on a form and move them so that their boundaries overlap. One component is on top of all the rest — it has the highest Z-order. The component that's overlapped by only the one that has the highest Z-order has the next-highest Z-order, and so on.

Figure 3-9:
Use the
Delphi Edit
Tab Order
dialog to
put your
components
in correct
Tab order.

Z-order is rarely as important as Tab order — it's not even a property. But when you need to set Z-order, it's just as easy as setting Tab order. Suppose you have three components that overlap each other. Click the one that should be on top of all the rest and choose Edit⇨Send to Back from the menu. Click the one that should be in the middle and send it to the back. Finally, click the one that should be below the other two and send it to the back. That's all there is to it!

Chapter 4

Standard Components

● ●

In This Chapter

▶ Deciding which standard components to use

▶ Grouping radio buttons and check boxes so that they work together

▶ Discovering how one Delphi component can enable and disable another

▶ Creating a password-entry dialog

▶ Creating a program that lets you edit AUTOEXEC.BAT and keep a backup

▶ Using a list box to sort the lines of a text file in order

▶ Adding color and graphics to a list box

▶ Controlling the form's color using scroll bars

● ●

*T*he Delphi standard components are a perfect match for on-screen elements supported by Windows 95, and they come with added features that make them easy to use. Nearly every Windows program uses these components, so it's important that you select the right component for the job. As Figure 4-1 shows, Delphi puts the components you use the most on the first page (called the Standard page) of the Component palette.

Figure 4-1:
The
Standard
page on the
Delphi
Component
palette.

Choosing Standard Components

At first, it might seem like the Delphi Component palette gives you *too* many choices. In fact, every component has a particular purpose and is the best in a given circumstance. To see these components in use, you can look at any Windows program, including Delphi itself. Refer to Table 4-1 any time you're not sure which standard component to choose.

Table 4-1	Problems Solved by Standard Components
Task	*Component*
Activate a feature in your program.	Push button. See "You're Pushing My Buttons!"
Choose between two or more mutually exclusive options.	Radio button. See "Punching Radio Buttons."
Choose one or more nonexclusive options.	Check box. See "Checking Off Your Options."
Associate groups of related radio buttons, check boxes, or other components.	Group box. See "Join the In Group."
Add an identifying label to a component.	Label. See "Pinning Labels on Components."
Take one-line input from the user.	Edit box. See "Fill in the Blank in an Edit Box."
Take multiline, justified, or scrolling input from the user.	Memo box. See "Take a Memo."
Display a list of items for single or multiple choice.	List box. See "I've Got a Little List."
Display a list of items for single choice using minimal space on the form; optionally allow the user to enter a value not on the list.	Combo box. See "A Two-Player Combo (Box)."
Display or adjust the value of a continuous numeric quantity.	Scroll bar. See "Belly Up to the (Scroll) Bar."

Okay, if you look really closely, you notice that the panel component on the Standard page in the Component palette isn't covered in this chapter. Panel is *not* a standard Windows component, and its purpose is mostly related to the look and feel of a form, so I discuss it in Chapter 7, on graphical components. And the menu and pop-up menu components, also on the Standard page, are so important that all of Chapter 6 is devoted to them.

You're Pushing My Buttons!

In the real world, buttons that you press make things happen. Use the Delphi push button component to make things happen in your program.

Properties

The most visible property for a push button is its Caption property. A caption for a push button should be a short action word that describes what the button does. Try picturing a caption as a line of dialog for the Terminator: OK, Yes, No, Load, Run, and Shoot are all good possibilities.

An ampersand in a button caption makes the character that follows a mnemonic access key for the button. Pressing Alt with the access key is the same as clicking the button.

Some captions have special meanings based on the way most Windows programmers use them. OK means shut down the form and accept its data, Cancel means shut down the form and throw away its data, Help means HELP! Don't use different words for these functions, or your program will be ostracized for talking funny. Of course, the captions that you select yourself must be consistent. If you use Load for the name of a button that opens a file in one form, and Replicate for the same purpose in another form, you confuse the poor user.

Setting a button's Cancel property to True associates that button with the Esc key; Esc becomes the access key for the button. Commonly, the caption for a button with Cancel set to True is (suprise!) Cancel. A button with the Default property set to True is activated when the user presses Enter, unless the user has tabbed to another button. The standard caption for a Default button is OK. Only one button with the Cancel property and one button with the Default property should be active at any given time — one per form or one per page on a multipage form. (This default button behavior sounds a little complicated, but you've been *using* it for as long as you've been using Windows.)

When a form has lots of components, it can be difficult to find enough distinct access keys to go around. Don't bother giving an ampersand-style access key to a button with the Default or Cancel property.

A push button doesn't have a Color property because its color is rigidly dominated by the color settings in the Windows Control Panel. Separate Control Panel settings exist for the button face, the text on the button, the shadow along the bottom and right edges, and the highlight along the top and left edges. You can control the font used for the button's caption as far as size and typeface go, but don't bother setting a font color. No matter what vivid color you choose, Windows will sneer and discard your choice, replacing it with the button text color set by Control Panel.

The ModalResult property is useful only in secondary forms that function as modal dialogs. A modal dialog is a form that gets in the user's face and won't go away until it gets a response. The rest of the program can't continue until the user closes the modal dialog. When you set a button's ModalResult property to a nonzero value, pressing that button closes the modal dialog and returns the ModalResult value to the calling program.

Events

It's no surprise that the big event for a push button comes when you push it. Most push buttons need to respond only to the OnClick event, nothing more. When you double-click a push button in the Form Designer, Delphi creates a skeleton for an OnClick event handler in the Editor window.

On a new form, place an edit box, place a button, and change the button's caption to OK. Double-click the button. You flip into the Code Editor with the cursor on a line between the words *begin* and *end.* Type the following:

```
Close;
```

Run the program. Press Enter vigorously; nothing happens. Click the button to end the program, change the button's Default property to True, and run the program again. This time when you press Enter, it wipes out the program, just like clicking the button. What a difference Default makes!

Start a new project and then do the following:

1. **Choose File⇨New Form from the menu.**

2. **Drop a button on the secondary form.**

3. **Set the button's Caption property to OK.**

4. **Set the button's Default property to True.**

5. **Set the button's ModalResult property to mrOK.**

6. **Size the secondary form so that it's just a little bigger than the button and set its properties as follows:**

Property	Value
BorderIcons.biSystemMenu	False
BorderIcons.biMinimize	False
BorderIcons.biMaximize	False
BorderStyle	bsDialog
Position	poScreenCenter

7. **Switch to the main form and place a push button with the caption &Show Form2.**

8. **Put this line in the button's OnClick event handler:**

```
Form2.ShowModal;
```

9. **In the Code Editor page for Unit1, the first form's unit, scroll all the way to the top and find a line that contains the lone word uses.**

10. **Type** Unit2, **to the end of this line (don't forget the comma).**

11. **Choose File⇨Use Unit and choose the secondary form's unit.**

The short way to describe what you did by inserting the name Unit2 is: "Add Unit2 to the uses clause." When you run this program, clicking the Show Form2 button displays the secondary form, and clicking the OK button on that form closes it. You don't have to write any code to close Form2; setting the OK button's ModalResult property to mrOk is enough.

When you see a table of property names and values like the one in the preceding instructions, set each property to the specified value. If a property name contains a period, such as BorderIcons.biMaximized, you should find the first portion of the property name and double-click to explode it and then find the second portion in the exploded list.

Join the In Group

Group boxes keep other components neatly corralled on the form. They associate related components visually and logically. In fact, a group box takes on some of the capabilities of a form — it's a kind of straw boss to the components it contains. When you place a component in a group box, its ParentColor, ParentShowHint, ParentFont, and ParentCtl3D properties refer to the group box — not to the form. The Left and Top properties of a component in a group box are relative to the top left corner of the group box. If you move the group box, all the components it contains will move, too.

On a new form, place a group box. Place one radio button on the group box and another on the form outside the group box. Drag the second radio button onto the group box. Move the group box and watch what happens — the first radio button moves with it, but the second is left behind.

This little experiment reveals that you can't fool a group box. If you want a group box to contain a particular component, you have to create the component in the group box. Dragging it in after the fact just won't work. If you've invested time and effort in setting a component's properties only to realize later that it should be inside a group box, there *is* hope. Click the component and press Ctrl+X to cut it to the Clipboard. Then click the group box and press Ctrl+V to paste the component into the group box.

Often when you paste a component into a group box, it seems to disappear. That's because its Left and Top properties are measured from the top-left corner of the group box, and the box isn't as big as the form. To avoid this problem, *move* the component to the top left corner of the form before you cut it to the Clipboard. If you pasted the component and forgot to move it first, use the Object Inspector window to set the Left and Top properties of the component to 0. How do you use the Object Inspector when you can't see the component in the first place? Pull down the component list at the top of the Object Inspector; you find your lost component there.

Group boxes have no important properties beyond the common ones described in Chapter 3. They *can* respond to the common keyboard, mouse, and system events, but they almost never do.

Punching Radio Buttons

These days, car radios are digitally controlled miniatures of home stereo systems, with CD audio and digitally controlled tuning. *Some* of us remember when we had to twist a knob to tune the radio, or punch a button to choose a favorite station. It took some oomph to push those buttons because they dragged the tuner to the specified location. And when you pushed in one button, any other pushed-in button would pop out. This nostalgic trip explains the origin of the name for Windows radio buttons. They always come in groups (visibly marked by a group box), and only one button per group can be pushed in at a time. Each radio button has a circle next to its caption, and the one that's pushed in has a filled circle.

Use radio buttons to let the user choose between two or more options that are mutually exclusive. For example, the Delphi Find dialog uses radio buttons to let you choose a forward or backward search. At any given time, you can search in one direction or the other, but never in both.

Properties

The Alignment property for a radio button determines whether the caption appears to the right or left of the circle. Normally it's on the right, but you can set Alignment to taLeftJustify to put the caption on the left.

A radio button's most important property is the Checked property. This property is True only for the one radio button in the group that's selected. It's possible for all the radio buttons in a group to start off with Checked set to False, but if you try to set a second button's Checked property to True, even at design time, Delphi will change the first one to False.

Place a group box and a push button on a form and then add three radio buttons inside the group box. Give the three radio buttons different captions, each with a different access key, for example, &Curly, &Larry, &Moe. For each button in turn, set the Checked property to True — note that it remains True only for the button you set last.

Run the program. Press Tab repeatedly and note how the focus moves back and forth between the push button and the selected radio button. Press the access keys for the radio buttons — they all work. Now fool around with the arrow keys. The down and right arrow keys move the selection through the group of radio buttons, staying within the group box. The up and left arrow keys do the same thing in reverse.

Events

The average radio button only shows whether it's the lucky selected button. That's all handled without any effort on your part. When the program needs to know which button is selected, it peeks and sees which one of them has Checked set to True. However, you may want to tweak other components on your form, depending on which radio button is checked. Adding a handler for the OnClick event enables you to tweak the components on your form.

On a new form, first place a group box and then place a push button. Set the push button's caption to OK and its Default property to True. Double-click the push button and fill in its OnClick event handler with the single line:

```
Close;
```

Now put two radio buttons in the group box, with captions &Enabled and &Disabled. Set the Checked property of the first to True. Double-click the Enabled, radio button and fill its OnClick event handler with this line:

```
Button1.Enabled := True;
```

Double-click the Disabled button and do the same for its OnClick event handler, but replace True with False. Now run the program. If you click Disabled, the OK button is disabled; click Enabled and it works again.

Radio buttons and group boxes have a special relationship that Delphi celebrates by marrying the two in its RadioGroup component. A RadioGroup is a group box whose purpose in life is to display radio buttons. Its Items property is a list of captions for the radio buttons, and its ItemIndex property indicates which button is checked. If ItemIndex is –1, none of the radio buttons is checked. The radio buttons will be neatly arranged in as many columns as the Columns property specifies. Any time you want a group box with only radio buttons inside, it's much simpler to just use a RadioGroup.

Checking Off Your Options

Like radio buttons, check boxes normally come in groups. However, you can check off as many of them as you like. For example, a form for ordering pizza may use radio buttons to choose a thick or thin crust, but check boxes to select any or all of the dozens of available toppings.

Usually the check box caption is to the right of the box itself, but in Delphi 3, you can reverse their positions with the Alignment property. Besides a True/False Check property, check boxes also have a State property with three values: cbChecked, cbUnchecked, and cbGrayed.

You use the cbGrayed state to show that the choice represented by the check box is not clearly one way or the other. Suppose the check box indicates that the text in your word processor is Politically Correct. If the selected text is "The old horse is dead," the box isn't checked. If the text is partially Politically Correct, ("The temporally gifted horse is dead"), the box is grayed. Clicking on a grayed check box causes it to be checked; in this example it also translates the sentence to "The temporally gifted equine companion is metabolically challenged."

Clicking a checked check box causes it to be unchecked. (Say that ten times fast!) If the AllowGrayed property is True, clicking an unchecked check box turns it to grayed; otherwise, it turns it to checked. Most of the time, you can avoid this confusion by leaving AllowGrayed set to False. Like radio buttons, check boxes are occasionally used to control the status of other items on the form through an OnClick event handler. Most of the time, though, your programs will simply peek at the Checked or State property.

Pinning Labels on Components

The label component has two main purposes. First, it can serve as a caption for another component that doesn't *have* its own caption, such as the list box or edit box components that you read about later in this chapter. Second, it can display read-only information for the program's user; an example of this is the score in a Solitaire game. A label can have a mnemonic access key, too, but pressing that key gives the focus to the caption-impaired component associated with the label. If you'd rather forgo the mnemonic access key and gain the ability to use the ampersand freely in the label's Caption, set the ShowAccelChar property to False.

The Alignment property determines whether a label's caption is left, right, or center justified within the space allowed. When the AutoSize property is True (the default), the label sizes itself to fit its Caption. Setting an autosized label to right alignment pins the right edge of the label to the form. If a right-aligned autosized label needs to grow larger, it grows to the left.

The FocusControl property determines which of the other components on the form will get the focus when the label's access key is pressed. Click the down arrow next to its value and choose from a list of components on the form. If you later change the name of that component, Delphi cleverly changes the FocusControl property to match the new name.

Occasionally, you may want to use a multiline label rather than several single-line labels. In that case, set the WordWrap property to True and be sure to make the label tall enough to accommodate multiple lines.

A label's background color is normally controlled by the Color property. If you set the Transparent property to True, though, the background disappears. Place a large rectangular label on the form so that it nearly fills the left half of the form, and place another that nearly fills the remaining space. Set the Color property of one to clFuchsia and of the other to clLime. (All right, you can choose any two colors that strike your fancy.) Now create a third label that overlaps the first two. Repeatedly double-click the third label's Transparent property, toggling it from False to True and back. You can use this property to place labels on top of Image components and other graphical components, as Figure 4-2 shows.

Figure 4-2: When a label's Transparent property is True, its background vanishes and only the text shows.

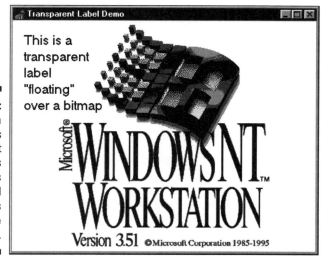

Fill in the Blank in an Edit Box

Computer programs are always asking questions. What is your name? What is your quest? What is your favorite color? You may select a quest or color from a list of what's available, but no computer can offer a list of all possible names. An *edit box* permits the user to enter anything.

Properties

An edit box has no caption. When you first place an edit box on the form, the all-important Text property is set to the edit box's name. In Delphi 3, you can delete this initial value, change it to a different default value, or have your program set the value just before displaying the edit box. Delphi 3 allows the Text property's length to be as long as the operating system allows. Windows 95 supports 32,767 characters as the limit. In Windows NT, text length is limited only by available memory. You can enter more text in an edit box than will fit in the boundaries of the box, but it's awkward to do so. As you add text at the end of the string, the beginning gets shoved out of sight. Use MaxLength to restrict the number of characters that can be entered and to set the physical size of the edit box large enough to hold that many characters. Make the edit box a little extra large, because different combinations of screen resolution and font size change the meaning of "large enough." If you need one super-long line of text or multiple lines, use a memo box, which I describe in the next section.

By default, an edit box has a single-line border around it to help users estimate just how much text they can enter. Never set the BorderStyle property to bsNone; it will only confuse users.

If the PasswordChar property is anything but ASCII character zero (#0), every character that's typed will show up as that character. This way, someone looking over the user's shoulder can't find out what was entered. The asterisk (*) is the usual password character, but you can use X or / or even a smiley face — any character will do.

ReadOnly means what it says — look but don't touch. The user can peruse the edit box's text, select and copy parts of it, and scroll it around, but that's all. Your program can turn this property on and off at run time, if necessary.

If AutoSelect is True (as it is by default), the text in the edit box is automatically selected any time the user tabs to the edit box. Be careful: This setting makes it easy to wipe out the contents of the edit box. That's because Tab followed by any character wipes out the selected text and replaces it with that character. It's your choice: make it easy for your users to replace text in edit boxes, or protect them from trashing text accidentally.

When an edit box isn't the active control, you can't see whether any text is selected. That helps the user keep track of which box is active. If you set the HideSelection property to False, however, the selection shows up even when the edit box isn't active. This is handy when your program displays another dialog that acts on the selected text, such as a Find and Replace dialog.

AutoSize is also True by default, but you probably want to set it to False. When this property is True, the edit box's height increases as necessary to accommodate a larger font. The problem is that the other components on the form don't automatically move to make room for the taller edit box, so this action may result in some ugly territorial squabbling.

Events

Most of the time, an edit box just gathers its input without any intervention from the programmer. The OnChange event occurs every time the value of the Text property changes, which can be useful. And you can use the OnKeyPress event to modify or prohibit certain keystrokes.

Be extremely careful if you put code in an OnChange event handler that makes a change to the Text property. Why? Because that change will trigger another OnChange event, which may trigger another, and another, indefinitely. Your program could go off to chase its own tail forever and crash Windows 95. (But a tail-chasing program can't knock out Windows NT!)

1. **Place an edit box on a new form and set the box's MaxLength property to 4.**

2. **Type these lines in its OnKeyPress event handler:**

```
IF ((Key < '0') OR (Key > '9')) AND (Key <> #8) THEN
BEGIN
  MessageBeep(0);
  Key := #0;
END;
```

3. **Use these lines for its OnChange event handler:**

```
WITH Sender AS TEdit DO
IF (Length(Text) > 0) AND
  (StrToInt(Text) > 4999) THEN
  BEGIN
    MessageBeep(0);
    Text := Copy(Text, 1, Length(Text)-1);
    SelStart := Length(Text);
  END;
```

4. **Click the edit box and press Ctrl+C.**

5. **Press Ctrl+V twice to paste two copies of the edit box into the form.**

6. **Arrange the three edit boxes so that they don't overlap.**

7. **Delete the Text property of all three boxes.**

The edit boxes in this program accept only numeric keys, and you can't enter a number greater than 4999. Try it! If the OnKeyPress event handler detects a key that's neither a digit nor a backspace (#8), it beeps and sets the Key parameter to ASCII #0. This tells Delphi to censor the key — it never reaches the edit box. And if the user types a digit that brings the number above 4999, the OnChange event handler beeps and cuts off that last digit. Delphi doesn't have a cut-off-last-character function, so you use the built-in Copy function to copy everything except the last digit.

Yes, I warned you earlier not to change the Text property in an OnChange event handler, and now I'm doing it. However, in this case, cutting off the last digit of the text does indeed trigger a second OnChange event, but no infinite tail-chasing chain of changes occurs because the second OnChange event doesn't make any further changes to the text.

Exercise your edit box control by building a password-entry dialog.

1. **Start a new project and choose File⇨New from the menu.**

2. **Flip to the Projects page and select the Fixed-Size Form project.**

3. **Change the form's Ctl3D property to False and change its caption to Change Password.**

4. **Add three labels, three edit boxes, and two buttons to a new form, arranging them as shown in Figure 4-3 and assigning their captions as shown in the figure.**

Figure 4-3:
Retype the final character of the password; the OK button will be enabled instantly.

5. **Create the labels and edit boxes from top to bottom, and the buttons from left to right.**

This arrangement is important because in the following code, I assume that the first button is Button1, the third label is Label3, and so on.

6. Set the OK button's Default property to True.

7. Set the Cancel button's Cancel property to True.

8. Select the OK button and the lower two labels and edit boxes, and set their Enabled property to False.

9. Select all three edit boxes, delete their text, set AutoSize to False, and set their PasswordChar property to the @ symbol.

10. Set each label's FocusControl property to the corresponding edit box.

11. Double-click the OK button and set its OnClick event handler to:

```
Close;
```

12. Double-click the Cancel button and set its OnClick event handler to:

```
Close;
```

13. Double-click the top edit box and insert these lines in its OnChange event handler:

```
Edit2.Enabled := Edit1.Text = 'Delphi';
Edit3.Enabled := Edit2.Enabled;
Label2.Enabled := Edit2.Enabled;
Label3.Enabled := Edit2.Enabled;
```

14. Select both of the lower edit boxes.

15. Flip to the Events page in the Object Inspector window and double-click the OnChange event.

16. Insert the following lines in the resulting event handler, which will be called when the value of *either* of the two edit boxes changes:

```
Button1.Enabled := (Edit2.Text <> '') AND
(Edit2.Text = Edit3.Text);
```

17. Run the program.

The lower two edit boxes are disabled until you enter the super-secret password *Delphi* in the first edit box. The OK button is disabled until you enter the same new password in the lower two edit boxes. The password dialog you just created is similar to the one Windows 3.1 uses for changing the screen saver password. You can't change the password until you've entered the existing password, and it won't accept the new password until you've typed it twice exactly the same.

Take a Memo

An edit box is good for getting one fairly short line of text from the user. For anything fancier, you need a memo box. A memo box holds multiple lines of text and has quite a few properties that an edit box doesn't, making it much more flexible. Several memo box properties behave exactly the same as the corresponding edit box properties: BorderStyle, ReadOnly, HideSelection, and MaxLength.

The text you enter in an edit box is always left-aligned with the box's border. If you want right or center justification, even for a single line of text, use a memo box and set the Alignment property to the style you want. (Don't confuse the Alignment property with the Align property. With the Align property, you can set a memo box so that it automatically sizes itself to fill either a portion of the form along any of the four edges or the entire available area of the form.)

The ScrollBars property lets you give the memo box a horizontal scroll bar, a vertical scroll bar, both, or neither. The WordWrap True/False property determines whether the text you enter automatically wraps at the end of the visible line. If you set WordWrap to True, you must not give the memo box a horizontal scroll bar — the two concepts are contradictory.

Normally the Tab key moves the focus around among the various components on a form, and the Enter key activates the default button. If your memo box needs to accept Tab as just another character, set the WantTabs property to True. If you want Enter to simply start a new line in the memo box, set the WantReturns property to True.

Even if you don't set WantTabs or WantReturns to True, you can enter Tab characters by pressing Ctrl+Tab, and you can start a new line by pressing Ctrl+Enter. This is true in the Delphi memo boxes as well.

The most important property for a memo box is the Lines property. Click the ellipsis button (. . .), and a dialog opens that lets you type numerous lines of text. These lines show up in the memo box at design time, and are its initial contents at run time. When your program needs to refer to the contents of the memo box, it looks at the Lines property.

The memo box's Lines property is actually an object itself, with its own special capabilities. Most impressively, it can load itself with text from a file and write its contents back to a file!

1. **Place a memo box on a new form and change the form's caption to AUTOEXEC Editor.**

2. **Set the ScrollBars property of the memo box to ssBoth and its Align property to alClient.**

3. Insert these lines in the form's OnCreate event handler:

```
Memo1.Lines.LoadFromFile('C:\AUTOEXEC.BAT');
Memo1.Lines.SaveToFile('C:\AUTOEXEC.BAK');
```

4. Insert this line of code in the OnCloseQuery event handler:

```
Memo1.Lines.SaveToFile('C:\AUTOEXEC.BAT');
```

Do you realize what you just did? You've created a simple editor devoted to editing AUTOEXEC.BAT! If your system boots from a different drive, change each occurrence of C: to the boot drive for your system. Now, did you think you'd be writing a text editor in this chapter?

I've Got a Little List

A list box stores a list of items and lets the user select one or several of them. You can preload the list at design time, or your program can add and remove items. A single-selection list box serves much the same purpose as a set of radio buttons — it lets the user select one of a number of mutually exclusive choices. But a list box can easily hold dozens or even hundreds of items, whereas the same number of radio buttons would overflow even the largest form. Also, you can easily build the list of choices at run time.

A multiple-choice list box lets the user select any number of choices, like a group of check boxes. Use a list box instead of the check boxes when there are more than eight or choices or when the choices aren't known at design time.

Properties

The Delphi list box component has an Align property, just like the memo box. You can set it to hug any of the four sides of the form or to occupy all available space on the form. The Items property in a list box is like the Lines property in a memo box. It's a collection of lines that you can preload at design time, and your programs can call on the Items property to load itself from a file or save its contents to a file. Your programs can treat Items as an array of strings, and the run-time-only ItemIndex property is the index of the selected item. For example, this line in an OnClick event handler displays the selected item in the label Label1:

```
Label1.Caption :=
ListBox1.Items[ListBox1.ItemIndex];
```

Most of the time, you leave the Style property set to its default of lbStandard. If it's lbOwnerDrawFixed, your program must take over the task of drawing the list box items (normally handled by Windows). If it's lbOwnerDrawVariable, your program has to draw the items and let Windows know how high each item is.

If you set the Sorted property to True, items inserted into the list box at run time will automatically be put in sorted order. At design time, any lines you've entered in the Items property are put into order when you set Sorted to True. If you then add more lines that aren't in order, Delphi cleverly sorts them as soon as you click OK to close the list editor.

You can use nonvisible sorted list boxes for minor sorting tasks in your programs. Delphi 3 programmers can take advantage of the fact that Windows 95 permits over 32,000 items per list box and puts no limit on the total string length. Windows NT doesn't even limit the number of items!

1. **Place a label in the top left corner of a new form.**

2. **Place an edit box to the right of the label.**

3. **Put another label and edit box just below the first pair.**

4. **Set each label's FocusControl property to the adjacent edit box.**

5. **Caption the labels &Input file and &Output file and delete each edit box's text.**

6. **Place a list box on the form and set its Visible property to False and its Sorted property to True.**

7. **Place a push button on the form with the caption &Sort, and fill in its OnClick event handler with these lines:**

```
ListBox1.Items.LoadFromFile(Edit1.Text);
ListBox1.Items.SaveToFile(Edit2.Text);
MessageDlg(Edit2.Text + ' sorted!', mtInformation,
        [mbOk], 0);
```

8. **Run the program and type into the first edit box the name of an existing small-to-medium text file.**

9. **Type a filename that's not already in use into the second edit box.**

10. **Click the Sort button and — presto! — the file is sorted.**

With just three lines of code, you've written a simple file-sorting program. But that's not all you've accomplished. Some potent protection against errors is built into any Delphi program, including the one you just wrote. If you omit the input or output filename, or use an invalid name, your program automatically pops up a warning to the user. The user also gets a warning if the input file is too big to fit in the list box.

The fancy name for this protection is *exception handling*. Try it and see what it's like. But first, open the Environment dialog (under the Tools⇨Options) and clear the box next to the Break on exception option. If you don't do that, the Delphi debugger traps the exception and displays a scary message box.

When the MultiSelect property is False, only one item in the list can be selected. If you click another item, the first one is deselected. If you set this property to True, though, you can select any or all of the items. Just how you select depends on another property, ExtendedSelect. When ExtendedSelect is True, you just click one item and Shift+click another to select the two items and all items between them. And you Ctrl+click any item to select or deselect it without affecting other items. When Extended-Select is False, each click on an item in the list box turns the selected state of that item on or off. You get a more versatile multiple selection list box when ExtendedSelect is True.

The Selected property isn't available at design time, but when your program is running it tells which items of a multiple choice list box are selected. For example, to find out if item number 10 is selected, you can do this:

```
if ListBox1.Selected[10] then...
```

Setting the Columns property to a nonzero value changes the look of a list box. The box's items are lined up in as many columns as you specify, and the scroll bar is horizontal. Few Windows programs use this type of list box, but it *can* come in handy. The four small list boxes in Figure 4-4 contain the same list of items but have different values for the Columns property.

If IntegralHeight is set to True, the list box automatically adjusts its height so as not to show a partial item at the bottom; see the rightmost list box in Figure 4-4 for an example of this. The height of items can change depending on the user's Windows setup, so adjusting it on your system at design time isn't enough. Note that it isn't possible to make a list box line up top and bottom with another component if IntegralHeight is True. The next-to-right list box in Figure 4-4 lines up correctly with its neighbors to the left, but the bottom portion of its last item is cut off.

List boxes are made for displaying text, but if you set the Style property to lbOwnerDrawFixed, your program can draw anything at all for the list box's items. Well, anything that fits in a rectangle. The ItemHeight property controls how high the items in an owner draw list box are. Set Style to lbOwnerDrawVariable and the items don't even have to be the same height.

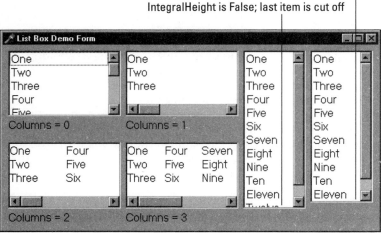

IntegralHeight is True; bottom of list box is not aligned

IntegralHeight is False; last item is cut off

Figure 4-4:
The four list
boxes have
different
Columns
property
values; the
two taller
list boxes
differ in
their
Integral-
Height
settings.

Events

A list box's OnClick event is triggered, logically enough, when you click it with the mouse. However, it's also conveniently triggered when you change the selection using the arrow keys.

In addition to the usual mouse, keyboard, and system events, list boxes respond to OnDrawItem and OnMeasureItem. These events occur when the list box has one of the two owner draw styles. A program responds to OnMeasureItem by indicating the height of the specified item. It responds to OnDrawItem by drawing the item. Try this example:

1. **Place a list box on a new form.**

2. **Set its Align property to alClient.**

3. **Set its Style to lbOwnerDrawVariable.**

4. **Enter 16 items in the Items property.**

   It doesn't matter what they are, as long as there are precisely 16 of them; you can enter the names of your 16 closest friends.

5. **Flip to the Events page and enter this line of code for the list box's OnMeasureItem event handler:**

```
IF Odd(Index) THEN Height := 2*Height;
```

6. Create an OnDrawItem event handler containing these lines:

```
WITH ListBox1.Canvas DO
BEGIN
  IF odFocused IN State THEN Brush.Color := 0
  ELSE Brush.Color := $FFFFFF;
  FillRect(Rect);
  Rect.Left := Rect.Left + 12;
  Brush.Color := $111111 * Index;
  FillRect(Rect);
END;
```

7. Run the program and scroll through the items in the list box.

Because of the OnMeasureItem event handler, every odd-numbered line is double-height. Because of the OnDrawItem event handler, instead of text, each item contains a different shade of gray, with a black marker at the left of the selected item.

A Two-Player Combo (Box)

Combo boxes (which combine edit boxes and list boxes) come in three types: simple, drop down, and drop-down list. The simple type looks like a list box with an edit box grafted onto its head. The drop-down type keeps the list rolled up out of sight like a window shade until you press the down arrow button to the right of the edit box. And the drop-down list type doesn't let you type anything in the edit box part; you can only choose an item from the list.

The simple type of combo box isn't very common because it doesn't provide the main advantage of a combo box — reduced space on the form. A combo box of any other type keeps its list portion rolled up, so it takes very little space, yet manages to display its current selection.

Naturally, the combo box shares many properties and events with the list box and edit box. Its Text property holds the text for the edit box portion. Items, ItemHeight, and Sorted behave just like those list box properties.

The Style property in a combo box determines whether this combo box keeps its list rolled up and whether the user can enter a value in the edit portion. If Style is csSimple, the list is always visible, like a list box, and the user either chooses from the list or types into the edit box. A style of csDropDown tells the combo box to keep the list rolled up when not in use. And csDropDownList keeps the list rolled up and restricts the user to choosing from the list instead of typing in anything. The DropDownCount property determines how many items appear at once in the list.

The csOwnerDrawVariable and csOwnerDrawFixed styles give you a drop-down list type combo box in which you control what's displayed, just like in an owner draw list box. If either of the owner draw styles is selected, you use the OnDrawItem event handler to draw the individual items. And if lbOwnerDrawVariable is the style, the event handler for OnMeasureItem lets you set the height of each item separately.

1. **Place a combo box on a new form and set its Sorted property to True.**

2. **Set its Style to csSimple.**

   You have to resize it to see the list part.

3. **Flip to the Events page and double-click OnKeyPress.**

4. **Type this code:**

```
IF Key = #13 THEN
BEGIN
  ComboBox1.Items.Add(ComboBox1.Text);
  ComboBox1.Text := '';
  Key := #0;
END;
```

5. **Run the program and enter some lines into the combo box.**

After you press Enter (which is the key whose code is #13), the line you typed is inserted into the list portion of the combo box, in sorted order.

Belly Up to the (Scroll) Bar

Memo, list box, and combo box components can have scroll bars built-in, but you can also place independent scroll bars on a form. You use these for setting a value that can vary continuously between two fixed extremes, like the volume sliders on your stereo's graphic equalizer. You can grab the movable "thumb" with the mouse and drag it to a new position or you can click the scroll bar to move in predefined increments. Clicking the arrows at either end moves the thumb a small increment, whereas clicking the bar itself either above or below the thumb moves it a large increment.

Properties

Scroll bars can be horizontal or vertical, depending on the value of the Kind property. A newborn scroll bar is always horizontal — when you switch the Kind to sbVertical, it pivots on the top left corner. The Max and Min properties control the range of the scroll bar, and Position reports the current position in that range. SmallChange determines how far the thumb will move in response to a click on the arrows at the end of the scroll bar, and LargeChange affects how far it moves when you click the scroll bar itself.

Events

The big event for a scroll bar is OnChange. Any change to the position of the thumb causes an OnChange event. OnScroll is a more low-level scroll bar event triggered by *any* activity on the scroll bar, even if it doesn't move the thumb. For example, if the scroll bar's thumb is already at the top, clicking the up arrow generates an OnScroll event but not an OnChange event.

1. **Start a new project using the Fixed-Size Form template and set the form's properties like this:**

Property	*Value*
Caption	Color Changer
Ctl3D	False
Color	clWhite

2. **Place three horizontal scroll bars on the form, spacing them evenly and sizing them to almost the full width of the form.**

3. **Select all three bars and set their properties as follows:**

Property	*Value*
LargeChange	16
Max	255
Position	255

4. **Keeping all the bars selected, flip to the Events page and double-click OnChange.**

5. **Put this statement in the OnChange event handler:**

```
Color := RGB(ScrollBar1.Position,
ScrollBar2.Position,
ScrollBar3.Position);
```

When you run the program, it will look like Figure 4-5. Use the mouse to tweak the scroll bars: The top one controls the amount of red in the form's color; the middle one, the amount of green; and the bottom one, the amount of blue. The left and up arrow keys scroll the focused scroll bar left one unit (SmallChange); the right and down arrow keys scroll right one unit. PgUp scrolls left 16 units (LargeChange), and PgDn scrolls right 16 units. Home and End go to the left and right ends of the scroll bar, respectively.

These standard components are the lowest-level building blocks of the Windows interface. Master them and you've graduated from Windows novice to journeyman.

Figure 4-5:
Scroll bars
control
values such
as the
amount of
red, green,
and blue in
a form.

Chapter 5
A Dialog with Windows

- -

In This Chapter

▶ Creating a simple text editor program that loads and saves text files

▶ Modifying the text editor to display its text in any font, style, or color

▶ Adding font selection to the simple editor

▶ Setting the system-wide printer configuration from any program

▶ Adding printing to the simple editor

▶ Adding search and replace capabilities to the simple editor

- -

*S*tandardized Windows on-screen elements such as buttons, list boxes, and menus have always given Windows applications a helpful consistency. It's a bit humdrum, compared to the exciting world of DOS-based programs, where you never know whether help is F1, F3, ?, or Ctrl+Alt+Shift+H. But if you know how to use one Windows application, you have a head start on using every other Windows application.

Windows 3.1 raised this consistency to new heights with *common dialogs*. Now every Windows program can use the same dialogs for selecting files, choosing fonts or colors, finding text, and printing. Windows 95 adds more power to the common dialogs, and Delphi 3 makes these supercharged dialogs available. Use the common dialogs whenever you can; you save time and effort.

Common Habits of Common Dialogs

The Delphi common dialog components all live together on the Dialogs page in the Component palette and have a lot of traits in common. At design time, the components all appear on your form as little icons that can't be resized, and at run time, none of them appears. To make a common dialog component show up in response to an event, you execute it. No, put down that guillotine! You call its Execute method, as in the following example:

```
OpenDialog1.Execute;
```

The File, Color, and Printer dialogs basically take over. Your program can't continue until you click OK or Cancel, at which point the Execute function returns True (if OK was clicked) or False (otherwise).

The Find and Replace dialogs are more egalitarian. Their Execute function returns right away, and the dialog shares space with your program until you get tired of it. That way, you can leave the dialog open and click Find Next repeatedly to continue finding occurrences of the item you're looking for.

All the common dialog components have a Ctl3D property. The Windows 95 common dialogs used in Delphi 3 are always 3-D, but the property still exists so existing code doesn't need to be rewritten. All common dialog components also have a HelpContext property, and each component's Options property has a subproperty that enables a Help button. If that subproperty is True, clicking the button brings up the Help system page with the number that matches HelpContext. (That is, this happens if you have a Help system attached to your program.) Each common dialog except the Print Setup dialog has its own specialized Options property that explodes into a set of True or False properties specific to the component.

The File, Color, and Printer dialogs don't have any events associated with them. Your program simply executes them and acts on the user's choices. The Font, Find, and Replace dialogs all have associated events, triggered by clicking buttons on the dialog. For example, clicking the Font dialog's Apply button generates an OnApply event, giving you the opportunity to apply the user's changes to some text without closing the Font dialog. Now you can get down to details.

Opening Data Files

It's a rare program that doesn't use some kind of file storage for data. Thanks to the Open File common dialog shown in Figure 5-1, all Windows 3.1 and Windows 95 programs can open files in similar ways. And the overwhelming set of options enables you to fine-tune the dialog to address your program's particular needs.

Properties

By default, the caption of an Open File common dialog is just Open. You probably want to change that to something appropriate to your program. That's easy — just set the Title property to, for example, Open Completely Different File (which is used in Figure 5-1).

Figure 5-1:
The
Windows 95
Open File
common
dialog is set
up for
loading
various
types of
graphics
files.

The Filename property is the payoff for using the dialog. After the user clicks OK, the dialog disappears from view, and your program can retrieve the selected file from the Filename property. If you want the dialog to start with a particular filename displayed, your program should fill in the Filename property just before executing the dialog. Otherwise, your program retains the value it had the last time the dialog was used.

InitialDir specifies what directory the dialog should display at first. If you leave it empty, the dialog starts in the directory that your program last accessed. If you put a value in it, the dialog always starts in the specified directory.

Setting a default extension with the DefaultExt property isn't all that useful, but you may as well do it. If the user painstakingly types in a filename, rather than simply pointing and clicking, and runs out of steam before typing an extension, the Open File common dialog appends the default extension. Also, the dialog warns you if the user chose a file with an extension different from the default extension.

You probably noticed that file common dialogs display a set of choices at the bottom left — a drop-down list box labeled Files of type (refer to Figure 5-1). The Filter property enables you to create a list such as this for yourself. Until Delphi came along, creating this list was a laborious process. You had to build one long string containing the description and file specification for every type. One misplaced character could throw the whole thing off. In Delphi, however, you just double-click the Filter property and fill in the names and file specifications as in Figure 5-2. Notice that one filter can include multiple file specifications, separated by semicolons.

FilterIndex indicates which of the filter items should be selected initially. Just leave it at its default value of 1 and put the most popular filter at the beginning of the list.

Figure 5-2:
The Delphi
Filter Editor
simplifies a
tedious
Windows
programming
task.

The FileEditStyle property enables you to enhance the basic Windows file common dialog by changing the filename edit box into a combo box. The HistoryList property gives access to the combo box's list of items. The name gives it away; you normally use the list to store recently loaded files.

That leaves only the Options property, but what a property it is! After you double-click it, it explodes to more than a dozen individual True or False properties.

Options that affect the display

Some elements of the Open File dialog are optional. The Help button, for example, is absent unless you set the ofShowHelp option to True. The Read Only check box disappears if the ofHideReadOnly property is True. This check box is useless by itself in any case. If it's present, your program is responsible for opening the file in a way that doesn't permit changes. Unless you really *need* to enable read-only file viewing, you want to hide the check box. The Open File dialog in Figure 5-1 has ofShowHelp set to True and ofHideReadOnly set to False.

Delphi 3 supports the standard Windows 95 Open File dialog, which has a Network button and displays long filenames. You can suppress the Network button by setting ofNoNetworkButton to True, and force old DOS-style filenames by setting ofNoLongNames to True. You can even go for the totally retro-chic Windows 3.1 style by setting ofOldStyleDialog to True!

Options that affect what you can do

If your user politely chooses a file from the list using the mouse, you're pretty much guaranteed a safe and correct result. However, users are permitted to improvise by typing a filename directly into the common dialog, and users are amazingly talented at creating incorrect filenames. By default, the Open File dialog rejects an entry that contains invalid characters. You can turn off this behavior by setting ofNoValidate to True, but why would you want to?

If you don't want to deal with read-only files, just set ofNoReadOnlyReturn to True and the dialog doesn't let the user to choose read-only files. Notice that this is unrelated to the read-only check box on the dialog. ofNoReadOnlyReturn controls what files can be selected; the check box simply carries a message saying whether the user wants to open the selected file in a read-only mode.

What does your program do if the user tries to open a file that doesn't exist yet? You need to decide whether this is permitted or not. If not, set ofFileMustExist to True and the common dialog rejects nonexistent files. If new files are allowed, you may want to set ofCreatePrompt to True. This action causes the dialog to ask for confirmation before creating a new file — a handy wake-up call in case users thought they were typing an existing filename.

Even if you feel expansive enough to enable users to create new files, you may draw the line at creating new directories to hold those files. Set ofPathMustExist to True and the common dialog doesn't accept a filename unless it's in an existing directory.

Set ofShareAware to True if you're using the dialog to choose database files that may be in use by some other person or application. The Delphi database file components have file-sharing capability built-in. If this option is False, the Open File dialog doesn't let the user to choose a file that's already in use. That's the more prudent course if your program is opening a file without using the database components.

Other options

The Open File dialog has a few other useful options and a few that aren't good for much. If you set of NoChangeDir to True, the dialog returns to its starting directory after it's finished. And ofAllowMultiSelect enables the user to select multiple files; the list of files turns up in a run-time-only property named, appropriately, Files.

The ofOverwritePrompt option doesn't mean anything in an Open File dialog — it's there only because the Save File dialog uses the same set of options. The same is true of ofNoTestFileCreate. You can check of Extension Different after executing the Open File dialog to see whether the user selected a file with a different extension from the default, but you rarely have any reason to do so.

The ofReadOnly option holds the state of the read-only check box in the dialog. The expression for checking it is as follows:

```
IF ofReadOnly IN OpenDialog1.Options
```

The common dialog is just a messenger here — it's up to your program to *do* something about this check box. Unless the program actually provides some method for opening a file for nothing but viewing, you should hide the read-only check box.

Brother, Is Your Data Saved?

Every time a program opens an existing file, the program should use the Open File dialog. And every time a program saves a file for the first time or saves it under a new name, the program should use the Save File dialog. The two dialogs have a lot in common — in fact, their property lists are identical.

Properties

The only difference between the properties of the Save File dialog and the Open File dialog is in the meaning of some of the options. OfCreatePrompt isn't relevant here, but ofOverwritePrompt causes the dialog to warn users if they choose to save to an existing filename. OfReadOnly is simply irrelevant in this dialog.

Build a simple text editor

You can use these components to make a simple text editor. In the process, you're going to use a bevel component. You haven't been properly introduced to the bevel in this chapter, but don't be shy. Pretend you're friends now; you get a full introduction in Chapter 7. You find the bevel on the Additional page of the Component palette. So just follow these steps:

1. **Place a bevel component on a new form and set its Align property to alTop.**

2. **Place four buttons on the bevel. Caption them &Open. . . ., &Save, Save &As. . . , and E&xit.**

   The three-dot ellipsis at the end of two of the names is a secret Windows code that means clicking the button displays a dialog instead of performing some immediate action.

3. **Drop a memo box on the form with its properties set as follows:**

Property	*Value*
Align	alClient
ScrollBars	ssBoth
Lines	(blank)

4. **Change the form's Caption to My Editor.**

5. **Now drop an Open File dialog on the form and give it the following properties:**

Property	*Value*
DefaultExt	TXT
FileEditStylefs	ComboBox
Options.ofHideReadOnly	True
Options.ofFileMustExist	True
Options.ofNoReadOnlyReturn	True
Title	Open Text File

6. **Double-click the Filter property to open the Filter Editor.**

7. **Fill in the first two lines in the Filter Name column with Text files and All files and type the corresponding filters *.TXT and *.* in the Filter column.**

8. **Place a Save File dialog on the form and give it almost the same set of properties:**

Property	*Value*
DefaultExt	TXT
Options.ofHideReadOnly	True
Options.ofOverwritePrompt	True
Options.ofNoReadOnlyReturn	True
Title	Save Text File

9. **Fill in the same set of filters as you did for the Open File dialog.**

10. **Create an OnClick event handler for the Exit button with just the command** Close; **in it.**

11. **For the Open button OnClick event handler, use these lines of code:**

```
WITH OpenDialog1 DO
  IF Execute THEN
    BEGIN
      Memo1.Lines.LoadFromFile(Filename);
      HistoryList.Add(Filename);
      Caption := 'My Editor - ' +
        ExtractFilename(Filename);
      SaveDialog1.Filename := Filename;
      Filename := '';
    END;
```

Notice that *Filename* is the name I give to a variable, not something you're supposed to replace with your own filename.

12. **Double-click the Save button and enter the following line for its OnClick event handler:**

```
Memo1.Lines.SaveToFile(SaveDialog1.Filename);
```

13. **Finally, use the following lines for the Save As. . . button:**

```
WITH SaveDialog1 DO
  IF Execute THEN
    BEGIN
      Memo1.Lines.SaveToFile(Filename);
      Caption := 'My Editor - ' +
        ExtractFilename(Filename);
    END;
```

Leaping Lizards! As Figure 5-3 shows, you've written a simple text editor. It can load, edit, and save small to medium files; its capacity is roughly the same as the Windows Notepad accessory. You can cut, copy, and paste text by using the standard Windows keystrokes. And each file you open is added to a history list in the Open File dialog in case you want to open it again soon. You return to this project later, so save it now. Name the unit MYEDITU.PAS and the main project MYEDIT.PRJ.

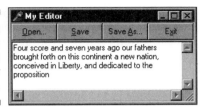

Figure 5-3:
Building
this simple
text editor
is a snap.

Taking Advantage of Windows Fonts

If you use any Windows word processor, you've probably seen the Font common dialog many times. Even the puny little Write accessory uses it. Choose Character⇨Fonts. . . from Write's menu bar and you see the Font common dialog. (You can access the Font dialog also by double-clicking the Font property of any Delphi component.) Figure 5-4 shows a Font common dialog with all its elements in use.

Figure 5-4:
The Font
common
dialog
provides a
standard
method for
choosing
from the
available
Windows
fonts.

Properties

Some fonts are designed to display beautifully on the screen, some are optimized for printing, and some are good for both. The Font dialog's Device property determines which types of fonts are displayed: screen, printer, or both.

The Font dialog component has a Font property, just as do most other Delphi components, but this particular Font property doesn't control the font for the dialog itself. Rather, you use it to pass font information into and out of the dialog. Typically, you copy the current font into the Font property before calling the dialog, and you retrieve the selected font from this property after the dialog closes.

Like the two file common dialogs, the Font dialog has an Options property that explodes into a number of True or False options.

Options that affect screen elements

If you set fdShowHelp to True, a Help button appears on the dialog. Clicking this button displays the program's Help file at the page specified in the Font dialog's HelpContext. The fdEffects option is the only option that's True by default. If you set it to False, the portion of the Font dialog that enables you to set the Underline and Strikeout effects disappears.

Options fdNoFaceSel, fdNoSizeSel, and fdNoStyleSel eliminate the initial display of a default value in the Font (typeface), Font size, and Style sections of the dialog. You use these options only if you're using the dialog to set the font for a chunk of text that currently includes more than one typeface, size, or style.

Options that affect which fonts are available

The remaining options restrict the type of fonts that appear. The fdAnsiOnly option limits the list to fonts that use the normal Windows character set in case you don't see any need for your users to type their memos in Symbols or Wingdings or other nontext fonts. And fdTrueTypeOnly rejects fonts that aren't the flexible Windows TrueType style. The fdFixedPitchOnly option cuts out variable-pitch fonts, leaving only the fonts in which every character is the same width.

TrueType fonts make it especially easy for the user to choose a ridiculously huge or tiny font size. The fdLimitSize option enables you to ban fonts so big that one letter fills the screen or so small that the characters can't be read. Set it to True and put your desired minimum and maximum sizes in the MinFontSize and MaxFontSize properties.

You need a master's degree in fontology to understand the restrictions corresponding to fdNoOEMFonts, fdNoSimulations, fdNoVectorFonts, and fdWysiwyg. Best bet: Leave these set to False.

Finally, fdForceFontExist means that the Font dialog should display an error message if the user types in a typeface name that doesn't exist. Always set this option to True, unless you happen to develop an amazing technique for automatically inventing fonts based on nothing but the name. How would you represent Slartibartfast Bold Italic?

Events

The Font common dialog responds to one special event, OnApply. This event is triggered after you click the Apply button in the dialog. Don't get frantic looking for the Apply button, The Options.fdApplyButton property enables you to pointlessly force an Apply button to appear even without an OnApply method. The purpose of this button and its event is to apply the changes that you've made in the Font dialog without closing the dialog.

Load the MyEdit project you made earlier in this chapter and place a Font dialog on the form. Move the Exit button to the right and insert a button captioned &Font between Save As and Exit. Put the following code in the new button's OnClick event handler:

```
WITH FontDialog1 DO
  IF Execute THEN
    Memo1.Font := Font;
```

Put this single line in the Font dialog's OnApply event handler:

```
Memo1.Font := FontDialog1.Font;
```

Run the program again and load a file into it. Select a font by using the Font button. Choose something wild — use all the options. The file is displayed in the typeface, size, style, and color you selected. Open the Font dialog again and move it so that it doesn't obscure the editor itself. Make some changes and click the Apply button. The change takes effect right away, but the Font dialog doesn't close. This makes it easier to fiddle around with different possibilities. Notice that, in this sample program, after you use the Apply button, you can no longer truly cancel your changes. That's not a problem; if you don't like the font you applied, just reselect the one you were using before.

Save the updated MyEdit project; now it includes the capability to change fonts!

You may be wondering if you're going to be giving the simple editor the capability to apply fonts to just *some* of the text. Maybe you'd like to put the heading in bold 16-point type and underline every occurrence of your name. The answer is — you're not going to be doing that yet. The memo component at the heart of our editor depends completely on the Windows multiline edit box element, which simply doesn't have the capability to display more than one font at a time. In Chapter 12, you look at the Windows 95 rich edit component, which has text formatting capabilities to rival most word processors, along with nearly unlimited capacity.

A Rainbow of Color Dialog

You probably already used the Color common dialog in Delphi itself. If you double-click the Color property of any component, you see the Color dialog. If your programs need to enable users to choose a color, this dialog — shown in Figure 5-5 — does the job for you.

The Color dialog's Color property doesn't affect the color of the dialog itself. Instead, it determines what color is selected initially. After the user has made a selection, this property contains the chosen color.

The CustomColors property is a list of up to 16 strings that have the same format as the lines in the Custom Colors section of CONTROL.INI. Each line consists of a color name (from ColorA to ColorP), an equal sign, and the hexadecimal value of the particular custom color, as in this example:

```
ColorA=5AEBD6
```

Figure 5-5:
The Color common dialog is fully opened; it can also display only its left half.

As you see shortly, Delphi makes it easy to load the color dialog with CONTROL.INI's official custom colors and to save any changes back to CONTROL.INI.

After the first three dialogs, which were jam-packed with options, you may dread the thought of another Options property. But this time, it's no big deal. If cdFullOpen is True, the dialog starts life fully open, with the gaudy "curtain" of all possible colors showing. If cdPreventFullOpen is True, the Define Custom Colors button is disabled and the user is forced to choose from existing basic and custom colors. And if cdShowHelp is True, a Help button appears on the dialog. Clicking it opens the program's Help system to the page with the number stored in the dialog's HelpContext property.

The Windows 95 Color dialog, available in Delphi 3, adds the cdSolidColor and cdAnyColor options, but they're fairly lame. Use cdAnyColor, and the user can choose colors that don't appear correctly in the current video mode. And rather than forcing all the colors in the dialog to the nearest solid color by using cdSolidColor, you'd be better off using the Delphi Color Grid component that I introduce in Chapter 7. Follow these steps:

1. **Drop a Color dialog on a new form and set its Color property to clWhite.**

2. **Set the form's Ctl3D property to False and make its color clWhite as well.**

3. **Put the following lines in its OnDblClick event handler:**

```
IF ColorDialog1.Execute THEN
   Form1.Color := ColorDialog1.Color;
```

4. **Run the program and double-click the form to change its color.**

That's all you need to do to add a Color dialog to your program.

If you want to load and save the custom colors from CONTROL.INI, you need a little more code. Delete the lines you just entered and replace the begin..end pair for the OnDblClick event handler with the following lines:

```
VAR N, P : Word;
begin
  WITH TIniFile.Create('CONTROL.INI') DO
    try
      WITH ColorDialog1 DO
        BEGIN
          ReadSectionValues('Custom Colors',
            CustomColors);
```

(continued)

(continued)

```
          IF Execute THEN
            BEGIN
              Form1.Color := Color;
              FOR N := 0 TO CustomColors.Count-1 DO
                BEGIN
                  P := Pos('=', CustomColors[N]);
                  WriteString('Custom Colors',
                    Copy(CustomColors[N], 1, P-1),
                    Copy(CustomColors[N], P+1, 255));
                END;
            END;
        END;
    finally
      Free;
    END;
end;
```

Now page up to the top of the file and add IniFiles to the uses clause. (Remember, that means you find the word *uses* at the start of a line and add *IniFiles* and a comma after it.) Now each time you double-click the form, the color dialog's custom colors are loaded from CONTROL.INI. If you add or change custom colors and click OK, the changes are written to CONTROL. INI. Do notice that, although Windows 95 still has a CONTROL.INI file, it stores its *internal* custom colors as a chunk of binary data in the registry. I am not going to discuss modifying the registry; the potential for disabling your system is simply too great!

Calling on Windows to Configure Printers

In the old DOS days, many a programmer sank into terminal despair on confronting the Printing Problem. To send anything but the most basic plain text to a printer, you needed to know the control codes for that printer. But you had hundreds of sets of codes, with more appearing every month. Not only that, but you had no way to query the printer to find out what set of codes it knew.

The great thing about Windows is that it is in charge of printing. Your programs don't need to know the detailed control codes for a zillion and one printers, because Windows knows. The Print Setup dialog component (its icon has a picture of a printer and a wrench) gives you an easy way to select and configure Windows printers.

The Print Setup dialog gives you a break — it doesn't respond to any events, and you don't need to set values for any of its handful of properties.

Load the MyEdit project again and drop a Print Setup dialog on it. Stretch the bevel component downward so that you have room for a second row of buttons. Place two new buttons labeled &Print. . . *and* P&rint Setup. . . in the second row. Create the Print Setup button's OnClick method with the following single line of code:

```
PrinterSetupDialog1.Execute;
```

Run the program and click the Print Setup button (the Print button doesn't do anything yet). You see a dialog similar to the one shown in Figure 5-6. Now click Properties or Options (one or the other is present) and you get another dialog; its look varies depending on your printer driver. Notice carefully what the existing options are before you make any changes.

Figure 5-6: In the Print Setup common dialog, you can select which of the installed printers to use.

Preparing to Print

You use the Print Setup dialog (found in the Dialogs components page) to select and configure the printer. Concerning what gets printed, the Print dialog, shown in Figure 5-7, is in charge. (Just in case you get a last-minute urge to change printers, the Setup button in the Windows 3.1 style Print dialog displays the Print Setup dialog.)

Several of the remaining properties control the initial values of items in the dialog and report those values after the user's changes. If Collate is True, the Collate check box is checked, and multiple copies of multipage documents are printed a whole document at a time. If Collate is False, all copies of page 1 are printed and then all copies of page 2, and so on. The check box is disabled if the selected printer doesn't support uncollated copies.

Figure 5-7:
In the Print
common
dialog, you
can select
what is
printed.

The Copies property corresponds to the Number of copies box in the dialog and should generally be set to 1. If the user increases this number, your program is responsible for printing multiple copies. FromPage and ToPage control the range of pages that gets printed, and MaxPage and MinPage define the valid range for FromPage and ToPage.

The value of PrintRange corresponds to one of the three radio buttons in the Print Range group box; FromPage and ToPage are ignored unless the PrintRange property's value is prPageNums. Finally, PrintToFile goes with the Print to file check box on the dialog. If this box is checked, your program is responsible for getting a filename from the user and performing the print to file operation.

You don't always need all the information that the Print dialog can gather, so the Options property's subproperties enables you to selectively disable portions of the dialog. The Print to file check box disappears if poPrintToFile is False. If poPageNums is False, the Pages radio button isn't available. If poSelection is False, the option to print only the selected text is turned off. If poWarning is True, the dialog automatically warns if no default printer is selected. And poHelp determines whether a Help button appears on the dialog.

Add a Print dialog to the MyEdit project, leaving all its properties set to their default values. Double-click the Print button and replace the begin..end pair supplied by Delphi with the following code:

```
VAR
  POutput : TextFile;
  N       : LongInt;
BEGIN
  IF PrintDialog1.Execute THEN
```

```
      BEGIN
        AssignPrn(POutput);
        Rewrite(POutput);
        Printer.Canvas.Font := Memo1.Font;
        FOR N := 0 to Memo1.Lines.Count - 1 DO
          Writeln(POutput, Memo1.Lines [N]);
        CloseFile(POutput);
      END;
END;
```

Scroll to the top of the unit and add Printers to the uses clause. (Find the line near the top of the file that starts with the word uses. Add the unit name after this word, and follow it with a comma.) Select the Font common dialog and set its Device property to fdBoth to restrict its choices to fonts that are available for both the printer and the screen.

You just added printing to the simple editor. It doesn't attempt to print or collate multiple copies, but you can print the editor's contents in the font of your choice. And by using the Print Setup dialog, you can select the printer, paper orientation, and configuration options that are specific to your printer.

Searching for Text in All the Right Places

What if you loaded a good-sized text file into your simple editor and you needed to search for a particular word or phrase in the file? You wouldn't want to page through the whole file; after all, you may blink and miss what you're looking for. Finding stuff is the kind of job computers are good at, so Windows and Delphi provide a Find common dialog. Unfortunately, all the dialog does is find out what the user wants to look for; your program has to do the legwork to actually find it.

Properties

The FindText property holds the text the user entered in the dialog. Most of the time, you don't set this in advance. The only properties you normally set for a Find dialog are the numerous options.

The basic Find dialog has two check boxes that enable users to choose whether to match the exact case (so they don't find *CAT* if they're searching for *Cat,* for example) and whether to match whole words only (so they don't find *catastrophe* if they're looking for *cat*). It also includes a pair of radio buttons that enable users to specify whether they want to search forward or backward from the current cursor position.

If you want to hide these three options from users, you can use the frHideMatchCase, frHideWholeWord, and frHideUpDown properties. If you'd rather tantalize users by displaying the three user-option controls without allowing input, just disable the controls. The options for this purpose are frDisableMatchCase, frDisableWholeWord, and frDisableUpDown. There's also the frShowHelp option — if it's True, a Help button appears.

The remaining options are used in the Find dialog's OnFind event to enable you to know which button the user clicked and which options are current. frMatchCase, frWholeWord, and frDown indicate the current state of the user options. If frFindNext is True, the user clicked the Find Next button. The remaining options, frReplace and frReplaceAll, are used only by the Replace dialog. (I cover that dialog in a minute.)

Events

A Find dialog responds to just one event, OnFind. After the user clicks the Find Next button, it triggers the OnFind event. That's all the help you get from this component — your program is responsible for doing the required searching.

Making Replacements

A Replace dialog is almost the same as a Find dialog. It has all the same properties plus ReplaceText, which holds the text entered by the user on the Replace line. And it has one added event, OnReplace, which is triggered by clicking the Replace or Replace All buttons.

Load the MyEdit project and set the memo box's HideSelection property to False. Drop a Find dialog and a Replace dialog on the form and select them both. Double-click the Options property and set frHideMatchCase, frHideWholeWord, and frHideUpDown to True. Add buttons labeled Fi&nd. . . *and* Rep&lace. . . to the second row of buttons. Use the following line for the Find. . . button's OnClick event:

```
FindDialog1.Execute;
```

Use the following line for the Replace. . . button:

```
ReplaceDialog1.Execute;
```

Run the program and try the Find. . . and Replace. . . buttons. Each displays the corresponding dialog, but using them is frustrating; they don't do anything yet.

Select the Find dialog, flip to the Events page and double-click the OnFind event. Replace the begin..end pair inserted by Delphi with the following rather formidable-looking block of code:

```
VAR
  Buff, P, FT : PChar;
  BuffLen : Word;
begin
  WITH Sender AS TFindDialog DO
    BEGIN
      GetMem(FT, Length(FindText) + 1);
      StrPCopy(FT, FindText);
      BuffLen := Memo1.GetTextLen + 1;
      GetMem(Buff, BuffLen);
      Memo1.GetTextBuf(Buff, BuffLen);
      P := Buff + Memo1.SelStart + Memo1.SelLength;
      P := StrPos(P,  FT);
      IF P = NIL THEN MessageBeep(0)
      ELSE
        BEGIN
          Memo1.SelStart := P - Buff;
          Memo1.SelLength := Length(FindText);
        END;
      FreeMem(FT, Length(FindText) + 1);
      FreeMem(Buff, BuffLen);
    END;
end;
```

After you're finished, click the Replace dialog, flip to the Events page in the Object Inspector, and click the down arrow next to the slot for the OnFind event handler. From the resulting list, select the same event handler you just created for the Find dialog. Create an OnReplace event handler for the Replace dialog that contains the following lines:

```
WITH Sender AS TReplaceDialog DO
  WHILE True DO
    BEGIN
      IF Memo1.SelText <> FindText THEN
        FindDialog1Find(Sender);
      IF Memo1.SelLength = 0 THEN Break;
      Memo1.SelText := ReplaceText;
      IF NOT (frReplaceAll IN Options) THEN Break;
    END;
```

Wow, that was quite a handful of code. It would have been simpler if it didn't need to compile under Delphi 3. But it would have been even more complicated if I hadn't skipped the various options, such as match case and search up or down! Save the program, run it, and load a file. Now you can use the Find button to locate a given string in the loaded file. It must be an exact match, and only the text after the current cursor position is searched.

Click Replace and you can use the dialog to replace a particular string with another. In the Replace dialog, Replace All replaces every instance that occurs after the current cursor position. I could make the find and replace code more complicated, but this should be enough for now. Hey, Notepad doesn't even offer Replace!

Figure 5-8 shows the final form of the MyEdit project with a Replace dialog in action. Be sure to save the project, because you can continue to enhance it.

What's missing in that last picture? What does almost *every* Windows program have that our simple editor doesn't? A menu, of course. On to the next chapter for more about menus!

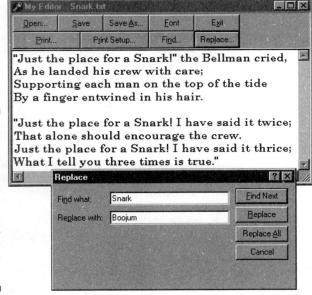

Figure 5-8: This simple editor relies heavily on the Delphi common dialog components, such as the Replace dialog.

Chapter 6
What's on the Menu?

● ●

In This Chapter

▶ Designing menus visually with Delphi

▶ Enhancing simple text editors

▶ Enabling right-click pop-up menus

▶ Merging a child window's menu into the main menu

▶ Using pop-up menus that "know" where they were popped up

● ●

*I*n a big, complicated program, a button for every feature may leave no room on the form for anything else. And finding a particular button among the masses is tough. Solve both problems by using a menu to launch your program's features. The main menu lists general categories of activity in a menu bar, which is always visible across the top of the form. After you click each main menu item, a submenu appears; this submenu disappears after you make a selection.

Preparing a Tasty Menu

The main menu component is the first item on the standard Component palette — its icon looks like a menu with a submenu pulled down. Dropping a main menu component on your form has no immediate visible effect, but as soon as you add a menu choice to the component, the main menu appears across the top of the form. Even during the design phase, you can pull down submenus, and if you click a submenu item, Delphi takes you to the OnClick event handler for that item.

The main menu component

A main menu component has just four properties — AutoMerge, Items, Name, and Tag — and responds to no events. (I introduce Name and Tag in earlier chapters; you look at the AutoMerge property later in this chapter.) The Items property is the list of menu items. After you click the ellipsis button next to the Items property or double-click the menu component's icon, Delphi fires up the Menu Designer, which is shown in Figure 6-1.

Add a main menu item here

Add a main menu item here

Figure 6-1:
The Delphi
Menu
Designer
works with
the Object
Inspector to
enable you
to build
menus.

Separator

Add a submenu item here

Like everything else in Delphi, the Menu Designer is visually oriented. To start creating a new menu, just open the Menu Designer and type the caption for the first item on the menu bar. After you type that first caption, you add new main menu items in the empty rectangle at the right end of the menu bar. You add submenu items in the empty rectangle at the bottom of the active submenu. You can see both rectangles in Figure 6-1. To insert a series of submenu items, click the Caption line in the Object Inspector, click the empty rectangle at the bottom of the submenu, and just start typing captions. Each time you press Enter, you move to the next item. After you get the items in a submenu to fall naturally into groups, you can insert a separator line (visible in Figure 6-1) by adding a menu item with a lone hyphen for its caption.

The chances are good that your first attempt at a menu structure isn't perfect. That's not a problem, however, because redecorating is simple — you just move individual items or whole submenu structures by dragging them around the menu. You can also right-click anywhere on the Menu Designer to display a pop-up menu that (among other things) enables you to insert and delete menu items. Notice that the Insert command inserts a new item before the highlighted item, and the Delete command deletes the highlighted item.

Remember that right-clicking *doesn't* select the item you right-click. Get in the habit of left-clicking to select and right-clicking to open the pop-up menu.

Menu item components

Every item on the main menu bar and every item in a submenu is represented in your program by a menu item component. These components don't appear on the Component palette; only the Menu Designer can create them. After you create the components however, you use the Object Inspector to set their properties and events just like ordinary components.

The absolutely essential property of a menu item is its Caption property, which tells the user what this item does. Top-level menu items must have one-word captions; that's because users can easily mistake two-word captions for two items. You can be a bit more verbose with submenu items, but captions should still be as short as possible. Delphi automatically derives a name for the item from the caption.

As with other components, an ampersand (&) in the caption underlines the next character and makes it a mnemonic access key. For main menu items, the access key is Alt plus the underlined character. To select a submenu item, pressing Alt is optional. To select the &Open item from the &File menu, for example, either press Alt+F and then Alt+O or press just Alt+F, O.

The ShortCut property defines an always-available shortcut key for a submenu item. Pressing this key has the same effect as selecting the menu item but without having to open the menu. As Figure 6-2 shows, if you choose a shortcut key for a submenu item, Delphi puts the name of the shortcut key to the right of the caption in the menu, lined up against the right edge of the submenu.

Figure 6-2:
The shortcut key for a submenu item appears right-aligned after the caption and is available even if the submenu isn't open.

You can open a list of values for the shortcut key, but that list contains only the simplest keystroke combinations. Instead, try typing key combo names that aren't on the list, such as Ctrl+Up or Ctrl+Shift+Alt+A. If Delphi doesn't gripe, the combination is valid.

If a menu item's Checked property is True, a check mark appears to the left of the caption. The last two items on the Delphi View menu are good examples of checkable menu items. A common practice is to separate related groups of checkable items with separator lines, such as the line above SpeedBar in the Delphi View menu.

Delphi 3 uses the GroupIndex property with the RadioItem property to create groups of menu items that act like radio buttons — you can check only one at a time. (As you can see later, in Figure 6-3, the check mark morphs into a circle for menu items that use the RadioItem property. Delphi programmers call them "checked" menu items regardless, because the Checked property controls the mark.)

Sometimes a group of checkable menu items represent independent options, such as the SpeedBar and Component palette items in the View menu. Other times, the menu items are mutually exclusive choices, such as the different Sort by items in File Manager's View menu. In either case, it's up to your program to check and uncheck the items.

If your submenu is overloaded with items, you can set the Break property of an item to mbBreak. This setting forces the submenu to begin a new column of menu items. Setting the Break property to mbBarBreak does the same thing and also places a vertical bar before the new column. (Peek ahead to Figure 6-3 for an example.) Always leave this property set to mbNone for top-level menu items — they never get a break! Now try these steps:

1. **Drop a main menu component on a new form and double-click the component to enter the Menu Designer.**

2. **Give the first main menu item the caption** &Test.

3. **Click the blank submenu item just below the main item and type captions** &A, &B, &C, &I, &J, **and** &K, **pressing Enter after each.**

   This step should create a submenu with six items. Notice that Delphi has named the items A1 through K1.

4. **Now, if you want, replace each caption with a word that starts with that letter, such as** &Apple, &Bridge, **and so on.**

   Give your menu items personalized captions right away. Delphi assigns default *names* to menu components based on their initial caption; the code that follows assumes that those names are &A, &B, and so on.

5. **Click the item that starts with** *I*.

6. **Right-click to display the pop-up menu.**

7. **Choose Insert.**

8. **Set the caption of this item to a single hyphen (-) for a separator.**

9. **Click the A item and set its Checked property to True.**

10. **Click A, and then Shift+click C to select the first three items.**

11. **Set RadioItem to True and GroupIndex to 1 for all three items.**

12. **Flip to the Events page in the Object Inspector and double-click the OnClick event.**

13. **Put the following lines in the event handler:**

```
WITH Sender AS TMenuItem DO
    Checked := True;
```

14. **Select items I, J, and K and create an OnClick method for all of them with just the following line:**

```
WITH Sender AS TMenuItem DO Checked := Not Checked;
```

15. **Set the GroupIndex property for these three items to 2.**

16. **Run the program.**

As you first run the program, only the A menu item has a solid circle. Choosing the B or C item *moves* the mark to that item. Items A, B, and C act as radio buttons; you can check only one of them. Set RadioItem to True for all related menu items and give them a GroupIndex different from all the other items. In their OnClick event handler, set Checked to True for the item that you click; Delphi handles unchecking the other items. Choosing I, J, or K from the menu toggles the check mark — if the check mark is there, it disappears; if it's not there, it appears. Items I, J, and K act as check boxes. Any time you want a menu item to toggle its checked state on each click, use an OnClick event handler such as the one for I, J, and K.

Using the same project, open the Menu Designer again. Assign the shortcut key Ctrl+A to the A item, Ctrl+B to B, and so on. Click the separator item and either press the Del key or right-click and select Delete. Click the menu item that starts with *I* and set its Break property to mbBarBreak. (You don't see the result of changing the Break property until the program runs.) Run the program again and press Ctrl+I, Ctrl+J, and Ctrl+K. Click Test or press Alt+T and you see that all three items are now checked, just as if you selected them from the menu. Also, as shown in Figure 6-3, the two sets of three items are in two parallel columns, separated by a vertical bar.

Figure 6-3:
Two types of checkable menu items, each with a shortcut key.

You can check only one of the items in this column

You can check or uncheck any of the items in this column independently

As the figure shows, the shortcuts for the second column of menu items aren't visible. You think that looks bad? Break the menu into three columns and it gets worse — much worse. The shortcuts for items in the second column appear in the third column! The problem lies in the combination of Windows 95, multicolumn menus, and menu shortcuts. Eliminate any one of the three and you have no problem. Because Windows 95 is here to stay (that is, until the *next* Windows version comes along), the simplest rule is to avoid using multicolumn menus and menu shortcuts together.

Go back to the Menu Designer for the same project and add another main menu item called &SuperTest. To do this, click the empty rectangle to the right of the Test item and type the caption. Use the mouse to drag the Test item to the submenu location below SuperTest. Don't get frustrated if the submenu hanging from Test obscures the place you want to drag to. If you drag directly to the right and then down, you can see the target.

You just created a cascading submenu. Run the program and select SuperTest. Notice that the Test submenu item has a sort of cuneiform wedge after its name, like the one in Figure 6-4. That wedge is the signal that the item has a cascading submenu. Click Test and the original six submenu items appear. Notice that the shortcut keys Ctrl+A and so on still work even though the corresponding menu items are one level deeper in the menu. Another way to create a cascading submenu is to highlight any submenu item, right-click, and choose Create Submenu from the pop-up menu.

Figure 6-4:
One cascading submenu is open and another is indicated by the symbol to the right of its name.

Cascading submenu indicator

Cascading submenu

Standard Menu Templates

Part of the charm of Windows is that programs *try* to do things the same way. In all but the most antisocial programs, the submenu option to load a file from disk is called &Open, and it's in a main menu named &File. Delphi makes conforming to standard usage easy by enabling you to store menu layouts as templates. Use templates provided by Delphi or build your own. Unless your program is totally bizarre, you find that some elements of the standard templates fit your needs. Start your menu by installing all appropriate templates. Then simply delete any of the standard items that don't apply and add items specific to your program.

To add a template by using the Menu Designer, first click the empty rectangle on the menu bar where the template should go. Then right-click and select Insert From Template from the pop-up menu. Choose the template you want, click OK, and you're done.

File menu

Just about every program uses files in some way. For the rare program that doesn't, you usually have a File menu anyway, with just the Exit item. You can now create a template for the File menu. (Yes, Delphi already includes templates for File, Edit, and Help menus, among others, but you discover more by building them yourself.) Follow these steps:

1. **Drop a menu component on a new form and double-click the component to enter the Menu Designer.**

2. **Type** &File **and press Enter.**

3. **Now refer to Figure 6-1 and type each of the menu item captions below File** (New, Open, Save, **and so on**).

4. **Insert an ampersand (&) before the underlined character in each name and press Enter after each.**

    Remember to enter a hyphen for each separator line's caption and don't try to include the shortcut keys in the item name. After you finish entering the captions, go back and add the shortcut keys if you want.

5. **Right-click and choose Save as Template from the menu that pops up and name this template** My File Menu.

That's it! You created a reusable menu template. If you made a mistake or if you want to fine-tune the template, load it into an otherwise empty main menu, make your changes, and save the modified menu as a template.

As I mention in Chapter 5, some menu items have an ellipsis (…) after the item name to tell you that choosing this item displays a dialog. Follow this convention as you create menu items of your own. For any item that activates a dialog, tack those three dots onto the end of the item name.

Edit menu

After you load a file, you probably want to edit it, so the Edit menu comes next. You can build this template as well. If the Menu Designer is still open from the previous exercise, select the File menu and delete it. Click the

Caption line in the Object Inspector and then click the empty rectangle at the top left of the Menu Designer. You're ready to type in another list of menu captions. This time, use the items shown in Figure 6-2, starting with &Edit for the top-level item name.

Assign the standard shortcut keys to Undo, Cut, Copy, and Paste. (These keys are, respectively, Ctrl+Z, Ctrl+X, Ctrl+C, and Ctrl+V.) Now save this template as My Edit Menu. Most of these items should be familiar to you from the Delphi Edit menu. A few of them, Paste Link and Links, are strictly related to OLE. You may want to create a separate template without these two items and use the template for projects that don't require OLE.

Help menu

In a perfect world, every Windows application would have a standard Windows Help file. Alas, we don't live in a perfect world, but our world *does* contain utilities that ease the process of creating Help files. After you've managed to build a Help file for a project, the first three choices on the standard Help menu invoke the Windows Help program in three specific ways. You can either use the Delphi Help menu template or build your own to match Figure 6-5.

Figure 6-5:
The Help
menu
standardizes
access
to the
application's
Help file.

The Contents item displays the Help file's contents page, just like the corresponding item on the Delphi Help menu, and the Search for Help On item is equivalent to Topic Search on the Delphi menu. Selecting How to Use Help accesses a Help file associated with the Windows Help program itself.

You always rename the About *<program>* item to refer to your program's name. The item should display an About box, which is a secondary form that tells the name and version number of the program and supplies copyright information. In Chapter 19, you build a fancy About box that displays all kinds of useful information. For now, follow these steps:

1. **Add a menu component to a new form and double-click the component to enter the Menu Designer.**

2. **Right-click and add the Help menu template.**

3. **Use the following three lines of code as the OnClick event handlers for the three standard menu choices:**

Menu choice	*OnClick event handler*
Contents	Application.HelpCommand (HELP_CONTENTS, 0);
Search for Help On . . .	Application.HelpCommand (HELP_PARTIALKEY, 0);
How to Use Help	Application.HelpCommand (HELP_HELPONHELP, 0);

4. **Choose Project⇨Options from the menu bar and turn to the Application page.**

5. **Click the Browse button next to the Help file edit box and select the Delphi Help file, DELPHI.HLP.**

6. **Choose File⇨New from the menu bar.**

7. **Click the Forms page.**

8. **Click the Copy radio button.**

9. **Choose the About Box template.**

10. **Type the following line in the About menu item's OnClick event:**

```
AboutBox.ShowModal;
```

11. **Add Unit2 to the main form's uses clause.**

As you run this program, you find that the standard Help menu items work fine. You can open the contents page of the Delphi Help system, search for Help on a given topic, or get Help on using help in general. And clicking the About menu item open the as-yet-unfinished About box.

Beautify the simple text editor

Remember the MyEdit project from the last chapter (if you've gone through the last chapter)? Remember how busy it looked, with so many buttons across the top? Load it up again or go to Chapter 5 and make it. You're going to build a menu for this project using the templates.

Drop a menu component on the MyEdit form and double-click the component to enter the Menu Designer. Place a standard File menu template in the menu, click the separator after Save As, and choose Insert from the pop-up menu — use **&Font . . .** as the caption for the new menu item. Now add a top-level menu item, **Fi&nd**, with submenu items **Fi&nd . . .** and **&Replace . . .** below it. For each item on the menu except File⇨New, attach the existing OnClick method for the corresponding button. The Open button was named Button1, for example, so in the Object Inspector's Events page for the Open menu item, you click the right arrow next to OnClick and select Button1Click. If you're not sure which name was used for a particular button, just click the button and look in the Object Inspector.

Double-check to make sure that you connected each of the menu items to the correct event handler. Now delete all nine buttons and the bevel. Instead of wasting space on the form with buttons, you've put all the actions into a tidy menu. You can open, edit, save, and print files just fine.

Add some polish to the tiny editor. Right now, the editor enables you to exit or switch to a new file without reminding you to save your existing file, and the File⇨New menu item doesn't do anything. You can fix that! In the event handler for the Open menu item, find the line that begins

```
Memo1.Lines.Load...
```

Insert the following line after it:

```
Memo1.Modified := False;
```

The event handler for the Save menu item contains just one line at present. Replace that line with the following line:

```
IF SaveDialog1.Filename = '' THEN
  SaveAs1.OnClick(Sender)
ELSE
  BEGIN
    Memo1.Lines.SaveToFile(SaveDialog1.Filename);
    Memo1.Modified := False;
  END;
```

In the event handler for the Save As menu item, find the line that begins

```
Memo1.Lines.Save...
```

Insert the following line after it:

```
Memo1.Modified := False;
```

Now create an OnCloseQuery event handler for the form, with these lines:

```
IF Memo1.Modified THEN
  CASE MessageDlg('File ' +
      ExtractFileName(SaveDialog1.Filename) +
      ' has changed. Save now?',
      mtConfirmation, mbYesNoCancel, 0) OF
    idYES    : Save1.OnClick(Sender);
    idNO     ::
    idCANCEL : CanClose := False;
  END;
```

Highlight the lines you just typed and press Ctrl+C to copy them to the Clipboard. Go back to the event handler for the Open menu choice, place the cursor immediately after the begin line, and press Ctrl+V to insert a copy. Then change the line that begins with the word idCancel as follows:

```
idCancel : Exit;
```

Highlight the lines you typed for the form's OnCloseQuery event handler and press Ctrl+C for another copy. In the File menu, click the New item to start an OnClick event handler for it and paste in the confirmation code. Change the line that begins with idCancel as follows:

```
idCancel : Exit;
```

Now add the following three lines after the pasted-in code:

```
Memo1.Clear;
SaveDialog1.Filename := '';
Caption := 'My Editor';
```

With those additions, this simple editor is now a *safe* editor. You can't accidentally throw away your work without saving. Speaking of saving, save the MyEdit project now.

Pop-Up Menus

All visible Delphi components have a property called PopupMenu. After you right-click the component, the attached pop-up menu pops into view. Of course, before you can hook up a pop-up menu, you must build the menu. That's what you do next.

The most important property of a pop-up menu is AutoPopup. If this property is True (the default), right-clicking a component that's hooked to this menu causes the menu to pop up. The Alignment property determines where this menu pops up. The menu's top edge is at the height of the cursor, and — depending on whether Alignment is paLeft, paCenter, or paRight — either the left, center, or right of the top edge is at the cursor.

Designing a pop-up menu easier than designing a main menu because no menu bar is across the top. However, don't add cascading submenus to the pop-up by using the Create Submenu choice from the Menu Designer's *own* pop-up menu. Pop-up menus are supposed to be speedy and convenient.

Most of the time, pop-up menu items don't have mnemonic access keys because no built-in way exists to pop up the menu itself by using just the keyboard. However, you *can* get a lot of mileage out of assigning shortcut keys to pop-up menu items. You do so by using the ShortCut property. Even if the menu itself isn't hooked to any component and never shows on-screen, the shortcut keys remain available throughout your program.

A pop-up menu component receives the OnPopup event just *before* it appears on-screen. This is the chance for the pop-up menu to make any last-minute preparations, such as disabling unavailable items or adjusting check marks. To create a neat pop-up menu, follow these steps:

1. **Drop a memo and a pop-up menu component on a new form.**

2. **Double-click on the component to enter the Menu Designer.**

3. **Put three items in the menu; name them** Cut, Copy, **and** Paste.

4. **In each of the three items' OnClick methods, use these lines:**

   Memo1.CutToClipboard;   (in the Cut item)

   Memo1.CopyToClipboard;   (in the Copy item)

   Memo1.PasteFromClipboard;   (in the Paste item)

5. **Delete the contents of the memo's Lines property, set its ScrollBars property to ssBoth, and set its PopupMenu property to the name of the pop-up menu component.**

6. **Set the memo's Align property to alClient.**

Run the program and type some text. Highlight a word or two by dragging with the mouse and then press the right mouse button. Choose Cut from the pop-up menu and the text disappears. Move the text insertion point and right-click again, this time choosing Paste. The text reappears. You created a pop-up menu that enables you to cut and paste with the mouse in one hand while holding an ice cream cone in the other. Cool, huh?

Using the same program, select the pop-up menu from the list in the Object Inspector. Flip to the Events page, double-click the OnPopup event, and insert the following code:

```
Cut1.Enabled := Memo1.SelLength > 0;
Copy1.Enabled := Cut1.Enabled;
Paste1.Enabled := Clipboard.HasFormat(CF_TEXT);
```

Add ClipBrd to the uses clause of the unit, run the program again, and you see that the pop-up menu's Cut and Copy items are disabled if you have no selected text to cut or copy, and the Paste item is disabled if you have no text to paste. The point of the OnPopup event is to enable you to tweak the pop-up menu to match current conditions.

Many different components on the form can be associated with the same pop-up menu through their PopupMenu property. The pop-up menu's PopupComponent makes that connection in reverse. It tells the pop-up menu component which component it's popping up over.

Follow these steps:

1. **Place a pop-up menu and six or eight edit boxes on a new form.**

   Make sure that the form's font is one that supports both bold and italic.

2. **Select all the edit boxes and set their PopupMenu property to point to the pop-up menu.**

3. **Double-click the pop-up menu itself and add four menu items with captions Bold, Italic, Underline, and Strikeout (naking their names Bold1, Italic1, and so on).**

4. **Set the Tag property of the four items to 0, 1, 2, and 3, respectively.**

   These numbers directly correspond to the font style constants fsBold, fsItalic, fsUnderline, and fsStrikeout.

5. **Put this code in the pop-up menu's OnPopup event handler:**

```
WITH (PopupMenu1.PopupComponent AS TEdit).Font DO
  BEGIN
    Bold1.Checked := fsBold IN Style;
    Italic1.Checked := fsItalic IN Style;
    Underline1.Checked := fsUnderline IN Style;
    Strikeout1.Checked := fsStrikeout IN Style;
  END;
```

6. **Highlight all four of the submenu items in the Menu Designer.**

7. **Flip to the Events page in the Object Inspector.**

8. For all of the submenu items, create an OnClick handler containing the following code:

```
WITH (PopupMenu1.PopupComponent AS TEdit).Font DO
  BEGIN
    Style := Style - [TFontStyle((Sender AS
        TMenuItem).Tag)];
    IF NOT (Sender AS TMenuItem).Checked THEN
      Style := Style + [TFontStyle((Sender AS
          TMenuItem).Tag)];
  END;
```

9. Run the program and right-click one of the edit boxes.

The choices in the pop-up menu are checked or unchecked depending on the edit box you click. Click any of the menu items to *change* the box's font.

Caution: Merging Menus

Now that you have some menu experience under your belt, you can tackle two advanced items: the main menu's AutoMerge property and the GroupIndex property of individual menu items. In a plain, simple program with just one form, AutoMerge is useless. Only if you have a main form and one or more secondary forms does menu merging makes sense. If a secondary form menu's AutoMerge property is True, its menu items merge with the main form's menu if that secondary window is active. Suppose that you write a program that includes secondary windows for limerick editing and graffiti design. If the limerick window is active, the Limerick menu item appears among the items of the main window's menu bar. When the graffiti window is active, the Graffiti item replaces that item.

Never set AutoMerge to True in the main form's menu. If you do, the menu attempts, at run time, to merge with the cosmic even-more-main form . . . and it disappears.

The GroupIndex is relevant for all level menu items. The GroupIndex of top-level menu items controls how the secondary form's menu merges into the main menu. Going from left to right across the menu bar, the GroupIndex for each item must never be less than the GroupIndex for the previous item. If you raise one item's GroupIndex to 3, for example, Delphi checks all items to its right and makes sure that their GroupIndex is at least 3. If you attempt to set an item's GroupIndex lower than the previous item, Delphi complains.

Items with the same GroupIndex form a group. If a group from a secondary menu merges into a main menu, one of two things happens. If the main menu has a group with the same index, the group from the secondary menu completely replaces the group from the main menu. If no same-numbered group is in the main menu, the secondary group inserts into the main menu in GroupIndex order. It sounds complicated, but the process is easier to understand when you see it happening.

On-again off-again merging

Start a new project and select the MDI Application template. You see a working skeleton of a Multiple Document Interface program. Try it — run the program and choose File⇨New a few times. Now quit the program.

Back in the Form Designer, double-click the main window's main menu. Select the Help menu item and set its GroupIndex to 2. Now open the MDI child form. (If you don't see the child form, choose View⇨Forms from the menu.) Drop a menu component on the child window and open the Menu Designer. Name the top-level menu **&Test** and set its GroupIndex to 1. Invent some creative item names to put in the Test item's submenu.

Run the program again. After you open a child window, the Test menu appears in the main window's menu (see Figure 6-6). If you close the last child window, the Test menu disappears again. Exit the program and change the Test menu item's GroupIndex to 2. Now when you run the program, the Test menu *replaces* the Help menu anytime a child window is open.

Figure 6-6:
The Test menu belongs to the child window; it merges into the main menu only if a child window is open.

With no child window, the Test menu is absent

Child window

The Test menu appears if the child window is open

Multiple-choice merging

The aphorism "Different strokes for different folks" becomes "Different menus for different venues" in Windows. All the child windows in the preceding MDI example are the same type, but nothing says they *must* be the same. Delphi itself has *lots* of different window types: the Form Designer, the Code Editor, the Object Inspector, and so on. If you want, you can give each type of child form its own set of menu items. Whichever child form is active has its menu merged into the main form's menu. Follow these steps:

1. **Put this code in a new form's OnCreate event handler:**

```
Left := 0; Top := 0;
Width := Screen.Width;
ClientHeight := 0;
```

2. **Place a menu component on the form with just two top-level menu items, &File and &Help.**

3. **Set the GroupIndex property of the second one to 2.**

   Don't worry about submenus; this is just a demonstration.

4. **Choose the New Form item from the Delphi File menu twice to add two more forms to the project.**

5. **For each form, set Visible to True and BorderIcons.biSystemMenu to False.**

6. **Drop a menu component on each form and set the menu's AutoMerge property to True.**

7. **In the menu for Form2, create a top-level menu item, set the menu item's caption to Form&2, and the menu item's GroupIndex to 1.**

8. **Repeat Step 7 for Form3 but set the menu item's caption to Form&3.**

The commands in the main form's OnCreate method cause the main form to take over the top of the screen, just as Delphi does. The two secondary windows appear wherever Windows chooses to place them. If you click one of the secondary windows to activate it, its menu merges into the main menu. This can be a handy way to keep the menu activity for a multiform application centralized, while keeping it relevant to the current context.

In the next part, you meet components that you can use to build *extraordinary* programs. For example, if you're interested in graphical components to make your program above-average, you can read all about them in the next chapter.

Part III
More Components

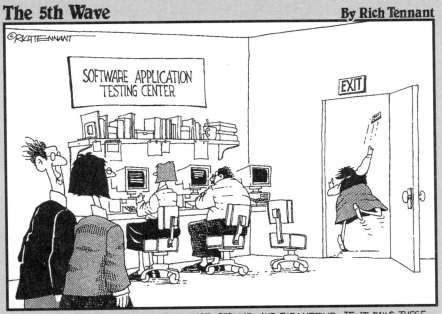

"WE TEST FOR COMPATIBILITY, PERFORMANCE, SERVICE, AND FORMATTING. IF IT FAILS THESE, THEN IT'S TESTED FOR THE DISTANCE IT CAN BE SAILED ACROSS THE PARKING LOT AND ONTO THE EXPRESSWAY."

In this part . . .

At the Delphi Diner, you can order bland components that duplicate and enhance the basic Windows screen elements. But that's only the beginning for the component gourmet. The graphical components I show you in Part III spice up forms and serve to display information visually. The tedious task of loading, saving, and displaying bitmap images is a snap with Delphi.

Delphi has components to implement simple controls that Windows forgot, and components to let you create customized file-selection forms. At the top of the food chain, you find potent components such as the media player, which plays multimedia files or devices. Along the way through Part III, you activate OLE objects in your own programs.

To top off this feeding frenzy, you work with powerful and versatile Delphi database components. Delphi database support is modern and high-tech. It supports specialized field types, such as images and variable-length memos, and can easily scale up from local database applications to client/server. Just hook up a handful of components and write a line or two of code!

For dessert, you can dip into the delicious collection of Windows 95 user-interface components. Whether you're running under Windows 95 itself or Windows NT, these components enhance your programs with truly up-to-the-minute power and flexibility.

Chapter 7

Look-and-Feel Components

● ●

In This Chapter

▶ Using shape components to stack up a Towers of Hanoi puzzle

▶ Building unlimited shapes by using the paint box component

▶ Creating a simple graphic file viewer

▶ Creating a toolbar with flyover Help, just like the Delphi toolbar

▶ Building a status line that automatically displays hints for the current component or menu choice

▶ Using the Bevel component to set off form elements with 3-D "dips" and "bumps"

▶ Controlling your form's scrolling with a scroll box

● ●

*T*he standard components, dialogs, and menus handle all the mundane aspects of building a Windows user interface for your programs. Useful? Indubitably! Exciting? Alas, no. Computer users these days are jaded. Even the most supremely effective program gets short shrift unless it *looks* like the user's idea of a supremely effective program.

In this chapter, you examine some components that add color and style to your forms and that provide new ways to organize mundane components. These components deal with the "look and feel" of your program, not with accomplishing its grunt work. You can use these components to add crown moldings, decorative finials, tail fins, a good paint job, or whatever's necessary for your programs to grab the attention of even the most finicky user.

Choosing Look-and-Feel Components

Use Table 7-1 to locate the component that best suits your needs. You find most of these components on the Additional page of the Component palette, although a few appear on the Samples page.

Table 7-1	Problems Solved by Look-and-Feel Components
Task	*Component*
Place a simple geometric shape on your form.	Shape. See "Get into Shape with Shapes."
Display a nonstandard or complex shape.	Paint box. See "Paint Any Shape You Like."
Have the user choose one of the 16 simple solid colors for the foreground and the background.	Color grid. See "Color Control with Color Grid."
Put a pretty picture on your form.	Image. See "Image Is Everything."
Display the progress of an ongoing process.	Gauge. See "Gauging Your Progress."
Create a toolbar or status bar, with optional flyover help.	Panel. See "Introducing Our Panel."
Create dividing lines or rectangles on your form.	Bevel. See "Bumpy and Dippy Forms."
Limit the portion of your form that can scroll.	Scroll box. See "Controlling Scrolling."

Get into Shape by Using Shapes

The shape component can take on six shapes, all of them variations on the ellipse and rectangle. Sorry, no triangles, hexagons, or enneagrams. You often use shape components to create backgrounds and borders for other components. For example, you could put a dark gray rectangle behind a light gray data entry field to give it a shadow effect. You can also create wholly visual programs in which the user interacts with the program by manipulating shapes.

Properties

The most important properties of a shape component are Shape, Pen, and Brush. The Shape property determines the shape that appears — ellipse, circle, rectangle, square, round-cornered rectangle, or round-cornered square. Pen is an exploding property that determines how you draw the shape's border with subproperties Color, Mode, Style, and Width. Color is the border's color, and Width is the width of the border. Style selects a solid, dotted, or dashed line for the border, but the nonsolid styles have no effect unless the pen's width is 1. Follow these steps to get a feel for Shape:

1. **Drop two Shape components on a new form.**

2. **Select the components and set the component's shapes to stEllipse.**

3. **Set the pen width to 16.**

4. **Select just one Shape component and set its pen style to psInsideFrame.**

In Windows, if you draw a shape by using a wide pen, the border is drawn so that its *center* comes right to the edge of the shape's boundary rectangle, and any bits that hang outside the boundary are unceremoniously chopped off. The psInsideFrame style exists to avoid this problem. Delphi, however, automatically fits the whole shape inside its boundary, so the psInsideFrame style makes the shape too small, as Figure 7-1 demonstrates.

Figure 7-1:
If you set a shape component's pen style to psInside-Frame while the width is 2 or more, it doesn't fill the entire boundary rectangle.

The Brush property controls what's drawn inside the shape. Brush, too, is an exploding property, with subproperties Color and Style. If Style is bsClear, the interior of the shape is transparent; if Style is bsSolid, the interior fills in with the brush's Color. The other styles yield various patterns. (You can see one crosshatch pattern in Figure 7-1.)

Events

A shape component responds only to the OnMouseDown, OnMouseUp, and OnMouseMove events, along with the drag-and-drop events. The following exercise is a classic graphics-only puzzle program called the Towers of Hanoi, implemented by using shapes that you can drag and drop.

If you made any changes to the Form Designer's sizing grid, choose Tools⇨ Environment Options from the menu bar. On the Preferences page, in the

Form Designer rectangle, put an X next to Display grid and Snap to grid, and set both grid sizes to 8 pixels. Now your grid settings match the assumptions in the instructions that follow. Follow these steps to create the Tower:

1. **Start a new project and choose the fixed-size form template that I tell you how to build in Chapter 2.**

   This project requires you to use the fixed-size template instead of the blank project template.

2. **Place eight shapes on the new form, as shown in Figure 7-2.**

   Look at the figure as you follow the next few instructions.

3. **First, draw a rectangle 3 grid units high and 8 grid units wide.**

Figure 7-2:
This is the
Towers of
Hanoi
puzzle,
implemented
using the
Delphi
shape
components.

4. **Draw five more rectangles below the first, each one extending 1 grid unit farther to the left and 1 grid unit farther to the right than the rectangle above it.**

5. **Select the largest rectangle and copy the rectangle you select to the Clipboard.**

6. **Paste two copies of the rectangle onto the form, lining the copies up in a horizontal row with the original.**

7. **Select the three largest rectangles and set their Brush.Color properties to clGray.**

8. **Set the Brush.Color property of each of the other five rectangles to a different bright color.**

   I used clRed, clYellow, clLime, clBlue, and clFuchsia.

Does this stack of rectangles look like anything to you? Perhaps a Mayan pyramid with two parking lots for tourists? Well, it's supposed to be an edge-on view of three flat bases with five disks of decreasing size stacked on the left-hand base. This figure is a representation of a very old puzzle called the

Towers of Hanoi. All you need to do is move the disks from the left base to the right base. That task would be simple, except for two restrictions: First, you can move only one disk at a time. Second, you can never, even for an instant, stack a larger disk on top of a smaller disk.

Change the form's caption to Towers of Hanoi and size the form to fit around the shapes you drew. Change the Name property of the left, middle, and right large rectangles at the bottom of the form to *L, M,* and *R,* respectively. Change the Name property of the five disk rectangles stacked on top of the large rectangle on the left to *A, B, C, D,* and *E,* from top to bottom.

Set the DragMode of the smallest disk, *A,* to dmAutomatic, meaning that you can move this disk. This is the only disk that you can move at the beginning of the game.

To force obedience to the rules, your program must know how each disk relates to the disk above it and to the disk below it. You can use the Hint property for this purpose, because it's not otherwise occupied. Set each shape's Hint to a two-letter string in which the first letter is the name of the shape below it and the second letter is the name of the shape above it; use *X* if no shape is either above or below it:

Rectangle	*Setting*
A (top)	BX (B is below it and nothing is above it.)
B	CA (C is below it and A is above it.)
C	DB (D is below it and B is above it.)
D	EC (E is below it and C is above it.)
E	LD (L is below it and D is above it.)
L (left base)	XE (Nothing is below it and E is above it.)
M (middle base)	XX (Nothing is above it or below it.)
R (right base)	XX (Nothing is above it or below it.)

Select all the shapes except the smallest (*A*) and create an OnDragOver event handler for them containing the following lines:

```
Accept := ((Sender AS TShape).Hint[2] = 'X') AND
  ((Source AS TShape).Width < (Sender AS TShape).Width);
```

Remember the rule that forbids placing a larger disk on a smaller one? This event handler already enforces that rule. It says that a disk (Sender) can accept having another disk (Source) dropped on it only if the width of the dragged disk is smaller. And, of course, the disk must be at the top of its stack, with nothing above it. Source and Sender are important parameters passed by Delphi to every OnDragOver event handler. Source is the component that's dragged; Sender is the component that's dragged over. These could be any old type of component, but you know they are both shapes, so you use the AS keyword to share that knowledge with Delphi. So (Source AS TShape) refers to the dragged disk and (Sender AS TShape) is the dropped-on disk. Got that?

Run the program and try dragging the top disk around the form. The cursor turns to the slashed-circle No symbol at first. Drag the disk over either of the two empty bases, however, and they welcome the disk by changing the cursor to an arrow with a rectangle. Sorry, nothing happens if you try to drop the disk; you write the code to do that next.

Again select all the shapes except the smallest. Switch to the Events page of the Object Inspector and double-click the OnDragDrop event. Replace the begin..end lines of the OnDragDrop event handler supplied by Delphi with the following code:

```
VAR Moved, Still : TShape;
begin
  Moved := Source AS TShape;
  Still := Sender AS TShape;
  Moved.Top := Still.Top - Moved.Height + 1;
  Moved.Left := Still.Left + (Still.Width DIV 2)
    - (Moved.Width DIV 2);
  WITH FindComponent(Moved.Hint[1]) AS TShape DO
    BEGIN
      IF Name <= 'E' THEN DragMode := dmAutomatic;
      Hint := Hint[1] + 'X';
    END;
  Moved.Hint := Still.Name + 'X';
  Still.Hint := Still.Hint[1] + Moved.Name;
  Still.DragMode := dmManual;
  IF (L.Hint = 'XX') AND (M.Hint = 'XX') THEN
    Caption := 'Towers of Hanoi - DONE!';
end;
```

The OnDragOver event handler was clunky because of all the repetitions of (Source AS TShape) and so on. This new event handler would have been even clunkier, so I solved that problem by declaring two local variables. The Moved variable represents the shape that moved and the Still variable represents the shape that stood still; the first two lines of the event handler set these variables to the Source and Sender parameters. The rest of the handler uses these simple names to refer to the two disks.

The first step is to set the Top and Left properties of the moved disk to center it above the shape you dropped it on. Next, you use the handy FindComponent method of the main form to locate the disk that was previously beneath the moved disk. The FindComponent method locates a component on the form by name, and the desired name here is the first character of the moved shape's Hint.

If the newly uncovered shape isn't one of the three base rectangles, you set its DragMode to dmAutomatic, making it movable. You also set the second character of its Hint to *X,* because now nothing is above it. You adjust the Hint properties of the moved and still shapes to reflect that one is now above the other, and you set the still shape's DragMode to dmManual so that you can't move it. Finally, you check to see whether all the disks are now stacked on the right-hand base, in which case the puzzle is solved.

That's it! The program is complete. The OnDragOver event handler enforces the rules of the puzzle by permitting only valid moves, and the OnDragOver handler takes care of shuffling the disks around after you make a move. The minimum number of moves to solve this puzzle is 31 — can you get all the disks to the right-hand base in just 31 moves?

To increase the difficulty, you can add more disks between disk *E* and the left-hand base, naming the disks *F, G,* and so on. Adjust all the Hint properties to include the new disks. For each additional disk, you double the previous minimum number of moves and add one. With 6 disks, for example, the puzzle takes 63 moves (which is $31 \times 2 + 1$). With 16 disks (the most you can use without suffering a "name collision" with the base named *L*), the puzzle requires 65,535 moves.

The legendary Towers of Hanoi reside in an undisturbed temple deep in the jungle. (Which jungle? It doesn't matter!) It consists of 64 polished brass disks, and shifts of silent black-robed monks continually move one disk at a time from one stack to another. After they finish, the universe ends. Well, that's what the story says! If they manage one move per second, the solution takes about half a trillion years, so don't change your weekend plans.

Paint Any Shape You Like

Shape components can be useful, but they're limited to representing variations on the ellipse and rectangle. Also, they have only two colors, one for the border and one for the interior. The paint box component enables you to draw any shape or combination of shapes in any color you want. Of course, along with control comes responsibility — you're completely in charge of painting every aspect of the paint box component.

A paint box has all the common properties, but the only ones that show a visible effect at design time are the ones controlling on-screen size and position: Left, Top, Width, Height, and Align. The Color property becomes the default brush color; you can use Font.color to pass a pen color into the paint box's OnPaint method. This essential method gets called whenever the paint box needs to repaint itself. The code in the OnPaint method completely determines what a particular paint box looks like. To see what I mean, follow these steps:

1. **Place a paint box component on a new form (making the component roughly square), set the box's Color property to clWhite, and create an OnPaint event handler for it by using the following code:**

```
WITH Sender AS TPaintBox, Canvas DO
  BEGIN
    Brush.Color := Color;
    Pen.Color := Font.Color;
    Polygon([Point(Width DIV 2, 0),
      Point(Width DIV 5, Height),
      Point(Width, 2U(Height DIV 5)),
      Point(0, 2U(Height DIV 5)),
      Point(4U(Width DIV 5),Height)]);
  END;
```

If you run the program, it displays a five-pointed star. The interior of the star matches the paint box's Color, and the border matches its Font.Color. You do have one little problem; the points of the star are filled in but not the center.

2. **Go back to the OnPaint event handler and insert the following line just before the line that begins with the word Polygon:**

```
SetPolyFillMode(Handle, WINDING);
```

Now the star is completely filled in. SetPolyFillMode is a function of Windows itself — it's not part of Delphi. But Delphi automatically gives you access to every one of the thousands of functions built into Windows. This particular function determines what method Windows uses to fill a polygon with border lines that cross each other.

In the OnPaint event handler that you just built, you're calling methods and setting field values for the paint box's run-time-only Canvas property. This property is an object itself, but it's not a visible component that can stand alone on the form. (Look up TCanvas sometime in the Delphi online Help to see a list of properties and methods for this object.) This object can do a lot! Now, however, you can teach the paint box a few more tricks. Place another paint box on the same form and make this one twice as wide as it is high. Start an OnPaint event handler for it and replace the Delphi begin..end pair with the following code:

```
VAR
  R : TRect;
  N : Word;
CONST
  Rainbow : ARRAY[0..4] OF TColor =
    (clRed, clYellow, clLime, clBlue, clFuchsia);
begin
  WITH Sender AS TPaintBox, Canvas DO
    BEGIN
      R := ClientRect;
      R.Bottom := 2UR.Bottom;
      Pen.Width := 8;
      Pen.Style := psInsideFrame;
      FOR N := 0 TO 4 DO
        BEGIN
          Pen.Color := Rainbow[N];
          WITH R DO
            Ellipse(Left, Top, Right, Bottom);
          InflateRect(R, -8, -8);
        END;
    END;
end;
```

Most of the time if you type in the code for an event handler, you just enter lines between the begin..end pair supplied by Delphi. Be alert for examples such as the one here, in which you *replace* the begin..end pair with lines you type.

This event handler is a little more complicated than most you've written, but that's the price of using a paint box. You can draw whatever you want, as long as you can figure out how to write the code to do it. This code draws a rainbow. Actually, it draws five ellipses of different colors, one inside the other, but because the bottom half of each ellipse is outside the paint box, it looks like a rainbow.

Add yet another paint box to the project you're working on. Set its properties as follows:

Property	*Value*
Align	alTop
Color	clYellow
Font.Name	Arial
Font.Style.fsBold	True
Height	41

Create an OnPaint event handler for this paint box, replacing the begin..end pair supplied by Delphi with the following lines:

```
VAR
   a16th, N, X : Word;
begin
WITH Sender AS TPaintBox, Canvas DO
    BEGIN
       Brush.Color := Color;
       FillRect(ClientRect);
       WITH ClientRect DO
          Rectangle(Left, Top, Right, Bottom);
       a16th := PixelsPerInch DIV 16;
       N := 0; X := 0;
       WHILE X < Width DO
          BEGIN
             MoveTo(X,1);
             LineTo(X, 6U(1+(Byte(N MOD 2=0) +
                Byte(N MOD 4=0) +
                Byte(N MOD 8=0) +
                Byte(N MOD 16=0))));
             Canvas.Font := Font;
             IF (N > 0) AND (N MOD 16=0) THEN
                TextOut(PenPos.X+3, PenPos.Y-16,
                   IntToStr(N DIV 16));
             N := N + 1;
             X := X + a16th;
          END;
       END;
end;
```

Try to guess what that event handler does before you run the program. Did you guess? It draws a ruler across the top of the form. The FillRect function fills the entire paint box with color, and the Rectangle function draws a border. (So far, this code isn't doing anything a shape component couldn't do.) Next, you calculate approximately how many pixels correspond to $1/16$ of an inch. You set variables N and X to 0 and start a loop that draws a vertical line every $1/16$ of inch across the width of the paint box.

Within the loop, the MoveTo function moves the pen to the top edge of the paint box, at the pixel position defined by X. The LineTo function draws a line from that position down; the longest lines come at the 1-inch marks, the next shorter lines come at $1/2$-inch marks, and so on down to the shortest lines at $1/16$-inch marks. For a 1-inch mark, the TextOut function writes the correct number just to the right of the mark. Each time through the loop, variable N increases by 1 and variable X increases by the number of pixels in $1/16$ of an inch.

The very first line is numbered 0, so look at line number 1, the first $^1/_{16}$-inch mark. It's not divisible by 2, 4, 8, or 16, so its length is 6. How about the 1-inch mark (line 16)? It is divisible by 2, 4, 8, and 16, so its length is 5×6, or 30 pixels. This handy calculation yields the correct length for lines representing whole inches and for each fraction down to $^1/_{16}$ of an inch.

Color Control with Color Grid

The Color common dialog enables you or your users to choose any of the 16,777,216 colors that Windows is theoretically capable of displaying — about 16 million more choices than you need. If your system is set up to display 256 different colors, Windows usually gives you a dithered color instead of the exact color you choose. That is, it displays a pattern of dots in two or more solid colors that approaches the color you asked for. If you just want to select a solid color, the color grid component is a better bet. You find the color grid on the Samples page of the Component palette. (See Chapter 3 for more about the Samples page.)

Properties

If you drop a new color grid onto a form, you get a 4-by-4 array of colored boxes. The GridOrdering property enables you to rearrange the boxes in 8 or 16 rows or columns instead. By default, the color grid tracks foreground and background colors, but you can set ForegroundEnabled or BackgroundEnabled to False to disable one of these. Don't disable both unless your users have shown a tendency to choose really vile combinations. The ForegroundIndex and BackgroundIndex properties indicate which of the 16 boxes you select for each, and the run-time-only ForegroundColor and BackgroundColor properties hold the actual color.

Events

A left-click on a color box sets a new foreground color, and a right-click sets a new background color. If the user changes the foreground or background selection, the color grid receives an OnChange event. You can also respond to the OnClick event, which occurs anytime the user clicks the grid, but OnChange is usually all you need.

Place a big shape on the form. Set the shape's Shape property to stEllipse and it's Pen.Width to 8. Place a color grid on the form below the shape, and set its GridOrdering property to go8x2. Match its width to that of the shape, and set its height so that the boxes are roughly square. Set its BackgroundIndex property to 15. Put these lines in the color grid's OnChange event handler as follows:

```
WITH Sender AS TColorGrid, Shape1 DO
   BEGIN
      Pen.Color := ForegroundColor;
      Brush.Color := BackgroundColor;
   END;
```

Run the program (as shown in Figure 7-3) and try left- and right-clicking the color grid. If you left-click, the outline of the shape changes to match the color, and *FG* appears in the box you clicked. If you right-click, the shape's interior changes color and *BG* appears in the box. If you make the foreground and background the same, the box holds *FB*. Notice, too, that you can use the arrow keys to move the highlight around the color grid and press the *F* or *B* key to set the foreground or background color.

Figure 7-3:
The color grid component enables users to choose foreground and background colors from a set of 16 solid colors.

Image Is Everything

An image component displays a bitmap, an icon, or a Windows metafile. Delphi wizards can even arrange to register other graphic file formats for the image component's use. If you ever meet any old-time Windows programmers, *don't* show them the image component! They'll start an hour-long harangue about how difficult it was to display bitmaps in the "good old days" and how kids these days just don't know the value of honest work.

Properties

An image component's *Picture* property is an object that holds the bitmap, icon, or metafile you want displayed. Load an image into the Picture property at design time or at run time. If the Stretch property is True, the picture stretches or shrinks to fit the bounds of the image component. Otherwise, it stays the size you gave it at design time. If the picture is too big, it is clipped at the image bounds; if it's too small, blank space is around it.

Events

Images respond to the standard mouse events — clicks, double-clicks, dragging, and so on. Most of the time, however, images don't need to do anything except display a pretty picture, as the following steps show:

1. **Drop an image component on a new form and set Stretch to True.**

2. **Set the component's Align property to alClient so that it fills the form.**

3. **Set the form's caption to Image Viewer and add an Open File dialog with the following properties:**

Property	*Value*
DefaultExt	BMP
Options.HideReadOnly	True
Options.FileMustExist	True
Title Open Image	File

4. **Double-click the dialog's Filter property to access the filter list and create filters named Bitmaps, Icons, and Metafiles, with values *.BMP, *.ICO, and *.WMF, respectively.**

5. **Place a menu on the form and give the form a simplified File menu, with just the** &Open. . . **and** E&xit **items.**

6. **Put the single command Close; in the Exit menu item's OnClick event handler and enter the following lines for the Open item:**

```
WITH OpenDialog1 DO
  IF Execute THEN
    BEGIN
      Screen.Cursor := crHourglass;
      try
        WITH Image1.Picture DO
          BEGIN
            LoadFromFile(Filename);
            WindowState := wsNormal;
            ClientWidth := Width;
            ClientHeight := Height;
          END;
```

(continued)

(continued)

```
        Caption := ExtractFilename(Filename);
    finally
        Screen.Cursor := crDefault;
    end;
END;
```

Loading a bitmap from disk can take a little time, so you set the cursor to an hourglass while the loading is going on. Rather than change the cursor for the form or one of its components, you change it globally for the Screen object.

7. Run the program and load any bitmaps you have handy.

The form first sizes itself to match the image. But if you resize or maximize the form, the image stretches to fit. Oh, one thing — icons don't stretch.

If you use this viewer on some of the tiny bitmaps designed as Windows wallpaper, the result is some squashed-looking, very tiny pictures. That's because the size of the bitmap ties to the size of the form, and the form can't shrink small enough to display these particular bitmaps at their actual sizes.

Gauging Your Progress

Computers do things in the blink of an eye that you or I would take hours to do by hand. Still, some tasks would take a person years, and those tasks take more than moments even for a computer. A program that's cranking away at a job needs to keep the user apprised of its progress. That's what the gauge component is for. It represents a process's progress visually in several different ways. The gauge component resides in the Sample page of the Component palette.

The Kind property determines which type of gauge appears, as follows:

- ✔ A pie-type gauge gradually fills a circle as the process progresses.

- ✔ A bar-type gauge fills either from left to right or from bottom to top.

- ✔ A needle-type gauge is similar to the gas gauge on your car; it's shaped like a semicircle and has a needle that moves to track the process.

- ✔ A text-only gauge displays the percentage-complete information as text only. (All the gauges — not just this one — display this information as text unless you set the ShowText property to False.)

Set BorderStyle to bsNone for the pie and the needle gauges. Otherwise, a rectangular border surrounds the circular or semicircular gauge. The BackColor property sets the color of the entire gauge, and the ForeColor property sets the color of the filled portion of the gauge. Properties

MaxValue and MinValue determine the range of values reports, and your program reports progress by setting the aptly named Progress property. The percentage the gauge display is relative to the position of Progress between MinValue and MaxValue. As with the Color Grid, the gauge has a PopupMenu property.

Figure 7-4:
The gauge component offers five ways to report the progress of a process.

1. **Shift+click the gauge component's icon and place five gauge components on a new fixed-size form, arranged as shown in Figure 7-4.**

   Here's the value of the Kind property for each component:

Gauge component	*Value of the Kind property*
Big circle	gkPie
Half circle	gkNeedle
Small square	gkText
Horizontal bar	gkHorizontalBar
Vertical bar	gkVerticalBar

2. **Set the nonrectangular gauges' BorderStyle property to bsNone.**

3. **Place a button on the form (next to the small square gauge), give it the caption &Add 10, double-click it, and put the following code in its OnClick event handler:**

   ```
   Gauge1.Progress := (Gauge1.Progress + 10) MOD 100;
   Gauge2.Progress := Gauge1.Progress;
   Gauge3.Progress := Gauge1.Progress;
   Gauge4.Progress := Gauge1.Progress;
   Gauge5.Progress := Gauge1.Progress;
   ```

4. **Run the program and click the button repeatedly.**

The gauges go up by 10 percent with each click of the button. After they pass 100 percent, they reset to 0 percent. Notice how the percentage-complete text changes color as the color bar passes it. You use the gauge control in other projects.

Introducing Our Panel

The panel component is the building block from which you build status bars and SpeedBars. If you place a panel component at the top of your form and drop a few speed buttons (which I introduce in the next chapter) on it, you have a SpeedBar. If you place a panel component at the bottom of the form and arrange to have useful information appear on it, you have a status bar.

Properties

The most important property of a panel component is Align. If you set it to alTop, the panel moves to the top of the form and expands to the form's full width. If you set it to alBottom, the panel fits itself to the bottom of the form. Likewise, alLeft and alRight snug the panel against the left and right edges, respectively, and alClient causes it to fill the entire client area of the form.

But wait — there's more! If you run the program and resize the form, the panel automatically resizes to match. If more than one component has the same Align value, they stack up along the specified edge. A panel with the alClient Align value fills the entire client area of the screen that's not occupied by other panels. And MDI child forms (which I discuss in Chapter 6) correctly use only the part of the form that's not occupied by panels. (Don't confuse the Alignment property with Align. Alignment simply determines where the panel's Caption appears: left, right, or center. Frequently, you delete the caption entirely.)

A panel automatically has a 3-D look and a handful of properties dedicated to adjusting that look. BevelInner and BevelOuter set the panel's inner and outer edges to look raised, lowered, or flat. BevelWidth and BorderWidth set the width of the bevel and the panel's border.

To create a panel, start a new form and follow these steps:

1. **Place a panel on the form; set its height to 57 and its width to 97.**

2. **Make eight copies of the panel and arrange the nine panels in three rows of three.**

3. **Select all the panels and delete the panels' captions.**

4. **Set the panels' BevelWidth and BorderWidth properties both to 2.**

5. **Select the top row of three panels and set BevelInner to bvLowered and Caption to *H* (make sure that it's a capital *H*).**

6. **Select the middle row of three panels and set BevelInner to bvNone and Caption to *m* (small *m*).**

7. **For the bottom row of three panels, set BevelInner to bvRaised and Caption to *G* (capital *G*).**

   Why these captions? You find out shortly!

8. **Select the left column of three and set BevelOuter to bvLowered.**

9. **Set BevelOuter for the middle and right columns to bvNone and bvRaised.**

10. **Select each panel in turn and append a letter to its caption — capital *H* if it's in the first column, small *m* for the second column, and capital *G* for the third column.**

11. **Now select the form itself, double-click its Font property, choose Wingdings for the font, and set the size to 20.**

Surprise! With that last step, it all makes sense. Each bevel contains two pictographs from the Wingdings font (see Figure 7-5). The first represents the value of BevelInner and the second the value of BevelOuter. A down-pointing hand means bvLowered; an up-pointing hand means bvRaised; and a big zero means bvNone. Save this project and load it any time you need to check what a particular combination of bevel styles looks like.

The ShowHint property is useful if you have a panel full of speed buttons or other components. You can set the panel's ShowHint property to True without enabling hints for every component on the form. The background color of all hint boxes in your program is controlled by the HintColor property of the invisible Application object. The Application object's HintDelay property is the number of milliseconds the mouse must rest on a component before the flyover help appears. You use all these properties shortly.

Figure 7-5:
Adjust the
inner and
outer
bevels of
the panel
component
to get a
variety of
different
effects.

Events

Frequently, a panel doesn't need to respond to any events; its job is to maintain its alignment, hold other components, and display flyover help. Occasionally, you add an OnResize event handler to take care of the arrangement of components that the panel contains. Panels that display information directly are more likely to respond to OnClick or OnDblClick events. In Word for Windows, for example, a subpanel of the bottom status bar indicates whether overwrite mode is on, and double-clicking that panel toggles overwrite mode on or off. Follow these steps to connect an event to a panel:

1. **Place a panel on a new form and delete the panel's caption.**

2. **Set the panel's Align property to alTop and its ShowHint property to True.**

3. **Insert the following line in an OnCreate event handler for the form:**

```
Application.HintColor := clAqua;
```

4. **Put a smaller panel inside the first panel and set its properties as follows:**

Property	*Value*
BevelOuter	bvLowered
Caption	CAP
Font.Color	clGray
Hint	"Toggles CapsLock"
Tag	20

5. **Size the smaller panel to fit snugly around the caption and center it vertically in the larger panel.**

6. **Make two copies of the subpanel but, to make sure that they're owned by the same big panel, click the subpanel, press Ctrl+C, click the main panel, and press Ctrl+V.**

7. **Drag the copies into a horizontal line.**

8. **Change the captions of the other two panels to NUM and SCR and their Hints to Toggles NumLock and Toggles ScrollLock.**

   The Tag for the NUM panel should be 144; for the SCR panel, 145. (In case you're wondering, the values 20, 144, and 145 are the numbers Windows uses internally to represent the CapsLock, NumLock, and ScrollLock keys, respectively.)

9. **Run the program and move the mouse cursor over any of the three subpanels.**

If the mouse is still set for $^8/_{10}$ of a second, the flyover help appears. However, clicking the panels doesn't *do* anything yet.

10. Select all three subpanels and create an OnClick method for them, replacing the default begin..end pair with the following code:

```
VAR KS : TKeyboardState;
begin
  GetKeyboardState(KS);
  WITH Sender AS TPanel DO
    KS[Tag] := KS[Tag] XOR 1;
  SetKeyboardState(KS);
end;
```

Now, if you click one of the subpanels, it toggles the corresponding light on your keyboard — try it and see! Each time you click the CAP panel, for example, the CapsLock light turns on or off. And it's functional too, as you notice if you type anything. Unfortunately, you can't yet make this project *display* the current state of the three shift locks. You won't be introduced to a component that's essential for fixing up that kind of display in this chapter. Save the project as LOCKS, and you can add the state-display capability in the next chapter.

Status symbols

One popular style of window dressing is a status line at the bottom of the form that displays a brief hint for the control or menu item that has the focus. Setting up this kind of status bar in Delphi is simple; you just use the status bar component! Follow these steps:

1. Drop a panel on a new form and set its properties as follows:

Property	*Value*
Align	alBottom
Alignment	taLeftJustify
BevelInner	bvLowered
Caption	(none)

2. Create an OnClick event handler for the panel; it should contain the following single line:

```
Panel1.Caption := Application.Hint;
```

Now comes the tricky part.

3. **Go to the Object Inspector's Events page and** *delete* **the panel's connection to this event handler.**

   Use the editor's Find and Replace feature to change every occurrence of Panel1Click to DoShowHint.

4. **Put the following line in an OnCreate event handler for the form:**

   ```
   Application.OnHint := DoShowHint;
   ```

   Before you continue, note that you created a method for your form that is *not* an event handler for the form or any of its components. Rather, it's an event handler for the *Application* object — the invisible object that owns all forms. After the mouse passes into or out of a component that has a Hint property, the OnHint event triggers.

5. **Drop a bunch of components on the form — it doesn't matter what type as long as they're visible as the program runs — and set the Hint property of each to a short descriptive string or to any short string.**

   Be creative!

6. **Drop a menu on the form and open the Menu Designer.**

7. **Add a template or two and fill in a short hint for each menu item.**

8. **Run the program and move the mouse around.**

Whenever the cursor is over one of your components, the hint for that component appears in the status line. Skid the mouse up and down a pull-down menu, and the hint for the highlighted menu item shows up on the status line.

Using flyover help and status bar Help at the same time can be trouble, because the text for a status bar hint is usually longer than the text for flyover help. Don't worry! Delphi enables you to enjoy the best of both worlds. For each component's Hint property, use the short flyover help text, a vertical bar character (|), and then the longer status bar hint text. Your program uses the short hints for flyover help and the longer ones for status bar Help.

A template with status

That status line form is pretty darn valuable, and you're sure to want to use it again. Clean it up and save it as a template. First, delete the mess of components you dropped on the form for experimental purposes. Change the panel's name to StatusLine and make any final adjustments in the size, font, and so on for the panel.

The Delphi object repository stores projects and forms in a simple manner. First, save the status line form and the project that contains it into a new subdirectory of the OBJREPOS directory, which is below the main Delphi directory. Make sure that this directory contains *only* files related to the status line form project. Now open the Project Manager, right-click it, and choose Add To Repository from the pop-up menu. Enter Hinted Form as the title and type a description. Select Projects from the Pages combo box and enter your name under Author. Then click OK.

From now on, whenever you open a new project, you can optionally start out with a working status line already in place.

Bumpy and dippy forms

Often you don't need all the features that the panel component brings along — sometimes you don't even need all four sides of a panel! In that case, the Bevel component may be just what you need. A bevel doesn't own components the way a panel does; as you move the bevel, the components stay put.

Like a panel, a bevel has an Align property. Its Style can be simply bsLowered or bsRaised. But the most important property is Shape. The bsBox shape is like a simple panel that's just raised or lowered relative to the form. BsFrame yields a rectangle with a raised or lowered rim. The remaining four styles display just one of the four sides of the rectangle, again either raised (a bump) or lowered (a dip). That can be handy for creating a dividing line on your form. Figure 7-6 shows a form with raised and lowered frames and lines.

Follow these steps to create the example in Figure 7-6:

1. Drop a Bevel component onto a new form.

Raised frame and line (bumps)

Lowered frame and line (dips)

Figure 7-6:
Use the Bevel component to define areas of your form with frames and lines.

2. **Set the component's Align property to alTop and its Shape property to bsBottomLine.**

   You now have a horizontal dip on your form.

3. **Change the Style property to bsRaised.**

   The dip becomes a bump.

In general, to create a dividing line that maintains a constant distance from one side of the form, set the Align property to that side and the Shape property to the opposite side. To make a line that stays in place relative to the left side of the form, for example, set Align to alLeft and Shape to bsRightLine.

Bevels don't do as much as panels, so they don't consume as much of the resources of Windows. Always use a bevel rather than a panel unless you *need* a feature that a bevel just doesn't have.

Controlling Scrolling

A Delphi form is smart — if any of its components protrude off the edge of the form, the form automatically sprouts scroll bars so that the user can scroll around and see the entire form. Unfortunately, this isn't always the right behavior. Want to see something ugly? Try the following steps:

1. **Place two panels on a new form, setting their Align properties to alTop and alBottom.**

   These represent the SpeedBar and status bar of an elegant program.

2. **Place a button near the bottom right corner of the form and shrink the form so that the button hangs off its right edge.**

   A horizontal scroll bar appears and pushes the status bar up.

3. **Widen the form again and resize it so that the button is off the bottom of the available space.**

   Now a vertical scroll bar appears on the right, cutting off the tips of the two panels.

Clearly, you don't want the SpeedBar and status line to be included in the part of the form that scrolls. That's why the scroll box component exists — to enable you to redefine the scrolling portion of the form. A scroll box is similar to a panel minus the 3-D effect. It has many of the same properties and events, but most of the time you can leave its properties set at their default values.

Using the same form, cut the button to the Clipboard and drop a scroll box in the middle of the form. Set the scroll box's Align property to alClient and paste the button back onto it. Now, after you resize the form, the scroll bars that appear stay within the area between the SpeedBar and status bar panels.

Chapter 8
Additional Components

● ●

In This Chapter

▶ Building your own digital clock

▶ Using a Delphi program to generate bitmap glyphs to use in other Delphi programs

▶ Using data entry components that force correct input

▶ Creating multipage forms like the ones Delphi uses

▶ Adding headers that enable you to resize columnar information on your form

▶ Decorating your programs with speed buttons and bitmap buttons

▶ Enhancing the simple editor with a SpeedBar

● ●

*T*he last chapter's graphical elements add pizzazz to user interfaces built by using standard Windows components. The real fun begins with this chapter, however, because the sky's the limit as far as what a Delphi component can accomplish.

This chapter discusses some additional components that are pretty simple in what they can do. Chapter 9 discusses additional components that are more advanced.

Choosing Additional Components

Naturally, you find *most* of the additional components on the Additional page in the Component palette. A few of the additional components are on other pages, however, and several move to the Win 3.1 page in Delphi 3. You can consult Table 8-1 anytime you're not sure which components to use.

Table 8-1   Problems Solved by Simple Additional Components

Task	Component
Trigger an event every so often or create a delay.	Timer. See "Wake Up with a Timer."
Enable the user to enter a numeric value or tweak an existing value up or down.	Spin edit. See "Putting the Best Spin on Things."
Send general up or down messages to a component.	Spin button. See "Putting the Best Spin on Things."
Force the user's input to match a predefined mask (for example, for phone numbers).	Masked edit box. See "Who Was That Masked Edit Box?"
Create a form with multiple tabbed pages.	Tabbed notebook. See "Compositions in a Tabbed Notebook."
Create a form with multiple pages, a set of tabs, or both.	Tab set and notebook. See "Gluing Tabs on a Notebook."
Display a header with resizable columns.	Header. See "Using Your Header."
Trigger a program feature with a button that has a picture or colored text.	Bitmap button. See "Brighten Your Forms with Bitmap Buttons."
Launch processes from buttons on a SpeedBar.	Speed button. See "Get Up to Speed with Speed Buttons."

Wake Up with a Timer Component

Programmers say that Windows is a cooperative multitasking system, but Windows 3.1 is anything but cooperative. What *cooperative multitasking system* really means, regarding Windows 3.1, is that, if even one program *doesn't* cooperate, the whole system comes to a grinding halt. Experiencing this kind of crash is a rite of passage for Windows 3.1 programmers. Typically, such a crash happens because of a program loop that continues until a particular Windows 3.1 event occurs. The result is that the program spins madly in its loop, like a dog chasing it's tail, giving Windows no chance to process messages. And because Windows 3.1 can't process messages, the program never gets the message that would enable it to break out of the loop. Catch-22! Tight loops are still a problem in 32-bit Windows 95 programs, but they don't bring the whole system to a halt — just the offending program.

The solution to never ending loops lies in the Delphi timer component, which ties into the built-in Windows timer. If your program performs a long, repetitive task, set a timer for a very short time and perform one portion of the task each time the timer ticks; Windows isn't tied up, because it processes all other pending messages before getting around to your timer. You can also use the timer to update your program's display, perhaps reporting its progress with a gauge or updating an on-screen clock. Finally, you can set up a timer for a one-shot time delay, simply by turning the timer off after the OnTimer event occurs.

Properties and events

The timer component has just four properties. The Tag and Name properties are similar to the other components that I discuss in the previous chapters. The Interval property specifies a number of milliseconds; it's initially set to 1,000, or one second. Roughly each time that interval passes, the timer receives an OnTimer event. Why "roughly"? Windows queues up events as they happen, but it permits most other events to cut in line ahead of timer events. Setting the Enabled property to False turns off the timer and stops the flow of OnTimer messages.

Don't bother setting Interval to a value less than 55. Windows uses the hardware timer interrupt as the basis for its timers, and that interrupt occurs about every 55 milliseconds. What? You don't like approximations? Okay, the timer interrupt occurs once every 65,536/1,193,180 second. Better?

Inside Windows, timers are a limited resource. Windows 3.1 has just 32 timers, which all applications in the system share. In 32-bit Windows 95 and Windows NT, you have virtually no limit, but you still shouldn't use more timers than necessary. You can use one timer for multiple time intervals, if you choose the interval correctly. To set timers at 8, 24, and 60 seconds, for example, you could set the interval to 4,000 milliseconds (4 seconds) and trigger the 8-second action every other event, the 24-second action every 6th event, and the 60-second action every 15th event.

Follow these steps:

1. **Start a new project by using the fixed-size form template.**

2. **Place a label on the form, set its caption to 00:00:00 PM, and make sure that its AutoSize property is True.**

3. **Choose an interesting font for the label, and make the font big.**

   I used 72 points.

4. **Set the label's Align property to alClient and its Alignment property to taCenter.**

5. **Size the form so that it nicely surrounds the label and set its caption to** Digital Clock.

6. **Locate the timer component on the System page of the Component palette and drop one on the form, leaving its Interval property set to the default of 1,000.**

7. **Create an OnTimer event handler containing this single line of code:**

```
Label1.Caption := TimeToStr(Now);
```

8. **Give the form an OnCreate event handler containing just this line:**

```
Timer1Timer(Timer1);
```

With just two lines of code, you build an attractive digital clock. Figure 8-1 shows one possible clock — yours may look different depending on the font you choose.

Figure 8-1:
A timer
component
keeps this
clock
ticking.

Locks again

In Chapter 7, I promise you that you can teach the shift-lock program to stay synchronized with the keyboard. The timer component is the key.

Load the LOCKS project that I ask you to save in Chapter 7. Drop a timer on the form, set its Interval to 100, and give it an OnTimer event, with these lines replacing the begin..end pair supplied by Delphi:

```
VAR KS : TKeyboardState;
begin
  GetKeyboardState(KS);
  IF Odd(KS[VK_CAPITAL]) THEN
    Panel2.Font.Color := clBlack
  ELSE Panel2.Font.Color := clGray;
  IF Odd(KS[VK_NUMLOCK]) THEN
    Panel3.Font.Color := clBlack
  ELSE Panel3.Font.Color := clGray;
```

```
   IF Odd(KS[VK_SCROLL]) THEN
      Panel4.Font.Color := clBlack
   ELSE Panel4.Font.Color := clGray;
end;
```

After you run the new Locks program, you see that the panels corresponding to the three shift locks are gray if the corresponding shift is off and black
if it's on. And as you toggle the shift on and off from the keyboard, the
corresponding panel synchs up within 1/10 second. Timer components are
great whenever your program needs to stay current with real-world events.

Putting the Best Spin on Things

Computers love numbers, but computer users can very easily enter numbers *incorrectly*. In earlier chapters, you build an edit box component that
accepts numbers only in a certain range. That's handy if users are entering
brand-new numbers. If your aim is to tweak an existing numeric entry up or
down, a spin edit box is a better choice. Users can still enter numbers
directly in a spin edit box, but they can also finagle the number up or down
by clicking an attached spin button. For other situations that involve
tweaking values up and down, you can skip the edit box entirely and use a
standalone spin button.

The SpinButton and SpinEdit components both reside on the Delphi
Samples page. You don't find them built into the Help system, but you *do*
find them useful! Many Windows applications use them. Windows 95 *does*
have a spin button control built-in; Delphi implements this control as the
UpDown component. You meet this component in Chapter 12.

Properties

The properties special to a spin button include DownGlyph and UpGlyph,
which represent the glyphs on the down and up arrow portions of the spin
button. The default glyphs are boring down- and up-pointing triangles, but
you can draw your own glyphs to replace them. If you increase the spin
button's size, you want to use a *larger* pair of triangles! The tiny default
triangles look dopey if the spin button gets big. The FocusControl property
determines which control gets the focus if you select the spin button.

A spin edit box's properties mostly mirror those of a regular edit box, and you can't change the glyphs for the built-in spin button. A few properties are absent, most notably Text. If you want to check or set the text of a spin edit box, you work with its Value property. Properties special to a spin edit box include MaxValue, MinValue, and Increment. As you'd expect, the first two control the range available to the spin edit, and the last is the amount by which the value changes after you click the up or down button.

Events

A spin edit box responds to precisely the same set of events that a regular edit box does. The special events for a spin button are OnUpClick and OnDownClick, which are triggered by a click on the up or down portion of the button. Notice that you can click and hold the button to spin through its values rapidly — hence the name. To create a spin box, follow these steps:

1. **Place four spin edit components on a new form.**
2. **Set the MaxValue of the last three components to 100.**
3. **Set the Increment of the third component to 10.**
4. **Set the MinValue of the fourth component to 50.**
5. **Run the program and enter values into the four spin edit boxes.**

Notice that you can't enter nonnumeric characters in the edit boxes. You can enter values outside the range from MinValue to MaxValue, but if you move the focus to another component or tweak the value by using the spin buttons, the value in the spin edit component snaps into range.

The first spin edit box in this sample program has MaxValue and MinValue as the default value, 0. You can spin this spin edit box through the full range of –2,147,483,648 to 2,147,483,647 (that is, if you're prepared to spend the next ten years or so with your finger on the mouse button). The others are restricted to the range 0..100 or 50..100. The third spin edit box spins by tens rather than by ones.

I don't have much more to say about spin edit boxes. Use them any time you want the user to either enter a number or adjust an existing number.

Delphi as artiste

Anytime that you make a spin button bigger than the rather tiny default size, you need to supply it with up and down glyphs appropriate to its size. I don't know about you, but I'm no artist. Anytime I need to draw a bitmap, I try to find a way to make Delphi draw it for me. To do so, follow these steps:

1. **Drop two image components on a new form.**

2. **Set the height of both components to 33.**

3. **Set the width of the first component to 17 and the second to 33.**

4. **Put the following lines in the OnCreate method for the form itself:**

```
WITH Image1, Canvas DO
  BEGIN
    Font.Name := 'Wingdings';
    Font.Size := 20;
    TextOut(0,0,'G');
    Picture.SaveToFile('FINGUP.BMP');
    TextOut(0,0,'H');
    Picture.SaveToFile('FINGDOWN.BMP');
  END;
WITH Image2, Canvas DO
  BEGIN
    Brush.Color := clLime;
    Pen.Color := clLime;
    Polygon([Point(1, Height),
      Point(Width DIV 2, 0),
      Point(Width-1, Height)]);
    Picture.SaveToFile('TRNGUP.BMP');
    Brush.Color := clWhite;
    FillRect(ClientRect);
    Brush.Color := clRed;
    Pen.Color := clRed;
    Polygon([Point(0, 0),
      Point(Width DIV 2, Height),
      Point(Width, 0)]);
    Picture.SaveToFile('TRNGDOWN.BMP');
  END;
```

5. **Run the program.**

Watch Delphi mix its paints, daub them on the palette, measure the subject with squinted eye and thumb . . . whoops! It goes by too fast to see all that. In fact, as soon as the program comes up on-screen, it's finished generating the four bitmap files (though you only see two of them). The first two contain the up- and down-pointing finger characters from the Windows Wingdings font, and the second two contain large up- and down-pointing triangles. Hang onto this program in case you want to generate different bitmaps. Play around with it; change the size and color of the triangles or choose different characters for the character-based glyphs.

You may notice that the up-pointing triangle is two pixels narrower than the down-pointing one. That's because the spin button component checks the color of the bottom left pixel of the glyph and treats that color as transparent anywhere it appears in the glyph. If you hadn't made the triangle narrower, its *green* color would be transparent — ugly!

Organizing the vertically challenged

A lone spin button can have its uses independent of any edit box. For example, you can use it to move the selected item up and down in a list box. Just follow these steps:

1. **Start a new form and place two spin buttons on it.**

2. **Stretch both the spin buttons to several times their normal size.**

3. **Set the UpGlyph and DownGlyph properties of one spin button to FINGUP.BMP and FINGDOWN.BMP.**

4. **Set the UpGlyph and DownGlyph properties of the other spin button to TRNGUP.BMP and TRNGDOWN.BMP.**

5. **Adjust the size of the spin buttons to match the glyphs.**

6. **Now decide which button you prefer and delete the other.**

7. **Place a list box on the form and double-click its Items property.**

8. **Enter the names of Snow White's seven vertically challenged companions.**

    If you don't remember their names, check Figure 8-2.

9. **Set the FocusControl property for the spin button to the name of the list box.**

10. **Create an OnUpClick event handler, replacing the Delphi begin..end pair with the following lines:**

```
VAR I : Integer;
begin
  WITH ListBox1 DO
    IF ItemIndex > 0 THEN
      BEGIN
        I := ItemIndex - 1;
        Items.Move(ItemIndex, I);
        ItemIndex := I;
      END;
end;
```

11. **Highlight the code you typed and press Ctrl+C (copy to Clipboard).**

12. **Start an OnDownClick event handler for the spin button by highlighting the begin..end pair supplied by Delphi and pressing Ctrl+V to replace those lines with a copy of the OnUpClick event handler.**

13. **In the copy, replace ItemIndex-1 with ItemIndex+1.**

14. **Find the line** `IF ItemIndex > 0 THEN` **and replace it with this line:**

```
IF (ItemIndex >= 0) AND (ItemIndex < Items.Count-1) THEN
```

Figure 8-2 shows the final program, with spin buttons displaying both pairs of specialized glyphs. Anytime you write a program that needs to enable the user to reorder items in a list, steal this code!

Figure 8-2:
This program uses either of the two spin buttons to move the selected list box item up or down.

Who Was That Masked Edit Box?

Even without its spin button, the spin edit has a useful talent — it accepts only numbers. Well, the masked edit box can do that trick and quite a few more. You can set it up to automatically format input as phone numbers, zip codes, and so on, by using a coded text string called a *mask* that controls what characters are permitted. If none of the prebuilt masks suits your purposes, you can create your own.

The event list for a masked edit box is identical to that of a plain edit box, and the property list is almost the same. A few properties are absent, and the essential property EditMask is added. The EditText property contains the text the user enters, with any literal characters from the mask incorporated. If the Save Literal Characters option for the mask is True, the Text property's value is the same as that of EditText; otherwise, Text contains precisely the text the user enters, without any additions. Follow these steps:

1. **Place several masked edit boxes on a new form, with a label next to each.**

2. **For each edit box, double-click the EditMask property and choose a different predefined mask type from the dialog.**

3. **Double-click the first box to create an OnChange event handler with the following single line of code:**

```
Label1.Caption := MaskEdit1.Text;
```

4. **Create a parallel OnChange event handler for each of the other masked edit boxes, setting the corresponding label's Caption property to the value of the masked edit box's Text property.**

5. **Run the program and try entering data in the various edit boxes.**

You can easily see which is a zip code, which is a date, and so on. Enter a partial value, such as a single digit of a phone number, and try to move to another field. The program complains that the input isn't valid, because it's incomplete. Enter a time such as **99:99:99PM**, however, and you see that it's accepted. Masked edit boxes don't care about anything beyond making sure that the right type of character is in each position. Notice, too, that the label associated with each edit box holds the exact contents of the box.

Go back into the same little program. For each masked edit box, double-click the EditMask property and uncheck the Save Literal Characters check box. Now whenever you run the program, only the characters typed into the masked edit box appear in the label's caption. The phone number 800-555-1212, for example, appears as 8005551212. The phone number string with separators is 30 percent longer than without. If you plan to store thousands or millions of phone numbers, that 30 percent may represent megabytes of disk space.

Add a new masked edit box to the same form and set its EditMask property to the following value:

```
!>0LLL000;0;_
```

If you run the program, you find that the new masked edit box accepts only strings that start with a digit, followed by three uppercase letters and three digits. That's the current format for auto license plates in California. But how does that mask produce this effect?

The mask is broken into three fields, separated by semicolons. Working backward from the end, the underscore is the character that displays blanks. You can change it to anything you want, as long as you don't confuse users. The middle field is 0 if you want to strip the mask characters from the Text property; 1 if you don't. The first field is the mask itself, with each cryptic character having a special meaning. The following lines show what the characters in this particular case mean:

!	Leading blanks are removed.
>	All alphabetic characters change to uppercase (until a < character is encountered).
0	The user must enter a digit.
L	The user must enter an alphabetic character.

You can use many more hieroglyphics in edit masks; check the online Help. Most of the time, however, the built-in collection of masks serves you well.

Compositions in a Tabbed Notebook

Delphi uses many multipage dialogs — in the Object Inspector window, the Editor window, and most of the options dialogs, to name a few. Each page has a tab with its name, and clicking a tab flips to that page. You can add this absolutely fabulous feature to your own programs in two ways. The simpler way is to place a tabbed notebook component on your form, enter a list of names for the pages, and just start placing components on the different pages. The business of flipping pages and moving rows of tabs is handled for you. The other method, which I discuss in the next section, involves writing code to manage the connection between two separate components that represent the tabs and the pages.

In Delphi 3 (and also Delphi 2.0), these tab and notebook components are shoved off onto the Win 3.1 page of the Component palette. Their place in the limelight is usurped by the Windows 95 TabControl and PageControl components; Delphi 3 itself uses these components. If your programs need to stay compatible with Delphi 1.0 (and also Windows 3.1), however, you must forgo the thrill of using the Windows 95 components directly. In Delphi 3, however, the tabbed notebook is actually a PageControl in disguise. So if you use tabbed notebooks in your Delphi 1.0 programs, they automatically modernize themselves if compiled under Delphi 3!

The Pages property of the tabbed notebook component is an array of strings, which contains the names for the tabs on the notebook's pages. You enter the names in a special dialog that includes the capability to reorder the pages if necessary.

After you start placing components on the pages, do *not* try to move a page by deleting its name and inserting it elsewhere in the list! Doing so destroys all the components on that page.

ActivePage contains the name of the currently active page, and PageIndex contains its index, starting with 0 for the first page. The Font property for a notebook passes along to any components on the pages that have ParentFont set to True. If you want to set the font for the tabs, use the TabFont property. To do so, follow these steps:

1. **Place a tabbed notebook on a new form and set its Align property to alClient.**

2. **Double-click the Pages property to enter a list of page names.**

3. **Click the Edit button and change the first page's name from Default to One.**

4. **Add pages named Two through Eight.**

5. **Try reordering the pages by using the Move Up and Move Down buttons (but make sure that you organize them correctly before you close this dialog).**

6. **Set the TabsPerRow property to 4 and watch the tabs line up in two rows.**

7. **Set the TabsPerRow property to 8 and the tabs all scrunch into the same row.**

8. **Try setting the property to 2.**

   Whoops! Delphi doesn't permit that, because the minimum is 3. (Alas, in Delphi 3, the tabbed notebook's TabsPerRow property has no effect.)

9. **Right-click the tabbed notebook.**

   Notice that its pop-up menu has items titled Next Page and Previous Page. These enable you to flip through the pages at design time.

10. **Add a few components to each page.**

11. **Run the program and flip through the pages.**

You notice that if you choose a page with a tab that isn't in the front row, the tabs shift to bring that row to the front. The top half of the form in Figure 8-3 is a tabbed notebook with eight pages, just like what you built. This component makes organizing complicated forms incredibly easy by putting each set of related components on a different page.

Figure 8-3:
The top is a
tabbed
notebook
component,
and the
bottom half
is a
notebook
component
connected
to a tab set
component.

Gluing Tabs on a Notebook

The bottom half of the form in Figure 8-3 is a notebook component with a tab set component glued onto it. A few lines of code are required to keep the tabs and notebook pages in synch, but the effort is minimal. The Delphi multipage dialogs are built this way. One more thing — tabs in a tab set point down, while tabbed notebook tabs point up.

You can use the tab set and notebook separately. You may, for example, use a set of radio buttons or a list box full of page names to select which page to display in a notebook component. You can also use the tab set to provide a quick way to jump around in a phone book database. Tab sets and notebooks really shine, however, if you use them together.

Properties

Both the notebook and the tab set components have the Align property. You almost always want the tab set aligned at the bottom and the notebook aligned to occupy the rest of the window's client area. The tab set's Tabs property is the list of names for the tabs. It corresponds directly to the notebook's Pages property, and generally the two lists should be the same. Tab set's TabIndex and Notebook's PageIndex both represent the selected tab or page. In addition, Notebook's ActivePage property holds the name of the active page.

That's about it for shared properties. Tab set has a number of other properties related to its on-screen image. EndMargin and StartMargin define the distance from the edge of the window to the first and last visible tab, and SelectedColor and UnselectedColor define the colors you use for tabs. You almost always leave AutoScroll set to True — if the window gets too small to show all the tabs, this property causes left and right arrows to appear for scrolling through the tabs. (You can see the arrows at the bottom of Figure 8-3.) If you set AutoScroll to False, your program must take charge of the dreary task of displaying off-screen items by changing the value of FirstIndex, which controls which tab is drawn at the leftmost position.

If you change the Style property from tsStandard to tsOwnerDraw, you can take charge of how the tabs are drawn. No, you can't round them or make *any* change to the basic tab shape, but the tsOwnerDraw style does enable you to draw pictures on the tabs or color-code them. Tabs in a Delphi tab set always point downward.

Events

The main event for a tab set is OnClick — after the user clicks a tab, you want something to happen. This method includes a line like the following:

```
NoteBook1.PageIndex := TabSet1.TabIndex;
```

This line causes the notebook to flip to the corresponding page after the user clicks a tab. If you forget this line, your tab set becomes an ineffectual Milquetoast.

An OnChanging event occurs just before the TabIndex changes. This event is an opportunity to validate the data on the page that's losing visibility and to refuse for the pages to flip if the data isn't valid.

The special event for a notebook is OnPageChanged. Whereas the tab set's OnChanging event occurs just *before* the active page changes, the notebook's OnPageChanged occurs just *after*. Programs respond to this event by preparing to display the newly activated page.

If you actually start building a multipage form by using these two components, you must set the notebook's PageIndex property to the page that's under construction. Nine times out of ten, you forget to reset it before running the program. The result? The highlighted tab doesn't match the active page. To avoid embarrassment, insert the following line in the form's OnCreate event handler:

```
NoteBook1.PageIndex := TabSet1.TabIndex;
```

Now follow these steps:

1. **Drop a tab set on a new form and set its Align property to alBottom.**

2. **Add a notebook and set its Align property to alClient.**

3. **Double-click the notebook's Pages property and create pages named One, Two, and Three.**

4. **Put these lines in the form's OnCreate method:**

```
TabSet1.Tabs := Notebook1.Pages;
Notebook1.PageIndex := TabSet1.TabIndex;
```

You almost always want the tabs to have the same name as the corresponding pages, so the easiest thing to do is set them the same at run time, in the form's OnCreate event handler. That way, if you add or reorder pages, the tab set automatically matches up.

5. **Put the following line in the tab set's OnClick event handler:**

```
NoteBook1.PageIndex := TabSet1.TabIndex;
```

6. **Set the notebook's ActivePage property to One.**

7. **Drop a label on the notebook, set the label's caption to This Is Page One, and set its FontSize to 24.**

8. **Right-click the notebook and choose Next Page from the pop-up menu.**

The label disappears, because the first page isn't showing.

9. **Place a similar label on the page that *is* on-screen (the second page) and set the label's caption to This Is Page Two.**

10. **Give the last page a label with the caption This Is Page Three.**

You have two other important events for a tab set, OnMeasureTab and OnDrawTab. Your tab set receives these events only if its Style is set to tsOwnerDraw. By default, tabs are just wide enough to hold their text — you can change that width by responding to OnMeasureTab. As for what appears on the tab, you take charge of that by responding to OnDrawTab.

Use the same project and change the tab set's Style property to tsOwnerDraw. Set the Font.Color property of the labels on the three pages to clRed, clBlue, and clLime, respectively.

In the tab set's OnMeasureTab event handler, put the following single line:

```
TabWidth := 48;
```

This action gives you tabs 48 pixels wide. In the OnDrawTab handler, put the following lines:

```
WITH TabCanvas, Brush DO
  BEGIN
    CASE Index OF
      0 : Color := clRed;
      1 : Color :=clBlue;
      2 : Color :=clLime;
    END;
    FillRect(R);
  END;
```

Now, whenever you run the program, the three tabs appear marked with red, blue, and lime-green rectangles instead of names. Clicking a tab accesses the page with the label of the same color.

Melding a tab set and a notebook into a multipage form takes work. Unless you're desperate for down-pointing tabs, owner-draw tabs, or some other special feature, use a tabbed notebook instead.

Using Your Header

To see an example of a header component, open the Delphi Project Manager view. Just below the SpeedBar, you can see a gray bar with the headings Unit, Form, and Path. After you put the mouse cursor over one of the vertical lines on this bar, it turns to a left-right arrow, and you can drag the bar left or right to control the relative widths of the three headings, which in turn control the width of the columns below them. (The gray bar in Project Manager is actually a Windows 95 HeaderControl. Chapter 12 shows off the HeaderControl and its Windows 95 cohorts.)

Properties

The most important property of a header component is Sections, a list of heading strings naming the sections. AllowResize determines whether users can resize the headings at run time. If you set AllowResize to False, you pretty much defeat the purpose of having a header component. You also have a run-time-only SectionWidth property, which gives your program access to the widths of the individual sections.

Events

The two big events for a header are OnSized and OnSizing. OnSizing
is triggered by every incremental mouse-move while the user is resizing
the sections. OnSized occurs after the user stops resizing the headers.
Follow these steps:

1. **Place a header component on a new form and set its Align property
   to alTop.**

2. **Double-click the Sections property and enter two strings, Section One
   and Section Two.**

3. **Place a list box on the form with Align set to alLeft, and then add
   another list box with Align set to alClient.**

4. **Use the *right* mouse button to drag the dividing line between the
   header's two sections until it's right above the line that separates the
   two list boxes.**

   You must use the right button to resize the sections during form design
   because the left button is dedicated to the form design process.

5. **Enter this single line in an OnSized event handler for the header:**

   ```
   ListBox1.Width := Header1.SectionWidth[0];
   ```

6. **Run the program and drag the header's dividing line back and forth
   (by using the *left* mouse button).**

After you stop dragging, the list boxes resize so that their shared edge lies
just below the dividing line. While you're dragging, the header and the list
box are out of synch, as Figure 8-4 shows.

Using the same project, click the header and flip to the Events page in the
Object Inspector window. Click the down arrow next to the OnSizing event
and select the OnSized event handler that you already created. This time, as
you run the program and drag the header's dividing line, the list boxes
resize while you're dragging.

 If the screen elements that are resizing in response to changes in the header
are *slow* to redraw themselves, resize them only in the OnSized event. If, as
with the list boxes here, they can redraw themselves quickly, your program
seems more responsive as long as you resize them in the OnSizing event
as well.

Figure 8-4:
If a header
component
acts only on
the OnSized
event, it can
get out of
synch with
the forms.

Brighten Forms with Bitmap Buttons

Standard push buttons are sartorially dismal. You can dress them up with a fancy font, and you can set their text to any color you want — as long as you want black. Bitmap buttons spice things up a bit. Not only can you set their text color, you can actually put a picture on the button. Standard pictures for buttons that mean Yes, No, OK, and so on are provided automatically.

Bitmap buttons respond to all the same events as regular push buttons. They also have all the same properties, plus a few more. Most important is the Kind property, which tells what kind of button this is. The values bkAbort, bkAll, bkCancel, bkClose, bkHelp, bkIgnore, bkNo, bkOk, bkRetry, and bkYes give you standard pictures appropriate to these ten standard buttons. Choosing any except bkHelp or bkClose sets the ModalResult property to the corresponding value. If you want to take control of the picture yourself, leave Kind set to bkCustom.

The Glyph property is the bitmap picture that appears on the button. You can draw simple button pictures for bkCustom buttons yourself by using the Delphi Image Editor, or you can write short programs to create the pictures (as you do earlier in this chapter for the spin button component). To match the glyphs on the standard buttons, set your bitmap's size to 18 by 18.

The NumGlyphs property indicates how many different glyphs are in the bitmap you supply. A bitmap button can have different bitmaps for its normal state, disabled state, and pressed-down state. If your bitmap is precisely two or three times as wide as it is high, Delphi automatically assumes that the image contains two or three bitmaps. (You see how this works shortly.)

By default, the glyph is to the left of the caption, but by using the Layout property, you can put it on the right, the top, or the bottom. The Spacing and Margin properties control the location of the glyph and the caption within the button. Margin is the distance of the glyph from the layout edge; if the distance is –1, the glyph and caption center on the button face. Spacing is the distance from the glyph to the caption; if the spacing is –1, the two center between the margin and the opposite edge. If you have a vertical row of bitmap buttons, the glyphs and captions line up best if you set both margin and spacing to a small positive value, such as 4 or 6.

Because the user can change the color of button faces, you've got a problem if you want the background of your glyph to match the button face background. If you select the default gray, it looks awful if a user with no color sense selects maroon! Delphi gets you out of this dilemma by checking the color of the bottom-left pixel in the glyph and treating all pixels of that color as transparent. Any part of the glyph that matches this color isn't drawn — the button face shows through.

The Style property determines whether the bitmap button emulates the Windows 3.1 button style or uses the Windows 95 button style. Leave this property set to its default of bsAutoDetect, and your buttons automatically match the operating system in use. That is, your buttons look like Windows 3.1 buttons under Windows 3.1, and they look like Windows 95 buttons under Windows 95.

The last paragraph may be confusing in one instance: programming cross-compatibility between Windows 95 and Windows 3.1. You can write a program in Delphi 3 for Windows 3.1 or Windows 95. But the same program may not always run under both Windows 3.1 and Windows 95.

To see the button variety, follow these steps:

1. **Place ten bitmap buttons in two columns of five on a new form and set their Kind properties to bkAbort, bkAll, and so on, skipping bkCustom.**

2. **Start a new column of two buttons and set their captions to Left and Right.**

3. **Place two more buttons side-by-side below these.**

4. **Set the width of the two buttons from Step 3 to the height of the standard buttons and set their height so that they line up, as shown in Figure 8-5.**

5. **Set the captions of these last two buttons to Top and Bot.**

6. **Now draw a 54-by-18 bitmap with three equal-sized sections representing, from left to right, the normal glyph, the disabled glyph, and the pressed-down glyph.**

   This triptych doesn't need to be a work of art — I drew a red circle, a gray circle, and a red circle with an arrow in it.

Figure 8-5:
Bitmap
buttons
give you
standard
pictures,
custom
pictures,
and colored
text.

7. **Set the Glyph property of the last four buttons — the buttons with the Kind property at the default value bkCustom — to this bitmap.**

Notice that you must set them one at a time — normally you wouldn't use the same bitmap for multiple buttons.

8. **Set the layout of the Right button to blGlyphRight and set its Enabled property to False.**

9. **Set the layout of the two vertical buttons to blGlyphTop and blGlyphBottom.**

10. **Select all the buttons and set their Margin properties to 4.**

11. **Add four more bitmap buttons in a fourth column.**

12. **Set the caption of the first button to Win 3.1 and set its style to bsWin31.**

13. **Set the captions of the remaining buttons to RED, WHITE, and BLUE.**

14. **Select the last three buttons, set Font.Size to 12, and then set Font.Color for each to the color corresponding to its caption.**

Get Up to Speed with Speed Buttons

Speed buttons are another special type of button, specifically designed to provide fast access to menu choices. If you place a few of them on a panel component, you have an instant SpeedBar.

Properties

Speed buttons can function as radio buttons so that pressing one button in a group causes the others to pop up. Several speed button properties are devoted to managing this behavior. Buttons with the same nonzero value in their GroupIndex property are treated as a group. The property determines whether it's permissible for none of the buttons in the group to be pressed down. AllowAllUp is False by default, and it's ignored if GroupIndex is zero. The Down property is True for the button in a group that's "stuck" down and False for the rest.

If you set AllowAllUp to True and GroupIndex to a nonzero value that's different from every other speed button, you get a speed button that acts as a check box. One click and it sticks down; another click and it pops up again.

As does a bitmap button, a speed button has a picture defined by its Glyph property, and any pixels in the picture with a color matching the color of the pixel in the lower left corner of the glyph are see-through. NumGlyphs defines how many separate glyphs are included in the bitmap. A speed button, however, has a fourth possible bitmap for a fourth possible state — stuck down.

The next little program builds an 18-by-72 bitmap containing four glyphs. If you're feeling creative, you can draw the bitmap yourself. Remember, from left to right, the bitmaps represent a button that's normal, disabled, pushed down, and stuck down. (What's the difference, you ask? A button that's pushed down pops out after you release the mouse button; a button that's stuck down doesn't.) Follow these steps to see what I mean:

1. **Place an image component on a new form and set its width to 72 and height to 18.**

2. **Put the following lines in an OnCreate event handler for the form:**

```
WITH Image1, Canvas DO
  BEGIN
    FillRect(ClientRect);
    Font.Name := 'Wingdings';
    Font.Size := 12;
    Font.Style := [fsBold];
    TextOut(0,0,'K');
    TextOut(36,0,'m');
    TextOut(54,0,'J');
    Font.Color := clGray;
    TextOut(18,0,'L');
    Picture.SaveToFile('FOURGLYP.BMP');
  END;
```

3. **Run the program to generate the bitmap file and then start a new project.**

4. Place a panel component on the form, delete its caption, and set its Align property to alTop.

5. Place a speed button on the panel and sets its Glyph property to FOURGLYP.BMP.

6. Press Ctrl+C to copy the button to the Clipboard.

7. Click the panel and press Ctrl+V repeatedly to paste four copies of the button onto the panel.

8. Place the first three buttons so that they're touching.

9. Place the fourth and fifth buttons so that they're separate.

10. Select the three buttons that are touching and set their GroupIndex property to 1.

11. Set the first button's Down property to True and the very last button's Enabled property to False.

12. Run the program and look at the buttons.

As you can see in Figure 8-6, two of the first three buttons show neutral faces; one appears pushed in and shows a happy face. If you push a different one of the first three, the one that was pushed down before pops out. The last button is disabled and shows a gray frowning face. If you click and hold the mouse on the fourth button (or any of the first three), it shows an empty circle.

Figure 8-6:
The first three speed buttons act like radio buttons; the other two buttons are independent.

Go back into the Form Designer and set the AllowAllUp property to True for the three grouped speed buttons. Now, whenever you run the program, you can click the button that's down to pop it up again.

Events

OnClick is the default event for a speed button. If you're using the speed button to launch a process in your program, you do it in the OnClick event handler. Speed buttons also respond to OnDblClick, but only if they're stuck down. You don't use OnDblClick very often.

Load the MyEdit project yet again; that's the project you start in Chapter 5 and enhance in the Chapters 6 and 7. Drop a panel on the form, delete its caption, and set its alignment to alTop.

Starting from the left, place two speed buttons on the panel so that they don't touch each other. Place three more speed buttons on the panel so that they do touch each other; set their AllowAllUp property to True and set their GroupIndex properties to 1, 2, and 3. Place three more speed buttons so that they touch each other and set the GroupIndex property of all of them to 4. Set the Down property of the first one in this last group to True.

Set the Font.Name for the first two buttons to Wingdings and their captions to 1 and <, which appear as an open folder and a diskette. Set the captions for the next three buttons to *B, I,* and *U* and set their font styles to bold, italic, and underline, respectively. Set the captions of the last three to <, =, and >. Now go back and adjust the font size for each button individually so that the single-character caption fills the button.

Set the first button's OnClick event handler to the existing handler that the Open menu choice uses and the second to the handler for the Save menu choice.

Set the Tag properties of the next three buttons to 0, 1, and 2, respectively. Create an OnClick event handler for all three as follows:

```
WITH Sender AS TSpeedButton, Memo1.Font DO
  IF Down THEN
    Style := Style + [TFontStyle(Tag)]
  ELSE
    Style := Style - [TFontStyle(Tag)];
```

For the next set of three buttons, assign Tag properties 0, 2, and 1 (in that order) and create an OnClick event handler for these three as follows:

```
WITH Sender AS TSpeedButton DO
  Memo1.Alignment := TAlignment(Tag);
```

Replace the code for the Font menu choice's OnClick event with the following code:

```
FontDialog1.Font := Memo1.Font;
WITH FontDialog1 DO
  IF Execute THEN
    BEGIN
      Memo1.Font := Font;
      SpeedButton3.Down := fsBold IN Font.Style;
      SpeedButton4.Down := fsItalic IN Font.Style;
      SpeedButton5.Down := fsUnderline IN Font.Style;
    END;
```

Finally, for each speed button, fill in the Hint property with a short phrase that describes what the button does. Set the panel's ShowHint property to True.

You just added a SpeedBar to the simple editor. The speed buttons enable you to open and save files, change font styles, and choose left, center, or right justification for the text. The file open and save speed buttons (buttons you use to trigger dialog boxes that open and save files) launch an action because their GroupIndex is 0. The font style buttons can be up or stuck down independently of each other, because they have AllowAllUp set to True and they each have a unique GroupIndex. And you can select precisely one of the justification buttons at a time, because they have the same group index and AllowAllUp is False.

I use simple characters on these speed buttons just to show that you don't always need to provide a glyph bitmap. You're welcome to draw and use tiny bitmaps for each. Remember — I'm not an artist!

Notice that you can make speed buttons and bitmap buttons do almost the same things. Take a bitmap button, delete its caption, and shrink it to speed button size, and you hardly know the difference. Or take a speed button, give it a caption, and stretch it. The main difference is that speed buttons can act in groups, similar to radio buttons, and bitmap buttons already have predefined for them the handy types such as OK, Cancel, and so on. Speed buttons are also designed to use up fewer Windows resources, so if you need gobs of buttons, use speed buttons.

With all the enhancements you've added, the MyEdit project is hardly a simple editor any more. It has dozens of components and hundreds of lines of code. How many additional components do you suppose it would need to do something really complicated, such as play multimedia sound or video files? If your answer is "One," you're ready for the next chapter.

Chapter 9

Advanced Additional Components

. . . . (continued)

In This Chapter

▶ Playing sound files, movies, and audio CDs on your multimedia computer

▶ Displaying Windows INI files in outline form

▶ Building a quick stand-in for the Windows character map accessory

▶ Building a program to extract the icons from other programs

▶ Displaying and choosing dates from a perpetual calendar

▶ Activating OLE objects inside your programs

. . . .

*C*ertain areas of Windows programming have long been the domain of experts only, because those aspects of Windows programming are just so darn hard to work with. The high-level super-powerful Delphi additional components blow the lid off these so-called difficult topics and make them as simple as anything else!

Choosing Additional Components

If you've got an idea for a project but don't know which component to use, make sure that you check Table 9-1.

Table 9-1 Problems Solved by Advanced Additional Components

Task	Component
Play or record with multimedia devices.	Media player. See "The Media Player Is the Message."
Display hierarchical data in outline form.	Outline. See "Let Me Outline My Plan. . . ."
Display in grid form items that are either stored elsewhere or calculated.	Draw grid. See "Cookin' with the Draw Grid(dle)."

(continued)

Table 9-1 *(continued)*

Task	Component
Display in grid form strings or String objects that are stored with the grid.	String grid. See "Super Lists in a Grid."
Display a calendar and choose a date.	Calendar. See "I'll Check My Calendar."
Communicate with other programs by using Object Linking and Embedding.	OLE control. See "¡Ole! ¡Ole! ¡Ole!"

The Media Player Is the Message

If your computer doesn't jabber at you, you're not on the cutting edge. Multimedia is *a real* hot topic in computers today. In fact, you can hardly find a new system that doesn't at least have a sound card, and most CD-ROM drives can play audio CDs as well. The massive removable storage capacity of CD-ROMs also enables applications to incorporate video clips without overflowing your hard disk.

Multimedia programming in Windows is a convoluted topic that rates a whole volume of its own in the Windows Software Development Kit documentation. The Delphi media player component handles the tough stuff *for* you and gives instant access to this incredible sensory world. Play WAV and MIDI files, audio CDs, digitized video, or any multimedia file or device that you can control through the Windows MCI (Media Control Interface).

Properties

A media player component shows up on your form as a button bar containing up to nine buttons. The button bar resembles the control panel for a VCR or CD player. VisibleButtons, ColoredButtons, and EnabledButtons are exploding properties that define what buttons appear on the bar and how they appear. All three have the same set of subproperties, btPlay, btPause, btStop, btNext, btPrev, btStep, btBack, btRecord, and btEject, and all are initially True. If the particular device you're writing for doesn't support a particular button, just set it to False in VisibleButtons. You can't eject a WAV file, for example, and you can't record on an audio CD. ColoredButtons gives default colors to the buttons — green for play, red for stop and record, yellow for pause, and blue for the rest. If this property is False, the corresponding button is black. Finally, EnabledButtons determines whether each button is initially enabled. Disabled buttons are grayed out.

Leave the AutoEnable property set to True; this setting makes the media player automatically enable and disable the buttons sensibly. The pause and stop buttons, for example, are disabled if nothing is playing. Leave AutoRewind True as well so that the media player resets to the start after it finishes playing. DeviceType identifies which of the many multimedia device types the component controls. If the particular device type is file-related, such as a WAV or video file, the Filename property specifies what file, and the device type is automatically determined from the filename.

If AutoOpen is True, the media player tries to open the selected device as soon as the program starts. Set it to False unless you're playing from a device or filename that's available after the program starts. Set AutoOpen to True for CD audio, for example, and to False for playing WAV files.

The media player has a large collection of run-time-only properties as well. By default, video plays in a separate window, but you can force it into your own program's window by using Display and DisplayRect. TimeFormat determines the format used for reporting the Length, Position, and several other properties. TrackLength, Tracks, and TrackPosition relate to the tracks on an audio CD. The media player has more properties, but these are the essentials.

Events

The OnClick event comes with an indication of which button is pressed, and OnPostClick occurs after the action caused by a click finishes. If your program directly calls media player methods such as Play, Rewind, and so on, and if it sets the property Notify to True beforehand, an OnNotify event occurs after the method finishes. In practice, however, you can do most of your multimedia programming without using any of these events.

Join the audio-visual club

Time to dive in and see just how easy multimedia programming can be with Delphi. You start with a general-purpose sound player. Follow these steps:

1. **Start a new project based on the fixed-size form template and drop a media player component on the form.**

2. **Double-click the VisibleButtons property to explode it and set all but the first three subproperties to False.**

3. **Set AutoOpen to False and position the media player near the top left corner of the form.**

4. **Place a speed button to the right of the media player and set its caption to the digit 1 and its font to 9-point Wingdings.**

   (Surprise! An open folder glyph appears on the speed button.)

5. **Put a horizontal bar gauge to the right of the speed button.**

6. **Select all three components, choose Edit⇨Size from the menu bar, and in the Height area choose Shrink to smallest.**

7. **Set the gauge's ForeColor to clAqua and stretch it to almost the width of the form.**

8. **Reduce the height of the form so that the same amount of space is around the components on all sides.**

9. **Set the form's caption to My Media Player.**

10. **Drop an Open File dialog and a timer on the form.**

11. **Set the timer's Interval to 100 milliseconds and set Enabled to False.**

12. **Set the Open File dialog's properties as follows:**

Property	*Value*
DefaultExt	WAV
Options. of HideReadOnly	True
Options.ofFileMustExist	True
Title	Open Sound File

13. **Double-click the Filter property and create two filters named WAV files and MIDI files, with corresponding file masks *.WAV and *.MID.**

14. **Put the following code in the speed button's OnClick event handler:**

```
WITH OpenDialog1 DO
  IF Execute THEN
    BEGIN
      Caption := 'My Media Player - ' +
        ExtractFilename(Filename);
      MediaPlayer1.Filename := Filename;
      Filename := '';
      WITH MediaPlayer1 DO
        BEGIN
          Open;
          Gauge1.MaxValue := Length;
          Gauge1.Progress := 0;
          Timer1.Enabled := TRUE;
        END;
    END;
```

15. Put the following single line in the timer's OnTimer event handler:

```
Gauge1.Progress := MediaPlayer1.Position;
```

That's all you need to do.

Figure 9-1 shows the resulting program. As long as your system has a sound card and Windows drivers installed, you should be able to play the sample WAV and MIDI files that come with Windows or any other sound files you may acquire. As the music plays, the gauge component tracks its progress.

Figure 9-1:
This program plays any WAV or MIDI files.

What's the difference between WAV files and MIDI files? A *WAV file* is like a tape recording of a series of sounds converted to digital form. A *MIDI file* is more like sheet music — a set of *instructions* for producing that series of sounds. MIDI files can pack a vast amount of music into a small amount of space, because the synthesizer on the sound card is responsible for producing the sound. On the other hand, WAV files can hold digitized voice, sound effects, and other nonmusical sounds that MIDI files can't handle.

These days, many Windows systems include drivers for playing video clips in one format or another. How much work do you suppose you'd need to do to make your sound player show movies as well?

If you guessed absolutely none, you win the prize! Simply select an AVI, QTW, or other video file for which your system has a driver loaded and press the play button. The video clip plays in its own window. You can enhance the media player just a little, however, to put the video inside its boundaries.

Start with the sound player project that you were just working on and update the Open File dialog's Filter property by adding three new names, Video for Windows files, Movies, and QuickTime files, with corresponding file masks *.AVI, *.MOV, and *.QTW. Change the dialog's title to Open Multimedia File. Explode the media player's VisibleButtons property and set btStep and btBack to True. You must rearrange the speed button and gauge to make room for the expanded media player.

Stretch the form to make it higher and place a bevel component on the form below the media player. Set its shape to bsFrame and return the form to its original height so that the bevel is just out of sight.

Double-click the speed button to jump into its OnClick event handler. Find the line that contains only Open; and insert the following lines of code immediately after it:

```
Display := Form1;
DisplayRect := Rect(Bevel1.Left+4,
  Bevel1.Top+4,0,0);
Bevel1.Width := DisplayRect.Right + 8;
Bevel1.Height := DisplayRect.Bottom + 8;
IF Bevel1.Height = 8 THEN
  Self.ClientHeight := Bevel1.Top
ELSE
  Self.ClientHeight := Bevel1.Height +
    Bevel1.Top + 8;
```

A few lines down, you see Timer1.Enabled := True;. Just after that line, add the following two lines:

```
Frames := 1;
Step;
```

As Figure 9-2 shows, the media player is now equipped to play movie-type files using itself as the screen. It resizes itself to match each video clip's preferred size and returns to its original size if you play a simple sound file. The Step command you added causes the video clip to display its first frame so that you can see what's coming before you press Play.

Turn your PC into a boom box

Playing audio CDs by using the media player is a little different from playing multimedia files. Mostly, playing audio CDs is easier. Hard to believe? Try it! Just follow these steps:

1. **Start a new project based on the fixed-size form template and place a media player component on it.**

2. **Double-click the VisibleButtons property and set btStep, btBack, and btRecord to False.**

3. **Set DeviceType to cdAudio, set AutoOpen to True and change the form's Caption to CD Player.**

4. **Resize the media player and the form so that they fit together nicely.**

Figure 9-2:
With just a
few added
lines of
code, the
media
player
program
plays video.

Here's a list of the steps you must follow before you can use this program to play audio CDs:

Put an audio CD in the CD-ROM drive.

Long list of steps, eh? That's really all you need to do. Try it now. You can start and stop the music, skip tracks forward and back (as long as the CD is playing), and even eject the CD from the drive. Without writing a single line of code, you've created an application that enables you to luxuriate in sounds ranging from Mozart to Pink Floyd to Weird Al Yankovic.

What's that great song that's playing right now? Can't tell? Add a track indicator, and you don't need to guess.

Set the form's Ctl3D property to False. Put a bevel on the form below the media player, with Style set to bsFrame. Make the bevel the same width as the media player and give it a height of 49.

Place a label inside the left end of the bevel. Set the label's properties as follows:

Property	*Value*
Caption	00
Font.Color	clLime
Font.Name	Courier New

(continued)

(continued)

Property	Value
Font.Size	16
Font.Style.fsBold	True
Transparent	True

Copy this label to the Clipboard and paste a copy onto the form. Set its caption to **00:00**, position it inside the right end of the bevel, and set Alignment to taRightJustify. Now set the form's color to clBlack.

Put a timer component on the form, with its Interval set to 100. Replace the begin..end pair of an OnTimer event handler with the following lines:

```
VAR Trk, Min, Sec : Word;
begin
  WITH MediaPlayer1 DO
    BEGIN
      Trk := MCI_TMSF_TRACK(Position);
      Min := MCI_TMSF_MINUTE(Position);
      Sec := MCI_TMSF_SECOND(Position);
      Label1.Caption := Format('percent.2d',[Trk]);
      Label2.Caption :=
            Format('percent.2d:percent.2d',[Min, Sec]);
    END;
end;
```

Add **MMSystem** to the uses clause at the top of Unit1.

Figure 9-3 shows the completed audio CD player with its minimalist display. On the left, you see the number of the track that's playing; on the right, the amount of time this track has been playing. You've turned your PC into a boom box!

Figure 9-3:
The media player plays audio CDs on your computer.

Let Me Outline My Plan. . . .

Some kinds of information are best presented in outline form so that you can choose the level of detail you want. The Windows 95 Explorer, for example, uses an outline to display the directory structure of your disk. You can collapse the outline right down to the root directory, expand it to show *every* directory, or display anything in between. The Delphi outline component is a flexible tool for displaying this kind of information. The outline component is located in the Win 3.1 page of the Component palette. You read about its replacement, the ListView component, in Chapter 12.

Properties

The essential function of the outline component is to display lines of text that have a hierarchical relationship to each other. The Lines property contains these lines. The lower an item is in the hierarchy, the farther to the right it's indented. The OutlineStyle property determines what other graphical elements are used to display the outline. Text is always present; other choices are a tree of lines, plus and minus icons indicating whether a particular icon can be expanded or collapsed, and folder and document icons that distinguish "leaf" items (those with no branches below them) and whether an item with branches below is open or closed. Figure 9-4 shows four of the possible combinations.

Figure 9-4:
The outline component can represent the hierarchical relationship of its elements in several different ways.

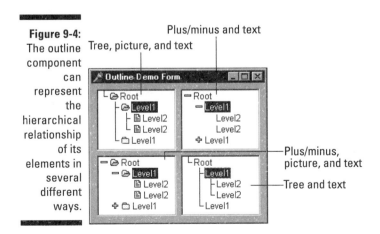

Follow these steps to create an executive-type outline:

1. **Place an outline component on a new form and double-click its Lines property to enter the string list editor.**

2. **Type** President **on the first line.**

3. **At the start of the second line, press Ctrl+Tab to insert a tab charac-ter and type** Vice President.

4. **On the next two lines, insert two tabs at the start and type** Bureaucrat.

5. **Click OK to close the string list editor.**

Now use the Object Inspector to select each possible value of the outline's OutlineStyle property, in turn. Take note of the different styles.

For further control over the look of the outline, you can set the PicturePlus, PictureMinus, PictureLeaf, PictureClosed, and PictureOpen properties to different bitmaps.

Notice that the Lines property has LoadFromFile and SaveToFile methods, just like the Items property of a list box. In the resulting file, the number of tab characters at the start of each line indicates the depth of that line in the outline.

The Options property explodes into three True and False subproperties. In Figure 9-4, a line connects the root of each outline to an unseen source beyond the top of the outline. If you set the ooDrawTreeRoot property to False, this line does not appear. The ooDrawFocusRect property controls whether a dotted focus rectangle appears around the selected outline item; it, too, is True by default. You generally want to set the ooStretchBitmaps property to True as well. This setting causes the bitmap pictures to adjust to the size of the text. If ooStretchBitmaps is False, the pictures may be cut off at the bottom.

The FullPath method of an item in the outline returns the full path from the outline's topmost level to that item. That is, it returns the item's text, preceded by the text of the item's parent and, before that, the text of the parent's parent, all the way back to the primordial root of the outline. The individual item strings are separated by the string specified in the ItemSeparator property. By default, this separator is a backslash (\).

Sneak a peek at INI files

Just about every Windows 3.1 application summarily dumps an INI file in your Windows directory, and some of them are as long as Bill Gates's stretch limo. As you skim through a big one, such as WIN.INI in Notepad, you can easily miss what you're looking for. But what if you could view just one section at a time? Follow these steps to see:

1. **Place an outline component, an Open File dialog, and a menu on a new form.**

2. Set the outline's OutlineStyle to osPlusMinusText and its Align property to alClient.

3. Set the Open File dialog's properties as follows:

Property	*Value*
DefaultExt	INI
InitialDir	C:\WINDOWS
Options.ofHideReadOnly	True
Options.FileMustExist	True
Title	Open INI File

This time, the Open File dialog gets just a single filter with the name INI Files and the mask *.INI.

4. Set the form's caption to INI Viewer.

5. Double-click the menu to enter the Menu Designer.

6. Create a simplified &File menu with just two submenu items, &Open. . . and E&xit.

7. In the OnClick event handler for the Exit menu choice, put the following single line:

```
Close;
```

8. Replace the begin..end pair supplied by Delphi for the Open item's OnClick event handler with the following lines:

```
VAR
  S : String;
  N, First, Last : Word;
  TS : TStringList;
begin
  WITH OpenDialog1  DO
    IF Execute THEN
      BEGIN
        Outline1.Clear;
        TS := TStringList.Create;
        try
          TS.LoadFromFile(Filename);
          TS.Insert(0, ExtractFileName(FileName));
          FOR N := TS.Count - 1 DOWNTO 1 DO
            BEGIN
              S := TS[N];
```

(continued)

(continued)

```
                    First := 1;
                    WHILE (First < Length(S)) AND
                      ((S[First] = ' ') OR
                       (S[First] = #9)) DO Inc(First);
                    Last := Length(S);
                    WHILE (Last >= First) AND
                      ((S[Last] = ' ') OR
                       (S[Last] = #9)) DO Dec(Last);
                    IF Last >= First THEN
                      BEGIN
                        S := Copy(S, First, Last-First+1);
                        IF (S[1]='[') AND
                           (S[length(S)]=']') THEN
                          S := #9 + S
                        ELSE S := #9#9 + S;
                        TS[N] := S;
                      END
                      ELSE TS.Delete(N);
                  END;
                Outline1.Lines := TS;
              finally
                TS.Free;
              END;
            END;
      end;
```

9. **Run the program, choose File➪Open, and choose an INI file.**

   The outline displays the INI filename along with the closed folder icon.

10. **Double-click that icon, and the outline expands to show the names of the INI file sections.**

11. **Double-click one of the sections, and it opens to show the key values it contains.**

12. **Double-click the INI filename again to close the whole outline.**

You can also use the keyboard to manipulate an outline component: Use the arrow keys to highlight the INI filename at the top and press the minus key; the entire outline collapses into that one line. Now press the asterisk and every branch of the entire outline expands. To expand or collapse just the current line, press the plus or minus key.

If something went wrong during the file-loading process, your program normally just displays an error message and merrily continues without executing the rest of the function. That's bad, because the function is responsible for freeing up the memory it allocated in creating the string list. The try..finally block beginning right after the call to TStringList. Create solves that problem. Even if a problem occurs within the try part of the block, the finally part always executes. In this case, the string list is always freed. This is an example of *exception handling,* a topic you can dig into in Chapter 15.

Events

Outline components don't *need* to respond to any events to be useful, as the preceding program shows. If your program needs to respond to changes in the selected outline item, use the OnClick event. You may, for example, display the value of the currently selected item in a label.

The OnExpand and OnCollapse methods occur if a branch of the outline is expanded or collapsed, either by the user or by the program itself. To expand the tenth item in the outline, the program would set Outline1.Expanded[10] to True.

Using the INI viewer project you just created, place a panel on the main form with the properties set as follows:

Property	Value
Align	alTop
Alignment	taLeftJustify
BevelInner	bvLowered
Caption	(none)

In the outline's OnClick event handler, insert the following lines:

```
WITH Outline1 DO
  IF SelectedItem > 0 THEN
    Panel1.Caption := Items[SelectedItem].FullPath
```

Next, change the ItemSeparator property of the outline to space, asterisk, space (*).

Run the program and click various lines in the outline. Figure 9-5 shows the result — if you click a key line, the panel's caption displays the INI filename, section name, and key separated by asterisks. Now, the next time a tech-support person asks you the value of the MaxRTEncodeSetting key in the [msacm.imaadpcm] section of your SYSTEM.INI, you can find it fast by using this INI file viewer!

Figure 9-5: After you pour the data into the Delphi outline component, it handles the display.

Cookin' with the Draw Grid (dle)

The draw grid component and the string grid component are grown-up relatives of the familiar list box. As does a list box, the grid components can hold a list of items. But unlike a list box, the number of items is virtually unlimited, and the items can be in a grid of multiple columns. You use the draw grid component if you can calculate the contents of a cell from the cell's position or if the contents of the cell are stored elsewhere. The string grid component stores strings and objects for display within itself.

Properties

The grids have a huge number of properties, but some are more important than others. You can just hit the high spots in this section. The ColCount and RowCount properties define the number of columns and rows in the grid. FixedCols and FixedRows tell how many of each are fixed nonscrolling headers — normally you use one or none of these. A special FixedColor property defines the background color for the fixed rows and columns.

By default, all columns and rows are the same size; this size is controlled by DefaultColWidth and DefaultRowHeight. DefaultDrawing (True by default) means that the grid handles the basics of drawing cells, such as indicating whether a cell is focused or selected.

The Options property contains a huge collection of options that control the look and action of the grid. The goRowSizing and goColSizing options determine whether you can resize rows and columns individually. If goRangeSelect is True, the user can select a range of cells by using the mouse, and if goDrawFocusSelected is True, the focused cell is the same color as the rest of the selection. If the goRowSelect option is True, the user must select whole rows of cells.

The goThumbTracking option controls whether the contents of the grid "track" as the scroll bars move or simply snap into place after the user releases the scroll bar. The former (tracking) makes finding a particular position in a large grid easier; the latter (snapping into place) is more practical if drawing the cells is time-consuming.

A draw grid has some other useful properties available only at run time. Row and Col are the row and column of the currently selected cell. TopRow and LeftCol are the row and column of the cell at the top left of the scrollable part of the grid. TopRow and LeftCol are both zero initially, but if some of the grid scrolls out of view, they change. ColWidths and RowHeights are arrays of integers holding the width and height of the individual columns and rows if sizing is permitted.

You must be reeling under this deluge of properties; I'll stop, I'll stop! You run across other properties for fine-tuning your grids after you start to use grids in programs.

Events

The big event for a draw grid is OnDrawCell. The OnDrawCell event handler is completely responsible for putting whatever text or image you want in each cell. Experiment with this event by following these steps:

1. **Start a new project and select the fixed-size form template.**

2. **Place a bevel on the form, and then set its Align property to alTop and its shape to bsFrame.**

3. **Place a draw grid on the form with the following properties:**

Property	Value
Align	alClient
ColCount	32
DefaultColWidth	18
FixedCols	0
FixedRows	0
Options.goRangeSelect	False
RowCount	7
ScrollBars	ssNone

4. **Size the form big enough so that the grid doesn't need scroll bars, but make the form small enough so that no blank space is outside the array of cells.**

5. **Create an OnDrawCell event handler for the grid. Put the following lines in it:**

```
WITH DrawGrid1.Canvas DO
  TextRect(Rect, Rect.Left, Rect.Top,
    Char((Row+1)*32 + Col));
```

6. **Place a combo box on the bevel, set its Style to csDropDownList, set its Sorted property to True, and stretch it so that it fills most of the width of the bevel.**

7. **Put the following lines in the form's OnCreate event handler:**

```
WITH ComboBox1 DO
  BEGIN
    Items := Screen.Fonts;
    ItemIndex := Items.IndexOf(Font.Name);
  END;
Caption := 'Font Display - ' + Font.Name;
```

8. **Create an OnClick event for the combo box as follows:**

```
DrawGrid1.Font.Name := ComboBox1.Text;
Caption := 'Font Display - ' +
  DrawGrid1.Font.Name;
```

You just created a program that displays all the characters in a font, similar to the Windows CharMap accessory. Run the program, and you see every character in the draw grid's current font. Choose various fonts by using the combo box. Figure 9-6 shows all the characters in the fabulous Wingdings font.

Figure 9-6:
With just a
few lines of
code, this
draw grid
displays
every
character in
the font of
your choice.

A bevel uses fewer Windows resources than a panel. In a program such as this one, where the specialized events and properties of a panel aren't needed, always use a bevel.

Super Lists in a String Grid

A string grid is just like a draw grid, except that you can store a string of text, an object, or both for every cell. You can set it up with one column and a zillion rows to create a list-box equivalent without the size limits of a list box. Or you can store an object, such as an icon, along with a descriptive string in each cell.

Properties and events

At design time, a string grid has the same set of properties and events as a draw grid, but it has a few additional run-time properties. The Cells property is a two-dimensional array of strings, and the Objects property is the corresponding array of objects. Another way to view the cells is through the Rows and Cols properties, which contain string lists corresponding to each row and column in the grid.

Four of the Options really make sense only in a string grid: goRowMoving, goColMoving, goEditing, and goAlwaysShowEditor. The first two options enable users to move rows and columns around at run time by dragging with the mouse. If goEditing is True, users can edit the contents of the cells. Pressing F2 displays the editor, unless you set goAlwaysShowEditor to True, in which case F2 isn't necessary.

The OnGetEditMask event gives you a chance to control the editing of cell data. This event occurs just before editing begins for a particular cell, and the event handler receives the row and column of the cell being edited. All your program needs to do is return an edit mask string (such as those used by the masked edit box component) for cells containing data that you want to control. Follow these steps:

1. **Place a string grid on a new form and set these properties:**

Property	*Value*
Options.goRowSizing	True
Options.goColSizing	True
Options.goRowMoving	True
Options.goColMoving	True
Options.goEditing	True
Options.goAlwaysShowEditor	True
Options.goTabs	True

2. **Create an OnGetEditMask for the string grid containing the following lines:**

   ```
   WITH StringGrid1 DO
     IF ACol = FixedCols THEN
       Value := '00000;1;_';
   ```

3. **Run the program and start typing — your input goes into the selected cell.**

   If the cell is in column 1, the first nonfixed column, you can enter only 5-digit numeric strings.

4. **Press Tab to step through the cells, left to right and top to bottom, entering something in each cell.**

5. **Click and drag the header cell of a column or row to move that column or row or drag the line between header cells to resize.**

Here I go gathering icons in May

Want to gather icons, too? Follow these steps:

1. **Create a new project based on the fixed-size form template.**

2. **Place a bevel on the form, set its Align property to alTop, and set its shape to bsFrame.**

3. **Place a string grid on the form and set its properties as follows:**

Property	*Value*
Align	alClient
ColCount	4
DefaultColWidth	144
DefaultRowHeight	64
FixedRows	0
FixedCols	0
Font.Name	MS Sans Serif
Font.Size	8
Options.goRangeSelect	False
RowCount	4

4. **Size the form high enough so that exactly three of the grid's four rows show and just wide enough so that a horizontal scroll bar doesn't appear.**

5. **Change the form's caption to** Icon Collector.

6. **Add an Open File dialog to the form and set its properties as follows:**

Property	*Value*
DefaultExt	ICO
InitialDir	C:\WINDOWS
Options.ofHideReadOnly	True
Options.ofFileMustExist	True
Title	Open Icon File

7. **Double-click the Filter property and enter two filter names,** All Icon files and All files, **with corresponding masks *.ICO; *.EXE; *.DLL (for All Icon files) and *.* (for All files).**

   Notice that you separate multiple file specifications with a semicolon.

8. **Place a push button on the bevel and set its Default property to True. Change its caption to** &Gather Icons. . . , **stretching it so that the caption fits.**

9. **Double-click the push button and replace the begin..end pair supplied by Delphi with the following long block of program code:**

```
CONST CurItem : LongInt = 0;
VAR
   pName : ARRAY[0..255] OF Char;
   fName : String[13];
```

(continued)

(continued)

```
   N      : Word;
   IcoH   : hIcon;
begin
   WITH OpenDialog1 DO
     BEGIN
       IF NOT Execute THEN Exit;
       fName := ExtractFilename(Filename);
       StrPCopy(pName, Filename);
     END;
   N := 0;
   WITH StringGrid1 DO
     REPEAT
       IcoH := ExtractIcon(hInstance, pName, N);
       IF IcoH <= 1 THEN Break;
       Col := CurItem MOD ColCount;
       IF (CurItem DIV ColCount) >= RowCount THEN
         RowCount := RowCount + 1;
       Row := CurItem DIV ColCount;
       Cells[Col,Row] := fName + ' #' + IntToStr(N);
       Objects[Col, Row] := TIcon.Create;
       WITH Objects[Col, Row] AS TIcon DO
         Handle := IcoH;
       CurItem := CurItem + 1;
       N := N + 1;
     UNTIL FALSE;
end;
```

Stop a second to let your fingers cool off. And don't worry; that's almost the entire program.

10. Give the string grid an OnDrawCell event handler, as follows:

```
IF StringGrid1.Objects[Col,Row] IS TIcon THEN
   StringGrid1.Canvas.Draw(
     Rect.Left+56, Rect.Top+24,
       TIcon(StringGrid1.Objects[Col,Row]));
```

11. Scroll to the top of the Unit1 file and add ShellApi **to the uses clause.**

(This action gives your program access to the all-important ExtractIcon function.)

12. Run the program and choose any ICO, EXE, or DLL file.

If the file contains icons, the icons show up in the string grid. For a real bonanza, choose PROGMAN.EXE or MORICONS.DLL from the Windows directory. Each icon is identified with the name of the file that contains it and the index of that icon in the file.

Having succeeded beyond all your expectations in extracting icons from files on disk, you may wonder if viewing is *all* you can do with them. Well, of course not!

Add a Save File common dialog to the Icon Collector project with the following properties:

Property	*Value*
DefaultExt	ICO
Options.ofOverwritePrompt	True
Options.ofHideReadOnly	True
Options.ofPathMustExist	True
Title	Save Icon File

Give the dialog just one filter named Icon files with *.ICO as the file mask.

Place a push button on the bevel with the caption &Save Icon. . . and use the following lines for its OnClick event handler:

```
IF SaveDialog1.Execute THEN
  WITH StringGrid1 DO
    WITH Objects[Col,Row] AS TIcon DO
      SaveToFile(SaveDialog1.Filename);
```

Figure 9-7 shows the resulting program with a number of icons loaded. Run it yourself and extract icons from EXE or DLL files; then choose an icon and click the Save Icon button to save it to an icon file. Of course simply commandeering these icons for your own use wouldn't be right, but you can use them for inspiration as you design your own icons.

The icon collector program can yank icons from either 16-bit or 32-bit files. Occasionally, however, a 32-bit file contains an icon with a format that doesn't match what the Delphi TIcon component expects. (The highlighted icon in Figure 9-7 is an example.) Save this icon to an ICO file and you've got pure poison. The Image Editor gags on it; you can't use it as an icon for your Delphi forms; and Resource Workshop reports that its dimensions are 0 by 222 pixels! Fortunately, icons such as this one are rare.

I'll Check My Calendar

The Delphi generalized grids have the potential to become just about anything in your programs. You can almost hear them chanting "I can be a chessboard . . . I can be a spreadsheet . . . I can be a calendar. . . ." Wait, did someone say calendar? Delphi actually supplies a specialized grid that functions as a calendar. This grid, found on the Samples page of the Component palette, is a fully functional calendar that you can use in any program.

You'd be alarmed if the main properties of a calendar were anything but Year, Month, and Day. The run-time-only property CalendarDate holds the entire date in the cryptic compressed form of Delphi. And the OnChange event occurs if the user chooses a new date. After you decide how your program enables the user to change the month and date, the PrevMonth, NextMonth, PrevYear, and NextYear methods handle the dirty work. Just follow these steps to see what I mean:

1. **Place a calendar component on a new fixed-size form.**

2. **Place two panels on the form and set their BevelInner property to bvLowered; delete their captions and place them above the calendar component, as shown in Figure 9-8; place spin buttons to the right of the two panels, as shown.**

3. **Create a one-line OnDownClick event handler for the left spin button containing the following line:**

```
Calendar1.PrevMonth;
```

4. **Use the following line for the left spin button's OnUpClick event handler:**

```
Calendar1.NextMonth;
```

Figure 9-8:
Double-
click any of
the five
masked edit
boxes in the
main form,
and the
date-
selection
calendar
form
appears.

5. **Make sure that the OnDownClick event handler for the right spin button contains the following line:**

```
Calendar1.PrevYear;
```

6. **Give the spin button an OnUpClick event handler with this single line:**

```
Calendar1.NextYear;
```

7. **Drop two bitmap buttons on the form and set their Kind properties to bkOK and bkCancel.**

8. **Put a panel in line with the bitmap buttons and sized the same; delete its caption and set its BevelInner property to bvLowered.**

9. **Double-click the calendar and put the following lines in its OnChange event handler:**

```
WITH Calendar1 DO
  BEGIN
    DateStr := DateToStr(CalendarDate);
    Panel1.Caption := LongMonthNames[Month];
    Panel2.Caption := IntToStr(Year);
    Panel3.Caption := DateStr;
  END;
```

10. **Locate the comment { Public declarations } near the top of the unit and add the following line below it:**

```
DateStr : String;
```

11. **Create an OnActivate event handler for the form itself; make sure that the handler contains the following lines:**

```
try
  Calendar1.CalendarDate := StrToDate(DateStr);
except
  On EConvertError DO;
end;
Calendar1.OnChange(Calendar1);
```

12. **Set the form's caption to Choose Date and its Name property to PickDate.**

13. **Right-click the form and choose Add To Repository from the pop-up menu.**

14. **Start a new project and place a masked edit box on the form.**

15. **Double-click the EditMask property and select the Date mask.**

16. **Choose File⇨New from the menu bar, flip to the Forms page, and choose the date-selection form.**

17. **Create an OnDblClick event handler for the masked edit box as follows:**

```
WITH PickDate, Sender AS TMaskEdit DO
  BEGIN
    DateStr := Text;
    IF ShowModal = mrOK THEN
      Text := DateStr;
  END;
```

18. **Go to the top of the program file and add Unit2 to the uses clause.**

19. **Run the program and type a date; then double-click the masked edit box.**

   If the date you type is invalid or incomplete, the calendar form just uses today's date. After you click OK, the date from the calendar is inserted in the masked edit box. You can use this form in any project that needs date input.

¡OLE! ¡OLE! ¡OLE!

OLE (Object Linking and Embedding), as Microsoft says, is the future of computing. After the Good Times arrive, you aren't going to use monolithic one-style-fits-all monster applications. Rather, you'll just snap together OLE-compliant miniprograms to create your own personal programs.

This lovely dream may or may not come to pass, but right now your Delphi applications can link or embed OLE objects of any type available on your system, from Paintbrush pictures to media clips to spreadsheets. Implementing OLE in a program is extremely complex, and even with help from Delphi, some of the complexity remains. Still, you can build a simple OLE container demo without straining your code muscles.

Rev-OLE-ution version number 2.0

To use the Delphi OLE container, follow these steps:

1. **Drop a menu on a new form, and give it a &File menu with just E&xit below it.**

2. **Double-click the Exit item and put this line in its OnClick handler:**

```
Close;
```

3. **Add another top-level menu item called &Edit and set its GroupIndex to 1; add the following menu items below it:**
   - &Select OLE Object. . .
   - &Paste Special. . .
   - &Object Properties. . .
   - &Change Icon. . .
   - - (hyphen)
   - Object

4. **Set the form's caption to Delphi 3 OLE Demo and set its ObjectMenuItem property to Object11.**

5. **Put a panel on the form aligned alTop and delete its caption; add another captionless panel aligned alBottom.**

6. **Place an OLE container component on the form and set its Align property to alClient.**

7. **Flip to the Events page in the Object Inspector and select Edit1 from the pull-down list of components.**

8. **Create an OnClick event handler for Edit1 by using the following lines:**

```
PasteSpecial1.Enabled := OleContainer1.CanPaste;
ChangeIcon1.Enabled := OleContainer1.State <> osEmpty;
ObjectProperties1.Enabled := ChangeIcon1.Enabled;
```

The OnClick handlers for the four menu items below Edit are each a single line. In order, they are as follows:

```
OleContainer1.InsertObjectDialog;
OleContainer1.PasteSpecialDialog;
OleContainer1.ObjectPropertiesDialog;
OleContainer1.ChangeIconDialog;
```

That's it! The dialog box displayed by the Select OLE Object menu choice is shown in Figure 9-9. After you choose Edit⊅Object Properties from the menu bar, you get a dialog similar to the one shown in Figure 9-10.

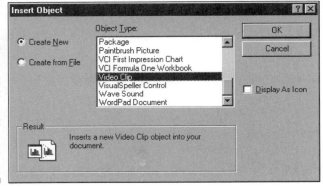

Figure 9-9:
The Insert Object dialog is built into the Delphi OLE component.

Figure 9-10:
The Object Properties dialog enables you to control the updating and display of an embedded OLE object.

This Object Properties dialog effectively replaces the Links dialog, but with a new twist or two. It adds the capability to convert the object to a different format (if conversion is available) or display it as an icon. Just which icon represents the object is determined by the Change Icon dialog, which is shown in Figure 9-11.

Figure 9-11:
Use the
Change
Icon dialog
to give the
embedded
object a
different
icon.

Well, that was a bit of work, but not *too* bad. Yes, you're ready to run the program. First try the Select OLE Object menu choice. You get a fancy dialog listing all the types of OLE objects registered on your system, and an invitation to create a new object or select a file. If you choose a file, you can either embed a copy of the file in your program or create a link to an existing file. And you can choose to display the object itself or just an icon in your program.

After the object is linked or embedded in your program, double-clicking it launches the appropriate program. If you link or embed a bitmap, for example, double-clicking it launches Paint. The Object menu choice under Edit is also replaced by a menu specific to the type of object.

If you embed an object, your program *owns* the embedded data. Any changes you make exist only within your program. If you link an object, the link just points to an external file. All changes are stored in the external file.

The Paste Special menu choice is probably grayed, indicating that it's not available. Load a bitmap into the Windows Paint accessory, select all or part of it, and copy it to the Clipboard. Now come back to the OLE demo and you see that Paste Special is enabled. If you click it, you can either paste a link to the bitmap file or embed the copied bitmap as an object.

The Links menu choice is enabled only if you've either pasted a link to a file or linked a file by using the Select OLE Object menu choice. Clicking Links displays the dialog shown in Figure 9-12, which enables you fool around with the links.

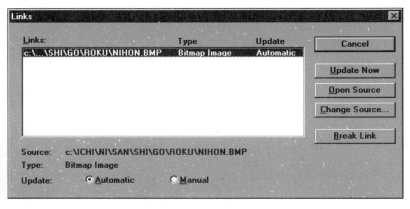

Figure 9-12:
The OLE
container
component
displays this
Links dialog
on demand.

And now you can add another feature to the OLE example.

Saving embedded objects to disk

The OLE container object has one more surprising capability: It can save and load its contents to disk.

Load the OLE demo program's main menu into the Menu Designer, highlight the Exit menu item, and press the Insert key four times. Fill in the new blank menu choices with **&Open. . .**, **&Save**, **Save &As. . .** and a lone hyphen separator. Place an Open File dialog and a Save File dialog on the form. Set the Filter property for both dialogs to a single line, with the name OLE files and the mask *.OLE. Set the rest of the Open File dialog's properties as follows:

Property	*Value*
DefaultExt	OLE
Options.ofHideReadOnly	True
Options.ofFileMustExist	True
Title	Open OLE file

Set the Save File dialog's properties as follows:

Property	*Value*
DefaultExt	OLE
Options.ofOverwritePrompt	True
Options.ofHideReadOnly	True
Options.ofPathMustExist	True
Title	Save OLE file

Find the File1 top-level menu item in the list of components in the Object Inspector and put the following lines in its OnClick event handler:

```
WITH OleContainer1 DO
  BEGIN
    Save1.Enabled := OleObjAllocated;
    SaveAs1.Enabled := State <> osEmpty;
  END;
```

Write an OnClick event handler for the Open menu item with these lines:

```
WITH OpenDialog1 DO
  IF Execute THEN
    BEGIN
      OleContainer1.LoadFromFile(Filename);
      OleContainer1.Refresh;
      SaveDialog1.Filename := Filename;
    END;
```

For the Save As menu item, use these lines as an OnClick event handler:

```
WITH SaveDialog1 DO
  IF Execute THEN
    OleContainer1.SaveToFile(Filename);
```

Put the following lines in the OnClick handler for the Save menu choice:

```
IF SaveDialog1.Filename = '' THEN
  SaveAs1Click(Sender)
ELSE OleContainer1.SaveToFile(SaveDialog1.Filename);
```

And finally, go back to the OnClick handler for the Select OLE Object menu item and insert the following line just before the end; line:

```
SaveDialog1.Filename := '';
```

Gee! I warned you this OLE stuff could get complicated. Run the program now, and you can save your OLE objects to a file and load them again. If you transfer such a file to a different system, however, that system must have the required server present.

Here's a free bonus: Server applications that are compatible with the OLE 2.0 specification have a capability called *in-place activation*. This term means that, after you activate the object, the server appears *within* your program. Its menu merges with your program's menu, and its SpeedBar and status bar do likewise.

Wow! OLE is certainly a lollapalooza. Too many programmers have accidentally burned out their brains trying to program OLE without Delphi. Even with help from Delphi, OLE is complicated, but manageable. Delphi 3 also simplifies the creation of OLE server programs and takes the pain out of OLE automation (by using OLE to remote-control other programs).

In this chapter, components display almost magical capabilities — playing CDs, gathering icons, displaying the calendar, even communicating by using OLE. You probably need a little time to absorb it all. Fear not; the next chapter is gentle with you. It's all about the mundane but essential Delphi file components.

Chapter 10
File Components

●●●

In This Chapter

▶ Creating your own customizable version of the file common dialogs

▶ Displaying all directories on your disk in outline form

▶ Building a directory-selection form and saving it as a template for later reuse

▶ "Stealing" the bitmaps representing different types of drives and displaying them as you please

▶ Creating a form like a File Manager directory window

●●●

*A*fter you turn off your computer, everything that's in memory goes pffft! All that's left is the information stored in files on the hard disk. As you crank up the computer again, it loads its operating system from *files* on the disk. The vast majority of programs deal with files in one way or another, whether to look up preferences in an INI file or to load and save scripts for the latest Hollywood extravaganza.

In Chapter 5, I discuss the Delphi common dialog components; they're great for common file-related tasks. Unfortunately, if you need to do anything even slightly out of the ordinary, the common dialogs don't help you. They're like seamless black boxes; you have no easy way to put anything into them or take anything out of them. The Windows 95 common dialogs also support handy tasks, such as renaming files and creating directories, but adding features yourself requires wizardly programming skills.

To help you with *un*common tasks, Delphi skillfully separates the four major elements of the Windows-style file common dialogs (the file list, directory list, drive list, and filter list) and enables you to use each separately, according to your own program's requirements. If the file common dialogs don't do *quite* what you want, you can just patch together the necessary file components.

Choosing File Components

The four main file components correspond to the four major elements of a file common dialog, and they reside on the System page of the Component palette. As a bonus, Delphi provides a sample directory outline for choosing any directory on your disk. Use Table 10-1 to quickly select the right component.

Table 10-1	Problems Solved by File Components
Task	*Component*
Display or process a list of files by matching a file specification box. See "Flipping through the File List."	File list
Select any directory in the current drive list box. See "Directory Assistance."	Directory
Display the available disk drives and their drive types combo box. See "A Combo Box with Real Drive."	Drive
Select from predefined file specification masks combo box. See "Filter Your Files with a Combo Box."	Filter
View and navigate through the entire directory tree outline. See "More Directory Assistance."	Directory

Flipping through the File List

The instant you drop a file list box on a form, it displays a list of files in the current directory. Aieee! It's alive! The obvious way to use such a thing is to enable your program's users to make choices from the displayed files. Perhaps less obvious is the fact that you can also *hide* a file list box and use it as a clandestine source of information about the files on disk.

Properties

If you set the ShowGlyphs property to True, the file list immediately displays a picture (a glyph) to the left of each filename. Executable files get a picture of a miniwindow, directories show a folder, and data files display as a piece of paper.

The FileType property enables you to choose which files show up in the box, based on their file attributes. The default is ftNormal — this type selects files with no attributes or with the read-only or archive attributes. You can include hidden or system files, directories, or the volume label by setting the appropriate options to True. If you want to display only read-only or archive files, just say No to ftNormal files.

The Mask property and the run-time-only Directory property also determine which files you see. The Directory property naturally specifies the directory in which you're seeking files. Mask is the wildcard file specification for the files. It's set to *.* (all files) by default, but you can specify any one or more wildcard file specifications. Multiple file specifications are separated by semicolons, such as *.FOO;*.BAR. and the Filename property at run time contains the currently selected filename. The FileEdit property associates an edit box on your form with the file list box. The edit box automatically displays the selected filename; before any file is selected, it displays the value of the Mask property.

If you set MultiSelect to True, users can choose multiple files from the file list. In most other ways, the file list box is similar to any list box. To determine which files are selected if MultipleSelect is True, for example, you peek at the Selected property. You get the list of files through the Items property.

Delphi 3 completes the picture with an ExtendedSelect property that controls how you select multiple files. It's True by default, which means that you can select multiple files by dragging or by clicking while holding Shift and Ctrl. If ExtendedSelect is False, each click of a filename reverses its selection state.

Events

The most important event for a file list box is OnChange. If the selected filename changes, this event triggers. Somewhat less useful is the OnClick event that occurs any time the user clicks the file list, even if the chosen filename doesn't change. You frequently hook the OnDblClick event to the same event handler that you use for a button that chooses the current file.

Follow these steps to create a File Dialog project for you to use in this chapter:

1. **Start a new project using the fixed-size file template you create in Chapter 2.**

2. **Set the form's Font to MS Sans Serif, 8 point, bold.**

3. **Place a label near the top left corner of the form, and an edit box just below it.**

4. **Set the label's caption to File &Name: and its FocusControl property to point to the edit box.**

5. **Now place a file list box below the edit box and set its ShowGlyphs property to True.**

6. **Stretch the list box so that it's wide enough to fit a reasonably long filename and make the edit box the same width.**

   Delphi 3 offers a file list component that supports long filenames, so you must settle for making the file list box wide enough for *most* filenames.

7. **Set the file list's FileEdit property to the name of the edit box.**

8. **Change the form's caption to File Dialog.**

9. **Run the program and click filenames in the list.**

   As you select a name, it appears in the filename edit box. If a filename is too wide for the file list box, click it and view it in the edit box. You can scoot it back and forth by using the arrow keys to see the whole thing. Well, that's a start!

10. **Save this project as FILEDLG; you're going to add to it throughout this chapter.**

Using the File Dialog form you just created, place a group box to the right of the file list box and set its caption to Attributes. Put seven check boxes in it with the captions Read Only, Hidden, System, Volume ID, Directory, Archive, and Normal, in that order. Set the Tag field for the seven check boxes to the numbers 0 through 6 and set the Normal box's Checked property to True. Select all seven and create a single OnClick event handler for them by using the following lines:

```
WITH Sender AS TCheckBox DO
  IF Checked THEN
    FileListBox1.FileType :=
      FileListBox1.FileType + [TFileAttr(Tag)]
  ELSE
    FileListBox1.FileType :=
      FileListBox1.FileType - [TFileAttr(Tag)];
```

Put the following single line in an OnCreate event handler for the form:

```
FileListBox1.Directory := 'C:\';
```

As you run this program, it initially displays all the normal files in the root directory of your C: drive. Fiddle with the check boxes and the program displays directories, the volume ID, and files with special attributes. Figure 10-1 shows the read-only, hidden, and system files in the root directory of a system with DOS, Windows 3.1, and Windows 95 installed. Quite a few files are hiding in there!

The file attribute group box was a flight of fancy; it isn't meant to be part of the final FILEDLG project. Delete it now, and the check boxes disappear as well. Flip to the Code Editor and delete the lines you entered in the OnClick event handler for the check boxes and the OnCreate handler for the form. Just delete what you typed; leave the begin..end pair alone. Now save the cleaned-up FILEDLG project.

File list boxes are good at undercover work, too. Whether they're visible or not, every time you change the Mask, Directory, or FileType properties, they immediately rebuild the list of names and you can use the rebuilt list in your programs. Try these steps to see what I mean:

1. **Place a file list box on a new form, double-click its FileType property, and set all the types to False except ftDirectory.**

2. **Place a panel on the form with the following properties:**

Property	Value
Align	alTop
Alignment	taLeftJustify
Caption	One moment, please...
BevelInner	bvLowered

3. **Size the panel so that it's about the height of the form's title bar.**

4. **Place an outline on the form and set its Align property to alClient.**

   This setting hides the file list box.

5. **Open the outline's Lines property and enter a single line containing C: (just *C* and a colon).**

6. **Switch to the Events page and double-click the OnExpand event.**

7. **Delete the begin..end pair supplied by Delphi and substitute the following code:**

```
VAR
  S : String;
  N : Word;
begin
  IF Tag > 0 THEN Exit;
  WITH Sender AS TOutline, Items[Index] DO
    BEGIN
      S := FullPath;
      IF length(S) = 2 THEN S := S + '\';
      FileListBox1.Directory := S;
      FOR N := 0 TO FileListBox1.Items.Count-1 DO
        BEGIN(
          S := FileListBox1.Items[N];
          S := Copy(S, 2, length(S)-2);
          IF S = '.' THEN Continue;
          IF S = '..' THEN Continue;
          Outline1.AddChild(Index, S);
        END;
    END;
end;
```

8. **In the outline's OnClick method, put the following lines:**

```
WITH Sender AS TOutline DO
  Panel1.Caption := Items[SelectedItem].FullPath;
```

9. **Replace the begin..end pair for the form's OnActivate event handler with the following lines:**

```
VAR N : Word;
begin
  Panel1.Refresh;
  WITH Outline1 DO
    BEGIN
      N := 0;
      REPEAT
        N := N + 1;
        Items[N].Expanded := True;
        Application.ProcessMessages;
      UNTIL N = ItemCount;
    END;
```

```
    Tag := 1;
    Panel1.Caption := '';
end;
```

As you run the program, it spends a few seconds building the directory outline. The OnActivate event handler steps through the outline's list of items, which initially contains just C:, and sets Expanded to True for each. This in turn causes an OnExpand event for the outline. The OnExpand event handler sets the directory for the hidden file list box to the current item in the outline. If the OnExpand event handler finds any subdirectories, it adds them as outline items under the current item. As the code steps through the outline's item list, the goal keeps receding because the list gets longer and longer. The end isn't reached until all directories are expanded. At this point, the event handler sets the form's Tag property to 1, which is a signal to the OnExpand handler that its work is finished. Whew!

As Figure 10-2 shows, the directory outline you created has all the features of the outline component. Double-click the root to close the entire directory outline. Now press the asterisk key (*) to fully expand the outline or press the plus key (+) to expand it by one level. Directories that contain subdirectories are represented as open or closed folders; directories without subdirectories show up as pieces of paper. After you click any item in the outline, its full path appears in the panel above. And all this happens because of a file list box that you can't even see!

Figure 10-2:
This
directory
outline gets
its data
from a
hidden file
list box.

Directory Assistance

The directory list box lists the directories of the selected drive in an expandable tree form, just as does the directory portion of a file common dialog. You could say that it shows the current branch of the directory tree along with a few twigs. Specifically, it shows the current directory, its parent, its parent's parent, and so on back to the root, as well as any subdirectories of the current directory. Suppose that the current directory is C:\FOO\BAR —

the directory list box shows C:\ at the top, FOO below it, and BAR below FOO. Any subdirectories of bar are also displayed. You can't ever see the whole tree, but you can navigate anywhere on the disk by backing up toward the root and following a different branch outward.

The DirLabel and FileList properties help integrate other components with a directory list box. The label specified in the DirLabel property displays the currently selected directory, and the file list box specified in the FileList property displays the list of files in the selected directory.

The run-time-only properties Drive and Directory are what rouse a directory list box to action. Change the Drive property and the list displays the current directory on the selected drive. And if you click a line in the list, the Directory property gets the full path for the selection. As with the file list box, the directory list box's main event is OnChange, which is called whenever the selected directory changes.

Load the FILEDLG project that you created earlier in this chapter. It has a column of components along the left: a label, an edit box, and a file list box. Make a second column to the right of the first column; the second column should contain two labels and a directory list box. Set the first label's caption to &Directories: and set its FocusControl property to point to the directory list box. Set the directory list box's DirLabel property to Label3 (the name of the other label) and set its FileList property to FileListBox1 (the name of the file list box). If this sequense is at all unclear, you can peek ahead at Figure 10-4, which shows the completed project.

As you run the updated FILEDLG project, you find that you can view the files in any directory that's on the current drive. The full path name of the selected directory appears in the label above the directory list box, and the file list box holds the contents of the selected directory. Save this enhanced file dialog project. You can either save the updated project in the file or specify a new project name, such as FILEDLG2.

A Combo Box with Real Drive

You've probably guessed that the drive combo box is a drop-down combo box that's suspiciously similar to the drive list in the file common dialogs. It displays all drives available on your system with a cute little glyph signifying a floppy drive, a hard disk, a RAM drive, a CD-ROM, or a network connection.

A drive combo box already does the hard work of figuring out what drives are available on your system, as well as the drive type for each. If you need drive availability and type information in a program, just use a hidden drive combo box. You can even "steal" the glyphs, as you can see later in this chapter.

The one significant property of a drive combo box is . . . you guessed it . . . Drive! At run time, this property returns the currently selected drive letter. And, of course, if the user chooses a new drive letter, the OnChange method is called. The DirList property holds the name of a directory list component. If the drive combo box's Drive property changes, the associated directory list box changes to display the directory structure of the new drive.

Load the good old FILEDLG project again. Add another label directly below the directory list box and place a drive combo box below the label. All the components in this column should be the same width and aligned at their left edge. Set the caption of the label to Dri&ve: and set its FocusControl to point to the drive combo box. Set the drive combo box's DirList property to the name of the directory list.

You are now one step closer to a complete homemade file dialog. Run the program, pull down the drive list, and note the different icons next to the drive letters. After you choose a new drive, a Rube Goldbergesque chain of events starts. The drive combo box sets the directory list box's drive property to the new drive letter. This action causes the directory list box to update the directory label and the file list box's directory. The file list box in turn updates itself to show the files in the new directory. It all happens so fast that you hardly notice. Once again, save the FILEDLG project.

About now, you may be asking why you're bothering to build a replica of the common file dialogs. Isn't it pointless? Well, the handmade version is more open to customization. You can make a version that omits the file list box and its associated label and edit box, for example, thus yielding a directory selection dialog. Follow these steps:

1. **Place a panel on a new fixed-size form and set its properties as follows:**

Property	*Value*
Align	alTop
Alignment	taLeftJustify
BevelInner	bvLowered
Caption	(none)
Height	25

2. **Drop a label on the panel, delete its caption, and set its Align property to alClient so that it fills the panel.**

3. **Below the panel, place two labels captioned &Directory: and Dri&ve:.**

4. Below the two labels, put a directory list box and a drive combo box, as shown in Figure 10-3.

5. Set the FocusControl property of each label to the file component below it.

6. Set the directory list box's DirLabel property to the name of the label on the panel.

7. Set the drive combo box's DirList property to the name of the directory list.

8. Place two bitmap buttons in the bottom right corner of the form with their Kind properties set to bkOK and bkCancel.

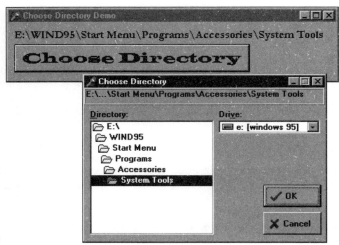

Figure 10-3:
You can use this form template in any project that requires users to select a directory.

9. Change the form's caption to Choose Directory and its Name property to ChooseDirForm.

10. Right-click the form.

11. Choose Add To Repository from the menu that pops up after you right-click the form.

12. Enter Choose Directory Form for the title, fill in a description, and set the Page to Forms.

13. Enter your own name as the Author and then click OK.

You've created a directory-selection dialog that you can use in any program. It should look something like the one in Figure 10-3, although, of course, you can redecorate it to suit your own fashion sense. Just follow these steps:

1. **Start a new project and choose File⇨New from the menu bar.**

2. **Click the Forms tab.**

3. **Select the Choose Directory form template you just created.**

4. **Place a label and a button on the main form.**

5. **Delete the label's caption and then set the button's caption to Choose Directory.**

6. **Put the following lines in the button's OnClick event handler:**

```
IF ChooseDirForm.ShowModal = mrOK THEN
   Label1.Caption :=
      ChooseDirForm.DirectoryListBox1.Directory;
```

7. **Add Unit2 to the uses clause of the main form's unit.**

Anytime you want to use a directory-selection dialog, all you need to do is add this template to your project and write a few lines of code.

Filter Your Files with a Combo Box

Your growing file dialog is coming along quite nicely, but it still lacks discrimination. You can choose any directory you want, but the file dialog insists on displaying all the files in that directory. By adding a filter combo box, you can give it the capability to choose files matching a set of file specifications.

The Filter property of a filter combo box holds a series of named file masks. Double-clicking it activates a special filter-entry dialog, with one column for the name and one for the mask. Each mask contains one or more wildcard file specifications, with multiple file specifications separated by semicolons. At run time, the Mask property holds the mask portion of the selected filter. I can hear you saying to yourself "Yeah, and I'll bet the OnChange event occurs after the user chooses a different filter, right?" It does get kind of predictable. . . . And, of course, the FileList property holds the name of a file list box with a Mask property that's updated to match the selected filter.

Place a label directly below the file list box in the FILEDLG project and a filter combo box below the label. Set the label's caption to List files of &Type: and its FocusControl to the filter combo box. Double-click the filter combo box's Filter property — it already contains a filter for All files. Add a filter named Text files with the mask *.TXT. Set the filter combo box's FileList property to the name of the file list.

Add three bitmap buttons in a column along the right edge of the form with their Kind properties set to bkOK, bkCancel, and bkHelp. Enter the following lines as the OK button's OnClick event handler:

```
IF ((Pos('*', Edit1.Text) > 0) OR
    (Pos('?', Edit1.Text) > 0)) THEN
  BEGIN
    FileListBox1.Mask := Edit1.Text;
    ModalResult := mrNone;
  END
ELSE
  BEGIN
    Filename := DirectoryListBox1.Directory;
    IF Length(FileName) > 3 THEN
      Filename := Filename + '\';
    Filename := Filename + Edit1.Text;
    ModalResult := mrOK;
  END;
```

Whoops! This code seems to be assigning a value to the Filename property, but your file dialog form doesn't *have* a Filename property. You can correct this situation. Page up through the unit in the editor until you see the comment { Public declarations }. Just below that line, insert the following:

```
Filename : String;
```

Click the file list box, flip to the Events page, and pull down the event list next to OnDblClick. Select the event handler you just wrote for the OK button. Change the form's Name property to MyFilDlg and then right-click the form and save it as a template or add it to the repository.

If you save a form in this way, it's automatically available anytime you choose File⇨New from the menu bar and click the Forms tab.

After you select a filter, its mask becomes the mask for the file list box, and the mask gets copied into the filename edit box. Just what happens after you click OK depends on whether the filename edit box contains any wildcards. If the file edit box does contain wildcards, its contents become the new mask for the file edit box. If the file edit box doesn't contain wildcards, the dialog closes and returns mrOK for its modal result. If you double-click a filename, the first click selects the filename and copies it into the edit box, and the second click has the same effect as clicking the OK button.

Congratulations! You've successfully simulated the look and feel of good old Windows 3.1 file common dialogs! Figure 10-4 shows the resplendent result.

Figure 10-4:
This
homemade
equivalent
to the file
common
dialog is 100
percent
customiz-
able.

So how do you use this dialog in a program? I thought you'd never ask!
Follow these steps:

1. **Place a label and a button on a new form.**

2. **Delete the label's caption and set the button's caption to Choose File.**

3. **Choose File⇨New from the menu and click the Forms tab.**

4. **Select the file dialog template you just created.**

5. **In the main form, add the following lines to the button's OnClick
   event handler:**

```
IF MyFilDlg.ShowModal = mrOK THEN
    Label1.Caption := MyFilDlg.Filename;
```

6. **Press Ctrl+Home to go to the top of the unit and add Unit2 to the uses
   clause.**

Incorporating the handmade file dialog into a program is as easy as that.
And because you built the file dialog yourself, you can modify or enhance it
in any way that suits you.

More Directory Assistance

The directory outline program you build at the beginning of this chapter is kind of fun, and it demonstrates the power of a hidden file list box. But I have a confession to make — it isn't entirely necessary. If you want a directory outline in your program, simply flip to the Samples page and use a directory outline component! As is the file list box, this component is a live wire. The minute you drop one on your form, you're viewing a directory outline for the current drive.

A few differences exist between the handmade outline and the directory outline component. The handmade one uses different glyphs to distinguish directories that can be expanded, can be collapsed, or can't be expanded. The handmade one also shows directories in sorted order, whereas the directory outline component doesn't. And the handmade outline correctly handles full expansion if you highlight the root and press the asterisk. The handmade outline, however, takes substantially longer than the directory outline component to initialize itself.

Properties and events

The directory outline in Delphi 3 is basically a subset of the properties of its ancestor, the plain old outline component. The outline's Lines, OutlineStyle, PicturePlus, and PictureMinus properties are not implemented in the directory outline component. The directory outline is a clean and spiffy component. An important point to remember is that the directory outline in Delphi 3 (and also in Delphi 2.0) and Delphi 1.0 are not 100 percent compatible.

The run-time-only Drive property tells the component which drive to display in outline form, and the Directory property holds the currently selected directory.

A directory outline's most important event is OnChange. This event occurs if the user changes directories; your programs normally use it to update a file list box. Yes, you must write code to perform that update; you have no equivalent to the directory list box's FileList property.

At the end of the section "Filter Your Files with a Combo Box," you create a simple project to demonstrate the use of the file selection dialog. If it's not still loaded in Delphi, take a minute to reconstruct it. In the file dialog, *delete* the directory list box and add a directory outline in its place. Choose Search⇨Replace from the editor's menu bar and replace all occurrences of DirectoryListBox1 with DirectoryOutline1. Create an OnChange event handler for the drive combo box; it should contain the following line:

```
DirectoryOutline1.Drive := DriveComboBox1.Drive;
```

Put these lines in an OnChange event handler for the directory outline:

```
FileListBox1.Directory := DirectoryOutline1.Directory;
Label3.Caption := DirectoryOutline1.Directory;
```

The change you made to the file dialog in this program affects *only* this program. It doesn't change the template.

Didn't I say this handmade file dialog was customizable? With one stroke, you replaced its standard directory list with a fully expandable directory outline. Figure 10-5 shows how it looks now (compare it with the file dialog in Figure 10-4). The directory list box shows a single branch of the directory tree (the current directory, all its ancestors, and one level of its subdirectories). The directory outline has the potential to show every little twig of the entire directory tree.

Figure 10-5:
This customized file dialog uses a directory outline instead of a directory list box.

Steal This Bitmap!

The file common dialogs provide one way of looking at files on disk. They're oriented toward choosing one file or a few files in a directory. You can assemble the same components differently to yield a form that's more like a File Manager directory window. Don't believe me? Well, just follow these steps:

1. **Place a drive combo box on a new form and tuck it into the top left corner.**

2. **Add a draw grid with properties set as follows:**

Property	*Value*
Align	alTop
ColCount	1
Color	clBtnFace
FixedRows	0
FixedCols	0
GridLineWidth	0
Height	26
Options.goHorzLine	False
Options.goVertLine	False
Options.goRangeSelect	False
RowCount	1

The draw grid hides the drive combo box; that's intentional.

3. In the form's OnCreate event handler, insert these three lines:

```
DrawGrid1.ColCount :=
   DriveComboBox1.Items.Count;
DrawGrid1.Col := DriveComboBox1.ItemIndex;
```

4. Create an OnDrawCell event handler for the draw grid, replacing the begin..end pair supplied by Delphi with the following lines:

```
VAR Temp: TBitmap;
begin
   WITH DriveComboBox1, DrawGrid1.Canvas DO
      BEGIN
         IF (gdSelected IN State) THEN
            BEGIN
               Brush.Color := clWhite;
               FillRect(Rect);
            END
         ELSE Brush.Color := DrawGrid1.Color;
         InflateRect(Rect,-8,-3);
         OffsetRect(Rect,-6,0);
         Temp := TBitmap(Items.Objects[Col]);
```

```
BrushCopy(Rect, Temp,
    Bounds(0,0,Temp.Width,Temp.Height),
    Temp.TransparentColor);
Font := Self.Font;
TextOut(Rect.Right+1, Rect.Top, Items[Col][1]);
    END;
end;
```

5. Add an OnResize event handler for the form as follows:

```
WITH DrawGrid1 DO
    IF ClientWidth < ColCount * DefaultColWidth THEN
        Height := 47
    ELSE Height := 26;
```

6. Give the program a whirl to make sure that it works so far.

You should see a row of icons across the top of the form representing the disk drives on your system. The images are hot property, stolen from the hidden drive combo box! If you make the form too narrow to hold all the drives, a scroll bar automatically appears across the bottom of the row of drive icons.

7. Now place a header component on the form, align it to alTop, and give it two sections called Directories and Files.

8. Use the right mouse button to drag the header's dividing line so that the sections are equal in width.

9. Drop a panel on the form with its properties set as follows:

Property	*Value*
Align	alBottom
Alignment	taLeftJustify
BevelInner	bvLowered
Caption	(none)
Height	26

10. Place a directory outline on the form, align it on the left, and size it so that its right edge is just under the dividing line in the header.

11. Place a file list box and set its Align property to alClient.

All the gears and gadgets are in place; you just need to connect them by attaching the pulleys and levers.

12. Put the following lines in an OnSized event handler for the header:

```
DirectoryOutline1.Width :=
  Header1.SectionWidth[0];
```

13. Create an OnClick event handler for the draw grid using these lines:

```
WITH DrawGrid1 DO
  DirectoryOutline1.Drive :=
    DriveComboBox1.Items[Col][1];
```

14. In an OnChange event handler for the directory outline, enter the following lines:

```
Caption := DirectoryOutline1.Directory;
FileListBox1.Directory :=
  DirectoryOutline1.Directory;
```

15. And finally, create an OnChange event handler for the file list box using the following line:

```
Panel1.Caption := FileListBox1.Filename;
```

Figure 10-6 shows the completely different file-selection form displayed by this project. It's similar to one of File Manager's directory windows; in fact, it could serve as the jumping-off point to *build* a directory window in a File Manager look-alike.

Program files, text files, spreadsheet files . . . all kinds of files are on your system. These file components help you perform high-level, generalized actions such as locating and displaying files. After Delphi gets down to business, however, it deals with one very special variety of files — *database* files. Database files are what Chapter 11 is all about.

Figure 10-6: You can assemble the same file components into this directory-browsing form.

Chapter 11

Database Components

In This Chapter

▶ Figuring out the jargon behind database programming

▶ Building data-entry forms with help from Delphi

▶ Defining calculated fields whose values are supplied by your program at run time

▶ Building a universal database program

▶ Connecting data-aware components for instant access to database tables

▶ Experimenting with SQL (Structured Query Language)

▶ Using the Delphi 3 database features

▶ Creating a form template for selecting database tables

*W*hat's a computer for? What's its excuse for existence? You can make a pretty good argument that *computer* is the wrong name for these gadgets. Sure, they can compute, but the main thing they do is store and retrieve data. Aunt Tillie's phone number, Arnold Schwarzenegger's shoe size, or every parking ticket that's ever blessed your windshield — just about any piece of information you can think of is stored in a database somewhere. Modern databases can even include images, sounds, and video!

Because data management is so important, Delphi devotes two whole pages in the Component palette to it. The Data Access page holds components for connecting to databases and peeking at their innards. The Data Controls page is loaded with data-aware components that have been carefully trained to display and edit database data. The Delphi 3 Database Explorer makes finding and understanding your available databases very easy. And the data module, a kind of nonvisual form for storing nonvisual database components, raises data worship to new heights.

Delphi relies on the near-omnipotent Borland Database Engine (BDE) to implement its database support. With the BDE (which comes with Delphi) you can just as easily connect to a remote Oracle database on a network server as to a local Paradox table on your hard disk. (For simplicity, I use local databases for the examples in this chapter.) Delphi insulates you from the painful details of database access so thoroughly that you can upsize a local database project to client/server with little effort beyond changing a few properties.

Walk the Walk, Talk the Talk

Quite a few ordinary English words take on special meanings in the techno-speak jargon used by database programmers. It's hopeless to try to avoid these words; all you can do is try to understand the language. Here's a basic dictionary:

- *Field* — The smallest element of data in a database. A field has a name and a type; for example, the type for a field named Company Name will probably be text. Some data types are text, numeric, currency, date, and time.

- *Record* — A collection of fields that contain related information. For example, a customer record might contain name and address information along with a unique customer ID number.

- *Table* — A collection of records that all have the same field structure. When a table is displayed in grid form, each row is one record and each column is one field.

- *Database* — A collection of related tables, usually identified by the directory that contains the tables or by an *alias* that names the database.

- *Index* — Just as the index to this book helps you find the topic you want, an index to a database helps locate records that have a particular field value.

- *Primary Index* — Required by many database functions, the primary index controls the order in which the records of the database are displayed. A primary index field must be unique; that is, no two records can have the same value in this field.

- *Secondary Index* — A more relaxed type of index that can be based on a combination of fields and needs not be unique. Secondary indexes are used in linking tables, a topic I cover in this chapter.

- *Query* — A statement in SQL (Structured Query Language) that selects records and fields from one or more tables. You use a query to get information *from* the database, for example, a list of all customers with unpaid bills.

Different database programs store database tables and fields in different ways, but when you access the data with Delphi, you don't have to worry about that.

The concept of alias deserves special mention. Desperadoes in the old West used aliases to hide from the law. The BDE's aliases have a more benign purpose: After you use the Database Engine Configuration program (found in the Delphi menu under the Windows 95 Start menu) to establish an alias for a particular directory on disk, you can refer to tables in that directory through the alias. If you move the files, or install them on a different machine, or move them to a shared directory on a network server, you don't have to make any changes in your program. Just whip out the configuration program and change the directory for that alias! Follow these steps:

1. **In the Delphi menu under the Start menu, find the Database Engine Configuration item and launch it.**

2. **Select the Aliases page of the resulting dialog and press the New Alias button.**

3. **Fill in the name Demos and leave the type set to Standard.**

4. **In the Parameters panel, set the PATH for this alias to the directory that contains the Delphi database example files.**

   The default path is C:\DELPHI\DEMOS\DATABASE. If you have any other dBASE or Paradox databases on your system, give them aliases as well.

5. **Choose File⇨Save from the menu bar and then close the configuration editor.**

I use this Demos alias in examples throughout this chapter.

Nurture Your Relationships

I define a database as consisting of one or more tables. The simplest kind of database is just a single table filled with any number of identically laid-out records. This humdrum table is called a flat-file database. Look at how this kind of database evolves into something more complicated.

Suppose that you want to devise a database to track your Christmas card list. You want to store the name and address of everyone you send cards to, and you also want to keep track of the cards you receive, noting when each arrived (before the Big Day or after), whether it included a handwritten note, and whether it included an Awful Xeroxed Christmas Letter (AXCL). To start, you simply dump all of these data elements into one big table, adding a new record for each correspondent each year.

However, there's trouble right here in Delphi City with a capital R — and that stands for Redundancy. If you've been exchanging Christmas cards with Bill Gates for ten years, he'll appear in ten different records in your database. At best, you're storing his name and address nine times more than you need to. At worst, you may have an inconsistent variety of addresses and names. Bill or William? WA or Wash.? Old address or new?

Here is the official motto of database designers everywhere: Never Store Anything Twice.

So the Christmas card database *should* store each name and address just once. In the simple-minded, one-table database, the name and address information is repeated with the specific data about each year's card exchange. A better solution is to store the name and address information in one table and the yearly card data in another. The two tables are linked in such a way that *one* entry in the names table can be connected to *many* entries in the card data table. If a friend moves, you must update the address only once. And if you get the urge to send a special Christmas message to anyone who blessed you with an Awful Xeroxed Christmas Letter (AXCL) last year, you can easily find out who's naughty and who's nice.

This kind of *one-to-many relationship* is extremely important in database design, and the Delphi database components devote special properties and methods to handling such relationships. Also, as you soon see, Delphi automates the process of creating database programs that link tables in this way.

Get Help from the Expert

Before you go any further, consult the world's expert on Delphi database programming — Delphi itself! Start with an empty project and follow these steps:

1. **Choose Database⇨Database Form Expert from the Delphi 3 menu bar.**

2. **Check the option to create a simple form and go on to the next page.**

3. **Pull down the combo box labeled Drive or Alias name and select the Demos alias.**

   Or, if you prefer, select another alias or navigate to a directory on your disk that contains database files.

4. **Highlight any table in the selected database and click Next.**

   The next page enables you to choose and order fields from the database.

5. **Select the fields one at a time by double-clicking in the order you want or by highlighting them and pressing the arrow button.**

   Or, if you prefer, move them all to the right-hand list box and order them using the up and down arrows.

6. **On the next page, choose the Horizontal form type and press Next.**

   After you press Create on the final page, Delphi creates a form for viewing or editing the selected database.

7. **Run this program.**

After you run the program, you see a form similar to Figure 11-1, which shows an instant database form for a BIOLIFE database example. The database navigator component, the one that looks like a cassette player's buttons, lets you step through the records forward or backward or flip to the first or last record in the database. You can even edit the database fields (but don't make any drastic changes, please). Yes, Delphi did all that for you. Follow these steps for insight into master/detail forms:

1. **Start a new project, discarding the database application you just created.**

   Hey, you can build it again any time!

2. **Open the Database Form Expert.**

3. **Choose Create a master/detail form.**

4. **On the next page, choose the Demos alias and select CUSTOMER.DB for the master table.**

5. **Select any or all of the fields and, on the next page, choose Horizontal placement.**

6. **For your detail table, choose ORDERS.DB, and again select any or all of the fields.**

   Be very sure to choose grid-style placement for the detail data.

7. **Choose the field that will link the two tables.**

8. **Pull down the combo box labeled Available Indexes and select ByCustNo or CustNo (this is a secondary index on the customer number in the ORDERS table).**

9. **Select CustNo in each column, press the Add button, go on to the next page, and generate the form.**

10. **Check the Form and Data Module radio button before pressing OK.**

Because the orders table may well have many orders for a single customer number, it can't have a *primary* index on CustNo. A primary index must be unique; you can't have two records with the same primary index.

As Figure 11-2 shows, this is a much fancier data entry form than the one in Figure 11-1. As you navigate through the customer records, the grid at the bottom changes to list all orders for that customer. And you still haven't written a single line of code!

Figure 11-2:
You can create a master/ detail form like this one just by answering questions posed by the Delphi Database Form Expert.

The Database Form Expert also creates a data module for your project. The first thing you notice is that all the nonvisual database components reside in the data module (see Figure 11-3) rather than in the main form in the Form Designer. Although tidiness may be next to godliness, the data module's *real* purpose is to add flexibility to database programming.

Figure 11-3:
The Delphi 3 data module stores non-visual database components.

If multiple forms in the program must access the same tables, they can all refer to the table and data source components stored in the data module. To give a new form access to an existing data module's database components, you just choose File⇨Use Unit from the menu and select the unit containing the data module. If two forms access the same data with two different table components, unpleasant wrangling over who owns the data can result. The data module avoids these synchronization problems.

Just about any time you're developing a database project, it makes sense to use the Database Form Expert. You get a head start by using the form it generates as the starting point for your own efforts, and in Delphi 3, the Database Form Expert automatically creates a handy data module. In the rest of this chapter, I delve deeper into the Delphi built-in database components.

DataBasics

Don't try to swallow everything about the Delphi database support at once. Just take a nibble to start. Meet a few carefully selected components: table, data source, data-aware grid, and data navigator. You can build fully functional database applications using only these four components.

Lay your cards on the table

Different database programs store their information differently, but it all boils down to rows and columns in the end. Each column represents a field — information such as name, birth date, salary, or hat size. Each row represents one record of data. A set of columns and rows is called a table, and the Delphi table component is your program's link to a particular table of data.

In a table component, the DatabaseName property specifies the database that holds this table; it's either an alias or the name of a directory containing table files. TableName is the holographically derivative cornfluster . . . naw, just kidding, it's what you thought — the name of the table. Setting the Active property to True opens the table, even at design time. You won't believe how convenient it is to have live data available when you're designing a form or writing code! If your table has a primary key, the records show up in order sorted by that key. To use a secondary key instead, you specify it in the IndexName property. Delphi 3's table component has a few interesting features, the most significant of which are *cached updates* and *filters*.

- ✔ *Cached updates* keep your program from constantly niggling the network for a little data here, a little update there. By storing changes locally and then blasting them back through the network all at once, the cached update feature can help your program be a good network citizen. There *is* a price — your program has to deal with the possibility that some other program may fiddle with the same records. If "transaction control" doesn't mean anything to you, leave CachedUpdates set to False.

- ✔ *Filters* let you temporarily put blinders on a table or query so that it sees only a subset of its data. When you take the blinders off, the whole data set is still available. If the Filtered property is True, the OnFilterRecord event handler that you supply is called for every record to determine whether or not that record will be accepted. This can be quicker than constructing a new query. Follow these steps to see what I mean:

1. **Place a table component on a new form and set its DatabaseName property to Demos or to any database on your system.**

   When you click the down arrow next to DatabaseName in the Object Inspector, you get a list of aliases.

2. **Click the TableName property, click the down arrow next to it, and make a choice from the list of tables in the selected database.**

3. **Set the Active property to True and try to change the DatabaseName or TableName.**

   Delphi informs you in no uncertain terms that you can't change these properties when the table is open.

4. **Set Active to False and change either DatabaseName or TableName so that it's no longer valid.**

   When you try to set Active to True again, Delphi won't let you; you can activate the table only when it has a valid DatabaseName and TableName.

Several of the table component's properties exist solely to set up two tables in a master/detail relationship. As you've seen, the Database Form Expert plugs values into these fields and voilà! A master/detail form! In the detail table, MasterSource is the name of the data source for the master table (hold on; I talk about data sources in just a minute), and MasterFields contains the name of the field or fields on which the two tables are linked. The linking field doesn't need to be the primary sorting key for the table, so the IndexName field holds the name of the index to be used.

If your table is hanging around a dark corner of some network server, someone else may want to access it at the same time you do. No problem. Delphi can share politely. If you set the Exclusive property to True, however, your program will hog the table for itself. Nobody else will be able to access the data while you're using it, and your program will run much faster. If you choose exclusive access and someone else is already using the data, you won't be able to open the table at all. If all you want to do is look at the data without making any changes, you can set ReadOnly to True.

Flip to the Events page in the Object Inspector, and you see a dizzying array of database events. The good news is, you can write complete and functional data-management programs that don't use these events at all! For now, forget 'em.

Get your data from the source

A table is a genteel component, much too sophisticated to hobnob with the riff-raff components that edit and display data. The data source component acts as a go-between in the exchange of data between a table and a data-aware component. Its DataSet property points to the table from which the fount of data flows. If AutoEdit is True, the data flows both ways. That is, changing data in a component connected to this data source automatically changes the data in the table. A data source receives notification events when data in a table or component changes and when its own state changes. For now, your programs can rely on the built-in handling for these notification events.

Instant view with a data grid

Displaying table data in a grid-style view is dead simple. Drop a data-aware grid on the form, set its DataSource property to a data source connected to the table, and you're ready to go. If you made the table active at design time, you see live data in the grid immediately. The data grid shares many properties with its cousin's string grid and draw grid, so I just talk about properties special to a data grid.

The Options property explodes into a mass of True and False subproperties. dgTitles controls whether the field names appear as column titles, and dgIndicator controls whether the wedge-shaped current-row indicator appears at the left of the grid. You can press Ctrl+Del to delete the current row; if dgConfirmDelete is True, the grid asks for confirmation first. The remaining options should be familiar from your experience with the string grid in Chapter 9.

You can set the font for the titles separately using the TitleFont property. If the grid contains live data, you can drag column headings to reorder the columns or drag the lines between column headings to resize columns.

By default, a data-aware grid displays fields in the order they appear in the table with the field names as column titles. However, you don't have to settle for the default. Double-click the table and the Dataset Designer dialog appears; it's shown in Figure 11-4. Using this dialog, you can control which fields are displayed and how. The next set of steps shows you what I mean.

Keep a live data grid hooked up to the table while you're using the Dataset Designer so that you can see the result of changes as you make them.

Figure 11-4:
The Dataset Designer lets you individually set properties for the fields of a table.

1. **Place a table, a data source, and a data grid component on a new form, and hook them up in series: grid to data source, data source to table.**

2. **Set the table's database name to the Demos alias and choose the COUNTRY.DB table.**

3. **Set the table's Active property to True.**

4. **Set the grid's Align property to alClient.**

5. **Double-click the table to enter the Dataset Designer.**

6. **Right-click the Dataset Designer and select Add fields from the pop-up menu.**

7. **Highlight a few fields and then click OK.**

   Only the fields you added appear in the grid. You can drag fields up and down the list to change their order.

8. **Add all the remaining fields.**

Note that as you click fields in the list, the Object Inspector displays properties specific to each field. You can set the column heading for a field by filling in the DisplayLabel property, or you can set it to left, right, or center Alignment. Each field can be independently set to ReadOnly, or you can set Visible to False to hide the field (that is, to prevent it from showing in a grid).

The exact set of properties present depends on the field type. For example, floating-point number fields have a True and False property to say whether they represent Currency. String fields have an EditMask property identical to that of a masked edit box.

Using the same form, return to the Dataset Designer, select the Population field, and set the Visible property to False. Right-click the Dataset Designer and select New field from the menu. Enter a field named ShortPop. Select FloatField from the Field type list and check the Calculated check box. Click OK. Back in the Dataset Designer, arrange the fields so that the first three are Name, Capital, and ShortPop. Select ShortPop and set its DisplayLabel property to

```
Pop. (millions)
```

and its DisplayFormat to

```
0.0
```

Select the Area field and set its DisplayFormat property to

```
###,###,### "sq.mi."
```

Close the Dataset Designer. Create an OnCalcFields event handler for the table itself containing these lines:

```
Table1ShortPop.AsFloat :=
  Table1Population.AsFloat / 1000000;
```

Run the program and you see the names and capitals of various nations in the Americas, along with their populations in millions, as shown in Figure 11-5. Because of the special display format, the Area column shows, for example, 1,967,180 square miles rather than the hard-to-read 1967180. You can change the capital of the U.S. from Washington to Washingtoon. (Truth in Advertising requires this change!) Because the rounded-off population figure is a calculated field, it's not subject to change.

Control columns for gorgeous grids

The data-aware grid in Delphi 3 has a nifty property called Columns that gives you a huge amount of control over the display, along with some powerful aids to data entry. Columns is a megaproperty that has its own personal Columns Editor, as shown in Figure 11-6. Some of its capabilities overlap those of the Dataset Designer, but the Dataset Designer affects *all* components connected to the table.

Figure 11-5:
This data grid's population column is a calculated field, and the area column was enhanced with a special display format.

Name	Capital	Pop. (millions)	Area	Continent
Cuba	Havana	10.6	114,524 sq. mi.	North America
Ecuador	Quito	10.6	455,502 sq. mi.	South America
El Salvador	San Salvador	5.3	20,865 sq. mi.	North America
Freedonia	Fireflyopolis	0.1	100 sq. mi.	Middle America
Guyana	Georgetown	0.8	214,969 sq. mi.	South America
Jamaica	Kingston	2.5	11,424 sq. mi.	North America
Mexico	Mexico City	88.6	1,967,180 sq. mi.	North America
Nicaragua	Managua	3.9	139,000 sq. mi.	North America

Land of the Brave and Free

The best way to get a handle on the Columns Editor is to use it. Limber up your fingers, because you're going to set a *lot* of properties!

Figure 11-6:
The Columns Editor sets the font and color of each column and title individually and allows specialized data entry modes.

1. **Start a new application and then choose File⇨New Data Module from the menu.**

2. **Place two tables in the data module, connecting Table1 to the ORDERS example table and Table2 to the CUSTOMER example table.**

3. **Set Active to True for both, and connect a data source to each.**

4. **Double-click Table1 to open the Dataset Designer, right-click, and choose Add fields from the menu.**

5. **Add OrderNo, CustNo, SaleDate, ShipDate, and ShipVia.**

6. **Choose New field from the pop-up menu.**

7. **Enter Customer for the field name and String for the type, and then click the Lookup radio button.**

8. **Choose Table2 in the Dataset combo box and CustNo in the Key Fields and Lookup Keys combo boxes.**

9. **Choose Company in the Result Field combo box and click OK.**

Just what did you *do* in the New Field dialog? You told Delphi to create a field called Customer, associated with Table1. The value of this field is obtained by a lookup into Table2. Delphi finds a record in Table2 whose CustNo matches the CustNo field in Table1. Then it returns the Company field from Table2. Why did you do that? Patience, patience — all shall be revealed!

10. **Switch to the main form and choose File⇨Use unit. . . from the menu to make the main form use the data module.**

11. **Drop a data-aware grid on the form, set its Align property to alClient, and connect it to DataModule1.DataSource1.**

    Take a moment to stop and marvel at the fact that the data source in a different unit appears in the pull-down list for the DataSource property.

12. **Double-click the grid's Columns property to open the Columns Editor.**

13. **Press the Add All Fields button, select CustNo, and then press the Delete button.**

14. **Select SaleDate and set the ButtonStyle to cbsEllipsis; do the same for ShipDate.**

15. **Select ShipVia, click the Pick List button, and enter the names of as many shipping companies as you can think of.**

16. **Go wild setting the color and font of each column and its title.**

    The result should look vaguely similar to Figure 11-7. Just one more thing, and then you can play with the program!

17. **Create an OnEditButtonClick event handler for the grid containing these lines:**

```
DBGrid1.DataSource.DataSet.Edit;
DBGrid1.SelectedField.AsDateTime := Date;
```

Setting the ButtonStyle to bsEllipsis for the two date columns causes an ellipsis button to appear in the cell during editing — clicking the button invokes this event handler.

Because the Customer field is defined as a lookup field, it sports a pull-down list displaying all the companies in the CUSTOMER table. Make a choice from the list and the nonvisible CustNo field is updated automatically. The ShipVia field has a more mundane pull-down list that simply displays the list of shipping companies you entered in the Columns Editor. And when you press the ellipsis button in either of the date columns, today's date is inserted automatically. That's a lot of program for two lines of code!

The great navigator

You've already seen a database navigator component in the forms produced by the Database Form Expert. This component is a collection of buttons that resembles the Media Player (which I introduce in Chapter 9), but its buttons are shortcuts for navigating through the database.

The database navigator's VisibleButtons property explodes into ten subproperties that determine which of ten buttons will appear. The most important buttons are those controlled by the properties nbFirst, nbLast, nbPrior, and nbNext. As you've surely discovered by fooling with them, these properties allow you to move to the beginning or end of the database and to the previous or next record.

If nbInsert and nbDelete are True, the navigator includes Insert and Delete buttons, symbolized by plus and minus signs. Clicking Insert adds a new blank row at the cursor; clicking Delete deletes the current row. If the ConfirmDelete property is True, the program asks for confirmation before deleting a row. The Edit button, the one with an up-pointing triangle, flips the associated table into edit mode. It's only needed when the data source's AutoEdit property is False.

Any changes you make to the data in a row are copied to the table as soon as you leave the row. The Post and Cancel buttons (check mark and X, respectively) give finer control over this process. Clicking Post accepts changes immediately, without leaving the row, and clicking Cancel discards changes. Finally, the Refresh button, with a curved arrow on it, refreshes the table's data from disk. This is only necessary when the data may have been changed by another user (or another program on the same machine).

Closing the table does *not* automatically post a modified record. To be safe, post your programs before closing.

The skinny indicator column at the left edge of the grid does more than just point an arrow at the current row. If the row is new and hasn't been posted yet, the arrow changes to an asterisk. If the row has been changed and the changes haven't been posted, the arrow changes to an I-beam shape.

The average user can't decipher the hieroglyphics on the navigator's buttons. Set the ShowHint property to True to enable flyover help for them. If you don't like the Delphi default hint strings, you can fill in ten hints of your own in the Hints property. These hints correspond to the ten buttons, in order, even if not all of the buttons are visible in your particular program.

The most important navigator property is DataSource. Click the down arrow next to DataSource and you get a list of available data source components in the form. A navigator that isn't connected to a data source is utterly useless.

Build a Database Editor

To start this project, get out another new form and follow these steps:

1. **Place a table and data source component and an Open File dialog on a new form, with the table as the data source's DataSet property.**

2. **Set the table's ReadOnly property to True and the data source's AutoEdit property to False.**

3. **Place a bevel component on the form, set its type to bsFrame, and set its Align property to alTop.**

4. **Set the Open File dialog's properties like so:**

Property	*Value*
DefaultExt	DB
Options.ofHideReadOnly	True
Options.ofFileMustExist	True
Title	Open Database File

5. **Double-click the Filter property and create two filters named Database files and All files, with matching file specifications U.DB;U.DBF (for Database files) and U.U (for All files).**

6. **Put a single speed button at the left of the bevel component, with its Caption set to the digit 1 and its Font set to Wingdings.**

   Surprise! This produces a button with an open folder on it.

7. **Place a database navigator to the right of the button.**

8. **Connect the navigator's DataSource property to the data source.**

9. **Set all but the first four VisibleButtons subproperties to False.**

10. **Set the navigator's ShowHint property to True.**

11. **Place a data grid component on the form, set its Align property to alClient, and connect it to the data source as well.**

12. **Change the form's caption to Universal Database Viewer.**

13. **Double-click the speed button and put this code in its OnClick event handler:**

```
WITH OpenDialog1 DO
  IF Execute THEN
    WITH Table1 DO
      BEGIN
        Close;
        DatabaseName := ExtractFilePath(Filename);
        TableName := ExtractFileName(Filename);
        Open;
      END;
```

That's it! You've built a viewer for all your database tables, simply by hooking up components and writing a few lines of code. As the following simple exercise shows, if you want to do more than look, all you have to do is change a few properties and your table viewer becomes a table editor.

In the database viewer project, set the table's ReadOnly property to False and the data source's AutoEdit property to True. Double-click the Visible-Buttons property of the navigator and set the subproperties nbInsert, nbDelete, nbPost, and nbCancel to True.

With those simple changes, the database viewer becomes an editor. Figure 11-8 shows the finished product. The navigator lets you step through the records forward or backward, or jump to the start or end of the data. You can also navigate by scrolling around the grid. Save this project as DBVIEWER.

Figure 11-8:
The Delphi database components do most of the work in this database viewer and editor.

NAME	SIZE	WEIGHT	AREA	BMP
Angel Fish	2	2	Computer Aquariums	(Blob)
Boa	10	8	South America	(Blob)
Critters	30	20	Screen Savers	(Blob)
House Cat	10	5	New Orleans	(Blob)
Ocelot	40	35	Africa and Asia	(Blob)
Parrot	5	5	South America	(Blob)
Tetras	2	2	Fish Bowls	(Blob)

Universal Database Viewer — Next record

Run the program and try making *minor* changes to the sample databases that come with Delphi. The changes take effect as soon as you leave the current row. You can also click the Post button (check mark) to post changes immediately, or click the Cancel button (X) to cancel changes before leaving a row.

Scroll to the bottom of the grid and press the down arrow to insert a new row, or click the Insert button (plus sign) to insert a new row anywhere in the table. If you leave the new row without entering anything, it disappears. In a table with a primary key, when you post the new record or leave the row, the row takes its place in order sorted on the primary key.

Remember that the changes you make in a Delphi database program are written to the file as soon as you leave the current row or click the Post button. There's no need to specifically save the file, though you should be sure to post before closing the table.

There's a Blob in Your Data

At first glance, the data grid seems to be a panacea for general database manipulation. A closer look, however, reveals some warts, most notably its failure to display BLOBs (Binary Large OBjects). Scan the BIOLIFE.DB sample table with the database viewer and look at the Notes and Graphic fields. These actually contain a variable-length memo and an image, but the general-purpose data grid can't display them.

For programs that work with one specific database, where the structure of the tables is known in advance, Delphi supplies a large group of data-aware components. (Visual Basic programmers like to call these *bound* components.) There are data-aware versions of the label, edit box, memo box, image, list box, combo box, check box, and radio group. Like the data grid, these all have a DataSource property that points to a data source within the project. They also have a DataField property to identify which field they display. In addition to these simple bound components, Delphi offers super-smart data-aware list box and combo box components that can reach out and grab data from another table. Delphi 3 offers smart versions of the lookup list box and combo box but retains the original pair for backward compatibility.

The data-aware components are not actually restricted to one-database, predetermined structures. You *can* create and connect these components at run time using code. However, that's not what most database programs need to do.

Awakening components to data

The best way to understand data-aware components is to start working with them. For safety's sake, work with a *copy* of one of the sample tables, not the original!

1. **Find and launch the Database Desktop application.**

2. **Choose File⇨Open Table from the menu and open the BIOLIFE.DB sample database.**

3. **Select Restructure Table from the Table menu and immediately save the table as BIOLIFEX.DB.**

   Now there's no chance that your experimenting will screw up the original table.

4. **Bring up the Restructure Table dialog again and use the down arrow to go one row past the bottom of the list of fields.**

5. Enter Large **for the name of the new field, set its data type to A for Alphabetic, and set its length to 3.**

6. **Add another field called Dominant Color, set its data type to A, and set its length to 8.**

7. **Save the table and then close the Database Desktop.**

8. **Start a new project and choose Database Form Expert from the Database menu in Delphi 3.**

9. **Follow the prompts to create a simple form for BIOLIFEX.DB containing all fields in a horizontal layout.**

10. **Click the table component in the resulting form and set its Active property to True.**

The Delphi components are incredibly useful for viewing and modifying database table information. When you want to *create* a table or change a table's structure, however, it's easier to use the Database Desktop.

When you choose either of the nongrid layouts, the Database Form Expert generates a simple bound edit box for every field. Like the grid, the edit box can't display variable-length memos or images, so the Notes and Graphic fields still don't display properly. You deal with them shortly.

Run the program and enter values for the Large field in a few records. If the fish is 100 centimeters or more, enter **Yes**; otherwise, enter **No**. Now go to the first record and enter **DUH**. Lightning does not strike you. Although you may intend for this field to contain just Yes or No, the program accepts UGH, GUK, YAP, XX, or any string of up to three characters.

Below the edit box on the form, place a data-aware check box that represents the Large field. Set its properties like this:

Property	*Value*
Caption	Large
DataSource	DataSource1
DataField	Large
ValueChecked	Yes
ValueUnchecked	No

Delete the edit box and associated label, and then resize and move the data-aware check box into its place. Run the program again and flip through the records. The check box will be checked if the Large field contains Yes, or unchecked if the Large field contains No. If the field is empty or contains something other than Yes or No, the check box will be grayed. You can use the data-aware check box to force a field to have one of two specific values. It's a lot easier to search for large fish when you know the field contains either Yes or No, not Yea, Nay, or Duh.

Select the edit box and label for the Notes field and drag them to the start of a new row of components. Now select just the edit box and cut it to the Clipboard by pressing Ctrl+X. Switch to the Code Editor, go to the very end of the program, and press Ctrl+V to paste the component as text. Change TDBEdit to TDBMemo in the first line. Cut the text description of the component to the Clipboard, flip to the Form Designer, click the edit box's previous location, and paste it back into the form. Enlarge the newly transformed field — you see the text of a note right away. Set its ScrollBars property to ssVertical.

Select the edit box and label for the Graphic field and move them down into the new row that holds the Notes field. As I discuss in the preceding paragraph, cut the edit box to the Clipboard, paste it into the Code Editor, and replace TDBEdit with TDBImage. Delete the line containing MaxLength, cut the modified description to the Clipboard, click the form where the field used to be, and paste it back in. Resize the image so that you can see the picture.

You can always cut and paste between a component on the form and a text description of the component in the Code Editor. When two component types are similar enough, you can transform one into the other by editing the text description.

Wow! The program isn't even running, yet it displays useful information in the Notes field and a picture in the Graphic field. It's a big improvement over the simple form originally created by the Database Form Expert.

Delete the label that says Dominant Color, and then cut the Dominant Color edit box and paste it into the editor. Change the object type from TDBEdit to TDBRadioGroup. Delete the line that defines MaxLength — that's a TDBEdit property that does not exist in TDBRadioGroup. Now cut the modified description and paste it back into the form. Enlarge the data-aware radio button group and set its caption to Dominant Color. Double-click its Items property and enter the four strings: Red, Yellow, Green, and Black. Rearrange the components on the form so that they look like Figure 11-9.

Run the program and step through a few records. If the fish has a dominant color, choose the appropriate radio button in the Dominant Color group. If it's large (over 100 cm), check the Large check box; otherwise clear it. End the program and load the BIOLIFEX database into the Database Desktop. Wherever you check a dominant color, the corresponding string is inserted in the database! When only a few possible values exist for a field, the data-aware radio button group makes entering a wrong value impossible.

Figure 11-9:
Data-aware
components
tailored to
the table's
fields
enhance
this form.

Before bidding this fishy form a fond farewell, perform one more amazing feat of transmogrification. Select the radio button group, cut it to the Clipboard, and paste it into the very end of the Code Editor. Change the object type from TDBRadioGroup to TDBListBox, and delete the line that defines the Caption property. Now cut the description to the Clipboard and paste it back into the form.

When you run the program now, the dominant color for each fish is highlighted in the data-aware list box. If no dominant color has been entered, none of the items are highlighted. This component (and the very similar data-aware combo box) is useful when the number of possible values for a field is fairly small but too large for a data-aware radio button group.

You could look it up!

Don't confuse the data-aware list box (DBListBox) with the *lookup* list box (DBLookupList). In both, the user chooses the value of a field from a list, true. But in the data-aware list box, the programmer defines the list of values in advance, whereas the lookup list box rips its list of possible values from another table. This is extremely handy when, for example, two tables are linked on a common field. You don't want to let the user accidentally enter a value in the detail table that's not even present in the master; a lookup list makes that error impossible by forcing the user to choose from a list of existing values. Try these steps to understand the lookup list box:

1. **Place a table component and a data source on a new form.**

2. **Connect the table to the example ORDERS.DB table and hook up the data source to the table.**

3. **Set the table's Active property to True.**

4. **Repeat Steps 1–3 to place a second table and a second data source in the same way, connecting the new table and source to CUSTOMER.DB.**

   You may want to put both tables and both data sources in a data module.

5. **Put a data grid and a navigator on the form, connecting both to the first data source.**

6. **Double-click the first table to open the Dataset Designer.**

7. **Add all the fields in the table, select CustNo, and set its Visible property to False.**

8. **Close the Dataset Designer.**

9. **Place a DBLookupCombo component on the form.**

   This component lives on the Win 3.1 page of the Component palette.

10. **Set the DBLookupCombo component's properties like this:**

Property	*Value*
DataSource	DataSource1
DataField	CustNo
LookupDisplay	Company;CustNo
LookupField	CustNo
LookupSource	DataSource2

11. **Run the program.**

As you scroll through the orders in the grid, the lookup combo box displays the name of the corresponding customer. When you enter a new order, you never type the customer number and thus never risk typing it *incorrectly*. Instead, you simply choose the customer name from the lookup combo box. Figure 11-10 shows a slightly fancier version of this same program that uses a lookup list box instead.

You can try the DBLookupListBox and DBLookupComboBox components, too. These two don't have the capability to display multiple fields, but they can be hooked directly to a lookup field that already exists in a table.

Figure 11-10:
This form uses a lookup list box to protect the user from mistyping the all-important customer number.

Try this: Take the preceding example program, delete the DBLookupCombo, and replace it with a DBLookupComboBox. Double-click Table1, right-click the Dataset Designer that appears, and select New field from the menu. Enter CompanyLook for the field name, select String for the field type, and click the Lookup radio button. Select Table2 from the Dataset pull-down list, and select CustNo for both Key Fields and Lookup Keys. Now choose Company from the Result Field pull-down list. Click OK to create the lookup field. Back in the main form, set the DBLookupComboBox's DataSource to Table1 and its DataField to CompanyLook. Bingo! The component immediately fills with data.

This grid is in control

Sometimes you feel like a grid; sometimes you don't. That's why the Delphi Database Form Expert creates either a grid or a form full of separate data-aware components. If you wanted something pretty much like a grid, but with a few fields for each record, you used to be out of luck. With the DBCtrlGrid, it's simple, as these steps show:

1. **Start a new project and right away choose File⇨New Data Module from the menu.**

2. **Click the main form, choose File⇨Use unit from the menu, and choose the unit containing the data module.**

3. **Select Explore from the Database menu to fire up the Database Explorer, shown in Figure 11-11.**

4. **Navigate into the Demos database and locate the EMPLOYEE table.**

5. **Drag the table from the Database Explorer into your data module.**

   Amazing!

6. **Add a DataSource component to the data module.**

7. **Connect the data source to the table and set the table's Active property to True.**

8. **Drop a DBCtrlGrid component on the main form and size it so that it nearly fills the form.**

9. **Set the DBCtrlGrid DataSource property to the data source in the data module, and set its RowCount to 4.**

10. **Add a navigator component connected to the same data source.**

11. **Flip back to the Database Explorer and fully expand the EMPLOYEE table so that you can see the list of fields.**

12. **Drag the fields one-by-one from the Explorer into the top section of the DBCtrlGrid.**

    As you drop each one, it explodes into a data-aware edit box and a corresponding label.

13. **Rearrange these components so that they occupy two separate lines in the top section of the DBCtrlGrid.**

14. **Run the program.**

Figure 11-11:
The Delphi 3
Database
Explorer
makes
developing
database
applications
easy.

As Figure 11-12 shows, each record occupies one band of the component, and four records are visible at once.

If you've ever programmed using Borland's Paradox for Windows, the DBCtrlGrid may look familiar. It's similar to Paradox's MRO (Multi-Record Object).

Figure 11-12:
The DBCtrl-
Grid is a
compromise
between
showing
one record
at a time
spread
out on a
form and
showing
records
jammed into
a grid.

Getting Results

If you're a data entry clerk, you naturally feel that the database exists so
that you can put data into it. Nothing could be further from the truth!
Databases exist so that you can get information *out* of them. Putting the data
in is just a necessary evil. The database proves its mettle when the boss
comes and asks for a list of everyone who has placed an order over $500,
but not ordered anything in the last two years, and lives anywhere in
California except the San Francisco and Los Angeles areas.

Information please — the query

A query component is another way of hooking your Delphi program to a
database. Like a table component, it has DatabaseName and Active properties, and it needs a data source as a go-between for connecting with data-
aware components. When your program opens a query component, it grabs
the information specified by the SQL (Structured Query Language) command in its SQL property. If you've set RequestLive to True, the query
attempts to access the database so that edits made using the query will feed
back into the database. This isn't always possible; the run-time property
ResultSetLive indicates whether it worked or not. If ResultSetLive is False,
the query gives you a copy of the *original data,* also known as canned, dead,
or offline data.

Delphi 3 supports the query component with most of the same goodies it heaped on the table component. Most importantly, queries in Delphi 3 support cached updates and filters. A query involving multiple databases on a busy network can take hours to complete. If you need to view a subset of the query's result, filtering can be *much* faster than sending off a new query.

The good news is that a query component brings the full power of SQL into your Delphi programs. The bad news is that SQL is a complex language. (And even worse, SQL comes in many flavors, unique to each SQL server vendor.) The really good news is that you don't have to know the whole language. All you really need to know is a few variations on the select command. Follow these steps to build a SQL scratch pad:

1. **Place a push button on a new form and set its caption to &Go.**

2. **Drop a memo box and set its Align property to alTop.**

   Don't worry if the memo box covers the push button.

3. **Set the memo box's ScrollBars property to ssVertical.**

4. **Place a query component on the form with its DatabaseName property set to the Demos alias.**

5. **Put a data source on the form and set its DataSet property to the query.**

6. **Add a data-aware grid with Align set to alClient, and connect it to the data source.**

7. **Create an OnClick event handler for the hidden button containing these lines:**

```
WITH Query1 DO
  BEGIN
    Close;
    SQL := Memo1.Lines;
    Open;
  END;
```

8. **Save the project as SQLPAD.**

You've built an SQL scratch pad, a program you can use to fool around with SQL statements. Type an SQL statement in the memo box and press Alt+G; the results of the query show up in the data grid. Try a few statements that pull data from the Delphi demo databases. Run the SQLPAD program and enter this statement:

```
select * from biolife
```

Press Alt+G and the grid should fill with all the data from the biolife table. Now enter this:

```
select category, common_name from biolife
```

This time only the two specified fields show up. Try this:

```
select species name from biolife
```

Whoops! The query gags on that statement. The problem is that the field name consists of two separate words. To make such a name palatable to the query, you must surround it with quotation marks *and* prefix it with the table name followed by a period, like this:

```
select biolife."species name" from biolife
```

The query component may also gag on field names that are the same as SQL command words. Any time an SQL command is unexpectedly rejected, try this: Find each field name in the command, surround it with quotation marks, and prefix it with the table name and a period. The table name itself may require quotation marks, too, if it must include a file extension or special characters. For example, queries on dBASE files must include the .DBF extension in the filename.

So the select command selects fields from a specified table. Use an asterisk to represent all fields. If you want to see only certain fields, you simply list their names separated by commas. You can fool with the SQLPAD some more. Take the preceding query and enter it with each word on its own line (but don't break up the quoted field name). Note that it works just jim-dandy. Now run this query:

```
select * from customer where state="HI"
```

As you'd expect, the grid now contains data only for customers in Hawaii. Now try this:

```
select * from customer where country<>"America" and
Company like "%SCUBA%"
```

You've selected all non-U.S.-residing customers with SCUBA in the company name.

The where clause is what makes the select command truly useful. With this clause, you can locate all records that match a simple or complex set of conditions. You can combine conditions logically using AND or OR. Try a few more where clauses. Here's a two-table query:

```
select orders.orderno, orders.itemstotal,
customer.company from orders,customer
where orders.custno=customer.custno and
customer.company like "%Dive%"
order by customer.company
```

This query pulls data from two different tables to display each order number, its total cost, and the company name, but only for customers whose name contains Dive. The last line contains a new SQL keyword, order by. As you might guess, this controls the sort order of the output. This particular command's output is sorted by company. If these SQL commands are making you dizzy, you may skip the next exercise. Still here? Good! Okay, for the grand finale, carefully enter this SQL statement:

```
select customer.company, items.orderno,
parts.description, vendors.vendorname
from parts, vendors, items, orders, customer
where parts.vendorno = vendors.vendorno and
items.partno = parts.partno and
items.orderno = orders.orderno and
orders.custno = customer.custno and
customer.company like "%SCUBA%"
order by customer.company, parts.description
```

The massive query you just entered displays data drawn from four different tables based on conditions defining relationships between data elements drawn from *five* different tables. For each customer whose company name contains SCUBA, the query displays the name of each item ordered, the vendor who supplies the particular item, and the number of the order. Figure 11-13 shows the result with rows sorted first by company and then by description.

Most of the time, your SQL statements won't come anywhere remotely near this level of complexity. The usual query is more like "Find me all the blacksmiths named Jones." But if you *need* to do something complicated, you can! Actually, a bona fide SQL-meister can use SQL statements to create new tables, delete rows, update fields based on a formula, and probably pay off the National Debt.

Get me that report!

The Delphi report component is an odd bird. It looks like almost any other component, and it has properties and methods like a component, but effectively it's just a door. Knock on the door by double-clicking and you find that you've activated ReportSmith, the reporting product that comes with

Delphi. Call the Run method of a report component and you're really running ReportSmith Runtime. This is all a subtle way of leading up to the fact that I'm not going to talk about the report component. ReportSmith is complex and powerful enough to merit a book all its own!

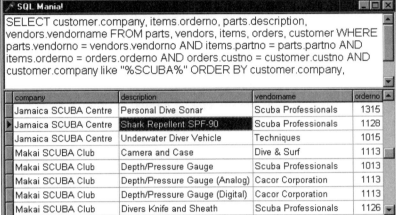

Figure 11-13:
This alarming SQL statement pulls together data from five different tables.

Database Guts

As you work with database components, you're constantly confronted with the seamy side of database society. You see lists of databases on the system, lists of tables in a database, lists of fields in a table, and so on. Because Delphi itself is written in Delphi, these lists must be available to your programs as well.

The list of databases and list of tables in a database emanate from the session component. The invisible and singular session component is present in any program that uses database components. It has methods that return a list of all database aliases on the system, or a list of all tables in a database. Add DB to your form's uses clause and you can call on the session component for help. The table and query components include a similar method that returns a list of field names. You can also request a list of indexes from a table.

A single-minded program that's obsessed with one particular database won't have any use for these methods. They only come into play in programs for generalized database access, like the database viewer you built earlier. Now you use them to create a table-selection form that lets the user make an informed choice. Just follow these steps:

1. **Start a new project based on the fixed-size form template.**

2. **Place an ordinary combo box near the top left corner, with a label captioned &Databases: above it.**

3. **Set the combo box's Style property to csDropDownList.**

4. **Below the combo box, place a label captioned &Tables: and below that, a list box with Sorted set to True.**

5. **Connect the FocusControl property of the two labels to the corresponding component.**

6. **Place another sorted list box next to the first so that the tops of the two list boxes line up.**

7. **Above the new list box, place a label captioned &Fields:.**

8. **Below the new list box, place another label and a short list box, giving the label the caption &Indexes:.**

9. **Connect the FocusControl property of the two labels to the corresponding list box.**

Check your layout against Figure 11-14.

Figure 11-14:
This
database
selection
form relies
on the
session
component.

10. **Put two bitmap buttons at the top right of the form, setting their Kind properties to bkOK and bkCancel.**

11. **Drop a table component on the form and set its Name property to WorkTable.**

12. **Create an OnActivate event handler for the form with these lines:**

The database component

Did you notice that I've gone through about 90 percent of this chapter without talking about the database component? Because I'm covering local database access here, the database component is simply not necessary. It becomes truly useful only when you start upsizing your projects to work with remote databases. At that time, you'll have to be concerned with passwords and user log-in procedures, which are handled by the database component. It also has the capability to maintain a connection with the remote database even when none of the tables are open.

When you move up to client/server, you also get to worry about how your program interacts with other completely separate programs — usually on completely separate machines — accessing the same data. The Delphi tables already supply transaction processing for remote tables. Basically, that means that, even if your program dies a horrible death, it can't corrupt the database. It will never give up the ghost halfway through updating a record because it doesn't commit the update permanently until all the data has been transferred. The database component's TransIsolation property controls precisely when other programs accessing the same data can see your program's changes. Aren't you glad you don't have to understand this . . . yet?

```
Session.GetDatabaseNames(ComboBox1.Items);
ComboBox1.ItemIndex := 0;
ComboBox1Change(ComboBox1);
```

13. **Put these two lines in an OnChange event handler for the combo box:**

```
Session.GetTableNames(ComboBox1.Text,
   '', True, True, ListBox1.Items);
```

14. **Now write an OnDeactivate event handler for the form using these two lines:**

```
ListBox2.Clear;
ListBox3.Clear;
```

15. **Double-click the first list box and enter these lines for its OnClick event handler:**

```
WITH WorkTable, ListBox1 DO
   BEGIN
      DatabaseName := ComboBox1.Text;
      TableName := Items[ItemIndex];
      TheDatabase := DatabaseName;
      TheTable := TableName;
      GetFieldNames(ListBox2.Items);      ListBox3.Clear;
```

(continued)

(continued)

```
      GetIndexNames(ListBox3.Items);
   END;
```

16. **Find the comment { Public declarations } near the top of the file.**

17. **Just after the comment, insert this line:**

```
TheDatabase, TheTable : String;
```

18. **Set the form's Name to PickTable and its Caption to Select Table.**

19. **Right-click the form to add it to the repository.**

20. **Load the DBVIEWER project from earlier in this chapter.**

21. **Choose File⇨New from the menu and flip to the Forms page.**

22. **Choose the newly created table-selection form from the repository.**

23. **Delete the Open File common dialog component.**

24. **Finally, replace the code in the speed button's OnClick event handler with these lines:**

```
WITH PickTable DO
   IF ShowModal = mrOK THEN
      WITH Table1 DO
         BEGIN
            Close;
            DatabaseName := TheDatabase;
            TableName := TheTable;
            Open;
         END;
```

Note the name of the unit associated with the table-selection form and add that name to the main form's uses clause. With the addition of this table-selection form, your simple database editor program can browse and edit tables on a wide variety of remote databases as easily as files on the local disk drive.

You can use this table-selection form (refer to Figure 11-14) in any general database access program you write. It's a lot easier to choose between ZPHDBBRX.DB and SLRTBFST.DB when you can see a list of the fields in each.

Database programming is a huge subject. I could go on and on with more and more examples, but you know enough now to go ahead on your own. The next chapter covers some truly phenomenal user interface components that encapsulate the Windows 95 look.

Part IV
Real Programming

Re·al Pro·gram·mers

Real Programmers have trouble supressing homicidal tendencies when asked "Are you sure?"

In this part . . .

In the previous parts, you had a field day tinkering with the incredibly rich set of tools in the Delphi parts cabinet. Talk about rapid application development! Getting a prototype running is usually just a matter of scattering components on the form and setting a few properties. And moving from prototype to finished program is mostly a matter of writing some event handlers.

So far, you've simply copied event handler code from this book. You've gained a clear enough impression of Delphi's language to pick it out in a police lineup:

```
+= ListPtr->ToppingPrice;
```

Sumimasen ga, ima wa nanji desu ka?

```
WITH Sender AS TListBox DO Clear;
```

Budtye idyotom, a nye parasitom.

```
LINE INPUT "Enter your name: ", Name$.
```

(You *did* choose the third item, right?)

In Part IV, I go into detail about the code that Delphi writes for you, and take a close look at the elements. No, not antimony, arsenic, aluminum, selenium, and so on — the elements that make up a program! Sooner or later you need to look at the Delphi manuals, but these chapters prepare you so that the experience isn't too much of a shock. To round out the section, I talk about what you can do when good programs do bad things.

Chapter 12

Windows 95 Components

• •

In This Chapter

▶ Giving your programs the genuine Windows 95 look and feel

▶ Tweaking numbers with track bar and UpDown components

▶ Displaying and editing a form's menu using a tree view

▶ Drawing bitmap images with transparent parts

▶ Using a list view to display and arrange a list of names

▶ Turning the simple text editor into a font-smart simple word processor

• •

*E*very Windows 95 program contains squared-off buttons, left-aligned captions, and tiny icons in the title bar. If you want your programs to truly have the look and feel of Windows 95, make use of the special user interface elements that Windows 95 brings to the game. With Delphi 3, you can use Windows 95 components in your programs. As an added bonus, the components work fine under Windows NT, too.

Choosing Windows 95 Components

Flip to the Win32 page in the Component palette and check out the Windows 95 components. If you don't know quite what to *do* with them, look at Table 12-1.

Delphi Has Its Ups and Downs

The spin button is among the nifty interface components that Windows 95 introduced as a built-in construction. Delphi 3 offers this component under the guise of the UpDown component.

Table 12-1	Problems Solved by Windows 95 Components
Task	*Component*
Enable the user to tweak a numeric value up or down.	UpDown. See "Delphi Has Its Ups and Downs."
Display status information at the bottom of the form.	Status bar. See "Bar Hopping."
Display and adjust the value of a continuous numeric quantity.	Track bar. See "Bar Hopping."
Display the progress of an ongoing process.	Progress bar. See "Bar Hopping."
Enable direct entry of shortcut keys like those used in menus.	Hotkey. See "Hot! Hot! Hotkey!"
Display bitmap images with "transparent" areas.	Image list. See "The Strong, Silent Image List."
Store images for use with tree view and list view components.	Image list. See "The Strong, Silent Image List."
Display and optionally edit hierarchical data outline form.	Tree view. See "View from a Tree."
Create a form with multiple tabbed pages.	PageControl. See "Keeping Tabs on Your Pages."
Display a set of selection tabs without associated pages.	TabControl. See "Keeping Tabs on Your Pages."
Display a multisection header with resizable and clickable columns.	HeaderControl. See "Two Headers Are Better Than One."
Display, organize, and edit a list of items, with icons representing each item.	List view. See "The Amazing List View."
Edit unlimited-size documents using multiple font and paragraph styles.	Rich text component. See "Get Rich (Text) Quick!"

Properties

As does a spin button, the UpDown component consists of two joined buttons with cuneiform wedges pointing up and down. Unlike the spin button, you can't change the triangular glyphs, but at least they resize along with the component. And by setting the Orientation property to udHorizontal, you can effectively transform it into a RightLeft component. (No, its name doesn't change!)

As the user clicks or holds one of the buttons, the Position property spins through the range of values defined by the Min and Max properties. If the Wrap property is True, trying to raise the Position property past Max makes it wrap back to Min (shades of Sisyphus).

UpDown components are gregarious; they like to hang out with their component buddies. Setting the UpDown component's Associate property to an edit box on your form produces the equivalent of a spin edit. The UpDown component leaps to a new position at the left or right of the edit box, depending on the value of the AlignButton property, and the "buddy" edit box displays the UpDown's Position property. If the Thousands property is True, the value shown in the edit box includes thousands of separators. Now you know the essential properties for an UpDown component.

Events

The ever-popular OnClick event happens whenever the user clicks one of the UpDown component's buttons. The OnClick event is also triggered repeatedly if the user holds down one of the buttons to spin through possible values. The OnClick event carries a parameter that tells which of the buttons you clicked.

Occasionally, you need to write an event handler for the OnChanging event, perhaps to require the user's confirmation before raising the Position property past a certain danger level. An OnChanging event handler can prevent the UpDown component's Position property from changing, if necessary.

You now have the keys, so why not take this component out for a spin?

1. **Drop two edit boxes and two UpDown components on a new form.**

2. **Set the AlignButton property of the first UpDown component to udRight and set its Max property to 9999.**

3. **Set the other's Min property to 50 and its Wrap property to True.**

4. **Associate one UpDown component with each of the edit boxes.**

5. **Add two list boxes to the form and fill their Items properties with names of friends, enemies, or whatever strikes your fancy.**

6. **Place two more UpDown components on the form and associate one with each list box — they stretch to fit.**

7. **Set the Max property for each UpDown component to one less than the number of items in its "buddy" list box.**

8. **Select the two new UpDown components and write an OnClick event handler for them containing the following two lines:**

```
WITH Sender AS TUpDown DO
   (Associate AS TListBox).ItemIndex := Max - Position;
```

The result should look something like Figure 12-1.

Figure 12-1:
The UpDown component combined with an edit box replaces the SpinEdit.

Ups and Downs

1,492

100

John
Paul
George
Ringo
(Pete)

Vulcan
Mercury
Venus
Earth
Mars
(Asteroids)
Jupiter
Saturn
Uranus
Neptune
Pluto
Persephone

9. **Run this program and try clicking the various UpDown components.**

The first UpDown paired with an edit box spins the value in its edit box from 0 to 9,999, adding thousands separators for numbers that need them. The other stays in the range from 50 to 100, wrapping back to 50 after it goes past 100 and vice versa. Clicking the UpDown that's associated with a list box selects the list box item corresponding to the UpDown component's position.

Actually, the connection between the UpDown component and the list box is reversed. If you literally set the list box item to the UpDown component's Position property, the up arrow moves the selection down and the down arrow moves it up. Confusing! To avoid this topsy-turvy situation, the OnClick handler subtracts the current position from the maximum value.

Bar Hopping

Like Las Vegas, Windows 95 has a lot of bars: status bars, progress bars, and track bars. All three of these components are similar to other components that you've already met. The progress bar works like a gauge, the track bar is a smarter and prettier scroll bar, and the status bar has a lot in common with a bottom-aligned panel. However, programs that use these spiffy components just *scream* "Windows 95 is spoken here!" If you're still thinking in Windows 3.1 terms, it's time to get used to working with these components in your Delphi 3 programs.

Progress bar properties and events

A progress bar's essential properties are Min, Max, and Position, corresponding to the gauge's MinValue, MaxValue, and Progress properties. A program can set the bar's Position, or it can call the StepIt method to advance the Position by the value of the Step property. If that seems too restrictive, free-spirited programmers can call the StepBy method to advance the position by any arbitrary amount. Events? Well, a progress bar does respond to the usual mouse and dragging events, but rarely do you need to write event handlers for one.

Where, you may ask, is the Color property? As it turns out, you can't control the color of a progress bar. The colored rectangles that show progress always use the system highlight color (clHighlight, in Delphi parlance).

Track bar properties and events

The Windows 95 track bar component looks as if it belongs on the front of a fancy stereo. As does a scroll bar, the track bar enables the user to slide a gadget back and forth or up and down. The Min and Max properties set the trackbar's range, and the Position property tells just where it's pointing. The Orientation property controls whether the trackbar is horizontal or vertical. That's where the similarity to a scroll bar ends, though. A number of other properties control the appearance and behavior of the trackbar. The TickMarks property determines where the tick mark lines appear (one side, the other, or both), and the TickStyle property controls the spacing. If TickStyle is tsNone, no tick marks appear. If the TickStyle property is set to tsManual, a tick mark shows up at each end of the trackbar, and the program can set additional tick marks with the SetTick method. And if the TickStyle property is set to tsAuto, tick mark spacing is controlled by the Frequency property; if Frequency is 5, for example, a tick appears at positions corresponding to 5, 10, 15, 20, and so on.

Sometimes highlighting part of a track bar's range is handy. For example, if the track bar controls a steam boiler's temperature, the low end is too cold to function, the high end is dangerously hot, and the highlighted middle is *just* right. The SelStart and SelEnd properties define this highlight. A triangular tick mark appears at the position defined by each, and the bar itself is highlighted in between. Like a scroll bar, the track bar is controlled using the keyboard. The LineSize property defines how many ticks the arrow keys move the slider, and the PageSize property controls how far the PgUp and PgDn keys move it. The big event for a track bar is OnChange. This event triggers after you move the slider by using the mouse or the keyboard.

Status bar properties and methods

By default, the status bar is aligned at the bottom of the form that you drop it on, and putting it anywhere else rarely makes sense. The status bar looks like a panel, but it has a kind of triangular tread in the bottom right corner that serves as an oversized resizing handle for the form. Setting the SizeGrip property to False hides the tread.

If all you want to do is display a simple line of text in the status bar, you can set the SimplePanel property to True and the SimpleText property to the text that you want. Simple! However, most of the time you want to create two or more subpanels within the status bar. For example, the first subpanel in the Delphi 3 Code Editor window displays the current cursor position.

To set up subpanels, you double-click the status bar's Panels property and use the Panels Editor dialog box that appears (see Figure 12-2). For each panel you create, you can set the text, width, and justification, as well as whether the panel's bevel edge is raised, lowered, or unchanged from the status bar itself. If you set the Style for a panel to Owner Draw, your program draws just about anything on the panel in response to the OnDrawPanel event.

Figure 12-2:
You can
create the
subpanels
of a
status bar
component
by using the
StatusBar
Panels
Editor.

The user can click or double-click a status bar, but your program must do a bit of head-scratching to determine which subpanel is clicked.

Visiting a few bars

You can have fun with some other bars; just follow these steps:

1. **Place a status bar on a new form and then add a scroll box with its Align property set to alClient.**

2. **Drop a progress bar and a track bar on the scroll box, both with the same width.**

3. **Set the Max property for both to 50 and set the track bar's Frequency to 5.**

4. **Create an OnChange event handler for the track bar using this line:**

```
ProgressBar1.Position := TrackBar1.Position;
```

Whenever you use a status bar, fill the rest of the form with a client-aligned scroll box, as in this program. Otherwise, if the user shrinks the form small enough so that scroll bars appear, the scroll bars interfere with the status bar.

5. **Double-click the status bar's Panels property.**

6. **In the Panels Editor, create four subpanels and leave the Text property blank for all of them.**

7. **Set the Width of the second subpanel to 120 and set the Style of the third to Owner Draw.**

8. **Place a second track bar on the scroll box, again stretching it to the width of the form. Set its properties as follows:**

Property	Value
Frequency	4
Max	212
Min	32
SelEnd	120
SelStart	80

9. **Create an OnChange event handler for the track bar containing the following lines:**

```
WITH Sender AS TTrackBar DO
  BEGIN
    StatusBar1.Panels[0].Text :=
      Format('%d°', [Position]);
    IF Position < SelStart THEN
      StatusBar1.Panels[1].Text := 'Too cold'
```

(continued)

(continued)

```
      ELSE IF Position > SelEnd THEN
         StatusBar1.Panels[1].Text := 'Too hot'
      ELSE StatusBar1.Panels[1].Text := 'Juuust right!';
   StatusBar1.Panels[2].Text :=
         StatusBar1.Panels[1].Text;
END;
```

10. **Put these lines in an OnDrawPanel event handler for the status bar:**

```
WITH TrackBar2 DO
   IF Position < SelStart THEN
      StatusBar.Canvas.Brush.Color := clAqua
   ELSE IF Position > SelEnd THEN
      StatusBar.Canvas.Brush.Color := clRed
   ELSE StatusBar.Canvas.Brush.Color := clLime;
StatusBar.Canvas.FillRect(Rect);
```

Figure 12-3 shows the resulting program. As you slide the upper track bar's slider, the progress bar follows. Sliding the lower track bar reports the temperature of a theoretical bowl of porridge. The first panel shows the temperature, the second displays a message based on the temperature, and the third panel is icy blue for too cold, blazing red for too hot, or calm green for just right.

Track bars

Progress bar

Figure 12-3:
The status bar, track bar, and progress bar add a Windows 95 look to your programs.

Status bar

Are you still worrying about why the OnChange handler for the second track bar sets the Text property of the third subpanel, the one that's set to Owner Draw? Good! That shows you're thinking! As it happens, a *change* to the subpanel's Text property triggers the OnDrawPanel event. That's perfect, because there's no need to redraw the colored panel except as the track bar's position moves into or out of the selected area.

Hot! Hot! Hotkey!

Remember the days of Windows 3.1? (Maybe it was before your time!)
Remember good old Program Manager? The Program Item Properties dialog
in Program Manager had a clever feature: To set the hotkey for a program
item, you simply select the item and press the key combination. You can use
the Delphi 3 hotkey component to jam this functionality into any program.

Properties and events

In a fit of self-reference, the most important property of a hotkey component
is Hotkey. The Hotkey property represents a specific key with a specific
combination of Ctrl, Shift, and Alt modifiers, and it's encoded in the same
way as the Shortcut property of a menu item (a fact you use later in this
chapter). The other two killer properties are InvalidKeys and Modifiers. By
setting subproperties of InvalidKeys to True, you can prevent the user from
entering hotkeys that use particular key combinations. By default, the
hkNone and hkShift subproperties are True — meaning that a hotkey with
no modifiers isn't valid, nor is a hotkey with only the Shift modifier.

The Modifiers property sits on the sidelines unless at least one of the
InvalidKeys subproperties is true. If the user selects an invalid key combination, the set of keys specified in Modifiers is used instead. By default, only
the hkAlt subproperty is True. Using the default values for both InvalidKeys
and Modifiers, if the user presses just *a* or *A,* the resulting hotkey is Alt+A.

Make sure that you don't set the Modifiers property to the same key combination represented by the InvalidKeys property. For example, if hcAlt is the
only True subproperty under InvalidKeys, don't make hkAlt the only True
subproperty under Modifiers. Mismatching these properties doesn't do any
harm, but it doesn't do any good either!

The hotkey component doesn't have an OnChange event. Its event list is meager,
consisting of just OnExit, OnEnter, and the three standard mouse events.

Follow these steps to see how hotkey components work:

1. **Drop a hotkey component on a new form and double-click its
   InvalidKeys property.**

2. **Set the hcShift subproperty to False.**

3. **Double-click the Modifiers property and set all four subproperties
   to True.**

4. **Run the program, click the hotkey component, and try pressing
   various key combinations.**

Press the letter *X* alone and the hotkey changes to Ctrl+Shift+Alt+X. That's because InvalidKeys.hcNone is True, meaning an unmodified key isn't valid.

5. **Run the program again after tweaking the InvalidKeys and Modifiers properties, to get a feel for the possibilities.**

The Modifiers property expands into hkShift, hkCtrl, hkAlt, and hkExt. The first three are clear, but what's hkExt? The Delphi Help file says that it means the Extra key is used as a modifier, but you don't find the Extra key on your keyboard. In fact, hkExt distinguishes the extended Alt and Ctrl keys at the right of many keyboards from the original left-side Alt and Ctrl and also distinguishes the extended navigation keys to the left of the numeric keypad from their numeric keypad equivalents.

The Strong, Silent Image List

The Delphi image list component stores a set of bitmap images and displays them on demand, optionally simulating a transparent background. The image list component is incredibly useful, but it does almost all its work at the bidding of other components. For example, the various images that appear in list view and tree view components reside in image lists. The image list Width and Height properties control the size of the stored bitmaps. Most of the other important properties for an image list are set not through the Object Inspector, but by using the ImageList Editor (see Figure 12-4), invoked by double-clicking the image list component.

The only event an image list generates is OnChange, triggered by a change to the component. Most programs simply use the image list without attaching any event handlers.

Figure 12-4:
You use the ImageList Editor to store one or more images in an image list component.

One image list feature is useful independent of any other component. Bitmaps are always rectangular, even if the images they contain are free-form. Displaying the bitmap draws the whole rectangle, including the useless background. An image list has the built-in capability to treat the background color as if it were transparent. All you do is call the image list's Draw method.

If you set an image list's BkColor property to a specific color, you disable the transparent-drawing feature. Leave BkColor set to clNone if you want to use a transparent color. Notice too, that if you use 256-color bitmaps in an image list, all your bitmaps must have exactly the same palette. Sticking with 16-color bitmaps and avoiding the palette problem is best.

Follow these steps for insight into transparency:

1. **Start a new project and place an image list component on it, setting the Width and Height properties to 32.**

2. **Double-click the image list to open the ImageList Editor, press the Add button, and select an icon whose image isn't rectangular.**

3. **Pull down the Transparent color combo box and select the color that represents the icon's background.**

4. **Set the form's Color property to $B3B3B3.**

   ($B3B3B3 shows up as a grainy dithered pattern in 256-color mode, but it doesn't show up at all in your box of crayons.)

5. **Double-click the form and put the following line in the resulting OnCreate event handler:**

   ```
   PtList := TList.Create;
   ```

6. **Page up until you see the comment { Private Declarations }, and add the line PtList : TList; immediately after.**

7. **Start an OnMouseUp event handler for the form, and replace the begin..end pair supplied by Delphi with the following code:**

   ```
   VAR R : TRect;
   begin
     PtList.Add(Pointer(SmallPoint(X, Y)));
     R := Bounds(X, Y, 32, 32);
     InvalidateRect(Handle, @R, True);
   end;
   ```

8. **Finally, create an OnPaint event handler for the form, delete the begin..end pair supplied by Delphi, and add the following lines:**

```
VAR N : Integer;
begin
  FOR N := 0 TO PtList.Count-1 DO
    WITH TSmallPoint(PtList[N]) DO
      ImageList1.Draw(Canvas, X, Y, 0);
end;
```

Figure 12-5 shows the resulting program.

Figure 12-5:
The image list correctly draws these happy circular icons while letting the background show outside the circles.

Image List Transparent Area Demo

Each click on the example form adds a point to the list stored in PtList. It also calls the Windows API function InvalidateRect, which triggers an OnPaint event. In response to this event, the form flips through the PtList list and draws the image list component's image at each point in the list. The background portions of the image don't cover the form's background or other images; they're effectively transparent. Many of the following examples use image list components.

View from a Tree

If you use the Windows 95 Explorer to poke around the files on your disks, you're already familiar with the tree view component. Explorer's left panel is a tree view representing all the drives and directories on your system. Explorer shows the hierarchical directory structure and uses a little icon at the left of the items to distinguish hard disks from directories, from CD-ROM drives, and so on.

The tree view component can represent any kind of data that has a hierarchical arrangement. You could define your company's organizational chart in a tree view — put yourself at the top!

Properties

The Images and StateImages properties of a tree view are both image lists. Images holds the bitmaps that represent the items themselves, like the disk drive images in Explorer. StateImages holds special images that indicate an item is in a particular state. What's a *state?* It's whatever you, the programmer, say it is!

The tree view's Items property is a collection of objects called TTreeNodes. The Items property has a whole set of methods named Add, AddChild, AddFirst, and so on for adding new nodes, each of which creates a node with the text you specify and returns the node in case you want to set some other properties. The most important properties of tree nodes are ImageIndex, SelectedIndex, and StateIndex. ImageIndex tells which image from the Images list represents the item, and SelectedIndex says which of those images gets used if the item is selected. Similarly, StateIndex is an index into the StateImages list. If StateIndex is something other than –1, the state image appears to the left of the regular image.

Other properties control the tree view's appearance. If HideSelection is True (as it is by default) the tree view's selection is hidden if it loses the focus. ShowButtons controls whether plus/minus buttons for expanding or collapsing parts of the tree appear. ShowLines determines whether or not the tree view displays lines connecting the nodes. If ShowRoot is True, the tree's root node is visible. Tree view has loads of other properties, but trying to absorb them all at once could be dangerous to your health.

Events

Unless you set the ReadOnly property to True, the user can edit the item captions. Two separate clicks (not a double-click) on the same node opens an edit window and triggers an OnEditing event. After the user finishes editing, the OnEdited event occurs.

An attempt to select a different node sets off the OnChanging event; your program can imperiously forbid the change by responding to that event and setting AllowChange to False. If the selection *does* change, an OnChange event bursts forth. The tree view component also spews events when the user expands or collapses a branch of the tree.

Tree views can sort themselves, and there's built-in support for user-defined sorting through the OnCompare event. An OnCompare event handler receives two tree nodes as parameters and responds by indicating whether the first is less than, equal to, or greater than the second. If you want to rig the sorting mechanism so that your friends always come to the top of the list, OnCompare is the place to do it!

Growing a menu tree

Though at times the overwhelming list of properties and methods of the tree view component seems to bury the practical uses, tree view can be very useful.

Make a tree by following these steps:

1. **Start a new project and drop a main menu component on the form.**

2. **Use the Menu Designer to add several templates.**

   Go wild! Don't worry about creating event handlers for the menu items; all you're trying to do is make a complicated menu structure.

3. **Create a new form and then switch back to the main form and choose File⇨Use Unit from the menu bar.**

4. **Select the secondary form's unit and click OK.**

5. **Drop a button on the main form and put the Form2.ShowModal; line in its OnClick event handler.**

The main form is now complete, so it's time to work on the secondary form. First, use the Image Editor to create seven 16-x-16 bitmaps. The first should suggest the root of a menu tree, and the next three should represent a top-level menu item, a submenu item, and a cascading menu item, respectively. The last three represent the top-level menu item, submenu item, and cascading menu item after they're selected. You can look back at Figure 12-4 to see some ideas for the last six bitmaps. Choose a little-used color such as clOlive for the parts of the image you want to be transparent.

If you get the order wrong in an image list's bitmaps, you can just drag and drop them into the correct order in the ImageList Editor.

Place an image list on the secondary form and load the seven bitmaps into it, setting the transparent color for each to clOlive. Put a tree view on the form and set its Images property to the image list you just created. Now double-click the form itself to start an OnCreate event handler, and replace the begin..end pair supplied by Delphi with the following code:

```
VAR
  Root : TTreeNode;
  N    : Integer;
  procedure StoreIt(TN : TTreeNode; TM: TMenuItem);
  VAR
    NewN : TTreeNode;
    N    : Integer;
  begin
    NewN := TreeView1.Items.AddChildObject(TN,
      TM.Caption, TM);
    IF TN = Root THEN NewN.ImageIndex := 1
    ELSE IF TM.Count = 0 THEN NewN.ImageIndex := 2
    ELSE NewN.ImageIndex := 3;
    IF NewN.ImageIndex > 0 THEN
      NewN.SelectedIndex := NewN.ImageIndex + 3;
    FOR N := 0 TO TM.Count-1 DO
      StoreIt(NewN, TM.Items[N]);
  end;
begin
  Root := TreeView1.Items.Add(NIL, 'Menu');
  WITH Application.MainForm.Menu DO
    FOR N := 0 TO Items.Count-1 DO
      StoreIt(Root, Items[N]);
  TreeView1.FullExpand;
end;
```

The modified event handler created in this code adds a root node to the tree view. Then it steps through the main menu of the main form and adds each menu item to the tree. For each node, the ImageIndex and SelectedIndex properties are set to the bitmaps that represent the corresponding menu item type, whether it's a top-level menu, a lone submenu item, or a cascading submenu. Next, you must perform a seemingly pointless ritual. Drop a main menu onto the secondary form, save the project, and then delete the main menu.

After you add a component to a form and save it, Delphi puts any necessary units in the uses clause automatically. Deleting the component doesn't change the uses clause. By adding and deleting a main menu, you gain access to the Menus unit, which is needed by the event handler you just wrote.

Place a bitmapped button component on the form and set its Kind property to bkClose. Then run the program. You find that after you click the button on the main form, the secondary form appears with the main form's menu structure displayed in a tree view. Each item has an image representing its type, and the selected item gets a special image. Wow!

But wait! There's more! Exit the program and choose the secondary form again. Add a hotkey component and set its Hotkey property to None. Place an ordinary button captioned Assign Hotkey on the form. Create three more 16-x-16 bitmaps, one representing changed text, one representing a changed hotkey, and one representing both. I used simple circles containing *T* (for Text), *K* (for Key), and *TK*. Place a second image list on the form and double-click it to open the ImageList Editor. Add the first image twice, and then add the other two; set the Transparent color for each to whatever color you used for the background. Set the tree view's StateImages property to this second image list.

Create an OnChange event handler for the tree view component and insert the following lines:

```
IF Node.Data <> NIL THEN
  HotKey1.HotKey := TMenuItem(Node.Data).Shortcut;
```

This code sets up the hotkey component to display the hotkey of the selected menu item. Now use the following lines to replace the begin..end pair of an OnClick handler for the Assign Hotkey button:

```
VAR P : Pointer;
begin
  P := TreeView1.Selected.Data;
  IF P <> NIL THEN
    BEGIN
      TMenuItem(P).Shortcut := HotKey1.HotKey;
      WITH TreeView1.Selected DO
        IF (StateIndex = 1) OR (StateIndex = 3) THEN
          StateIndex := 3
        ELSE StateIndex := 2;
    END;
end;
```

After you click the Assign Hotkey button, the menu item on the main form that matches the selected item in the tree has its Shortcut property changed to match the hotkey. Also, the tree node has its StateIndex set to 2 or 3, meaning that the hotkey changed or the hotkey and the text changed.

Start an OnEdited event handler for the tree view, and insert these lines:

```
IF Node.Data <> NIL THEN
  BEGIN
    TMenuItem(Node.Data).Caption := S;
    WITH Node DO
```

```
      IF StateIndex >= 2 THEN StateIndex := 3
      ELSE StateIndex := 1;
  END;
```

After the user edits an item in the tree view, the matching item in the main form's menu changes, and the tree node has its state set to 1 or 3, meaning the text changed or the text and hotkey changed.

Whee! You're finished! Figure 12-6 shows the resulting program. The secondary form displays the main form's menu as a tree. Selecting an item in the tree pours the shortcut key for that item into the hotkey component. Pressing the Assign Hotkey button dumps the hotkey component's hotkey back into the selected menu item. And editing an item's text in the tree view changes the caption of the corresponding menu item. A state icon appears to show that an item has had its hotkey, text, or both changed. And after you close the secondary form, you find the changes have indeed taken place in the main menu.

Figure 12-6: This form uses a tree view to display and change the captions and shortcut keys for the main form's menu items.

To sum up, each item in the tree has an image that's drawn from the tree view's Images property; the selected item has a special image. If an item's StateIndex property is greater than zero, an extra image drawn from the tree view's StateImages property appears to the left of the main image. The expand/collapse buttons appear if the ShowButtons property is True, and the connecting lines appear if the ShowLines property is True.

Keeping Tabs on Your Pages

The TabControl and PageControl components resemble the familiar TabSet and TabbedNotebook, but they're built into Windows 95. You want to use these for the Windows 95 look. The PageControl actually has some advantages over TabbedNotebook. As for TabControl, well, it's just another pretty face.

Properties

The TabControl's most important property is Tabs, a list of strings that become the tab captions. TabIndex is the index of the selected tab, and MultiLine controls how the TabControl reacts if it's too narrow to show all the tabs. If MultiLine is True, the tabs reorganize into multiple lines. If not, the control sprouts a pair of tiny arrow buttons pointing left and right. These buttons enable you to scroll all the tabs into view. It's worth pointing out that no provision is made for owner-draw tabs.

The PageControl has a MultiLine property that works in the same way, and its ActivePage property holds the name of the selected page. Surprisingly, it doesn't have a Pages property — at least not in the way the TabbedNotebook does. To add a new page, you right-click the control itself and choose New Page from the pop-up menu. Each new page is itself a component — a TabSheet. The essential properties for a TabSheet are Caption, TabVisible, and Enabled. Yes, you can easily hide or disable individual pages. By contrast, the TabControl's tabs are inseparable; you can't hide or disable one without the others.

Events

Like the TabSet component, a TabControl generates an OnChanging event after the user clicks a new tab and generates an OnChanging event when the change takes place. The OnChanging event handler can refuse to permit the user to switch tabs, perhaps because data entry is incomplete in the current tab.

The PageControl has the same set of events as the TabControl. The TabSheet's event collection is limited to the simplest mouse and dragging events. Try these steps to get some idea about how these components work:

1. **Drop a TabControl on a new form and set its Align property to alTop, and then double-click its Tabs property and add six or eight items.**

   Give it enough tabs so that they don't all fit on the form.

2. **Set its MultiLine property to True and adjust its height to just barely show all the tabs.**

3. **Place a PageControl on the form, aligned to fill the rest of the client area.**

4. **Repeatedly right-click the PageControl and choose New Page until, again, you have too many tabs to fit in the form's width.**

5. **Leave MultiLine set to False.**

6. **On the first page, place two check boxes captioned Sheet 2 visible and Sheet 3 enabled; set the Checked property to True for both.**

7. **Put this line in the OnClick event handler for the first check box:**

```
TabSheet2.TabVisible := (Sender AS TCheckBox).Checked;
```

8. **Use this line as the OnClick event handler for the second check box:**

```
TabSheet3.Enabled := (Sender AS TCheckBox).Checked;
```

9. **Place one or two components on TabSheet3 and then run the program.**

The result should look something like Figure 12-7.

Figure 12-7:
The
TabControl
has the
MultiLine
property set
to True; the
PageControl
has it set to
False.

Run the program and experiment. If you choose a tab in the back row of the MultiLine TabControl, that row moves to the front. Clicking the left and right buttons near the top right corner of the PageControl scrolls through the available tab sheets. If you remove the check from the first check box, the second tab sheet disappears. And if you remove the check from the second check box, the components on the third tab sheet are disabled, although the sheet itself can be selected.

No, the names on the tab sheets in Figure 12-7 don't represent a new line of microchips. They're the current names for the unstable elements with atomic numbers 104, 106, and 107. Unnilpentium (the hidden number 105) is also called neilsbohrium and rutherfordium. Whatever happened to short names such as lead, tin, or zinc?

Two Headers Are Better Than One

The Delphi Header component works, but it doesn't quite match the Windows 95 style — hence the new HeaderControl component. Like the Header component, HeaderControl holds column headings in its multiple sections and permits resizing of the sections. As an added bonus, the HeaderControl's sections can function as push buttons.

Properties

Sections is the only significant property of a HeaderControl. Double-click it to open the special Sections Editor. Each section has its own set of properties, including Text, Width, Alignment, and Min and Max (which constrain the resizing of the section). The Style property can be Text or Owner Draw, and if the Allow Click box is checked, the section functions as a button.

Events

If a particular section is marked as Owner Draw, you put code in the OnDrawSection event handler to draw it. OnSectionClick triggers after the user presses a section that allows clicks, and OnSectionResize occurs after a section is resized by the user. The OnSectionTrack event is more complex. It occurs once after section resizing begins, repeatedly during the resizing process, and once after section resizing ends.

What's the difference? Well, if you resize other components on your form in response to the OnSectionTrack event handler and the components are graphically complicated, your redrawing may be jerky. On the other hand, if you wait to resize other components until the OnSectionResize event occurs, your program may seem less responsive. It's a trade-off.

Time to get a feel for what's happening here. Follow these steps:

1. **Drop a HeaderControl on a new form and double-click its Sections property.**

2. **Add four sections named One, Two, Three, and Four.**

3. **Set the Min and Max properties for One to 50 and 100.**

4. **Remove the check next to Allow Click for section Two.**

5. **Set section Three's Alignment to Right justify.**

6. **Set Section Four's Style to Owner Draw.**

7. **Create an OnDrawSection event handler for the header using the following lines:**

```
HeaderControl.Canvas.Brush.Color := clRed;
HeaderControl.Canvas.Ellipse(Rect.Left+2, Rect.Top+2,
   Rect.Right-2, Rect.Bottom-2);
```

8. **Run the program and give it a whirl.**

You can resize all the sections, but the range of the first one is limited. All but the second section can be used like push buttons. And the fourth section has a red ellipse instead of a caption.

Drop an image component on the form, load a bitmap into it, and set its Stretch property to True. Move it to just below the header, and match its left edge and width to section Two. Now put the following code in an OnSectionResize handler for the HeaderControl:

```
IF Section.Text = 'One' THEN
  Image1.Left := Section.Left + Section.Width
ELSE IF Section.Text = 'Two' THEN
  Image1.Width := Section.Width;
```

In an OnSectionClick handler for the HeaderControl, use this single line:

```
Image1.Visible := NOT Image1.Visible;
```

Run the program again. Each time you resize the sections, the image moves to directly below section Two. Clicking any of the clickable sections toggles the image from visible to invisible and back.

Try one more trick. Create an OnSectionTrack handler for the Header-Control and put these lines into it. Be careful — they're not quite the same as the lines in the OnSectionResize handler:

```
IF Section.Text = 'One' THEN
  Image1.Left := Section.Left + Width
ELSE IF Section.Text = 'Two' THEN
  Image1.Width := Width;
```

Delete the lines you previously put into the OnSectionResize handler.

Don't delete the header portion of an event handler that you want to get rid of. Delete only the lines of code *you* added. Next time you save or run the program, Delphi neatly disposes of the empty event handler.

Now, whenever you run the program, the image moves or resizes while you're resizing section headers instead of snapping into place after the resizing operation finishes. Unless the image is very small or simple, however, it probably flickers as it moves.

The Amazing List View

You've met the tree view, which forms the left panel of the Windows 95 Explorer. What's in the right panel? A list view, of course. It's something like a list box, in the same way a jumbo jet is something like an oxcart. A list view can display a columnar list of items, but that's just one of its four display modes. In the large icons mode, it looks like an old Program Manager group window (ahhh! The good old Windows 3.1 days!) showing icons with titles beneath. In small icons mode, the titles appear to the right of the icons, which are arranged left-to-right in rows. You can move the icons around in either large or small icons mode (as long as the program includes code to move 'em). List mode is like small icons mode, but the items appear in columns and can't be moved around. Finally, details mode provides a multicolumn listing of any subitems associated with the items.

If these display modes aren't clear to you, just fire up Explorer and try them out. In Explorer, the details mode lists file date, time, size, and such trivia.

Properties

The Items property is the heart of a list view. It contains the list of items displayed by the component and their subitems as well. Double-clicking this property displays a specialized Items Editor. However, you're much more likely to create the item list under program control; I show you how in the section "A Liszt of composers."

The Columns property, which controls the columns displayed in details mode, also has its own special editor. For each column, you can set the Caption and Alignment. You can also specify whether the column width should initially match the widest item, the width of the header, or a fixed value.

As for those various display modes, they're controlled by the ViewStyle property. The icons and other images are stored in three image list properties named LargeImages, SmallImages, and StateImages. The first two clearly hold the images for the large icons and small icons display modes. StateImages is used to provide an extra icon indicating an item's state, like the same-named property in a tree view.

Events

The list view generates tons of events. Naturally, when the user selects an item, the OnChange event occurs. OnChanging is triggered first and enables a program to prevent the new selection. Item editing is built in, just as in the tree view, and the OnEditing and OnEdited events occur at the start and end of the editing process. The OnColumnClick event indicates that the user has clicked a column header. (You can set the ColumnClick property to False if you don't want to permit this scandalous behavior.) In Explorer, you click a column's header to sort by that column. Handily, the OnCompare event enabled your program to define how sorting takes place. Many more properties and events are associated with a list view, but we have enough of them now to give the list view a test drive.

A Liszt of composers

Follow these steps for some heavy list view insight:

1. **Place a list view on a new form and set its ViewStyle property to vsReport, set ReadOnly to True, and set DragMode to dmAutomatic.**

2. **Double-click its Columns property to fire up the Columns Editor.**

3. **Enter the column names: Composer, First Name, and Birth Year.**

4. **Choose the Item Width radio button for the first two and the Header Width radio button for the third.**

   The columns look all squished together after you finish, but don't worry. They straighten out as soon as the list view has some data to display.

5. **Double-click the form to start an OnCreate event handler, and replace the begin..end pair supplied by Delphi with the following impressive block of code:**

```
CONST
  Composers : ARRAY[0..9] OF String = ('Albinoni',
    'Buxtehude', 'Corelli', 'Dowland', 'Elgar',
      'Frescobaldi',
    'Grainger', 'Handel', 'Ives', 'Joplin');
  FirstNames : ARRAY[0..9] OF String = ('Tomaso',
      'Dietrich',
```

(continued)

(continued)

```
      'Arcangelo', 'John', 'Sir Edward', 'Girolamo',
         'Percy',
      'George', 'Charles', 'Scott');
   BirthYears : ARRAY[0..9] OF Word = (1671, 1637, 1653,
         1562,
      1857, 1583, 1882, 1685, 1874, 1868);
   Countries : ARRAY[0..9] OF Integer =
         (2,3,2,1,1,2,0,4,0,0);
VAR N : Integer;
begin
  WITH ListView1.Items DO
    FOR N := 0 TO 9 DO
      WITH Add DO
        BEGIN
          Caption :=  Composers[N];
          ImageIndex := Countries[N];
          StateIndex := 0;
          SubItems.Add(FirstNames[N]);
          SubItems.Add(IntToStr(BirthYears[N]));
        END;
end;
```

Whoops! I lied. There's actually very little code here. Most of what you typed is data. If you like, you can substitute your own favorite composers, but be sure to keep all four arrays in synch. Each number in the Countries array represents the composer's country of origin; in order from 0 to 4, the countries are U.S., U.K., Italy, Denmark, and Germany.

6. **Place an image list component on the form and set its Width and Height properties both to 32 (to create images to display next to these names).**

7. **Set the list view's LargeImages property to this image list; now find or draw 32-x-32 icons or bitmaps representing the flags of the United States, England, Italy, Denmark, and Germany, and add them to the image list in that order.**

8. **Place a second image list on the form and set the list view's SmallImages property to point to it.**

9. **Find or draw 16-x-16 bitmaps representing the same five countries and add them to this second image list.**

10. **You can add yet another image list, this one containing a 16-x-16 blank image, followed by a 16-x-16 image of musical notes.**

11. **Set the list view's StateImages property to this third image list.**

12. Place a radio group on the form, set its caption to View, set its Align property to alTop, and double-click its Items property.

13. Add four lines to the Items property: Large, Small, List, and Details.

14. Set its Columns property to 4 and its ItemIndex to 3.

15. Use these lines as an OnClick event handler for the radio group:

```
WITH Sender AS TRadioGroup DO
   ListView1.ViewStyle := TViewStyle(ItemIndex);
```

16. Set the list view's Align property to alClient.

17. Start an OnMouseDown event handler for it, and replace the Delphi-supplied begin..end pair with the following code:

```
VAR TheItem : TListItem;
begin
   IF Shift = [ssShift, ssLeft]THEN
      BEGIN
         TheItem := (Sender AS TListView).GetItemAt(X,Y);
         IF TheItem <> NIL THEN
            TheItem.StateIndex := TheItem.StateIndex XOR 1;
      END;
end;
```

18. Put the following two lines in an OnColumnClick event handler for the list view:

```
SortCol := Column.Index;
ListView1.AlphaSort;
```

19. Page up until you find the comment { private declarations }, and insert the following line immediately after it:

```
SortCol : Integer;
```

20. Back at the list view, create an OnCompare event handler and fill it with the following lines:

```
CASE SortCol OF
   0 : Compare := AnsiCompareStr(Item1.Caption,
      Item2.Caption);
   1 : Compare := AnsiCompareStr(Item1.SubItems[0],
         Item2.SubItems[0]);
   2 : Compare := AnsiCompareStr(Item1.SubItems[1],
         Item2.SubItems[1]);
END;
```

You're almost ready to roll; you have just a few more details to take care of.

21. Put this line in an OnDragOver event handler for the list view:

```
Accept := (Source = Sender);
```

22. Create an OnDragDrop event handler containing these two lines:

```
(Sender AS TListView).Selected.SetPosition(Point(X,Y));
(Sender AS TListView).Arrange(arDefault);
```

23. Go ahead and run the program.

Figure 12-8 shows two possible views of this program.

Figure 12-8: Two examples of the composers program show the large icons view and the details view; notice the large icon being dragged.

Experiment with all four views. Notice that you can reorder the icons only by dragging in the large and small icons views. Switch to the Details view and click each of the column heads. As you do so, the list is sorted by the column you chose. Shift+click an item in any view to toggle the state marker on and off. You can't edit the text, however, because the ReadOnly property is True. Hey, these guys are famous; they're not going to change their names just because you say so.

Get Rich (Text) Quick!

In this modern world, the editing capabilities of the memo box component are just too-too old hat. If you can't use four fonts in every sentence, why write at all? And if you're going to hit the wall with a mere 32,768 bytes of text, why bother? The Delphi 3 rich text component zooms to the rescue. The good news is, a rich text component handles every task a memo box can. The other good news (Hah! Got you!) is that it does a lot more. Its capacity is virtually unlimited. It enables the user to apply different font styles throughout the text, it includes paragraph formatting, and it even takes care of searching and printing its text for you.

Properties

As far as properties listed in the Object Inspector, the rich text component is a little different from a memo box. Set the PlainText property to True and you eliminate the capability to use multiple fonts and styles (and speed up the component's performance).

The spiffiest properties show up only at run time. The SelAttributes property holds the font attributes of the currently selected text. It has all the same properties as a TFont object, along with an additional one called ConsistentAttributes. This property indicates which font attributes are consistent throughout the selection. What's that mean? If half the selection is 12-point Arial and half is 14-point Arial, the font name is consistent but the font size isn't. If you change the properties of the rich text component's SelAttributes property, the change affects the entire selection.

Properties can themselves be objects, so it's not crazy or redundant to talk about the properties of the SelAttributes property.

A similar property named DefAttributes defines the attributes for newly inserted text. And the Paragraph property contains formatting information for the selected paragraph or paragraphs. Paragraph formatting includes bullets, tabs, alignment, and indentation.

Events

The rich text component generates all the events a memo box does, plus a number of additional ones. The simplest and most easily used is OnSelectionChange. This event is triggered any time the selection or cursor position changes. It's handy for reflecting the selection's formatting in a status bar.

Enriching the simple editor

Remember the simple editor project, last seen in Chapter 8? It's not so simple any more, and it's about to make another Great Leap Forward. Load that project now, delete the memo box that fills its main form, and replace it with a rich text component. In the Code Editor, press Ctrl+R and replace all occurrences of Memo1 with RichEdit1. Now set the rich text component's Align property to alClient, its ScrollBars property to ssBoth, and its HideSelection property to False.

Choose File➪Font from the menu bar. You're tossed into the Code Editor right at that item's OnClick event handler. Delete the event handler's code and replace it with the following lines:

```
WITH RichEdit1.SelAttributes DO
  BEGIN
    FontDialog1.Font.Name := Name;
    FontDialog1.Font.Size := Size;
    FontDialog1.Options := FontDialog1.Options +
      [fdNoFaceSel, fdNoSizeSel];
    IF caFace IN ConsistentAttributes THEN
      FontDialog1.Options := FontDialog1.Options -
        [fdNoFaceSel];
    IF caSize IN ConsistentAttributes THEN
      FontDialog1.Options := FontDialog1.Options -
        [fdNoSizeSel];
  END;
WITH FontDialog1 DO
  IF Execute THEN
    BEGIN
      RichEdit1.SelAttributes.Name := Font.Name;
      RichEdit1.SelAttributes.Size := Font.Size;
      RichEdit1.SelAttributes.Style := Font.Style;
      RichEdit1.SelAttributes.Color := Font.Color;
      SpeedButton3.Down := fsBold IN Font.Style;
      SpeedButton4.Down := fsItalic IN Font.Style;
      SpeedButton5.Down := fsUnderline IN Font.Style;
    END;
```

Delete the single line of code in the font dialog's OnApply method. Now double-click one of the font style speed buttons to reach the event handler they share. In the first line of code within that event handler, change RichEdit1.Font to RichEdit1.SelAttributes. Double-click one of the text alignment speed buttons, and in their shared event handler, replace RichEdit1.Alignment with RichEdit1.Paragraph.Alignment. Now choose File➪Print to go to its OnClick event handler. Delete the code in this event handler and replace it with the following two lines:

```
IF PrintDialog1.Execute THEN
  RichEdit1.Print('My Document');
```

Click the Find dialog, flip to the events page of the Object Inspector, and double-click the OnFind event. Delete all the code from the existing event handler, including the begin..end pair and the variables preceding the begin line. Then insert the following code:

```
VAR
  ST   : TSearchTypes;
  Rslt : Integer;
begin
  ST := [];
  WITH Sender AS TFindDialog DO
    BEGIN
      IF frWholeWord IN Options THEN ST := [stWholeWord];
      IF frMatchCase IN Options THEN ST := ST +
          [stMatchCase];
      Rslt := RichEdit1.FindText(FindText,
          RichEdit1.SelStart +
        RichEdit1.SelLength, RichEdit1.GetTextLen, ST);
      IF Rslt > -1 THEN
        BEGIN
          RichEdit1.SelStart := Rslt;
          RichEdit1.SelLength := Length(FindText);
        END;
    END;
end;
```

Place a status bar on the form and double-click its Panels property. Add two panels with the text Row and Col and add a third panel with no text. Start an OnSelectionChange event handler for the rich text component. Delete the begin..end pair that Delphi created and add the following code:

```
VAR ro, co : Integer;
begin
  WITH RichEdit1.SelAttributes DO
    BEGIN
      SpeedButton3.Down := (fsBold IN Style) AND
        (caBold IN ConsistentAttributes);
      SpeedButton4.Down := (fsItalic IN Style) AND
        (caItalic IN ConsistentAttributes);
      SpeedButton5.Down := (fsUnderline IN Style) AND
        (caUnderline IN ConsistentAttributes);
    END;
```

(continued)

(continued)

```
CASE RichEdit1.Paragraph.Alignment OF
  taLeftJustify  : SpeedButton6.Down := True;
  taCenter       : SpeedButton7.Down := True;
  taRightJustify : SpeedButton8.Down := True;
END;
ro := RichEdit1.Perform(EM_LINEFROMCHAR,
         RichEdit1.SelStart,
  0);
co := RichEdit1.SelStart -
         RichEdit1.Perform(EM_LINEINDEX,
  ro, 0);
StatusBar1.Panels[0].Text := Format('Row: %d', [ro+1]);
StatusBar1.Panels[1].Text := Format('Col: %d', [co+1]);
end;
```

Now, as the cursor moves, the status bar displays the current row and column, the font style speed buttons reflect the selection's style, and the alignment speed buttons change to match the current paragraph alignment.

You're almost finished! Click the File Open dialog, double-click the Filter property, and add a new filter called Rich Text Files with the mask *.RTF. For the Save dialog, double-click the Filter property and change the Text Files filter to Rich Text Files and change its mask to *.RTF. Select both and change the DefaultExt property to RTF. You've given the simple editor the capability to read either text files or rich text files and to save rich text files. You can change the font style for portions of the text and control the alignment of paragraphs. With this information, your introduction to the Windows 95 components in Delphi 3 is complete.

Chapter 13

Learn Programming
from the Master

· ·

In This Chapter

▶ Code Delphi writes for you

▶ Basic structure of programs and units

▶ Code you can edit and code you should leave alone

▶ Changes Delphi handles for you and changes you must take care of yourself

· ·

*B*y now, you've built dozens of programs while becoming intimate with the various Delphi components. Each time you start a new project, Delphi generates a project file for you, and each time you add a form to the project, Delphi whips up a unit file for it. If you plop a component on the form, Delphi inserts code to integrate it into your program. And whenever you're ready to write an event handler, Delphi provides the infrastructure. Sounds like Delphi's doing all the work, doesn't it? Well, Delphi leaves plenty more for you to do; but by first scrutinizing what Delphi does, you get a head start in understanding how to write your own great programs.

Dissecting an Empty Program

The moment a new, blank project appears on-screen, busy beaver Delphi has already written two pages of program code. The first page, initially named Unit1, is the code that handles the main form and all its components. The second, titled Project1 by default, isn't visible until and unless you choose View⇨Project Source from the View menu bar. Project1 — the main project file — pulls together all the forms in your program.

What's inside an empty unit?

Start a new project, click the Unit1 tab in the Code Editor, and expand the
window until you can see all (or most) of the code. It should look roughly
like Figure 13-1.

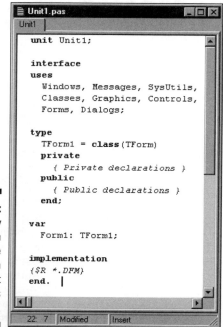

Figure 13-1:
Every
Delphi form
starts its life
linked to an
empty unit
such as
this one.

```
unit Unit1;

interface
uses
    Windows, Messages, SysUtils,
    Classes, Graphics, Controls,
    Forms, Dialogs;

type
    TForm1 = class(TForm)
    private
        { Private declarations }
    public
        { Public declarations }
    end;

var
    Form1: TForm1;

implementation
{$R *.DFM}
end.  |
```

The first line in a Delphi file generally tells you what kind of file you're
dealing with. This one is a *unit,* a code module that exists only to be used by
a main program or by another unit, and can never stand alone. The unit
name (in this case, Unit1) immediately follows the *unit* keyword. Whenever
Delphi creates a unit to go with a new form, Delphi always tries to call it
Unit1. If that name is taken, it tries Unit2, Unit3, and so on.

Julius Caesar said that all Gaul is divided into three parts; the same is true of
every unit (and it takes a lot of Gaul to make that comparison). The three
parts are the *interface section,* the *implementation section,* and the *initialization section.* The interface section is the smiling face the unit shows to the
world; whatever is in this section can be seen and accessed by any program
or unit that uses this unit. (So don't put anything incriminating in the
interface section!) Anything that appears solely in the implementation
section, on the other hand, is private, accessible only within the unit itself.
Finally, any commands that you put in the initialization section execute
automatically at the start of any program that uses the unit.

The interface section starts with the lone word *interface*. It continues until the start of the implementation section, which is a line that contains only the word *implementation*. Every unit must include these two sections, even if they're empty. The initialization section is optional, and Delphi doesn't build it into the form-based units it creates. If present, it starts with *initialization* and ends with *end.*, including the period. A unit that doesn't have an initialization section still ends with *end.*, but no matching *initialization* precedes it.

The interface section: the inside story

The first line in the interface section is the *uses clause* — a list of the other units that the unit in question relies on. The units Delphi builds for you are not rugged individualists; they're quite content to get along with a little help from their friends. The following units in the initial uses clause come standard with Delphi:

- *SysUtils* — a variety of system utilities such as string handling routines, date/time conversions, and file management functions

- *Windows* — provides access to functions in the core Windows libraries GDI, USER, and KERNEL (the ruling triumvirate of Windows) and holds data types and constant values used by the defined Windows functions

- *Messages* — Windows message number constants and data types associated with particular messages

- *Classes* — low-level basic elements of the Delphi component system.

- *Graphics* — graphical elements such as fonts, pens, brushes, and bitmaps

- *Controls* — mid-level elements of the Delphi component system.

- *Forms* — the form component and the invisible application and screen components

- *Dialogs* — the common dialog components

After the uses clause is a *type declaration block,* introduced by the word *type*. A type declaration block contains one or more definitions for *data types*. What are those? Well, deep down inside, all the data in your computer is stored as bits and bytes. You use data types to tell your program how to interpret those bytes. For example, the same four bytes could represent

- 78, 101, 105, and 108

- 25,934 and 27,753

- 1,818,846,542

- 1.128632 E+27

- 'Neil'

You find out everything you need to know about data types in Chapter 14.

The particular unit that you're dissecting defines just one data type, an *object class* named TForm1. The two-bit definition of an object is a collection of data elements combined with functions that act on the data. Sound familiar? Yes, forms and components are examples of objects. The process of wrapping up data in a nice package — an object — with the functions that act on that data is called *encapsulation* by object mavens.

The first line of the type definition is as follows:

```
TForm1 = Class(TForm);
```

It says that the TForm1 object *inherits* all the features and capabilities of the generic TForm object. Anything TForm can do, TForm1 can do too. For example, TForm has Caption and Color properties, so TForm1 has them, too. And because TForm has a Close method, TForm1 has a Close method, too.

This particular object class definition is effectively empty; both its *private* section and its *public* section just contain a comment. (I tell you more about comments in the section "The innards of an empty program".) If any lines of code were here, they would define the ways in which TForm1 is different from TForm. TForm1 extends TForm by adding new data fields, defining new methods, or overriding existing methods. Fields and methods in the private section are accessible only to the object itself; those in the public section are visible to any program or unit that uses this unit.

Programmers like to say that TForm1 is a *descendant* of TForm and that TForm is an *ancestor* of TForm1. If TForm1 had its own descendants, they would also be descendants of TForm, and TForm would be their ancestor. After hearing these warm fuzzy terms, you won't be surprised that programmers say objects have a family tree (technically, an object hierarchy).

Next comes a *variable declaration block,* signaled by the word *var*. A variable is a chunk of memory that your program reserves to store data. Every variable has a name so that it doesn't get lost in the crowd and a data type to tell Delphi what kind of stuff the variable stores. The next chapter has a lot to say about variables.

In the unit in Figure 13-1, Delphi declares a single variable with the name Form1 and the data type TForm1. In object-speak, Form1 is an *instance* of the object class TForm1. Notice that this variable declaration comes after the definition of the data type TForm1. That's the rule in Delphi: You can't use anything until after you define it!

The type definition and variable declaration I just reviewed come after the interface line and before the implementation line so that they're within the interface section of the unit and accessible to any other unit or program that uses this unit.

The implementation section: deep, dark secrets

A unit's implementation section is the back room where the real work happens; no distraction comes from outside influences. All contact with other code modules funnels through the interface section (which does the public relations for the unit, so to speak). A variable declared in the implementation section cannot be examined or changed by code outside the unit; a function declared only in the implementation section cannot be called by any code outside the unit.

The empty unit in Figure 13-1 contains only one line in its implementation section, the *compiler directive* {$R *.DFM}. This line tells Delphi to include all the hard work you put into designing the form; property information for the form and every component on it resides in the .DFM file. Delphi replaces the asterisk with the name of the unit, so this particular line includes UNIT1.DFM in the program. Never delete or change the {$R *.DFM} line!

Compiler directives are orders that go directly to Delphi, as opposed to commands that get translated into machine code for the final program. I tell you how to set compiler options in Chapter 1. Each of those options has a corresponding compiler directive. For example, {$S+} in a Delphi source file turns stack checking on, regardless of how you set the compiler options.

You can also add a second uses clause at the start of the implementation section for units that are required only by code in the implementation section. You must do this is if two units depend on each other. If unit Alfonse uses unit Gaston and Gaston uses Alfonse, Delphi goes around in circles. To fix this, add an implementation uses clause to one of the units.

The initialization section: last-minute preparations

Some units need to warm up their engines or do last-minute touch-up work at the start of a program. Program statements in the initialization section are executed at the beginning of any program that uses the unit, uses a unit that uses the unit, or uses a unit that uses a unit that uses the unit. . . . If anything in the unit must be initialized in some way before it can be used, you do it in the initialization section.

I give no example for the initialization section because normally Delphi doesn't need to create one. In fact, not a single example program in this book uses the initialization section. In general, if an initialization section exists, it's just a few lines.

The innards of an empty program

Now click the Project1 tab in the Code Editor to review the ridiculously tiny main program generated by Delphi. It should look like Figure 13-2.

Figure 13-2:
Delphi's
standard
main
program is
a mighty
mite.

The first line tells us this file defines a program with the name Project1. Unlike a unit, a program can and does stand alone. Immediately after the program line comes a uses clause, just as in the unit. This program uses two units, Forms and Unit1. Forms is the built-in Delphi unit that defines the form and application components. Unit1 is, of course, the unit you just looked at in the other page of the Code Editor.

Notice that Delphi has placed the name of the form corresponding to Unit1 in a comment after the unit name. This comment has no effect on the program code, but Delphi *does* use it to help associate the unit with its form. Never modify the comments Delphi inserts in the main program's uses clause.

Any text surrounded by braces {like this} or by parenthesis-asterisk pairs (*like this*) is ignored by Delphi as it compiles the program. With the exception just noted, comments exist for you! You should add comments to the programs you write. Otherwise, if you go to modify the code later, you may have no idea what it's supposed to do. The Delphi editor displays comments in a special color and font so that they stand out.

You can also use comment characters to comment out portions of your code. For example, if a certain part of your program is causing problems and you don't know why, you can try commenting out different parts to see what makes the problem disappear. For consistency, I suggest that you stick to braces {like this} for regular comments, and use parenthesis-asterisk pairs (*like this*) for commenting out code.

Comment delimiters surrounding a text string almost always mean a comment. The one exception is if the very first character of the string is a dollar sign. In that case, you have a compiler directive and not a comment.

After the uses clause comes a compiler directive that loads the resource file for the program. A resource file contains data that's compiled into the final executable program file. The .DFM file included in a Delphi-built unit is a kind of resource file. In a new empty program, the resource file contains nothing but the default icon.

Next comes the *main body* of the program, starting with begin and ending with end. (and the period after end must be included). It looks a lot like the initialization section of a unit, but in this case, it's not optional. In a typical Delphi program, the main body is really puny, because all the activity takes place in the units. This program has just two lines, one to initialize Form1 and associate it with the application and one to run the application.

One reason Delphi uses data types is to keep you from passing the wrong kind of variable to a method. If a certain method works on numbers, Delphi doesn't permit you to pass it a string of characters. If it works only on whole numbers, Delphi doesn't permit a number with a fractional part. But with objects, things get a little weird. Delphi methods that expect a TForm don't raise a fuss if they receive a TForm1 instead. Why not?

The answer lies in *polymorphism,* a ten-dollar word that means "many shapes." If a method expects to receive a certain kind of object, you can pass it any descendant of that object instead. It's not obvious at first, but this capability is one of the most powerful features of object-oriented programming.

A program by any other name . . .

As I discuss in the section "What's inside an empty unit?", Unit1 is a default name that Delphi gives to a unit. You can easily change the name to something more interesting (and mnemonic). Follow these steps:

1. **Choose File⇨Save Project from the menu bar.**

2. **Type** Barney **for the unit name and type** Fred **for the project name.**

   Look at the Code window and you see that Delphi has updated the tabs — they now read Barney and Fred. The first line of the unit is now unit Barney;, and program Fred; is the first line of the project file. Also, the project's uses clause now has Barney and BARNEY.PAS where it used to have Unit1 and UNIT1.PAS. Delphi has updated the source code files to reflect their new names.

3. Switch to the Object Inspector window and change the form's Name property from Form1 to Rubble.

Again Delphi changes the source code to match. The object type for the form changes to TRubble, and in the main project, even the comment is updated. Because the form's caption was *exactly* the same as its name, Delphi changed the caption, too. Figure 13-3 shows the main program as updated by Delphi.

Figure 13-3:
If you rename the form or save files under new names, Delphi handles all the internal changes.

```
Fred.dpr                    _□X
Barney  Fred
program Fred;

uses
  Forms,
  Barney in 'Barney.pas' {Rubble};

{$R *.RES}

begin
  Application.CreateForm(TRubble, Rubble);
  Application.Run;
end.

1: 1    Modified    Insert
```

Anything Delphi does for you is something you shouldn't do for yourself in the code. For example, if you want to give a unit or program a new name, don't edit the name by hand. Instead, use Save As or Save Project As to save it under the new name. And don't change the form object's name in the unit code — do it in the Object Inspector window. If you make these changes yourself, Delphi doesn't compile your program!

What a Difference a Component Makes

Building a framework for the main program and unit is just the beginning of the programming work that Delphi does for you. Every time you add or rename a component, Delphi integrates that component into your program.

Arrange the Form and Code Editor windows on the screen so that you can see both of them at once. Cover up the Object Inspector window if you must. In the Code Editor, flip to the Barney page and make sure that the type declaration section for TRubble is visible. Click the button icon in the Standard page of the Component palette and move the mouse over the form, but don't place the button yet. Focus your gaze on the TRubble definition and then click the mouse.

Did you see what happened? The definition of TRubble expanded to include the Button1: TButton; line. This line is a declaration of independence for the TRubble object type; it now marches to a different drummer. TRubble is different from a plain blank TForm because it has a data field named Button1 with the data type TButton.

Delphi deals with dependencies

If you add a component, Delphi sticks a line into the form object's definition. That line gives your program a name to holler if it wants to call on the component. A tad more preparation is required, but Delphi doesn't do it until you save the program.

Scroll the Code Editor so that the uses clause is visible. Watch the uses clause as you press Ctrl+S to save the file. Now delete the button from the form. After you save the file, the unit name StdCtrls popped into the uses clause. StdCtrls is the name of the unit that supports standard controls such as buttons, edit boxes, and list boxes. When you deleted the button from the form, the Button1 line in the TRubble object type declaration disappeared. StdCtrls, however, is still present in the uses clause.

Why doesn't Delphi remove the unit name, too? First, the StdCtrls unit supports many Delphi components — not just TButton, and not just the one specific TButton named Button1. To decide whether it's safe to remove the unit from the uses clause, Delphi would need to review every other component in the form. Second, and more important, *you* may have written code that requires that unit. Delphi knows all about its own code, but not yours. Thus, it's just not safe for Delphi to delete the unit from the uses clause.

Just about any component you place on a form expands the uses clause unless the support unit for that component is already present. If you're starting out with a new program, you may be in a creative frenzy, adding and removing components from the form with wild abandon. Chances are good that your final version includes units you don't need, and some of the code and data for those units can wind up in your compiled program. To avoid program bloat, delete all units from the uses clause that Delphi added to support particular components. Leave all the units that are present in a brand new form's uses clause (you can see them in Figure 13-1) and don't delete any unit names that you typed in yourself. Next time that you save the file, the units and unit names that are still necessary magically reappear.

A slight possibility exists that following this advice could give Delphi indigestion, as shown in Figure 13-4. If Delphi suddenly complains that your code contains an unknown identifier, you've deleted one unit too many. Don't panic! Consult the help system about the offending identifier to see which unit supports it and then add the name back to the uses clause.

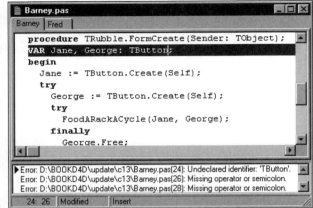

Figure 13-4:
Here,
TButton is
an unknown
identifier to
Delphi
because
you deleted
StdCtrls
from the
uses
clause.

Delphi 3 detects as many errors as it can before stopping and lists them all, as shown at the bottom of Figure 13-4. Clicking an item in the error list displays the line of code that caused the problem. Not only that, but Delphi warns you about code that has fine syntax but suspect logic, and it even gives you hints for better programming. What won't they think of next!

What's in a name?

If you change the Name property of a component by using the Object Inspector window, the name changes in the Code Editor as well. Delphi even renames any event handlers with default names based on this component. If you change Button1 to TikTok, Button1Click changes to TikTokClick. However, Delphi doesn't meddle with the code *you* wrote — only the code *it* wrote. If your code calls a component by its name, it stops working after you change the name.

The easiest way around this problem is to accept the default names supplied by Delphi. But, giving components names that relate to their function helps you keep track of what's going on in your program. The intended purpose of FormatHardDiskButton is obvious; Button42 is not. If you decide to use descriptive names, one simple rule saves you aggravation: Always name a component before writing any code that refers to the component. If you do change your mind about the name later on, be sure to change it in any code you've written yourself! Choose Edit⇨Replace from the menu to find the old component name and replace it with the new name.

You have another way around the name problem, one that we've already used quite a bit in example programs. Every event handler has a parameter called Sender that identifies the component that causes the event. Instead of referring to, say, Edit1, your code can use: (Sender AS TEdit). You get a

double benefit this way. First, Delphi doesn't depend on the name of the component button, and second, the same event handler can now easily service multiple components of the same type (in this case, TEdit).
As the song says, "Avoid any possible embarrassment or blame. Don't ever call your component by his name!"

Handling Event Handlers

You've written dozens of event handlers by now, and you surely take it for granted that Delphi generates the correct skeleton for each type of event. Take a closer look at those skeletons and see how many you can scare up.

Easy come, easy go . . .

Delphi creates empty event handlers at the drop of a hat, or at least at the click of a button. But if you don't use 'em, you lose 'em! Follow these steps:

1. **Start a new project, select the Events page of the Object Inspector window, and double-click the OnClick event for the main form.**

2. **In the Code Editor, scroll until you see the object class definition.**

   Besides supplying you with the framework for an OnClick event handler, Delphi adds that event handler to the definition of the main TForm1 object.

3. **With an eagle eye on the Code Editor, press Ctrl+F9 or choose Compile⇨Compile from the menu bar.**

   The event handler skeleton and its line in the object type definition appear as if by magic, and they vanish just as quickly after you compile the program. If an event handler contains no code, not even a comment, Delphi deletes it before compiling the program.

4. **Add a button to the form, double-click it, and put an empty comment { } in the OnClick event handler.**

5. **Now delete the button and compile the program.**

Notice several things here. For one thing, the event handler is part of the form object's definition; it actually belongs to the form, not to the button. If you delete the button, the event handler remains behind — another sign that it doesn't belong to the button. And because the handler isn't 100 percent empty, Delphi doesn't wipe it out at compile time.

If you want to delete an event handler, delete all the code except the skeleton Delphi originally provides. Delphi takes care of removing the skeleton and the declaration line the next time you compile.

But are we compatible?

In several of the sample programs you worked with earlier, you connected more than one component to the same event handler. For example, the interface for the simple editor project that you build in Chapter 5 is initially based on push buttons. You transfer the OnClick handlers for those buttons to menu items in Chapter 6 and then connect speed buttons to some of them in Chapter 8, all without any change to the event handlers. You can connect an event handler to events from multiple components or multiple events from the same component, as long as the events are compatible. What are compatible events? Stay tuned and just follow these steps:

1. **Starting with a new form, create an OnClick event handler.**

2. **Now select OnDblClick in the Events page and press the down-arrow button next to this event's value.**

   A list appears containing the single item FormClick. Do the same for OnClose, however, and the list is empty. What's happening?

3. **Go down the list of events and create an event handler for every single one of them.**

   Don't bother putting any code in the handlers; we're just interested in the skeletons Delphi builds. Maximize the Code Editor so that you can see as much code as possible.

Figure 13-5 shows part of the TForm1 object's declaration after performing this exercise. Notice that several groups of handlers have the same parameter list (the stuff in parentheses after the procedure name). The most popular parameter list is (Sender : TObject);.

FormDragDrop and FormDragOver have the same set of parameters, as do FormKeyDown and FormKeyUp.

Now, if you click the down arrow next to the OnClick method in the Object Inspector, you get quite a list of choices (Figure 13-6). Look back at the Code Editor and you see that all the handlers in the list have the same set of parameters. Delphi requires that the parameters for each handler are the same. If the parameter list matches, the event handler is compatible, even if you went behind Delphi's back and built it by hand. Remember: Delphi creates the event handlers' parameter lists, so you must never change them.

Figure 13-5:
If you
create
event
handlers for
every event,
you notice
a pattern
emerging.

Figure 13-6:
Any event
handler that
has the
same
parameter
list as
OnActivate
is a
compatible
replacement.

The fact that Delphi lists a particular event handler as compatible is no guarantee that you can use it successfully. Successful implementation depends entirely on the code in the event handler. The code may assume that the handler is called by a particular component or a type of component.

What Can You Edit in the Code?

To reiterate once more: Leave Delphi's work to Delphi. With some specific exceptions, if Delphi wrote a line of code, Delphi handles it. If you wrote the code, it's your responsibility. Now just what is under your control?

Event handler innards

Obviously you can create event handlers — you've been doing that for ages. Delphi builds a skeleton for you and adds the declaration line to the form object definition, and you fill in the rest. But never change the method header (the first line of the framework containing the method name and parameter list) and never change the declaration line in the form object definition. Within the event handler, you can do anything that's legal in Delphi programming language.

All right, if you're just desperate to rename an event handler, here's how you do it. Suppose that you want to rename Button1Click to GoSpeedRacerGo. Click on Button1 and then flip to the Events page in the Object Inspector. Highlight the event handler named Button1Click and change it to GoSpeedRacerGo. That's all you do. Delphi takes care of changing the code and makes the change for any other components that share this same event handler. The only time you'd need to edit the code yourself is if it includes a direct call to Button1Click from another event handler.

Adding units to the uses clause

Several of the sample programs require you to add something to your program's uses clause. Delphi starts you off with units that most programs need and automatically adds units to support the components you place on the form. However, if you start poking around in the Delphi manual and using the functions you find there, Delphi may hit you with an Unknown Identifier error message. Just look up the offending identifier in the Help system to get the name of the unit it's in. Insert the name into the uses clause and you're ready to roll.

You also need to add units to the uses clause if you start using Windows functions that don't live in the three core Windows DLLs — GDI, USER, and KERNEL. Delphi has an import unit for just about every Windows library, including COMMDLG, DDEML, LZEXPAND, MMSYSTEM, OLE, PENWIN, SHELLAPI, STRESS, TOOLHELP, VER, and WINMEM32. Again, look up the function in the Delphi Help system to find the unit name.

If your main form needs to call on a secondary form, you also must add the secondary form's unit to the main unit's uses clause. The main form doesn't know anything about a secondary form unless you give it access to the secondary form's unit.

Touch not the body!

By default, the main body of the project file contains only commands to create one or more forms and run the application. You hardly ever need to change this code, and if you do, Delphi may lose the capability to automatically maintain it.

After you become expert enough at programming that you need to make changes to the main program's body, be circumspect. Wait until the program is stable enough that you're sure you don't need to add or rename any forms.

My object all sublime

A few of the sample programs have required you to add a data field or two to the object definition. Nobody told you that's what was happening; you were just instructed to find the public or private declarations section near the top of the file and insert a specific line or two. You were busily extending an object definition without even realizing it!

You can add your own data fields to the object definition, define your own methods, or override existing methods. A method here, a method there . . . and pretty soon you're talking about real programming!

Always add fields or methods in the public or private declarations section, never to the top part of the form class declaration. The top part of the form class declaration is where Delphi generates its own declarations. If you put your declarations in the middle of the one Delphi created, Delphi complains about the infiltrators and asks whether it's okay to delete them.

Delphi Programming Basics

I don't give you a pop quiz on what I cover in this chapter — the print medium hasn't been made interactive yet! But the chapters that follow assume that you've absorbed at least most of the material from this chapter. If you're unsure, here's a quick run-down:

✔ For each project you start, Delphi writes a *program* file that gets turned into a self-contained EXE and one or more *unit* files that must be used by a program or another unit. Delphi program files tend to be small, with all the real action taking place in units.

✔ A unit has three parts. The *interface section* holds variables, functions, and type definitions that are available for all the world to see. Stuff in the *implementation section* is private to the unit. And any lines of code in the optional *initialization section* are executed at the start of a program that uses the unit.

✔ The *uses clause* at the beginning of a code module (program file or unit file) identifies other units this file depends on. A code module may have one or more *type definition blocks,* which define data types. It may also include one or more *variable declaration blocks.* Among the possible data types is the *object class.* An object is a collection of data fields *encapsulated* with functions that act on the data.

✔ An *object class* (or just *object*) is almost always defined in terms of an existing object. It *inherits* the features and capabilities of the existing object, and *extends* the object by adding new data fields, adding new methods, or overriding existing methods. The new object is called a *descendant;* the object from which the descendant inherits features and capabilities is called its *ancestor.*

✔ Normally, Delphi functions insist that the data passed to them match the data type of their parameters. If the type in question is an object type, however, any descendant is also acceptable — this is called *polymorphism.*

Next time the topic of object-oriented programming comes up at a cocktail party, remember the three big words: inheritance, encapsulation, and polymorphism. Just say them a lot, in various combinations, and people think you're a genius.

Chapter 14

Elements of Programming

● ●

In This Chapter

▶ Naming variables

▶ Choosing data types for maximum flexibility

▶ Making decisions in code

▶ Creating statements that repeat over and over and over . . .

▶ Keeping your programming skills growing

● ●

*D*id you ever take a radio apart when you were a kid? Taking it apart sure was a lot easier than putting it back together! You've picked apart the program code that Delphi writes, but putting a program together is going to require knowledge of all the nasty little pieces.

On the other hand, you received quite a stack of manuals with Delphi, and the help system tells you about any particular aspect of the Delphi programming language. So maybe I don't have to write this chapter.

Well, before you can get answers from a manual or a help system, you have to know the right questions to ask. That's where this chapter comes in. I don't waste your time regurgitating factoids from the manuals; rather, I help you reach the point where manuals become useful.

The techno-geek quotient of this chapter is above average, and the concepts you need to know are all wound up with each other, so it's hard to lay them out in any kind of order. If you find it tough sledding, try to plow through to the end anyway and pick up the general ideas. Take a break, walk the guinea pig, practice your figure skating, and then try reading through it again. It *is* easier the second time, I promise!

Datas De Way It Goes

You say DAY-ta, I say DAT-ta, you probably want to call the whole thing off . . . but you can't! Computers were invented to process data, and a big part of programming is finding the right way to represent data.

The Delphi data storage lockers are called *variables,* and each variable represents a specific *type* of data. In addition, Delphi programs use immutable data elements called *constants,* also with their own particular data type.

It depends on several variables. . . .

What do Delphi variables have to do with the price of gum in Singapore? Well, the price of gum in Singapore *is a variable.* Today it may be 50 cents and a week in jail; tomorrow it may be 75 cents and a public caning. You can say that chewing tobacco costs twice as much as gum without specifying today's price. It's the same in Delphi. When you want to refer to a particular piece of information without concern for its current value, you use a variable.

If time is nature's way of keeping everything from happening at once, variables are what Delphi uses to keep everything from happening in the same place. When you declare a variable in your program, Delphi reserves space in memory for that variable and makes sure that no other variable occupies the same space.

The word *var* begins a block of one or more variable declarations. Each declaration associates a variable name with a particular data type. I discuss data types in detail in the section titled "She's not my (data) type" in this chapter.

Scoping out variables

The dictionary says *scope* means "breadth or opportunity to function," and Delphi variables have the opportunity to function only within their scope. A variable declared outside any function has *global* scope; it can be used anywhere in the program. The main form variable in a Delphi unit is an example of a global variable. A variable declared inside a function, on the other hand, is *local* in scope. It's inaccessible outside the function that defines it. Global variables grab space in memory and hog it the whole time your program is running. Local variables exist only while the function that contains them is active.

Figure 14-1 shows an event handler from Chapter 9's CD player project. In this event handler and many others, you were instructed to *replace* the begin..end pair supplied by Delphi rather than just typing lines between begin and end. Surprise! When you type these event handlers, you define local variables!

Figure 14-1:
This event
handler
uses three
local
variables
named Trk,
Min, and
Sec (for
Tracks,
Minutes, and
Seconds).

```
CDPlayru.pas                                    _ □ ×
CDPlayru
  procedure TForm1.Timer1Timer(Sender: TObject);
  VAR Trk, Min, Sec : Word;
  begin
    WITH MediaPlayer1 DO
      BEGIN
        Trk := MCI_TMSF_TRACK(Position);
        Min := MCI_TMSF_MINUTE(Position);
        Sec := MCI_TMSF_SECOND(Position);
        Label1.Caption := Format('%.2d', [Trk]);
        Label2.Caption := Format('%.2d:%.2d', [Min, Sec]);
      END;
  end;

  1: 1              Insert
```

Use local variables instead of global variables whenever you can. Doing so conserves memory and makes it easier to keep track of what your program is doing. And, of course, always assign a value to a variable before you try to refer to its value!

What to name the new variable

Any combination of letters, digits, and the underscore character is a valid Delphi variable name, as long as the first character isn't a digit. You can name your variables _1, _2, _3, or VariableA, VariableB, VariableC, or Shadrach, Meshach, Abednego. Delphi doesn't mind!

However, you should give some thought to a variable's name and choose one that helps you remember the purpose of the variable. An expression such as IF X > Y doesn't have nearly as much punch as

```
IF ReactorCoreTemp > MeltdownDisasterLevel
```

The only time a nondescript name such as N really makes sense is when the variable *does* something nondescript, such as counting repetitions in a loop:

```
FOR N := 1 TO 12 DO Omelette.Add(Egg[N]);
```

Delphi doesn't let you use the same variable name twice in the same scope. You can't declare two global variables named SewageFlow, or one named STENCH and one named stench. (Delphi ignores the distinction between uppercase and lowercase.) If there's a conflict between global and local variables with the same name, the home team wins. For example, say you have a global variable called UnmatchedSocks and the current function declares a variable with the same name. When the function refers to UnmatchedSocks, it means the local one.

She's not my (data) type

Here's a quick quiz for you:

- ✔ What's "Cake" plus pi?
- ✔ How much is True times seven?
- ✔ What's the square root of "DUTT"?

Did you come up with any answers? Then you're thinking like a computer. If you answered 6.947, 7, and 37,614, you're *really* thinking like a computer! Computers are famous for wasting time trying to answer the wrong questions. Delphi data types help keep you out of this trap by squawking when, say, you try to take the natural logarithm of Tuesday. Every data type also has a particular size, so the data type tells Delphi how much memory to reserve.

A type declaration block in a Delphi program begins with the word *type*.

Choosing data types

Like the famous donkey sitting equidistant between two bales of hay, you could starve to death trying to decide which of the myriad Delphi data types to use. To cut through this muddle, memorize the half-dozen most important types:

Type	Data
LongInt	A whole number (no fractional part)
Extended	A number that may have a fractional part
Boolean	A True or False value
Char	One character, such as 'A'
String	A string of characters, such as 'Delphi'
PChar	A character string for use with a Windows API function

Whole numbers count

Computers, like people, do math fastest when they don't have to worry about fractions. Delphi has many whole number data types, but LongInt is the biggest and most flexible. LongInt can represent any number from –2,147,483,648 to 2,147,483,647 — over 4 billion values!

A LongInt takes 4 bytes of memory. The other whole number data types (Word, Cardinal, SmallInt, Byte, and ShortInt) use 2 bytes or 1, but their ranges are much smaller. CPU chips 386 and better talk to themselves internally in 4-byte numbers. Windows NT and Windows 95 are called 32-bit operating systems because they use 32-bit (4-byte) numbers internally. The Integer data type is adaptable — it uses 2 bytes (16 bits) in a 16-bit environment (like Windows 3.1) and 4 bytes (32 bits) in a 32-bit environment. The Cardinal type adapts in the same way, but it's an unsigned quantity. A Delphi 3 Cardinal can range from 0 to 2,147,483,647. However, LongInts are dependable 4-byte integers in either environment. LongInts rule!

I'll have just a fraction more

Whole numbers are nice, but a huge amount of scientific and business data can't be expressed in nice, whole numbers. To represent interest rates, pork belly prices, or the weight of an electron, you need numbers with a fractional part. Delphi represents these as floating-point numbers. That means that the decimal point isn't fixed in one place, so it's just as easy to represent 1 trillion or 1 trillionth.

Here's the catch. Think back to grade school, when you learned about decimals. To convert a nice, clean fraction such as $1/3$ into decimal, you wrote 0.3 and then kept adding 3s until your pencil wore out. A decimal expression for $1/3$ is never perfectly accurate. Other numbers, such as pi or the square root of 42, don't even have a repeating pattern.

The computer's floating-point numbers have the same problem, and they wear out their pencils after a fixed number of significant digits. To minimize the fuzziness of floating-point data, you want as many significant digits as possible. The 10-byte Extended data type has more significant digits and a larger range than other Delphi floating-point types (Single, Real, Double, and Comp). Its maximum possible value is roughly 10^{4932}. How much is that? Well, one estimate puts the number of subatomic particles in the measurable universe at a mere 10^{74}!

An Extended type variable is accurate to 19 significant digits. To get an idea of how accurate that is, consider the distance of the Earth from the sun, which is roughly 93 million miles, or 5,892,480,000,000 inches. An Extended type variable could represent the number of inches with six significant digits to spare. Therefore, you could store the distance from the Earth to the sun accurate to around a millionth of an inch — that is, if the Earth and the sun would hold still for the measurement. . . .

Most modern computers have an 80*x*87 math coprocessor. If the main processor is an 80487 DX or Pentium, the coprocessor is built into the main processor. Internally, the math coprocessor does its calculations using data in the same format as the Delphi Extended type.

That sounds logical

Delphi components are bursting with properties that have just two possible values: True and False. The data type for these properties is called Boolean, after George Boole, who was such a nut for logic puzzles that he invented a symbolic logic to solve them. Delphi uses 1 byte to store a Boolean variable; a byte with the value 1 stands for True, and a byte with the value 0 represents False.

A real character

Computers also have to store text — gobs and gobs of text! Text is made of characters, and the Char type stores a single character. A Char occupies 1 byte, and it can have 256 different values. The values from 0 to 31 are control characters, such as Tab and carriage return. In most fonts, characters 32 to 127 are letters, numbers, and punctuation, and those from 128 to 255 are foreign and other special characters. Try the following exercise to see a list of all characters from 32 to 255:

1. **Place a draw grid component on a new form and set its FixedRows and FixedCols properties to 0.**

2. **Set ColCount to 2 and RowCount to 224.**

3. **Insert these lines in the OnDrawCell event handler:**

```
WITH DrawGrid1.Canvas DO
  IF Col = 0 THEN
    TextOut(Rect.Left, Rect.Top,
      IntToStr(Row+32))
  ELSE
    TextOut(Rect.Left, Rect.Top,
      Char(Row+32));
```

4. **Run the program.**

    You get a list like the one in Figure 14-2 showing each character and its corresponding numeric value. Note that in the last line of the event handler, I use Char as if it were a function to convert the number that represents the current row into a character. The street runs both ways — Byte('A') is 65, for example.

The character sets represented by the Char data type were obviously invented by English-speaking people, with a few crumbs tossed to the European languages. Displaying Sanskrit or Cyrillic characters has always been difficult, if not impossible. The Unicode standard, used internally by Windows NT, allots 2 bytes to every character, making possible 65,536 different characters — enough for every known alphabet and then some. The WideChar data type in Delphi represents a Unicode character. However, neither Delphi nor Windows 95 uses Unicode internally. For now, writing a Delphi application that uses Unicode falls into the realm of "Delphi Programming for Rocket Scientists."

234	ê
235	ë
236	ì
237	í
238	î
239	ï
240	ð
241	ñ
242	ò
243	ó
244	ô
245	õ
246	ö
247	÷
248	ø
249	ù
250	ú
251	û
252	ü
253	ý
254	þ
255	ÿ

Figure 14-2:
Each value for a Char type variable corresponds to a numeric value from 0 to 255.

There are some strings on me

If you need to represent the Sex field in a personal data record (that's M or F, not Y or N!), a single character is enough, so use the Char type. For text-based data in general, though, you use a whole string of characters at once. The Delphi 3 ShortString data type can hold up to 255 characters, which is enough for most purposes. It is important to point out that Delphi 2.0 introduced the ShortString type to replace the String type in Delphi 1.0 (and for that matter, ShortString replaces String in Turbo Pascal and Borland Pascal as well).

A Delphi 3 ShortString is an array of characters that takes up 256 bytes of memory, but most of the strings your program uses won't be 256 characters long. So Delphi 3 reserves the first byte of a ShortString variable to hold a value representing the length of the text string it contains. If the value of the string is 'Stromboli', the length byte holds character number 9.

Old-time Turbo Pascal users know that you can fiddle with the length byte of a ShortString (that is, the old String type) by referencing the 0th element of the array. For example, this line shortens a ShortString variable by one character:

```
Dec(MarieAntoinette[0]);
```

Keep in mind that this programming trick works only in the ShortString.

Delphi also supports another type of string called a *PChar* (pronounced *pee-char*). A PChar is an array of characters, like a String, but it doesn't have a length byte at the start. Instead, it has a null (zero) character after the last in-use character, from which it gets the alternate name ASCIIZ *(askee-zee)* string. Just to confuse you further, some folks use the terms *zero-delimited string* and *null-terminated string*. Figure 14-3 shows how the same text string would be stored as a ShortString and as a PChar. The dash at the beginning of the ShortString variable is character #45 because the string is 45 characters long. The PChar data ends at the #0 character. The only reason to use a PChar rather than a string is if you need more than 255 characters or you're passing text to a Windows function. For now, don't worry about AnsiString, also shown in Figure 14-3 — I describe AnsiString in more detail in the next subsection titled, "Honey, I blew up the string."

Figure 14-3:
Storing a
string as
ShortString,
PChar, and
AnsiString.

You can declare a PChar in one of two ways:

```
VAR
   MyNonPointerPChar : ARRAY[0..300] OF Char;
   MyPointerPChar : PChar;
```

The first variable can be used immediately by your program. The second is a pointer (more about pointers in the section titled "Let me give you a pointer") and can't be used until you set aside some memory for it to point at.

A PChar can hold lots more text than a string, up to 65,535 characters! On the other hand, PChars are more awkward to use. A simple task such as assigning one PChar's value to another requires a call to StrCopy, one of the many PChar-specific functions Delphi offers. (They all begin with *Str.*) Delphi uses strings rather than PChars wherever possible and you should do the same. See Chapter 18 for some gory stories about the consequences of misusing PChars.

Honey, I blew up the string

People have problems with PChars, period. Yet Windows wants to wallow in them. Delphi 3 bridges a gap between a human distaste for PChar and Windows' predilection for them with AnsiString, a type of string with the best characteristics of both. Like a PChar, the AnsiString ends in an ASCII zero character. Like the ShortString, it has its length stored at the beginning. However, the stored length is a 32-bit quantity, and the length of an AnsiString is limited only by available memory.

Figure 14-3 shows the layout of an AnsiString. Three numbers are before the actual string: The size allotted to the string is the first value; the amount of the actual characters in the string is the third value. In between is a reference count — when you set one AnsiString equal to another, Delphi raises the reference count rather than making another copy of the whole string. The reference count feature means that working with AnsiStrings can be quite a bit faster than working with the older length-byte strings.

Almost all standard string manipulation routines work with AnsiStrings. The only significant thing you can't do is tweak their length by fiddling with the length byte. Delphi 3 provides the SetLength procedure to handle cases when you want to set an AnsiString's length to a specific value. When you need to convert an AnsiString to a PChar, you just typecast it. (I talk about typecasting later in this chapter under the subsection, "The typecasting couch.")

By default, "String" in Delphi 3 (and Delphi 2.0 before it) means AnsiString — old-fashioned length-byte strings are called ShortString. You can set a compiler option to bring back the good old days, so that String has the old-fashioned meaning. But why would you want to?

As if you don't have enough string types already, Delphi 3 has another jumbo-size string type, PWideChar. PWideChar is a zero-delimited character string like a PChar, but it's composed of 2-byte Unicode characters. As noted previously, neither Windows 95 nor Delphi uses Unicode internally, so programming with PWideChars is for super-duper experts only.

Roll your own types

The data types for many properties of Delphi components are complete fabrications. Really! They're made up. In Delphi code, you can define new types based on the ones that are built in to the compiler, or create new data types out of thin air. The simplest fictitious data type is the subrange. The NumGlyphs property for a bitmap button is an example. It's defined like this:

```
type TNumGlyphs = 1..4;
```

In the preceding line of code, the Delphi range-checking code rejects any attempt to assign a value outside the range from 1 to 4.

In a similar vein, you can define string data types that occupy fewer than 255 bytes of memory. Simply follow the word String in the declaration with the maximum number of characters enclosed in brackets. For example, the code for the common dialog components defines the file extension as a 3-character string:

```
type TFileExt = String[3];
```

Use a smaller string type to save memory only if you know that a particular string variable will *never* use more than that number of characters. What, never? No, never! If your *never* turns into *hardly ever,* you'll have big trouble.

With Delphi 3, you don't have to worry about the difference between ShortString and AnsiString. When you follow the word String with a length limit as shown here, Delphi knows that you're asking for a ShortString. Ain't it smart?

Finally, there are data types defined simply by listing (or enumerating) the possible values. You'll find a lot of these enumerated types in Delphi components. For example, the form styles are defined internally as

```
TYPE TFormStyle = (fsNormal, fsMDIChild,
  fsMDIFOrm, fsStayOnTop);
```

Generally, properties that show up in the Object Inspector as drop-down lists of values are enumerated types.

Any simple type that can be matched one-for-one to a whole number data type is called an ordinal type. Ordinal types include all the whole number types and the Char, Boolean, subrange, and enumerated types. Remember the name "ordinal type" because I use it to describe other aspects of Delphi programming.

The typecasting couch

Delphi uses data types to keep you from making mistakes. If you assign a value of one type to a variable of an incompatible type, Delphi gripes. Sometimes, though, you really want to do that. All you have to do is tell Delphi you know what you're doing by using the name of the desired type as if it were a function. This is called a *typecast,* and as long as it's possible, Delphi permits it. TFormStyle(0) equals fsNormal, and Word(fsMDIChild) is one, for example.

A typecast is always possible when the variable's actual type and the desired type are the same size. You can typecast a LongInt to a Single (a 4-byte floating point type) or to an array of four Chars, because they're all 4 bytes in size. That doesn't guarantee such a typecast makes sense, of course!

You use typecasting extensively in the sample programs, but in a slightly different way. The AS keyword tells Delphi to treat an object AS if it were a particular type. The Sender parameter for event handlers is defined as a simple TObject, but if you know that every component using this handler is really a TButton, you can typecast it with an expression like this:

```
WITH Sender AS TButton DO
```

Constant as the North Star

The rule is simple: Use variables to hold values that may change during the running of your program, and use constants for values that won't change. When Delphi compiles the program, constants are hard-coded directly in the machine code. Numbers such as 42 and $COFFEE are constants, as are literal strings such as 'Beware the Ides of March'.

You can also declare named constants to make your code easier to understand. Defining WM_ENTERMENULOOP equal to the number 529 doesn't make your final program any bigger, and it's a lot clearer. Named constants are defined in a constant block beginning with the word CONST.

```
CONST AnswerToUltimateQuestion = 42;
```

Check the Windows unit for a zillion named constants used in calling Windows functions!

Scientific breeding of variables and constants has produced a hybrid of the two: the typed constant. A typed constant starts life with an initial value, like a regular constant, but it's value can be changed in the program just like a variable. And a typed constant defined inside a function does not disappear when the function isn't active.

You use a typed constant in Chapter 9's Icon Viewer program to hold the number of the next icon. Its declaration looks like this:

```
CONST CurItem : LongInt = 0;
```

When the program starts, CurItem's value is 0. When the event handler containing this declaration is called, one or more icons are added to the collection, and CurItem's value is changed to match. Next time the event handler is called, CurItem retains the changed value.

Just to add to the confusion, in Delphi 3, typed constants can be changed only if you've checked the compiler option called Assignable typed constants. If you turn off this option, typed constants can't be changed, but VAR declarations containing a single global variable can include a value, like so:

```
VAR CurItem : LongInt = 0;
```

To preserve compatibility (and sanity), the programs in this book assume the Assignable typed constants option is ON.

Arrays, records, and sets: building structured data types

A structured data type is one that's cobbled together from a bunch of simple data types (or other structured types), and there are three main cobbling styles. An *array* is made up of identical elements, whereas a *record* is a crazy quilt of different types. The Delphi *set* type is like the mathematical sets you may remember from New Math homework. You don't have to tinker up your own structured data types right away, but you find plenty of them in the code of Delphi itself.

Array of hope

The Delphi SYSUTILS unit defines a general-purpose array of bytes like this:

```
TYPE TByteArray = ARRAY[0..32767] OF Byte;
```

Here 0 and 32767 are the lower and upper bounds of the array. (They must be constants, not variables.) In Delphi 3, array size is limited only by available memory, but you still shouldn't use more than you need. Like the mess hall cook says, "Take all you need, but use all you take!" The elements of an array can be any type, even another array type. To refer to the Nth element of the array named Foo, you'd use the expression

```
Foo[N]
```

Here, N is an *index* into the array Foo.

When it comes to passing arrays as parameters to functions, Delphi cuts you some slack. You don't have to say exactly what the lower and upper bounds are, as long as the element type of the array matches. The built-in functions Low and High return the lower and upper bounds. As a result, you can define functions like this:

```
FUNCTION Min(TheArray : ARRAY OF LongInt) : LongInt;
VAR N : LongInt;
BEGIN
  Result := MaxLongInt;
  FOR N := Low(TheArray) TO High(TheArray) DO
    IF TheArray[N] < Result THEN
      Result := TheArray[N];
END;
```

You can pass any array of LongInts into this function, and it returns the smallest one. An array parameter like this, where the bounds aren't specified, is called an *open array parameter*. Open arrays can appear only in parameter declarations, not in type or variable declarations.

A new world record

Visualize a database record in a file — it might store name, age, and salary using a string, a whole number, and a floating-point number, respectively. This Record type declaration defines a single data type holding those three disparate elements:

```
TYPE
  DataRecord = RECORD
    Name : String[20];
    Age : Byte;
    Salary : Single;
  END;
```

To access an individual field of a variable that's a record type, you simply add a period and the field name to the variable name. For example, if ActionRec is a variable of the type shown here, ActionRec.Salary refers to the salary field. (Yes, this is identical to the way you reference a property of a component.)

You may have noticed that this record doesn't follow the rules for choosing data types. It has String[20], Byte, and Single instead of String, LongInt, and Extended. Why? Using the default data types, the record's size would be 270 bytes. With the selected smaller types, it's 26 bytes — less than a tenth as big. Multiply that difference by, say, 1,000 records and you've got a *substantial* difference in file size.

The AnsiString type doesn't even have a fixed size, so the compiler steps in to keep you out of trouble. If you attempt to define a file of a certain record type and the record type contains one or more fields that are AnsiStrings, the compiler gags and refuses to process your code. The error message confusingly says the record type needs "finalization." Don't worry about that — just redefine the string field as a ShortString or an ARRAY OF Char.

When just a single variable is involved, use the large and flexible default choices. But when you have lots of variables in a file or array, use the smallest type that holds the needed data.

Set 'em up

Star Wars, The Empire Strikes Back, and *Tax Return of the Jedi* (whoops! I meant *Return of the Jedi*) make a set. Your video collection may include all of them, none of them, or any one or two. You may have multiple copies of one or all, but that's not important in determining whether you have a complete set. For each possible element in the set, either you own it or you don't — sets in Delphi are just like this!

Consider the BorderIcons property for a form. It explodes into four True or False subproperties: biSystemMenu, biMinimize, biMaximize, and biHelp. The value of BorderIcons is displayed as a pair of square brackets [] enclosing the names of the subproperties that are True. BorderIcons is a set. Specifically, its type is defined like this:

```
TYPE
  TBorderIcon = (biSystemMenu, biMinimize, biMaximize,
          biHelp);
  TBorderIcons = Set OF TBorderIcon;
```

In this case, the possible elements of the set are all values in the enumerated type TBorderIcon. A set can also be defined using a subrange. For example, in the DB unit you find

```
TYPE TDBFlags = Set OF 0..15;
```

The TDBFlags type is defined with 16 possible members. A set can be defined to have up to 256 possible members of any ordinal type. It'll be a *long* time before your *Star Wars* video collection overruns the capacity of a Delphi set!

An ordinal type is one that can be matched one-for-one with a whole number data type. All whole number, Char, Boolean, and enumerated types are ordinal. Strings, floating-point numbers, and structured types are not.

Delphi generates especially fast and efficient code for set types defined with a limited number of possible elements. Remember, each possible element of a set takes 1 bit in memory. In 32-bit Delphi 3, the limit is (as you've already guessed) 32.

Figure 14-4 is the event handler for the font speed buttons that you add to the simple editor project in Chapter 8. Each button's Tag property contains the numeric equivalent of one of the font styles. If the button is down, the code adds that style to the font's Style set; otherwise, it removes it. In Figure 14-4, the + means *union,* or add members of one set to another. The – means *difference,* or remove members of one set that are in another.

You can observe two different kinds of typecasting in Figure 14-4. The first line after the begin uses AS to typecast the Sender parameter to TSpeedButton. The two lines that change the font style typecast the Tag property (a LongInt) to the enumerated type TFontStyle. The typecast is necessary because Style is defined as a Set of TFontStyle.

Figure 14-4:
This event
handler
code uses
typecasting
to change
font styles.

```
MyEditor.pas
MyEditor
    procedure TForm2.SpeedButton5Click(Sender: TObject);
    begin
       WITH Sender AS TSpeedButton, Memo1.Font DO
          IF Down THEN
             Style := Style + [TFontStyle(Tag)]
          ELSE
             Style := Style - [TFontStyle(Tag)];
    end;

242: 1                    Insert
```

Nailing your files

You've written code by using Delphi components that load and save their
own data to files on disk, and you've used Delphi components to work with
database files. You probably find that it's easiest to use components for file
access whenever you can, for example, read small to medium text files by
loading them into a memo box and flipping through the lines.

On the other hand, when you come to a file problem that can't be solved
with a component, Delphi offers three types of file variables: TextFile, typed,
and untyped. They're defined like this:

```
VAR
   MyTextFile    : TextFile;
   MyTypedFile   : File OF MyType;
   MyUntypedFile : File;
```

If the file you want to read is human-readable text, use a TextFile file type. If
it consists of many identical chunks of data, use a typed file of a record type
that matches the layout of the data chunks. And if it has a complex structure
or no structure, use an untyped file. You can find example code for reading
and writing all three types in the Delphi manual and help system.

Let me give you a pointer

Pointers are the bane of budding programmers. They're single-handedly
responsible for the majority of hard-to-find bugs, and some programmers
never master them — that's the bad news. The good news is Delphi frees
you from most of the aggravation surrounding pointers. (Technically, Delphi
components *are* pointers, but you never have to think about it.)

So, what is a pointer? A pointer is an address of a location in memory; a pointer variable points to another variable. You define a pointer type by putting a caret (^) in front of an existing type name. To refer to the variable pointed to by the pointer, put a caret after the variable name, like so:

```
VAR MyPointer : ^LongInt;
...
MyPointer^ := -1161889074;
```

But there's a catch: The variable the pointer points to doesn't exist; there's no memory allocated to it. (When a programming concept spawns convoluted phrases such as "the variable the pointer points to," you just *know* it must be trouble!) Global variables occupy memory throughout the run of your program, and local variables are automatically created when the function that contains them executes. But the variable a pointer points to is created only when you, the programmer, write code to allocate memory for it. Once you do, it's like feeding a stray dog: *You* are also responsible for cleaning up the mess. You have to write code that frees up the memory the pointer was using and returns it to the general pool, like this:

```
VAR MyPointer : ^LongInt;
...
GetMem(MyPointer, 4);
MyPointer^ := -1161889074;
DoSomethingWith(MyPointer);
FreeMem(MyPointer, 4);
```

You've already met the PChar data type, which is a pointer to a zero-delimited array of characters. The AnsiString data type is actually a pointer, too, but it's a really weird one. A normal pointer points to the beginning of a chunk of memory; an AnsiString points to a location in the chunk. Specifically, an AnsiString's data consists of a header made of three 4-byte Integers representing the allocated length, the reference count, and the in-use length of the string, followed by the characters of the string itself. The pointer points to the beginning of the character data, *not* to the header. (Look back at Figure 14-3 if this is confusing.) Because the pointer points to the beginning of the character data, you can get away with simply typecasting an AnsiString to a PChar when you need to pass a PChar to a Windows function. Never meddle with AnsiString innards; the compiler handles it all behind the scenes.

Putting It All Together

By now you should have a pretty good handle on the kinds of data Delphi programs can store. So now you have data — but no data processing. To do anything with the stored data, you have to write code (no shock!). You experience writing Delphi code throughout the first part of this book; now I tell you why the code you wrote works.

Idiomatic expressions and hot operators

Operators operate on operands. More specifically, they modify or combine variables or constants in a way that's dependent on the data type. For example, the + operator between two numbers returns their sum. But if you put the + operator between two strings, whether they're old-fashioned length-byte strings or modern Delphi 3 strings, it glues them together: 'Two' + 'Two' equals 'TwoTwo'.

An *expression* is an operator with its operands. Here are some expressions:

```
X * Y
'Happy' + ' Birthday'
Bob = Leland
```

You can use an expression in place of a variable just about anywhere you're not trying to *change* that variable.

The four math operators (+, –, /, and *) work on any numeric type, as do the comparison operators (=, >, >=, and so on). If either operand in a math operation is a floating-point number, the result is a floating-point number. For whole numbers only, the DIV operator returns the whole number quotient of a division, and MOD returns the remainder.

Boolean operators combine logical expressions — the operators are AND, OR, XOR, and NOT. Suppose the Boolean variables A and B represent "Ivan is tall" and "Ivan is fat," respectively. A AND B is True only if Ivan is both tall and fat. A OR B is True if he's either tall or fat or both. A XOR B is True only if he is tall and thin, or short and fat — tall or fat, but not both. Finally, NOT A is True only if Ivan is not tall.

Figure 14-5 is a Delphi form that displays a truth table for AND, OR, and XOR. The cells in each table contain the result of combining the logical values in the row and column headers using the specified logical operator.

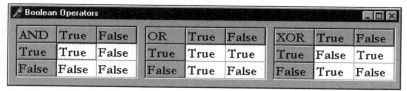

Figure 14-5:
This form
displays the
results of
combining
True and
False using
each of
three
Boolean
operators.

The logical operators can be applied also to whole numbers. In that case, they operate on each corresponding pair of bits in the two numbers. The most common use for this technique is to see whether a particular bit is set to 1, like this:

```
IF Flags AND WF_ENHANCED > 0 THEN
```

You almost never need to know that NOT $COFFEE equals $FF3F0011, or that $BEEF XOR $FACE is $4421.

About 99.44 percent of set operations use the *IN* operator to determine whether a particular member is present in a set. For example:

```
IF fsBold IN Font.Style
```

For those rare occasions when you have to perform gory mathematical operations on sets, the +, -, and * operators mean union, intersection, and difference, respectively. Thinking again of sets as video collections, the union of your set and mine includes all the videos that either of us own. The intersection is the ones we both have. The difference is the set of videos that you have but I don't — those are the ones I want to borrow!

The + and – operators have yet another set of meanings when used with PChars. Add 1 to a PChar and you get a pointer into the same text string, but one character further along. For example, if the PChar variable *Yahoo* contains 'Neil', then *Yahoo+1* is 'eil'. If I now change 'Neil' to 'Nell', *Yahoo+1* is 'ell'. Crazy? You bet! And misusing PChar math can make your program spew General Protection Faults (GPFs). The more you learn about PChars, the better Strings look. And of course, the AnsiStrings are the best of both worlds.

Making a statement

An old-fashioned DOS-based program is like a simple list of instructions for the computer to follow, one after another, whereas a Windows program is a set of contingency plans that are activated in response to events. When you start to pick apart those contingency plans, however, you find that deep down inside, each one is a list of instructions for the computer to follow, one after another. In either case, the instructions in the list are called *statements*. Just as you end an English sentence with a period, you end a Delphi statement with a semicolon. Statements come in two flavors: simple and compound.

Just a simple statement

Delphi accepts three kinds of simple statements: assignments, calls, and gotos. An *assignment* gives a value to a variable. A *call* executes a procedure, function, or method elsewhere in the program, and then returns to the line after the one that called it. A close encounter with the third kind, *goto,* is best avoided as I explain later in this section at the Technical Stuff icon.

You've used quite a few assignments in the sample programs you built earlier in this book. For example:

```
Button1.Enabled := False;
```

The := symbol is the assignment operator: It takes the variable that's to its left and gives it the value that's to its right. The value on the right can be any expression that's compatible with the data type of the variable.

A procedure call is an instruction to go execute a bundle of statements elsewhere in the program and then return. For example, when you define a button's OnClick method with the single statement

```
Close;
```

you are telling the computer to go execute the method called Close. A function call is the same as a procedure call, except that a function brings back a result value when it returns to the caller.

The third variety of statement is similar to a line that's common in opinion polls — "If your answer is no, skip to question 42." The *Goto* statement jumps to another statement in the program, such as a procedure call. However, it never returns. Gotos are considered gauche and ill-mannered, and you're better off pretending that they don't exist.

Compounding statements

Suppose that you want to tell your Delphi program to wash and wax the floor if it's dirty. You might write code like this:

```
IF IsDirty(Floor) THEN Wash(Floor);
Wax(Floor);
```

However, this code doesn't quite do what you wanted. The floor gets washed if it's dirty all right, but it gets waxed whether it's dirty or not. A compound statement solves the problem:

```
IF IsDirty(Floor) THEN
  BEGIN
    Wash(Floor);
    Wax(Floor);
  END;
```

To turn a series of statements into one big compound statement, you put **begin** before the first statement and **end**; after the last statement. You can use a compound statement anywhere that a simple statement is permitted. For example, the following is a valid (if pointless) Delphi statement:

```
BEGIN
  BEGIN
    BEGIN
      BEGIN
        BEGIN
        END;
      END;
    END;
  END;
END;
```

You use compound statements most often with the IF and WHILE statements (they're coming right up) and with the familiar WITH statement.

Conditional statements: decisions, decisions

The IF statement has made frequent appearances in our sample programs:

```
IF Odd(Index) THEN Height := 2*Height;

IF odFocused IN State THEN Brush.Color := 0;
```

```
IF Bevel1.Height = 8 THEN
  Self.ClientHeight := Bevel1.Top
ELSE
  Self.ClientHeight := Bevel1.Height +
    Bevel1.Top + 8;

IF OpenDialog1.Execute THEN
  BEGIN
  ...
  END;
```

The basic framework is always the same:

```
IF <Boolean expression> THEN
  statement
ELSE
  statement;
```

The ELSE portion is optional, and either or both of the statement parts can be a compound statement. If the Boolean expression (called the *condition*) is True, the first statement gets executed; otherwise, the optional ELSE statement gets executed.

When you start to type an IF statement, first type the framework:

```
IF THEN
  begin
  end
ELSE
  begin
  end;
```

Now go back and fill in the condition between IF and THEN, and type the appropriate statements between the two begin..end pairs. By doing this, you ensure that your begin..end pairs match up correctly and that they are aligned in the text, so you can easily see what matches what.

You can nest IF statements by using another IF statement as the statement part of the first IF. However, it's easy to mix up which ELSE goes with which IF. To avoid confusion, always use a begin..end pair around nested IF statements.

Sometimes you need to test a particular variable against a bunch of different values. If the variable is an ordinal type, the CASE statement is more effective than stacking up dozens of IF statements.

A CASE statement looks like this:

```
CASE <variable> OF
  <Label1> : statement;
  <Label2> : statement;
  <Label3> : statement;
  ...
  ELSE statement;
END;
```

The variable part can be any variable, expression, or function result as long as it's ordinal. The labels must be one or more constants or ranges of constant values separated by commas. For example, these are all valid:

```
'A' :
False, True:
fsBold..fsStrikeOut:
1..4, 6..10 :
```

The CASE statement is more efficient than multiple IF statements, and also easier to read.

Loops: going around in circles

Computers are good at doing stuff over and over again, performing repetitious tasks that would bore a human to death. Delphi provides three kinds of looping statements:

Purpose	*Loop type*
Repeat a statement a specified number of times	FOR..DO loop
Execute a statement once and keep doing it until a condition becomes True	REPEAT..UNTIL loop
Execute a statement only while a condition remains True	WHILE..DO loop

A FOR loop requires a local control variable of some ordinal type. It looks like this:

```
FOR N := lower TO upper DO
  statement;
```

You can look, but don't touch. That is, your program must not try to change the value of the control variable. After the FOR loop is over, Delphi makes no promises about the value of the control variable, so don't make any assumptions. Delphi 3 requires that the control variable *not* be a field of a record type — it has to stand alone.

The statement (simple or compound) is executed once for each number, starting with lower and going all the way to upper. You can also reverse it by putting the upper limit first and replacing TO with DOWNTO. The control variable *N* is available within the statement:

```
FOR N := 0 TO Memo1.Lines.Count-1 DO
  WriteLn(POutput, Memo1.Lines[N]);
```

A REPEAT..UNTIL loop always executes its statement part once. After executing the statement, it checks to see whether the UNTIL condition is True. If not, it does it all over again:

```
REPEAT
   statement;
UNTIL condition;
```

A WHILE..DO loop checks its condition first and repeatedly executes the statement part while the condition is True. If the condition is False to begin with, the statement is never executed.

```
WHILE condition DO
  statement;
```

What if you tell the computer to do something a million times, and a problem occurs the third time through? The Break statement helps in this situation — it breaks out of any of the three types of loop. A related statement, Continue, jumps to the next repetition without finishing the loop. Figure 14-6 shows the OnReplace event handler from Chapter 5's simple editor project. It uses a WHILE True DO loop, with Break statements to break out of the loop when the search text isn't found or when one replacement has been made and the Replace All option wasn't chosen.

What's my function?

You've called many different functions that are built in to Delphi, as well as a few built-in Windows functions. The Delphi help system lists and explains all the built-in Delphi and Windows functions. If you don't find a ready-made function to suit your purpose, you can write your own.

Figure 14-6:
The WHILE
True DO
loop would
execute
forever, but
the BREAK
procedure
breaks out
of the loop.

For example, if you find that several different event handlers in your program repeat the same chunk of code, you can move that code into a function and call the function from those several event handlers. As a result, your program's size is reduced, and replacing straight code with a function call has no noticeable effect on your program's performance. Also, if you need to change the code later, you can do it in just one place.

A function header starts with the word FUNCTION followed by the function name, parameter list, and returned data type. A procedure header starts with the word PROCEDURE followed by the name and parameter list only. The main body of the function consists of a begin..end pair surrounding one or more statements. Optional TYPE, VAR, and CONST blocks may precede the begin statement.

The purpose of a function is to return a value, so *somewhere* in the function's code you *must* assign a value to the function or to the implicit variable Result. If you forget this step, your function returns garbage!

Parameters are values passed by the code that's calling your function. Each parameter has a name and data type, like a variable. If the name is preceded by the word VAR, the calling code must pass a variable, not a constant, and the function can *change* the actual passed variable by changing the parameter. If the name doesn't have VAR before it, the calling code can pass a variable, a constant, or a function result, and any changes the function makes to the value won't affect the calling code.

When you're passing big variables, VAR parameters are more efficient because only the address of the variable is passed. When you use a value parameter, your function makes a copy of the entire passed parameter. The function can modify this copy, but not the original. Copying a number here and there isn't a big deal, but copying a 1,000-element array certainly is! If you want the efficiency of a VAR parameter without the risk of making unintended changes, put CONST in front of the parameter name. CONST parameters are passed as addresses, but Delphi doesn't allow any changes to them.

The Object under Discussion

In this chapter, I've told you about data and code separately. Now, imagine again if you will, objects that meld the two. Delphi forms and components are objects, and programming in Delphi is mainly a matter of combining and extending those objects. Now that you know more about the data and code that go into the objects you use, you have more freedom to extend them.

Strawberry data fields forever

When Delphi creates a form-type object, it automatically fills in the data fields that define the components on the form and the methods that implement their event handlers. Just before the end of the object type declaration, it inserts the private and public keywords. When you add data fields (and methods), you put them after the private or public keywords. If a field is meant for communication with the outside world, put it in the public section. Any fields that are just for your form's internal consumption go in the private section.

Data field declarations are just like variable declarations. You start with the variable name, add the data type after a colon, and finish with a semicolon.

Data fields in the main form object are like global variables, but better. You can keep them private to your form, yet have them freely accessible in the form. And if the program has multiple instances of the form (for example, child windows), each gets its own copy of the data fields. Anytime you're tempted to use a global variable, see if you can simply create a new data field instead.

A method to your madness

You've probably created a zillion methods with Delphi jumping in to help, but you can also build methods from scratch. Methods have the same advantage over functions that data fields have over global variables: You can make methods private or public, and the methods you write are accessible in any other method of your object. No matter how many instances of an object your program uses, there's only one copy of the code for its methods.

To declare a new method, first enter a normal procedure or function header right *in* the object declaration, in the public or private section. Copy it to the Clipboard, move down into the implementation section, and paste the copy. (Don't stick it inside another method!) Now insert the object's name and a period just before the function name, so Delphi knows who this method belongs to. Add a begin..end pair, enter your code between, and go-go-go!

It's always a good idea to lock in new concepts with a concrete example. How about a simple program that displays two list boxes and generates a list of random numbers in each? The top list box contains five random numbers between 0 and 1,000. When you click on any one of these numbers, you generate 20 random numbers in the bottom list box. The range of the numbers in the bottom list box is 0 to the value of the number selected in the top list box minus one. Piece of cake!

1. **Place a list box on a new form and set Align to alTop and Sorted to True.**

2. **Place another sorted list box, this one with Align set to alClient.**

3. **Put the following line in an OnCreate method for the form:**

```
GetTheData(1000, 5, ListBox1);
```

4. **Delete the begin..end in the OnClick event handler and insert the following lines in the event handler of the first list box:**

```
VAR Number, ErrorCode : Integer;
    S : String;
begin
  WITH ListBox1 DO BEGIN
    S := Items[ItemIndex];
    Val(S, Number, ErrorCode);
    GetTheData(Number, 20, ListBox2);
  END;
end;
```

5. **Page up to the private declarations section of the form object and add the following lines:**

```
PROCEDURE GetTheData(MaxNum, Count: Integer;
                     ListB : TListBox);
```

6. **Copy the line you just wrote to the Clipboard, page down to the start of the implementation section, and paste it in. Insert TForm1 and a period just before the procedure name in the copy you just pasted and add the following code so that the final method looks like this:**

```
PROCEDURE TForm1.GetTheData(MaxNum, Count : Integer;
                               ListB : TListBox);
VAR Number : Integer;
    S : String;
begin
  ListB.Clear;
  Randomize;
  WHILE Count > 1 DO BEGIN
    Number := Random(MaxNum);
    Str(Number, S);
    ListB.Items.Add(S);
    DEC(Count);
  END;
end;
```

This program avoids duplicating code by efficiently combining it into the single method GetTheData. The event handlers OnCreate (for the form) and OnClick (for the top list box) call the method GetTheData to generate the random numbers and place them in a list box. Each call has a different set of parameters and specifies a different list box.

The Key to Understanding Programming

If you just sit back and gawk at the sheer volume of stuff you need to know about programming, you'll probably freeze up in horror. So, don't look. Do! Seriously, if you want to know how to program, the important thing is to *do* some programming. When your ability is small, do something simple. When you get that working, build on it.

Think up something you want your computer to do, and just start working on it in Delphi. It doesn't have to be a simple project, as long as you have patience. Start adding components and building event handlers within the realm of your ability. Most important, always leave yourself with a program that compiles and runs.

When you get stuck, go snooping. Peek into the source code for Delphi components. Study the code for the sample projects in this book. Download code from your favorite on-line service. And of course, ask for help in the on-line forums. Borland has a considerable presence on CompuServe, but you'll find you can exchange tips with fellow Delphi users just about anywhere in Cyberspace.

As for the manuals, you can't memorize them, but try to at least page through them all. Keep one by your hammock, your bathtub, your favorite chair, or wherever you like to read. You don't have to understand the whole thing; just pass the contents in front of your eyes. Later, when you're trying to puzzle out some programming problem, a key word or phrase you've seen may pop into your memory. Look it up!

Many distinguished authors of prose and poetry set themselves a goal of writing something every day. Should an author of Delphi programs do any less? Keep programming, snoop through any code you can find, get at least moderately friendly with the manuals, and find a forum to ask for help. You'll figure this stuff out!

Of course, one of the most famous learning methods is trial and error. You find out about some errors right away because Delphi stops compiling your program and berates you. The tough mistakes are the ones that result in a program that runs but doesn't do what you meant it to. In other words, the program has a bug. In the next chapter, I show you how to work with built-in debugging resources in Delphi.

Chapter 15
Debugging

- -

In This Chapter

▶ Why compiler error messages deserve hearty applause

▶ Why the hints and warnings in Delphi merit a standing ovation

▶ How Delphi programs keep from crashing when errors happen at run time

▶ How to peek at your data while the program is running

▶ How to step through your code line by line

▶ Techniques for applying bug-repellent to your code

- -

*A*ccording to modern legend, the original computer bug was a real, live (well, actually dead) insect found fried in a relay by the late Admiral Grace Hopper. Modern computers don't have any such gross physical components, but if they do what you *tell* them to do instead of what you *mean* for them to do, you still blame the problem on "bugs." *Debugging* a program means correcting it so that it does exactly what you intended it to.

Some errors are so glaringly obvious that Delphi catches them as it compiles the program; Delphi refuses to continue until you correct the error. Other errors come up at run time if your program does something you didn't plan, such as dividing by zero; Delphi posts a run-time error box but still attempts to continue with the program. Logic bugs are the worst — silent, but deadly. The program compiles and runs just fine, but the results are plain wrong. If you run into a logic bug, be very thankful for the substantial built-in debugging features in Delphi.

Grammar Lessons

About the 20th time Delphi interrupts the compile process to grumble about an unknown identifier or something it "expected," you may be tempted to rub your magic lamp and wish all error messages to oblivion. Don't! Every message is helpful; every one is great! If a message is ignored, the compiler gets quite irate. Delphi speaks a very particular language, and if you make a grammatical mistake, you do not want Delphi guessing what to do. If you tell the program, "Throw the baby down the stairs a cookie," it darn well better ask precisely what you mean! If Delphi hits a snag during the compile process, it puts the cursor on the error and displays an error message on the status line. Press F1 to get detailed Help information about the error (though the information may or may not be useful).

If Delphi claims that a perfectly valid built-in function, variable, type, or constant is an Unknown identifier, this message usually means that you forgot to add a unit name to the uses clause. Click the identifier in question to clear the error message, and press F1 for Help. The Help system should tell you which unit contains the identifier.

The Delphi 3 compiler is one smart cookie! Sometimes it displays an error message and highlights a major error. Most of the time, if the compiler hits a syntax error in the code, the compiler continues checking for errors until it simply *must* stop. Instead of a single error message, you may get several at once, as Figure 15-1 shows.

Figure 15-1:
Delphi catches multiple errors at once, so you can correct them all before trying to compile again.

```
procedure TForm1.Timer1Timer(Sender: TObject);
VAR Trk, Min, Sec : Word;
begin
  WITH MediaPlayer1 DO
    BEGIN
      Trk := MCI_TMSF_TRACK(Position);
      Min := MCI_TMSF_MINUTE(Position);
      Sec := MCI_TMSF_SECOND(Position);
    BEGIN {<===}
      Label1.Caption := Format('%.2d', Trk);
      Label2.Caption := Format('%.2d:%.2d', [Minute, Sec]);
    END;
  end;

  end.
```

```
Error: D:\BOOKD4D\update\c15\cdpla32u.pas(39): Incompatible types: 'Array' and 'Word'.
Error: D:\BOOKD4D\update\c15\cdpla32u.pas(40): Undeclared identifier: 'Minute'.
Error: D:\BOOKD4D\update\c15\cdpla32u.pas(44): ';' expected but '.' found.
```

Each error message includes the filename and line number where Delphi detected the error. If you double-click a message, the program jumps to the corresponding source line. The sloppy programmer omitted the brackets around the variable *Trk* in line 39, and accidentally typed **Minute** instead of Min in the next line. Delphi 3 also points out a period in the spot where a semicolon should appear. The compiler not only catches all three errors, but also gives a clear explanation.

Many Delphi compiler error messages are self-explanatory. WHILE and DO go together like a horse and carriage, so Delphi doesn't let you forget the DO. If you use a variable where Delphi expects a type or vice versa, Delphi points out your error. Put a colon instead of an equal sign in a type declaration, omit the final bracket in an array, write an IF statement with no THEN; in every case, Delphi halts and complains at you.

If the error message doesn't make sense to you and the F1-invoked Help isn't any better, look for something wacky in your code. The most common source of confusion is mismatched begin..end pairs. These errors can be confusing because the point of discovery is often many statements past the actual cause. Perhaps you commented out some code and removed an *end* without its *begin*. If eyeballing the code doesn't turn up the problem, try this solution: Print the offending function, circle all the *begins* and *ends,* and draw lines connecting the matching pairs, starting at the outside and working inward. Then post the resulting abstract artwork on your fridge.

Anytime you write code that includes a begin..end pair, type the **begin** and **end** first and then go back and insert lines of code between them.

If you're new to programming, you're bound to suffer through a lot of compiler error messages. They're annoying, but they both force you and help you to remember the rules of grammar in Delphi. You inevitably spend time poring over code, bitterly convinced that Delphi is lying about the error, right up to the moment when you discover the problem. Trust me — using code gets easier. Before long, you'll routinely dash off code that compiles on the first try!

Can You Take a Hint?

If your program has multiple syntax errors (and many programs do!), Delphi 3 can catch several at a time. But the 32-bit compiler's skill at analyzing programs doesn't stop there. Given the chance, Delphi 3 warns you about elements of your code that are syntactically correct but may not be complete or may not do what you expect. If you want, you can have Delphi give you hints about improving your code; just check the Show Hints and Show Warnings boxes on the Compiler page of the Project Options dialog box. Figure 15-2 illustrates the difference between hints and warnings.

The aptly named *Incomplete* function returns True if its *I* parameter is odd. If not, it sets the local variable Useless to the square root of *I*. The Delphi 3 compiler notes a problem here — if *I* is not odd, the function's result isn't defined. A problem exists, but the function doesn't generate any syntax errors as such. Delphi 3 gives you a warning that the function's return value may be undefined.

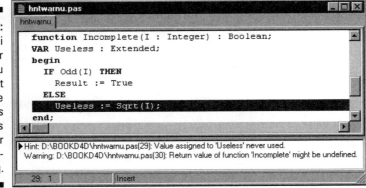

Figure 15-2:
The Delphi
compiler
warns you
about
possible
problems
and offers
hints for
better prog-
ramming.

Because the program doesn't *do* anything with the variable Useless, expend-ing computing power to set Useless to the square root of *I* is silly. You can better use computer power for some other task, such as calculating winning lottery numbers in the background. Delphi 3 hints that your program is more efficient if you avoid wasting effort on the Useless variable.

Delphi warnings help you improve your programming. Whereas compiler error messages catch flagrant syntax errors, warnings alert you to potential logic errors. Strive to write your programs so that Delphi doesn't give you any hints, and you end up writing better programs.

I Take Exception to That!

After your Delphi code passes the nitpicking grammatical scrutiny phase, it compiles and runs. And, as you may expect, while you run the program the run-time error messages kick in. In Turbo Pascal, the honored ancestor of Delphi, a run-time error usually brought the whole program to a screeching halt. Delphi programs are much more robust, surviving most run-time errors thanks to an ultra-modern feature called *exception handling*. I show you how to put this feature through its paces in this section. In a new project, start an OnCreate method for the form. Replace the begin..end pair with the follow-ing local variable declarations and lines of code:

```
VAR
   X, Y : Extended;
   Z : 1..4;
   F : File OF Byte;
begin
   {$S+}
   X := 1/0;
```

```
Z := 5;
Y := 0;
X := 1/Y;
Caption := FloatToStr(X);
Z := 4;
Z := Z + 1;
Caption := IntToStr(Z);
AssignFile(F, 'NOGOOD.BUM');
Reset(F);
FormCreate(Sender);
end;
```

If you run the program, Delphi 3 permits the division by zero (an error) and assigns X a value that represents an infinite number. However, as soon as you try to use the number, you have problems (actually you get error messages shown in Figure 15-3).

Figure 15-3: For most run-time errors, Delphi posts a warning message and continues.

Delete the line containing the division by zero and try again. If you try to run this program again, the compiler flags the line that assigns variable Z a value that is outside its range. Delete that line and recompile. Again, you get the divide-by-zero error from dividing 1 by Y (which is set to 0). The rest of the code in the event handler is skipped, but the program keeps running.

You may notice that the program uses the value of X as the program's caption immediately after assigning the illegal value of 1/Y to it. A method does exist in this madness! The Delphi compiler can optimize your programs by eliminating useless code and never-used variables. If the value of X weren't used in the program, no exception would be necessary, because the Delphi compiler effectively throws away the offending calculation!

Choose Tools⇨Options⇨Environment from the menu bar, click the Preferences tab, and put a check next to the Break on exception option in the
Debugging panel. Run the program again and you get the message box
shown in Figure 15-4. This message comes straight from Delphi, not from
your program. The message is a bit more detailed because it's aimed at the
programmer rather than the user. To correct this error, you can use the
exception name EZeroDivide in your code.

Figure 15-4:
Delphi
displays
this after
you check
the Break
on
exception
option box.

After you close this message box, your program goes into suspended
animation. You can use the techniques described later in this chapter to
poke and pry at the variables involved and find out what caused the error.
After you revive the suspended program, the user-style error box appears.

Comment out the X := 1/Y line and run the program again. This time, you get
a range-check exception on the line that attempts to give variable Z a value
outside its range. Comment out *that* line and try once more. Now, unless you
happen to have a file named NOGOOD.BUM (perhaps data on an ex-
spouse?), you see a File not found error box. In each case, your program
reports the error, skips the remainder of the method, and keeps on ticking.

To comment out one or more lines of code, surround them with braces {like
these} or with parenthesis-asterisk pairs (*like these*).

A peek into the Delphi Help system reveals that run-time error 202 is a
"stack overflow error." Basically, your program started chasing its own tail
and couldn't stop. The last line of the FormCreate method makes another
call to FormCreate, which makes another call to FormCreate, and so on.
As I describe in Chapter 1, each call uses up a little bit of stack space for
local variables, and eventually no stack space is left. Still, in Delphi, almost
all run-time errors get trapped and tamed by the default exception handling.
Delphi also tames the runaway stack overflow error. Time to be a bit brave
and try an experiment. Follow these steps:

1. Drop a label on a new form.

2. Start an OnCreate event handler for the form.

3. Replace the begin..end pair supplied by Delphi with this code:

```
procedure Overflow(I : Integer);
  begin
    try
      Overflow(I+1);
    except
      On EStackOverflow DO
        Label1.Caption := 'Repetitions before overflow:
        ' +
          IntToStr(I);
    end;
  end;
begin
  OverFlow(1);
end;
```

The Overflow procedure is a victim of runaway tail-chasing (called *recursion* at computer-nerd cocktail parties). It calls itself over and over, upping the ante each time by adding one to the parameter it received. If the stack overflows, however, the exception handler catches it and reports just how many repetitions *were* possible. Be aware that, although Windows NT is rock-solid, Windows 95 can become shaky if challenged by stack overflows.

By default, if your program traps an exception, the program reports it and skips the rest of the active function. If you prefer, however, you can tell the program precisely how to respond to each exception. In the OnCreate event handler you worked on, delete the tail-chasing last line and rewrite the rest of the code so it looks like the following:

```
Y := 0;
Try
  X := 1/Y
Except
  ON EZeroDivide DO X := 1.1E+4932;
End;
Caption := FloatToStr(X);
Z := 4;
Try
  Z := Z + 1;
Except
  ON ERangeError DO Z := 1;
End;
```

(continued)

(continued)

```
Caption := IntToStr(Z);
AssignFile(F, 'NOGOOD.BUM');
Try
  Reset(F);
Except
  ON EInOutError DO Rewrite(F);
End;
Caption := 'Success!';
```

For each potentially risky statement, you've given Delphi contingency instructions for exceptions. It tries to set *X* equal to 1 divided by *Y,* unless division by zero occurs, in which case *X* is just set to a Very Large Number. It tries to add 1 to *Z,* unless the result is out of range, in which case it "wraps" back to 1. And it *tries* to open the file NOGOOD.BUM, unless the file doesn't exist, in which case it creates a new file with that name.

Turn off the Break on exception option on the Preferences page of the Environment Options dialog box. Now, whenever you run the program, the three lines that previously caused problems are neutralized by your exception-handling code! The event handler runs all the way to its final statement, which sets the form's caption to "Success!"

A try..except exception handler reacts whenever an exception occurs. Another type of exception handler exists, however, that's proactive rather than reactive. The proactive handler ensures that a particular block of code executes whether an exception occurs or not and uses the keyword *finally* rather than *except*. Here's an example:

```
VAR TempStr : TStringList;
begin
  TempStr := TStringList.Create;
  try
    TempStr.LoadFromFile(InputFilename);
    DoSomethingWith(TempStr);
    TempStr.SaveToFile(OutputFilename);
  finally
    TempStr.Free;
  end;
end;
```

The code that creates the *TempStr* variable is responsible for freeing up the memory it occupies if it's no longer needed. Because the line that frees memory is in the protected block that follows the keyword *finally,* it executes regardless of whether an exception occurs in the try block. Try..finally blocks are useful anytime your program takes some action that requires a follow-up. Allocating and deallocating memory, opening and closing files, creating and destroying temporary objects — these are all candidates for try..finally exception handling.

In most cases in Delphi, the default exception handling prevents a run-time error from causing a program crash. By writing simple exception handlers for risky code sections, you can make your code nearly bulletproof.

Tiptoe through the Code Lines

Really blatant problems in your programs cause exceptions or run-time errors — those are the easy ones to find and correct. But what if the program compiles without error, runs smoothly . . . and produces the wrong result? The problem is with your logic, and only *you* can solve it. You need one of those miniature submarines that can cruise your program's bloodstream and spot clots in the code. Of course, Delphi provides you with all the equipment you need for that little expedition.

Gimme a breakpoint

If your mouse gestures tend to be on the wild side, you may have already discovered breakpoints by accident. Click in the very leftmost column of the Code Editor to set or clear a breakpoint on that line. The line turns red (unless you change the default colors) and a stop sign appears in the left column. Press the F5 key to set or clear a breakpoint on the current line.

If you run the program, it halts just before it executes the breakpoint line. This action enables you to examine your variables or to step through the code one statement at a time and watch for trouble. Figure 15-5 shows a breakpoint in a procedure that mysteriously locks up the system.

For a one-shot instant breakpoint, press F4. Delphi runs until it reaches the current line in the editor, and then halts. You can also choose Run⇨Program Pause (or press the Pause speed button) to suspend the program at whatever line it's currently executing.

Hot on the trace

Okay, your miniature submarine has surfaced at a breakpoint. What now? You could just choose Run again to put the program back in gear and wait for the next breakpoint. Most likely, you want to cruise along slowly, one statement at a time.

Figure 15-5:
Just before
the high-
lighted
breakpoint
line
executes,
Delphi
stops the
program so
that you
can look
around.

```
c15p10u.pas                              _ □ ✕

c15p10u

    procedure TForm1.FormCreate(Sender: TObject);
    VAR Mxyzptlk : LongInt;
    begin
        Mxyzptlk := 0;
►   WHILE Mxyzptlk < 10 DO;
            Mxyzptlk := Mxyzptlk + 1;
        Tag := Mxyzptlk;
    end;

29: 1   Modified    Insert
```

If you press F7, choose Run➪Trace Into, or press the Trace speed button.
Delphi executes just the current line of code and then halts again. If the
current line is a function call and the source code for that function is
accessible, Delphi dives right into it. You can trace through the lines of the
function and of any functions it calls, and so on. The current line is always
highlighted and marked by a triangle in the left margin. (You can see it just
below the breakpoint line back in Figure 15-5.)

Step on it

Sometimes the capability of Delphi to trace into functions is a bane, not a
boon. To avoid taking a pointless detour into a bug-free function, Step, don't
Trace. Press F8 or choose Run➪Step Over. The whole function executes at
full speed, and the program halts at the line after the function call.

The Trace Into speed button looks like a flea jumping into a box. The Step
Over speed button looks like a flea jumping over a box.

Advanced breakpoints

What if you suspect trouble on the thousandth time through a particular
code loop? You *could* put a breakpoint in the loop and run to that spot a
thousand times. (Hey, you *could* carve the program on stone tablets, too!)
But a pass-count breakpoint is a better solution. Just follow these steps:

1. **In a new project, create an OnClick method for the form with nothing
   in it but an empty comment, { }.**

2. **Click in the far left column of the method's end line or move the
   cursor to the line and press F5.**

3. **Run the program and click the form to trigger the breakpoint.**

4. **Choose View⇨Breakpoints.**

   You should see one breakpoint in the Breakpoint list window.

5. **Highlight it and then right-click and choose Edit Breakpoint from the pop-up menu.**

6. **Choose Properties from the pop-up menu.**

7. **In the Pass count line of the resulting dialog, enter** 10 **and click the Modify button.**

8. **Run this program and click the form repeatedly.**

   The breakpoint triggers every tenth time it's reached.

9. **After you reach the breakpoint, press F9 to get the program rolling again and keep clicking.**

What if you suspect a problem if variable *BabyBop* is larger than variable *Barney?* You can use the same Edit breakpoint dialog to set a *condition* for the breakpoint. In this case, you simply enter **BabyBop > Barney** on the Condition line. Now, each time you reach this line, Delphi checks the condition and breaks only if it's True. Figure 15-6 shows a sample program, its breakpoint list, and the Edit breakpoint dialog.

Figure 15-6:
You can set
breakpoints
to trigger
after a set
number of
passes or if
a certain
condition
is True.

After you set up a fancy pass-count or conditional breakpoint, you may want to keep it even if you're not debugging. Instead of deleting the breakpoint at the end of a debugging session, highlight it in the Breakpoint list window, right-click, and choose Disable Breakpoint. In the Code Editor, the stop sign and the line's highlight turn gray.

If you close the Edit breakpoint box by clicking the New button rather than Modify, you're creating a brand new breakpoint on the same line. Doing so enables you to set a conditional breakpoint and a pass-count breakpoint on the same line. If you put both types of breakpoint on the same line, the pass count advances only if you reach the breakpoint and the condition is True.

Demystifying Data

Now you know how to navigate your program's code, how to stop at a particular line of code, and how to run your program one line at a time. But *why* would you want to do so? The main reason is to check on the values of variables. Delphi can squawk if a variable's value goes completely out of range, but only a human operator can spot more subtle problems. You know how to navigate your code and follow the sequence of execution; now you need to raise the periscope and take a look around.

Don't hesitate — evaluate

Way, way back, many chapters ago, I discuss the Evaluate/Modify dialog. Ctrl+F7 displays this dialog any time (or you can choose it from the Run menu). You can use this dialog to perform simple calculations or to convert numbers from hexadecimal to decimal. But its real purpose is revealed in a hot and heavy debugging session — it enables you to peek at (and even modify!) variables. After the program stops, you can get the value of any global variable or any local variable accessible to the current line. Not only that, but if you suddenly realize the value is wrong, you can also patch it up and continue debugging the program. Of course, you need to remember to go back and correct the *code* so that the variable doesn't get the wrong value the next time around.

You can also evaluate expressions combining multiple variables and constants. Of course, you can't change the result; if you want to change the sum of Foo and Bar, you must change Foo or Bar — or both!

Watch it!

Suppose that you can see a variable has the wrong value, but you can't figure out how it got that value. You can try various breakpoints until you find a spot where the variable looks right and then step through the lines of code, evaluating the variable after each step. But if you'd rather just solve the problem as fast as possible, open the Watch list window instead.

If you press Ctrl+F5 or choose Run⇨Add Watch from the menu bar, Delphi asks for a variable name. After you add a watch variable, the Watch list window appears. (You can also choose View⇨Watches from the menu bar.) A variable in the Watch window has no more privacy than a goldfish. Every time the program stops at a breakpoint — every time you step into or over a line of code — Delphi updates the variable's value in the Watch window. *Now* stepping through the program watching for suspicious changes is practical! Just tap, tap, tap on the F7 key and keep your eye on the Watch window.

How'd I Get Here?

Delphi programs are surprisingly straightforward. Almost all the code *you* write is in the form of event handlers, and the event handler gets called if an event occurs. Rarely does any doubt exist about the sequence of function calls that led to a particular line of code executing.

If you ever *do* wonder about the path your program took to reach the current line, choose View⇨Call Stack. The list in the Call Stack window, as shown in Figure 15-7, starts with the currently active function. Next comes the function that called the active function and then the function that called it and so on all the way back to the granddaddy function that represents the main program. If you find anything unlikely in the call stack, select a line and right-click to view or edit the corresponding source code.

Figure 15-7:
This series
of function
calls leads
to a simple
OnClick
event.

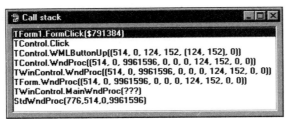

Bug-Repellent Programs

Nobody writes buggy programs on purpose. Bugs creep in because people are careless or don't understand exactly what they're doing. Spending a little extra time *thinking* about the code you're writing is far better than wasting days tracking down problems later on.

You can do some things to armor your programs against bugs. For example, whenever you can, turn logic errors into run-time errors. Really! If the variable Smee should always be in the range –12 to 12, define it to have that range. Now, if an error in the program sets Smee to 42, you're alerted by a range-check error. This method sounds a little like testing for land mines by clomping around in heavy boots, but an exploding run-time error truly is better than a lurking logic error.

Many program statements aren't fully under your control because they process the user's data. If possible, don't give the user the chance to enter invalid data. And use try..except blocks to protect any risky statements. What's risky? You find out as you go along, but for starters always protect statements involving division by a variable and input/output statements.

Delphi attempts to protect you from pointers, the world's biggest supplier of bugs. Mistakes with pointers can trash completely unrelated data in your program, and they're hard to track down because the tiniest change to your code may change their behavior. If you have a choice, don't use pointers; but if you must use them, *triple*-check your code. Make sure that you always allocate the necessary amount of memory and always deallocate precisely the same amount after you're through. Never access the variable before you allocate its memory or after you free its memory. Do all this and you still may have some pointer-related bugs, but they're fewer.

You discover how to program by programming, and you find out how to debug by debugging. Believe me, you'll have plenty of opportunities to master debugging. Keep writing code and debugging any errors you make.

Chapter 16

Working with Internet Components

● ●

In This Chapter

▶ An HTML form that allows you to visit Web sites

▶ An FTP form that allows you to copy files from a remote site

▶ A simple e-mail form-based application

● ●

*W*hat is the hottest topic in the world of computers today? Without any doubt, the hottest topic is the Internet, and it has taken the computer world by storm. Corporations, governments, users' groups, individuals, religious organizations, and every other kind of organization you can imagine (good or bad) are on the Internet. Want to learn about news from the Bee Gees? Go to the Internet. Would you like to check the weather in Phoenix, Arizona, today? Just use the Internet. Want to monitor the latest news or even listen to an FM station in another state? Use the Internet.

Delphi 3 offers a set of components that support programming forms that tap into the Internet. This chapter looks at sample Delphi applications that Borland includes with Delphi 3. Why use the applications in particular? Well, programming forms that tap into the Internet is no small task, believe me! By looking at the Delphi 3 sample Internet applications, you can save yourself a lot of code typing. You can find the sample Internet applications in the Internet folder, which is in the Demo folder.

Surfing The Net! (Fur Sure)

The Web alphabet soup *HTML* stands for HyperText Markup Language. HTML uses a strange set of tags that format the text you see in a Web page. (I use the terms *Web* and *Internet* interchangeably in this chapter; for the purpose of programming for them in Delphi, the terms are interchangeable.) Note that the Internet also includes e-mail, file transfer protocols, and other kinds of transactions.

The HTML folder in the Internet folder contains the WebBrows Delphi 3 project. Figure 16-1 shows a sample session with the WebBrows application while browsing at the www.borland.com site. The form contains the following relevant components:

- ✔ **The combo box:** This stores the list of Web site addresses (addresses are called *URLs* in Internet terms). The combo box stores the list of Web sites that you have typed in, so you can go back to a previous Web site without having to retype that site's address.

- ✔ **The Go speed button:** To visit a Web page, type its address in the combo box and click the Go button.

- ✔ **The Cancel speed button:** If the Web page takes a long time to load, you can click the Cancel button to stop loading that page.

- ✔ **The HTML component:** This displays the Web page.

As you view one Web page, you may be able to jump to another Web page. How can you tell? When the mouse pointer appears as a hand, the mouse is over a link to another Web page. If you click the left mouse button when the mouse pointer appears as a hand, you jump to the linked Web page.

Figure 16-1: The WebBrows application while browsing at the www.borland.com site.

The guts of Go

You can locate the HTML component of the Go button in the Internet page of the Components palette. The file MAIN.PAS in the WebBrows project contains the declaration and implementation of the class TForm1. When you click on the Go button, you trigger the code in the following event handler:

```
procedure TForm1.GoButtonClick(Sender: TObject);
begin
  if URLs.Items.IndexOf(URLs.Text) = -1 then
    URLs.Items.Add(URLs.Text);
  HTML1.RequestDoc(URLs.text);
  Statusbar1.Panels[0].Text := HTML1.RequestURL;
end;
```

This event handler does three things:

- First, the event handler adds the address of a Web site to the list box part of the combo box, if that site is not already in the list box. The expression URLs.Text stores the address of the targeted Web site.

- Second, and most important, the event handler asks the HTML component to find and load the page of the targeted Web site. This task takes place by applying the method RequestDoc to the HTML1 component. In case the term "applying" is new to you, it means the following: You call the method RequestDoc; however, because the method is not a regular procedure or function, calling it must be associated with a component. In this case, the component is the HTML1 component. The code — HTML1.RequestDoc( ) — places the dot after the name of the component and before the name of the method. You read this code as "Apply method RequestDoc to component HTML1."

- Last, the event handler displays the address of the targeted Web site on the left side of the status bar.

Canceling that View

The next two event handlers respond to the events related to when the HTML component retrieves the page of the targeted Web site:

```
procedure TForm1.HTML1BeginRetrieval(Sender: TObject);
begin
  CancelBtn.Enabled := True;
end;
```

(continued)

(continued)

```
procedure TForm1.HTML1EndRetrieval(Sender: TObject);
begin
  CancelBtn.Enabled := False;
end;
```

The first event handler enables the Cancel button while the HTML component is busy loading the page of the targeted Web site. This way, if you decide that you don't want to see the page of the targeted Web site, you can stop loading the page while the page is being accessed. The second event handler disables the Cancel button after the HTML component finishes loading the page of the targeted Web site.

What happens when you click the Cancel button while the application is loading a Web page? The program uses the following event handler to respond to the Cancel button:

```
procedure TForm1.CancelBtnClick(Sender: TObject);
begin
  HTML1.Cancel('test');
  CancelBtn.Enabled := False;
end;
```

This event handler invokes the method Cancel with the HTML1 component to stop loading the remaining part of the Web page. The event handler also disables the Cancel button because keeping it enabled makes no sense. You can't cancel the Cancel once you've canceled. Right?

The form contains the View menu with the Document Source command. When you select the Document Source command, the application displays the source text HTML code for the current Web page. The application uses the following event handler to respond to the Document Source command:

```
procedure TForm1.DocumentSource1Click(Sender: TObject);
begin
  with DocSourceFrm do
  begin
    Show;
    Memo1.Lines.Clear;
    Memo1.Lines.Add(HTML1.SourceText);
    Memo1.SelStart := 0;
    SendMessage(Memo1.Handle, EM_ScrollCaret, 0, 0);
  end;
end;
```

Now, I'm going to get down to the brass tacks here: This handler first displays the form, clears the memo1 component in the form, and then inserts the HTML source text in that memo component. The handler obtains the source text by applying the method SourceText to the HTML1 component. In addition, the handler inserts the HTML source text into the memo1 component by using the method Add with that component.

The WebBrows application is by no means a Cadillac of Web browsers; it's just a functional one! Even so, you can cruise the Net with the application — if you have an Internet connection and a modem.

Files to Go!

FTP is more Internet alphabet soup; it stands for File Transfer Protocol, a way of copying files. The FTP folder in the Internet folder contains the FTP Delphi 3 project. Figure 16-2 shows a sample session with the FTP application while visiting the ftp.borland.com site. The application uses a second small form to specify the FTP site to visit. The Delphi program supplies the Borland FTP site as the default one. How nice!

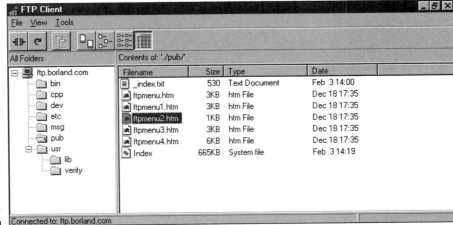

Figure 16-2: The FTP application while visiting the ftp. borland. com site.

The form displays the directories and files using a format similar to that of the Windows 95 Explorer (the directory tree appears on the left window pane, and the file list appears on the right window pane). You can view the files in a directory tree using large icons, small icons, or lists of the filenames with detailed information by clicking on the buttons in the toolbar (these buttons are fashioned after the ones in the Windows 95 Explorer). When you double-click a folder in the directory tree, you open that folder and cause the program to display the list of filenames in that folder.

Handling that FTP

The file MAIN.PAS in the project called Ftp contains the declaration and implementation of the class TMainForm. When you click the connect button (the leftmost button in the toolbar), the application uses the following event handler to connect you with (or disconnect you from) an FTP site:

```
procedure TMainForm.ConnectBtnClick(Sender: TObject);
begin
  if FTP.State = prcConnected then
    Disconnect;
  ConnectForm := TConnectForm.Create(Self);
  try
    if ConnectForm.ShowModal = mrOk then
      with FTP, ConnectForm do
      begin
        UserName := UserNameEdit.Text;
        Pwd := PasswordEdit.Text;
        RemoteHost := RemoteHostEdit.Text;
        RemotePort := StrToInt(RemotePortEdit.Text);
        Connect(RemoteHost, RemotePort);
        Root := DirTree.Items.AddChild(nil, RemoteHost);
        Root.ImageIndex := FTPServer;
        Root.SelectedIndex := FTPServer;
        DirTree.Selected := Root;
      end;
  finally
    ConnectForm.Free;
  end;
end;
```

This handler toggles between connecting to and disconnecting from the FTP site. The handler calls on the connect form to obtain the FTP site host name, user name, password, and port number. Fortunately, the application supplies default values to these fields that lead you to Borland's FTP site. The event handler applies the method Connect to the FTP component and specifies the names of the FTP host and port number using the variables RemostHost and RemotePort, respectively. After connecting you to the FTP site, the event handler displays the server name in the directory tree list.

Copying that file

The WebBrows program has a File menu that allows you to copy, to delete, and to rename a file, as well as to create a new folder. When you click the Copy command, the program copies the selected file to your system. You get a Save As dialog box to select the name, folder, and drive that will store the file you are about to copy. The program uses the following event handler:

```
procedure TMainForm.CopyItemClick(Sender: TObject);
begin
  SaveDialog1.FileName := FileList.Selected.Caption;
  if SaveDialog1.Execute then
    FTP.GetFile(NodePath(DirTree.Selected) + '/' +
                FileList.Selected.Caption,
                SaveDialog1.FileName);
end;
```

This event handler uses the name of the selected file as the default filename in the Save As dialog box (stored in variable SaveDialog1). The handler invokes the Save As dialog box by applying the method Execute to the variable SaveDialog1. If that method returns True, the handler gets the file you selected by applying the method GetFile to the FTP component. The method GetFile requires the name of the file on the FTP site and the name of the file in your system. Having different names for the source and destination files allows you to save a file that you are copying under a different name (for whatever reasons).

Zapping that file

When you click File⇨Delete, the program deletes either a folder or a file, depending on which you select. The program uses the following handler:

```
procedure TMainForm.DeleteItemClick(Sender: TObject);
begin
  if ActiveControl = DirTree then
    FTP.DeleteDir(NodePath(DirTree.Selected));
  if ActiveControl = FileList then
    FTP.DeleteFile(NodePath(DirTree.Selected) + '/' +
                   FileList.Selected.Caption);
end;
```

This event handler determines if the directory or file list is the currently active (the one that has the focus) component. When the directory list component is active, the handler applies the method DeleteDir to the FTP component and specifies the name of the selected folder to delete. On the other hand, when the file list component is active, the handler applies the method DeleteFile to the FTP component and specifies the name of the selected file to delete.

The miracle of (folder) creation

You can create a new folder (if you have the access privilege) on an FTP site by choosing File⇨New Folder from the menu. The program prompts you for the name of the new folder and then creates it. The program uses the following event handler to create a new folder:

```
procedure TMainForm.FileNewItemClick(Sender: TObject);
var.
  doorman: String;
begin
  if InputQuery('Input Box', 'Prompt', DirName) then
    FTP.CreateDir(NodePath(DirTree.Selected) + '/' +
                  DirName);
end;
```

The function InputQuery prompts you for the name of a new folder and stores that name in variable DirName. The handler then creates the new folder by applying the method CreateDir to the FTP component. The method specifies the name of the new folder.

Oh, Yeah! Wait a Minute, Mr. Postman!

Sending e-mail is one the most common things you do on the Internet. In fact, many local electronic bulletin boards offer Internet mail but not full Internet access (to Web pages and so on). The Simpmail folder in the Internet folder contains the Simpmail Delphi 3 project that offers a simple e-mail program. Figure 16-3 shows a sample session with the e-mail application. The program uses the SMTP (Simple Mail Transfer Protocol) and POP (Post Office Protocol) components. SMTP is used to transfer e-mail from one host to another. POP is used to download mail from a mail server.

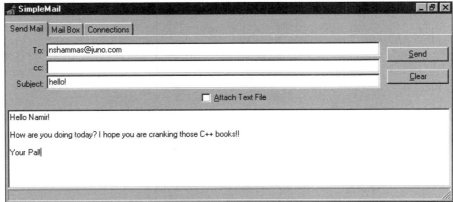

Figure 16-3:
The
Simpmail
application
sending
e-mail.

The form displays tabbed pages: Send Mail, Mail Box, and Connections. Click the Connection page to specify the host address and return address for the SMTP server. After you enter valid information in these edit boxes, you can then click the Connect button and switch to the Send Mail page. On this page you can specify the e-mail addressee, the names of other addressees who get a copy of the e-mail, the subject, and the e-mail text. You can also click the Attach Text File check box to send a text file with the message.

The file MAIN.PAS in the Simpmail project contains the declaration and implementation of the class TMainForm. When you click the Send button, the program uses the following event-handler to send your mail:

```
procedure TMainForm.SendBtnClick(Sender: TObject);
var
  Addressees: string;
begin
  if SMTP1.State = prcConnected then
  begin
    RecvVerified := False;
    SMTPError := False;
    Addressees := eTo.Text;

    if eCC.Text <> '' then
      Addressees := Addressees + ', '+ eCC.Text;
    SMTP1.Verify(Addressees);

    {wait for completion of Verify-Text message send}
    while SMTP1.Busy do
      Application.ProcessMessages;
```

(continued)

(continued)

```
     {Check global flag indicating addresses are in the
      correct format - if true, the text part of the
      message has been sent}
     if not RecvVerified then
     begin
        MessageDlg('Incorrect address format',
                   mtError, [mbOK], 0);
        Exit;
     end
     else
        if cbSendFile.Checked then
           SendFile(OpenDialog.Filename);
     end
     else
        MessageDlg('Not connected to SMTP server',
                   mtError, [mbOK], 0);
   end;
```

This event handler copies the name of the main addressee to the variable
Addressees and then appends the CC (carbon copy) addressees to that
string. The names are separated by a comma and a space. The handler then
sends the e-mail to the addressees by applying the method Verify to the
SMTP1 component. The event handler uses a WHILE loop to allow Windows
to process other applications while the SMTP1 component is busy sending
e-mail. The program uses the global variable RecvVerified to check for
errors. If there are no errors and you had checked the Attach Text File check
box, the event handler brings up an Open dialog box that allows you to
select a text file and then send that file. If the event handler detects any
error, it displays an error message.

Now, that wasn't so complex, was it? Well, maybe a little. Makes you wonder
what's so simple about Simpmail.

The Internet folder contains other Internet applications that support
chatting and online news. Delve into the folder to find out what other
Internet goodies and tools Delphi offers you.

This short chapter gives you a glimpse of the code involved in programming
Internet applications. Although Internet programming is not black magic, it's
not trivial either! At least for now, you may regard Internet programming as
something other than way above your head.

Chapter 17

Handling RadioActive(X) Materials

● ●

In This Chapter

▶ Reading about ActiveX forms

▶ Creating and using a simple ActiveX form

▶ Building a fancy ActiveX form that has a calendar

▶ Crafting an ActiveX form that has a counter, memo, and animation

● ●

*M*icrosoft created OLE (discussed in Chapter 9) to make Windows applications more versatile and more interconnected. The OLE controls (formerly known as OCX) permit software developers to create OLE components that others can insert in their applications. OLE controls are now known as ActiveX components. ActiveX components have a few additional bells and whistles. And by this time next year, who knows what these components may be called! (I am taking bets, by the way.) Chapter 9 discusses OLE 2.0 and Delphi. This chapter looks at the marriage between ActiveX and Delphi forms and how that marriage benefits Web pages.

You can insert ActiveX components not only in applications but also in Web browsers. And — yes — Delphi enables you to create ActiveX forms that you can insert in Web pages. On top of this, you can ask Delphi to deploy an ActiveX form in a sample Web page! This feature is major cool! Just think — you can create Web pages by using Delphi components that you program in Pascal and not Java. So while the whole world is going bonkers about Java, you can dish out neat Web pages that you create without learning another language (unless your boss demands that you do to keep your job — in that case, you better get *Java Programming For Dummies,* by Donald J. and David Koosis, or *Java For Dummies,* by Aaron E. Walsh, both published by IDG Books Worldwide, Inc.).

Creating an ActiveX Form

In this section, I show you how to create (and then send — what Delphi calls *deploy*) an ActiveX form, which Delphi affectionately refers to as an ActiveForm. You can create an ActiveForm that contains a simple edit box component and button component. After you click the button, it toggles the case of the characters in the edit box component. If the edit box component contains no text and you click the button, the form displays the text Hello World! in the edit box.

Making an ActiveForm

Here are the steps involved to create the beloved ActiveForm:

1. **Choose File⇨New from the menu bar.**

   Delphi responds by opening the New Items dialog box.

2. **Click the ActiveX tab.**

   You see the ActiveX tab, which shows a number of ActiveX items, including an ActiveForm. Figure 17-1 shows the New Items dialog with the ActiveX page displayed.

Figure 17-1:
The New Items dialog box with the ActiveX page.

3. **Click the ActiveForm.**

4. **Click the OK button to close the New Items dialog box.**

If the current project does not create an ActiveX library, Delphi displays a warning message and asks whether you want to create a new ActiveX library project. You see, an ActiveForm is stored in an ActiveX library, plain and simple. You must start with an ActiveX library to house, so to speak, the ActiveForm. If you see this warning message, click its OK button.

Adding boxes and buttons

After you create the basic ActiveForm, add the edit box and button components that I mention earlier. From the Standard page in the Component palette, select the edit box component and place it on the form. Likewise, select and place a button below the edit box. Change the Caption of this button into &Toggle. Double-click the button component and type in the following lines of code to replace the original begin..end block:

```
VAR BoxText : String;
begin
  BoxText := Edit1.Text;
  IF BoxText = '' THEN
    Edit1.Text := 'Hello World!'
  ELSE IF BoxText[1] IN ['a'..'z'] THEN
    Edit1.Text := UpperCase(BoxText)
  ELSE
    Edit1.Text := LowerCase(BoxText);
end;
```

The event handler uses the local string variable BoxText to store a copy of the text in the edit box component. The procedure uses an IF statement to first determine whether the variable BoxText contains an empty string. If the variable BoxText contains an empty string, the procedure assigns the string "Hello World!" to the edit box component. If the variable BoxText contains at least one character, the procedure determines whether the first character is lowercase. If the first character is lowercase, the procedure assigns the uppercase version of what's in BoxText to the edit box component. Otherwise, the procedure assigns the lowercase version of what's in BoxText to the edit box component. So the character conversion depends on the case of the first letter in the edit box component. I chose the approach of examining only the first character to make converting between upper and lower case easier.

Examine the listings for the form. Notice that its DPR file starts with the keyword library. You also notice that the form's source code file has a new kind of initialization section. (I cover this and other sections in Chapter 13.) The interface section declares a constant string that is a class ID.

Deploying the ActiveForm

Now that you created an ActiveForm, here's how to deploy it to your Web browser. Here are the steps involved:

1. **Choose Project⇨Options from the menu bar.**

   Delphi responds by opening the Project Options dialog box.

2. **Choose the Web Deployment page and set the Target Dir box to the location path of the ActiveForm DLL file.**

   Use the Browse button to select the project's current directory.

3. **Set the HTML Dir to the location as a path of the HTML file that contains a reference to the ActiveForm.**

   Use the Browse button to select the project's current directory.

4. **Copy the contents of the HTML Dir, paste it in the Target URL edit box, and click the OK button.**

5. **Choose Project⇨Build All from the menu.**

   Delphi responds by building the ActiveX library as a DLL file. This file contains the ActiveForm you created.

6. **Choose Project⇨Web Deploy from the menu bar.**

   Delphi creates the HTML file.

7. **Load your Web browser and load the HTML file that contains the ActiveForm.**

   Figure 17-2 shows the Web page containing the ActiveForm you created.

Now click the Toggle button and watch the text in the edit box change character case! Here is what the text of the HTML file may look like:

```
<HTML>
<H1> Delphi ActiveX Test Page </H1><p>
You should see your Delphi forms or controls embedded in
        the form below.
<HR><center><P>
<OBJECT
    classid="clsid:71A1660C-79C7-11D0-9970-444553540000"
        codebase="C:\Delphi97\Dummies\Ch17/C17p01.dll"
    width=350
    height=250
    align=center
    hspace=0
    vspace=0
```

Figure 17-2:
This Web
page
contains an
Active-
Form.

```
>
</OBJECT>
</HTML>
```

Notice that the class ID name and the DLL filename in the HTML file match the ID in the library source file and the DLL filename generated by Delphi.

It's about Time!

You can create a fancier ActiveForm that tells you the current date and time and shows you a calendar. If you deploy such a form to a Web page, you get a Web page that displays the current time. Cool and double cool, because you can offer this feature in Delphi and not Java!

Create a new ActiveForm by using the steps that I mention at the beginning of this chapter. Drop a calendar component and two UpDown components to the right edge of the calendar component. Also, drop two labels to the right of the UpDown components. Now drop a label below the calendar component and drop a timer component. Change the Min and Max properties of the top UpDown component to 1 and 12, respectively. These values represent the range of the number of months in a year. Change the Min and Max properties of the bottom UpDown component to 1980 and 2010, respectively. These values represent the range of years.

Double-click the Timer component and insert the following statement in the event handler of that component:

```
Label3.Caption := DateTimeToStr(Now)
```

This statement displays the current date and time in the label located below the calendar. Now double-click the top UpDown component and replace the original begin..end with the following code in the event handler of that component:

```
VAR aStr : String;
begin
  try
    Calendar1.Month := UpDown1.Position;
  except
    on EConvertError do begin
      Calendar1.Day := 1;
      Calendar1.Month := UpDown1.Position;
    end
  end;
  Str(UpDown1.Position, aStr);
  Label1.Caption := aStr
end;
```

This statement updates the calendar's month by using the value of the top UpDown component. The try..except block is in this code to catch run-time errors that may creep up if the new month does not have the day number of the previous month. For example, if you selected January 30 and you click the top UpDown component to move to February, the program selects February 1, because no February 30 exists! The preceding statements also update the text in the label component next to top UpDown component to reflect the current month. Now double-click the bottom UpDown component and replace the original begin..end with the following code in the event handler of that component:

```
VAR aStr : String;
begin
  try
    Calendar1.Year := UpDown2.Position;
  except
```

```
    ON EConvertError DO begin
      Calendar1.Day := 1;
      Calendar1.Year := UpDown2.Position;
    end
  end;
  Str(UpDown2.Position, aStr);
  Label2.Caption := aStr
end;
```

The preceding statements update the calendar's year by using the value of the bottom UpDown component. The code also contains a try..except block to catch run-time errors that may creep up if the new month does not have the day number of the previous month. The preceding statements also update the text in the label component next to bottom UpDown component to reflect the current year. Now double-click the form and insert the following code in the form's creation event handler:

```
Label1.Caption := '1';
Label2.Caption := '1997';
UpDown1.Position := 1;
UpDown2.Position := 1997;
Calendar1.Month := UpDown1.Position;
Calendar1.Year := UpDown2.Position
```

The preceding statements initialize the top two labels, the UpDown components, and the calendar component to show January 1997. (You're welcome to change the preceding setting to values that suite your needs.) Follow the instructions in the section "Deploying the ActiveForm," earlier in this chapter, to deploy the ActiveForm calendar you just created. If you browse at the HTML file generated by Delphi, you see a screen that looks like the one shown in Figure 17-3.

Web Page Animated Counter

Many Web pages contain counters that keep track the number of times a Web site is visited. Some Web pages may store additional information on file to retrieve that information later (perhaps the next time you visit the site). You can create an ActiveForm that shows you how many times you loaded it, displays simple animation, and contains a memo component that automatically saves and loads text. You can also throw in the feature of showing the current date and time. Just follow these steps:

1. **Create a new ActiveForm by using the steps that I mention earlier in this chapter.**

Figure 17-3:
This Web
page
contains an
ActiveForm
with a
calendar
and the
current
date/time.

2. Drop a memo component in the form and a label above that memo.

3. Set the caption of that label to Memo.

4. Insert an image component at the right edge of the memo component.

5. Drop two label components below the memo component.

6. Drop two Timer components anywhere on the form.

The first Timer component controls the display of the current date and time. The second Timer component handles the speed of animation.

7. Use the Paint accessory to create three bitmaps to for the animation.

The bitmaps resemble the three lights in a traffic light. The first bitmap (to be stored in file LITE1.BMP) contains the three circles with the colors red, yellow, and green. The second bitmap (to be stored in file LITE2.BMP) contains the three circles with the colors green, red, and yellow. The third bitmap (to be stored in file LITE3.BMP) contains the three circles with the colors yellow, green, and red. Place these bitmap files in the same folder as the project. The second Timer controls loading these bitmaps in the repeated sequence LITE1.BMP, LITE2.BMP, and LITE3.BMP.

8. **Insert the following declarations in the implementation section of the form's source code file:**

```
CONST MEMO_FILE = 'MEMO.TXT';
      COUNT_FILE = 'COUNT.TXT';
VAR ImageIndex : Byte;
```

9. **Double-click the first Timer component and insert the following statement in the event handler of that component:**

```
Label3.Caption := DateTimeToStr(Now)
```

This statement displays the current date and time in the bottom most label in the form.

10. **Double-click the second Timer component and insert the following statements in the event-handler of that component:**

```
ImageIndex := ImageIndex MOD 3 + 1;
  Case ImageIndex Of
    1 : Image1.Picture.LoadFromFile('LITE1.BMP');
    2 : Image1.Picture.LoadFromFile('LITE2.BMP');
    3 : Image1.Picture.LoadFromFile('LITE3.BMP');
  End;.
```

The preceding statements increase the value of the ImageIndex variable and then use the Case statements to load a bitmap (BMP) file.

11. **Double-click the form and insert the following code to replace the original begin..end in the form's creation event handler:**

```
VAR CountFile : TextFile;
    Count, ErrorCode : Integer;
    aStr : String;
begin
  { Read visitation counter }
  try
    AssignFile(CountFile, COUNT_FILE);
    Reset(CountFile);
    Readln(CountFile, aStr);
    Val(aStr, Count, ErrorCode);
    CloseFile(CountFile);
    IF Count < 0 THEN Count := 0
  except
    ON EInOutError DO
      Count := 0;
  end;
```

(continued)

(continued)

```
{ update counter, display it,
  and then store it }
Inc(Count);
Str(Count, aStr);
Label2.Caption := 'You are visitor # ' + aStr;
Image1.AutoSize := True;
ImageIndex := 1;
Image1.Picture.LoadFromFile('LITE1.BMP');
{ Write visitation counter }
AssignFile(CountFile, COUNT_FILE);
Rewrite(CountFile);
Writeln(CountFile, Count);
CloseFile(CountFile);
try
  Memo1.Lines.LoadFromFile(MEMO_FILE)
except
   { do nothing! }
end;
end;
```

The preceding statements initialize the form by reading the counter value from the file COUNT.TXT, increasing the counter value, initializing the image index variable, setting the AutoSize property of the image component to True, updating the counter value in file COUNT.TXT, and loading the text for the memo component from file MEMO.TXT. Whew! Did you get all that?

12. Double-click the OnDestroy event and insert the following statements in the form's closing event handler:

```
try
    Memo1.Lines.SaveToFile(MEMO_FILE)
except
    MessageDlg('Cannot write to file ' +
               MEMO_FILE, mtError, [mbOK], 0)
end;
```

The preceding statements write the text of the memo component to the file MEMO.TXT. Now follow the same instructions from the section "Deploying the ActiveForm," earlier in this chapter, to deploy the above ActiveForm. If you browse at the HTML file generated by Delphi, you see a screen that looks like the one shown in Figure 17-4. Load and close the Web page to observe how the counter increases and how the Web page remembers the text in the memo component.

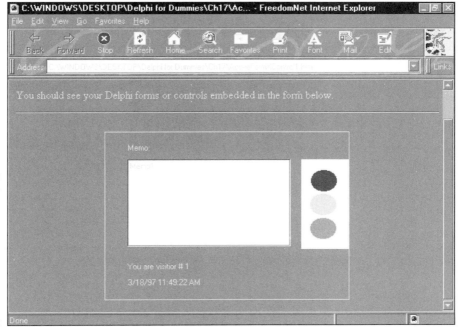

Figure 17-4:
This Web page contains an ActiveForm with a page counter and other fun stuff.

Part V
The Part of Tens

"NO, THEY'RE NOT REALLY A GANG, JUST A PARTICULARLY AGGRESSIVE LAN."

In this part . . .

There's so much to say about Delphi, this book could go on forever. But then you'd keep reading forever, and you'd never get around to programming. That's no fun! So Part V simply hits some of the high and low points along your programming path, and then lets you get on with your life. For example, by now you know how to debug Delphi programs — perhaps you'd like to *avoid* the most common bugs? Well, you get the low-down on their modus operandi in Chapter 18!

Windows is euphemistically called a "rich" programming environment, meaning that it contains more function calls than any sane person could possibly remember with names that nobody can spell. And of course 32-bit Windows ups the ante with more functions and still longer names. Delphi components and built-in functions handle almost all the programming tasks you run into, but occasionally you do need to dive down to the Windows API (Application Program Interface) level. When you do, start by checking out the ten fascinating functions in Chapter 19.

The secret of Delphi programming in three words is: components, components, components! But the code that defines components and the code you write yourself to enhance them — well, that code uses a bunch of functions that are built into Delphi. And after you get past the brouhaha of components demanding your attention, you find some demure objects lurking in the background, objects that can do quite a lot for you. You get an introduction to these fabulous functions and obscure objects in Chapter 20.

So when you feel the urge to expand your horizons, flip to this section and take off!

Chapter 18
Ten Common Mistakes

● ●

In This Chapter

▶ Recognizing and avoiding common programming errors

▶ Comparing floating-point numbers without being thrown for a loop by tiny errors

▶ Understanding range, stack, and integer overflow errors

▶ Observing the destruction that misused PChars can cause

▶ Preventing input/output errors from turning into time bombs

● ●

*W*hen you start debugging your programs, you're bound to find some real bloopers. Here's a preview of several mistakes that every programmer invariably makes at one time or another. If you pull one of these errors yourself, think of it as a rite of passage!

Fencepost Errors

Suppose that you need to put up a 100-foot free-standing fence between your swimming pool and the freeway so that passing motorists don't lose control while checking out your tan. The elegant Art Deco fencing you've chosen needs a post every 10 feet. How many posts do you buy? If you said 10, you just committed a *fencepost error,* more mundanely called an *off-by-one* error. You need a post at one end and then another post every 10 feet, for a total of 11 posts, not 10.

The equivalent question in Delphi might be: How many buttons are in an ARRAY[0..10] of TButton? Again, the answer is 11, not 10. If you want an array with 10 buttons, you need to set the array bounds to [0..9] or [1..10].

Another off-by-one problem surfaces in REPEAT..UNTIL loops, as follows:

```
Commandment := 1;
REPEAT
  Commandment := Commandment + 1;
  EngraveOnTablet(Commandment);
UNTIL Commandment = 10;
```

This loop looks like one that can handle engraving each commandment from 1 to 10, but it's not! In fact, it acts on *nine* commandments, from 2 to 10. The correction in this case is to set Commandment equal to 0 initially.

Most of the time, you can ferret out fencepost errors by "shrinking" the problem. For example, to put up a 20-foot free-standing fence with posts every 10 feet, you need three posts, one at each end and one in the middle. Every additional 10-foot section requires one more post, so the 100-foot fence needs 11 posts. In the REPEAT..UNTIL example, suppose that the condition were UNTIL Commandment = 2. The condition is True the very first time through the loop, so the loop executes once, not twice. Whenever you suspect a fencepost error, try shrinking the problem down to something more manageable.

Empty Statements and Spurious Semicolons

As I discuss in Chapter 14, every statement in the Delphi language must end with a semicolon. Delphi also permits completely empty statements, so lines such as the following are valid:

```
;;;;;;;;;;

(* World.Problems.Solve(Now) *);

begin end;
```

Empty statements are harmless, because the compiler doesn't generate any code for them. Empty statements can even be helpful! An empty statement for a particular value in a CASE statement makes clear that you didn't *forget* that value — you really, truly meant for the CASE statement to do *nothing*.

However, adding a semicolon where it doesn't belong can replace an important statement with an empty statement, and the consequences can be lethal. To see what I mean, follow these steps:

1. **Place an edit box, a Windows 95 UpDown component, a push button, and a list box on a new form, one below the other, all with the same width, as shown in Figure 18-1.**

2. **Set the push button's caption to &Hail and its Default property to True.**

3. **Set the Associate property of the UpDown component to the edit box.**

4. **Insert the following line in the button's OnClick event handler:**

```
HailStone(StrToIntDef(Edit1.Text, 0));
```

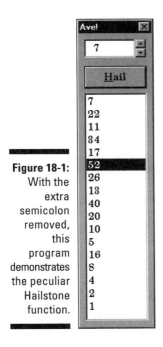

Figure 18-1:
With the extra semicolon removed, this program demonstrates the peculiar Hailstone function.

5. **Insert the following line in the private section of the main form's object definition:**

```
PROCEDURE Hailstone(N : LongInt);
```

6. **Now page down to just after the implementation line and enter the following code:**

```
PROCEDURE TForm1.Hailstone(N : LongInt);
BEGIN
  ListBox1.Clear;
  ListBox1.Items.Add(IntToStr(N));
  WHILE N > 1 DO;
    BEGIN
      IF Odd(N) THEN N := 3*N + 1
      ELSE N := N DIV 2;
      ListBox1.Items.Add(IntToStr(N));
    END;
END;
```

As written, this program loops nonstop. Do you see why?

The WHILE loop in this function is supposed to repeat the three lines of code between the BEGIN and END that follow for as long as *N* is greater than 1. However, the semicolon following DO turns the WHILE loop into a no-exit existentialist nightmare. The WHILE loop now executes the empty statement repeatedly as long as *N* is greater than 1. Because the empty statement doesn't change *N,* this loop runs forever (or until you press Ctrl+Alt+Del). The defective Hailstone procedure compiles just fine, but as soon as it's called with *N* greater than 1, it goes into a tailspin. A Delphi 3 program that's locked in a loop won't do you much good, but at least it doesn't take Windows 95 (or Windows NT) down with it!

You can use a compound statement anywhere a simple statement is valid, so the "orphan" begin..end block after the short-circuited WHILE loop is not a problem.

By the way, the Hailstone function is way cool. The rule is simple: If your number is odd, triple it and add 1. If it's even, divide it by 2. Repeat until the number reduces to 1. Graph the result and you see that it goes up and down wildly before converging on 1, like a hailstone bouncing up and down in storm winds. No way exists to predict how long a particular number takes to reach 1 or even to prove that every possible number does reach 1.

Put a semicolon at the end of every statement, but never insert a semicolon where it isn't needed. In the words of a famous patron of the arts, "Should these commands be ignored, a disaster beyond your imagination will occur!"

The Myth of Floating-Point Equality

Floating-point variables are fuzzy. No way exists to represent the vast majority of numbers with absolute precision, so I settle for as many significant digits as possible. The Delphi Extended data type offers 19 significant digits — enough to measure the distance from here to Alpha Centauri with just a few millimeters of error. Still, two numbers that differ by only that tiny margin are *not* equal.

Don't believe it? Try the following steps:

1. **Place four labels on a new form, one below the other, and set the Alignment property for all four to taRightJustify.**

2. **Set their captions to *X:*, *Y:*, *Y=X?*, and *Y-X:*.**

3. **Add four more labels in a parallel second column.**

4. **Replace the begin..end pair for the form's OnCreate event handler with the following lines:**

```
VAR X, Y : Extended;
begin
  X := 1995;
  Y := Sqr(Sqrt(X));
  Label5.Caption := FloatToStr(X);
  Label6.Caption := FloatToStr(Y);
  IF Y=X THEN Label7.Caption := 'YES'
  ELSE Label7.Caption := 'NO!';
  Label8.Caption := FloatToStr(Y-X);
end;
```

Figure 18-2 shows the result. Squaring the square root of a number *should* give you back the same number, and it *seems* as if it does. But the expression *Y=X* isn't True, and in fact, a teeny tiny difference exists between *X* and *Y*. The difference, about 0.0000000000000001, isn't *important,* but it *is a* difference. This problem can be hard to catch, because it depends on the exact numbers you use. For example, change 1995 to 1996 in the example and the diminutive discrepancy disappears.

Figure 18-2:
You don't need a faulty Pentium to gather tiny errors in floating-point calculations.

The Quite Fatal Monty Python Fig Oil

X : 1995

Y : 1995

X=Y ? NO!

Y-X : 1.11022302462516E-16

After you're over the shock of realizing that 1995 isn't always equal to 1995, you may be wondering what to do. Simply decide how close is close enough. Then, instead of testing whether two numbers are equal, test whether they're close enough.

Returning to the previous example, insert the following line right after the line that declares variables *X* and *Y:*

```
CONST epsilon = 0.000000001;
```

Now replace *IF Y=X* with the following line:

```
IF Abs(X-Y) < epsilon
```

The absolute value of the difference between *X* and *Y* is much less than one billionth, so the program now reports that *X* does indeed equal *Y*.

Don't Forget the Function Result

Picture this: You've worked all night to finish your tax return before the April 15th deadline. As the sun rises, you rub your eyes and carefully seal the envelope — without enclosing the tax forms! Doing the same thing is easy if you're writing a function, especially if you stay up all night programming. Your code may carefully calculate a dozen intermediate values, meticulously combine them into one temporary variable, and then neglect to assign that variable to the function's return value. Such a function returns pure unadulterated garbage, nothing but random bytes skimmed from your system's memory.

The best cure is to *avoid* that temporary variable entirely. Every Delphi function has an implicit local variable named *Result,* and you can and should use Result instead of a temporary variable. Here's a simple example:

```
FUNCTION DefaultExt(const FileName, Extension :
    String) : String;
BEGIN
  Result := UpperCase(FileName);
  IF Pos('.', Result) = 0 THEN
    Result := Result + '.' + Extension;
END;
```

This function converts the filename to uppercase and assigns it to *Result.* Then, if the *Result* variable does *not* contain a period, the function appends a period and the passed extension to the *Result.* No temporary variable needed here!

Ever vigilant, Delphi 3 catches this mistake. As you compile the program, a warning politely appears suggesting that the function result *may* be undefined. Don't mistake politeness for uncertainty! If the compiler says your function result may be undefined, you had better look long and hard at the function to see what's wrong.

Home In on the Range Errors

You should always do your development with the Range checking compiler option turned on. This built-in safety net catches an amazing number of errors! Yes, you can turn it off after you compile the final production version of your program; turning off the various run-time error-checking options shrinks the final EXE file substantially. But if your users report bugs and you need to dive back into the code, grit your teeth and turn those options back on.

You read in Chapter 1 that the Range checking check box on the Compiler page of the Project Options dialog controls range checking. Well, you can also turn range checking on or off by using a compiler switch in your code. {$R+} turns it on for subsequent lines of code, and {$R-} turns it off. These switches supersede the state set by the Range checking check box.

The simplest range errors occur when your program tries to set a variable to a value that's just not in its range. With range checking on, a run-time error occurs. With checking off, the results can be surprising. If you try to pour the four bytes of a LongInt into a two-byte container, the extra two bytes are simply lost. For example, dump the number 98,7654,321 into a *Word* variable and what's stored is 26,801. Who'd have thunk it? But wait — there's more! If you have range checking turned off and you try to access elements outside the bounds of an array, you can destroy the lives of innocent variables! Follow these steps to see what I mean:

1. **In a new project, build an OnCreate event handler for the form, replacing the Delphi begin..end pair with the following code:**

```
VAR
   Lawyer        : LongInt;
   Perpetrator   : ARRAY[1..2] OF LongInt;
   Bystander     : LongInt;
   Addr1, Addr2  : Pointer;
begin
   {$R-}
   Lawyer     := 0;
   Bystander  := 0;
   Addr1      := @Bystander;
   Addr2      := @Perpetrator[Lawyer];

   Perpetrator[Lawyer] := $DADABABA;
   Caption    := Format('%p =?= %p', [Addr1, Addr2]);
end;
```

2. **Set a breakpoint on the line of code that begins with the word Perpetrator.**

3. **Press Ctrl+F5 and add** Addr1, Addr2, **and** Bystander, x **to the Watch window.**

4. **Run the program to the breakpoint.**

5. **Press F7 to execute that one line of code.**

Figure 18-3 shows the dirty deed — the innocent Bystander variable's pristine zero value was stomped into the dust by a range error. The variables Addr1 and Addr2 have the same value, indicating that the nonexistent 0th element of the Perpetrator array occupies the same location as the Bystander variable. This kind of thing happens all the time when you forgo the protection of range checking. You Have Been Warned!

Figure 18-3:
Range error
can wreak
havoc on
nearby
variables.

Stacking Up Errors

Every program running on your system has a memory hunk reserved to hold its code, another hunk for global data, and a third hunk called the stack. This third hunk gets its name from the spring-loaded dish stacks in old-fashioned cafeterias. Take a dish off and the spring pushes the stack up so that the next dish is at the top. Add some clean dishes and they sink down again so that the top dish is at the same height.

Delphi programs don't wash dishes (too bad!), but they do stack *function calls*. After a function gets called, its local variables are pushed onto the stack. If the function calls another function, the variables remain on the stack — they just get pushed down farther to make room for the second function's variables. And after each function ends, its variables pop off the stack.

The Stack checking check box on the Compiler page of the Project Options dialog controls stack checking for your program. The compiler switch {$S+} forces stack checking on for lines of code that follow; {$S-} turns it off. These switches override the compiler options setting.

The only time you need to think about this stack thingie is if a stack error happens. If your program seizes up with a stack error, it may actually need more stack space. You can adjust your functions to use fewer or smaller local variables, or you can tweak the Stack size setting on the Linker page of the Project Options dialog. The 32-bit programs compiled under Delphi 3 have loads more stack space available, which is a good thing, because stack checking can't necessarily protect a 32-bit program with a stack that runneth over.

Most of the time, however, a stack error means that your program is stuck chasing its tail in a recursive loop. The dictionary entry for *recursion* says, "See recursion." If a function calls itself or calls another function that calls it back, that's recursion. If you forget to include a way for the function to break *out* of recursion, that's a stack error. Each time the function calls itself, it uses a little bit of stack space, and eventually the stack is just used up. You usually remember to provide a way out in a function that's supposed to be recursive. You run into trouble if the recursive call is accidental.

Make sure that you've checked the Stack checking check box on the Compiler page of the Project Options dialog. Then start an OnResize event handler for a new form, replacing the begin..end pair supplied by Delphi with the following lines:

```
VAR BigWaste : ARRAY[0..1023] OF Integer;
begin
   BigWaste[1023] := Width;
   IF Odd(Width) THEN Width := Width + 9
   ELSE Width := Width - 9;
end;
```

Run the program, and it crashes with a stack overflow. The BigWaste variable ensures that even the expanded stack of a Delphi 3 program overflows. What happened? Well, any change to the dimensions of a form, whether from mouse action by the user or code in the program, causes an OnResize event. This OnResize event handler changes the Width value, which generates another OnResize event, which changes the width, *et cetera ad nauseam*.

Windows 95 doesn't react *at all* well to stack overflows. If your program has stack checking turned off, a stack overflow could occur *inside* a Windows function. In that situation, Windows itself can crash. Leave stack checking turned on during development, and consider leaving it on in your production code as well. Windows NT is invulnerable to application stack overflows because NT system functions run on a system stack, not the application's stack.

Overflowing Integers

An integer overflow is like a range error, but sneakier. If you run your program with integer overflow checking off, you can suffer mysterious errors in calculations involving whole number variables. Cheer up! If you follow the recommendation in Chapter 14 and use LongInts for all your whole numbers, you almost never experience this one! The compiler switch to turn overflow checking on is {$Q+}; turn it off with {$Q-}.

Here's the deal. If you add, subtract, or multiply two whole numbers, they first get "promoted" to the smallest whole number data type that fits them both. If the result of the calculation doesn't fit in that data type, the extra bits are simply tossed out. I can show you this problem in action. Just follow these steps:

1. **Put six labels on a new form.**

2. **Replace the begin..end pair of an OnCreate method for the form with the following code:**

```
VAR
  B, B1, B2 : Byte;
  I, I1, I2 :SmallInt;
  W, W1, W2 : Word;
begin
 {$Q-,R-}
  B := 255;
  I := 32767;
  W := 65535;
  B1 := B*B; B2 := B+B;
  I1 := I*I; I2 := I+I;
  W1 := W*W; W2 := W+W;
  Label1.Caption := Format('%u*%u=%u',[B,B,B1]);
  Label2.Caption := Format('%u+%u=%u',[B,B,B2]);
  Label3.Caption := Format('%d*%d=%d',[I,I,I1]);
  Label4.Caption := Format('%d+%d=%d',[I,I,I2]);
  Label5.Caption := Format('%u*%u=%u',[W,W,W1]);
  Label6.Caption := Format('%u+%u=%u',[W,W,W2]);
end;
```

Figure 18-4 shows just what can happen if you turn off overflow checking. Weird, huh? You're better off leaving overflow checking on and using LongInt variables wherever possible.

Figure 18-4:
Overflow
checking
protects
you from
bizarre
results like
this.

New Math?

255 * 255 = 1

255 + 255 = 254

32767 * 32767 = 1

32767 + 32767 = -2

65535 * 65535 = 1

65535 + 65535 = 65534

PChar Panic — Error Galore

Delphi String variables and AnsiString variables are easy as pie to use because they're no different from other types of variables. The moment you declare one, it's available for use. You can assign the value of one String or AnsiString variable to another or glue several together by using the + operator, as follows:

```
ZooString := 'orang' + 'utan';
```

After you're familiar with Strings and AnsiStrings, you're likely to try using PChar variables in the same way. DON'T! That's about the most dangerous thing you can do in Delphi! The following steps show why:

1. **Start an OnCreate event handler for the main form of a new project and replace the begin..end pair supplied by Delphi with these lines:**

```
VAR Curly, Larry, Moe, Shemp : PChar;
begin
  Shemp := 'Nyuk nyuk nyuk!';
  Curly := 'Ow!';
  StrCopy(Curly, Shemp);
  Larry := StrNew('Woo-woo woo-woo!');
  Moe := Larry;
  StrCopy(Moe, 'Oh, a wise guy, eh?');
  IF (Moe=Curly) OR (Larry=Curly) THEN;
end;
```

2. **Set a breakpoint on the first line of code, and add** Curly, Larry, **and** Moe **to the Watch window.**

3. **Run the program and step through the event handler, keeping an eye on the Watch window (see Figure 18-5).**

Figure 18-5:
Treating
PChars as if
they were
Strings
makes this
function
extremely
dangerous.

This event handler is a real comedy of errors. The code says to set Larry to the string 'Woo-woo woo-woo!', but as you step through it, you see that it actually gets set to a portion of 'Nyuk nyuk nyuk!' And when the last line of code assigns a value to Moe, Larry gets the same value. Poor Larry!

The first two lines of code contain the same big mistake. They each set a PChar variable equal to a literal string constant. Remember, PChars are pointers, so the pointers now point to those literal strings *in the program's data segment.* The third line is a legitimate function that copies one PChar's value to another. Unfortunately, Curly's string has room for only the three characters Ow! The rest of the copied string spills over into the next part of your program's data segment in memory. Specifically, the program trashes the string 'Woo-woo woo-woo!' The line that sets Larry's value is a legitimate way to give a value to a PChar. The StrNew function allocates enough memory to hold the literal string and copies the string into that memory, and Larry points to that copy in memory. Unfortunately, the literal string that gets copied is the one that was trashed by the previous command.

For your next really big mistake, set Moe equal to Larry. If you set one String variable equal to another, the characters in the string get copied over. But PChars are pointers, so setting one PChar equal to another just gets them both pointing at the same *place* in memory. If the last line legally copies a value into Moe, it changes Larry, too.

What's the point of the last line, the one that checks whether any of the three PChars are NIL? Without that line, the Delphi 3 optimizing compiler wouldn't keep all three variables visible for us in the Watch window! One or more would be inaccessible at any given moment.

The program probably crunches to a halt with an Access Violation after the OnCreate method finishes. Choose Run⌐Program Reset from the menu bar to clear up the mess. Actually, these problems are pretty mild. Pointer errors can just as easily overwrite more significant parts of your program, causing inexplicable Access Violations in seemingly unrelated areas. Be forewarned: If you treat PChars the same as Strings, you turn your program into an accident waiting to happen.

Keep in mind that, in Delphi 3, String by default means AnsiString, the PChar/String hybrid. You can use an AnsiString in place of a PChar if you need to pass a string of characters to a Windows API function. All you need to do is typecast the AnsiString to a PChar. But don't go wild! Don't try to use PChar functions to *change* the value of an AnsiString! Treating an AnsiString as a PChar can be just as big a problem.

Let Sleeping I/O Errors Lie

If your program performs any kind of input/output task, such as reading a file or creating a directory, you risk having it interrupted by an I/O exception. That can be a shock to the user! To keep things running smoothly, your program can take over the handling of I/O errors. The {$I-} compiler directive turns off I/O error checking; {$I+} turns it back on.

If you do turn off I/O checking, your code must check the built-in IOResult variable after each I/O operation and deal with any errors. If you forget this step, an I/O error can get stuck in the gears of Delphi and go dormant, only to come flying out at the next I/O operation anywhere in your program.

Following these steps is the path to understanding I/O error checking:

1. **Start a new project and put the following lines in the form's OnCreate event handler:**

```
{$I-}
ChDir('C:\I\LOVE\YOU\YOU\LOVE\ME');
{$I+}
```

2. **Put this single line in an OnClick event handler for the form:**

```
ChDir('C:\');
```

3. **Run the program.**

As you run the program, nothing happens. The invalid directory name in the OnCreate method doesn't cause any trouble, because you turned off I/O checking. But because you didn't check the IOResult variable, the I/O error is still lurking. Click the form and an Invalid filename exception box pops up, even though nothing is wrong with the directory in *this* ChDir statement.

See, the problem in this simple program is easy, but what if you had a big project with dozens of forms? If you must turn off I/O checking, your code needs to check IOResult after every I/O operation!

Chapter 19

Ten Windows API Functions

In This Chapter

▶ Why you don't need to memorize hundreds of Windows functions

▶ Launching other Windows programs from your programs

▶ Building a utility to exit or restart Windows quickly

▶ Locating important Windows files

▶ Quizzing Windows about important system information

▶ Building fancy 32-bit About boxes that display useful system information

*W*indows makes hundreds and hundreds of API (Application Program Interface) functions available to the programmer. This seeming largesse is actually a mind-numbing disaster. You can spend hours, even days, paging through reference books looking for just the right function. The names get unwieldy, too, with tongue-twisters such as GetMenuCheckMarkDimensions, IsClipboardFormatAvailable, and DlgDirSelectComboBoxEx.

Delphi 3 supports programming in the world of 32-bit Windows 95 and Windows NT. Scads of additional functions (compared with good old Windows 3.1) are available, with even longer names such as Multinet-GetConnectionPerformance, DestroyPrivateObjectSecurity, and SystemTimeToTzSpecificLocalTime. Almost all the old Windows 3.1 functions are still present for backward compatibility, and many have new "extended" versions named by adding the suffix *Ex*. GetVersion becomes GetVersionEx, ExitWindows becomes ExitWindowsEx, and so on.

The Delphi components mostly insulate you from contact with this prickly style of programming. If you call on a component to load itself from a file or display itself on the screen, it may call dozens of Windows functions, but it politely keeps them out of sight. On the other hand, all the Windows functions are still completely available for your programs if you need them, and some are still useful even with Delphi, as you see in this chapter.

The Delphi 3 Windows unit appears in the uses clause that every unit Delphi 3 builds. The Windows unit gives direct access to the majority of the Windows API functions. Others are contained in special units such as MMsystem (for Multimedia functions) and OLE (for Object Linking and Embedding functions).

Where's the BEEP?

If you've enabled the Windows system sounds, each Windows session can start with the sound of a brass band and end with a lullaby. How about a bomb sound or a breaking window to go with critical errors? Four system sounds are tied to the four standard icons for a message dialog box. So how do you get to hear these sounds? Keep in mind that Delphi 3 does not automatically add sound to its message boxes. The programmer must call the API function MessageBeep before displaying the message box.

If you're unsure whether a particular event handler is getting called, insert a call to MessageBeep. If it squawks, clanks, or neighs, the handler was called!

To install the call, follow these steps:

1. **Start a new project with a fixed-size form captioned Beep Test.**

2. **Place four bitmap buttons and two regular buttons in a vertical column.**

3. **Assign these captions to the buttons, from top to bottom: MB_ICONINFORMATION, MB_ICONEXCLAMATION, MB_ICONQUESTION, MB_ICONSTOP, Default Beep (0), and Speaker Beep (65535).**

4. **Assign these six values to the Tag property of the buttons, from top to bottom: 64, 48, 32, 16, 0, 65535.**

5. **Select all four bitmap buttons and set their Height to 49, their Width to 257, and their Margin to 4.**

6. **Now select all six buttons and create an OnClick event handler for them containing just the following two lines of code:**

```
WITH Sender AS TButtonControl DO
  MessageBeep(Tag);
```

7. **Write an OnCreate event handler for the form and replace the begin..end pair supplied by Delphi with the following lines:**

```
VAR
  Ico : TIcon;
  N   : LongInt;
begin
  FOR N := 1 TO 4 DO
    WITH FindComponent('BitBtn' + IntToStr(N)) AS
        TBitBtn DO
      begin
        Glyph := TBitmap.Create;
        Ico := TIcon.Create;
        try
          CASE Tag OF
            64 : Ico.Handle := LoadIcon(0,
        IDI_ASTERISK);
            48 : Ico.Handle := LoadIcon(0,
        IDI_EXCLAMATION);
            32 : Ico.Handle := LoadIcon(0,
        IDI_QUESTION);
            16 : Ico.Handle := LoadIcon(0, IDI_HAND);
          end;
          WITH Glyph DO
            begin
              Height := Ico.Height;
              Width := Ico.Width;
              Canvas.Draw(0,0,Ico);
            end;
        finally
          Ico.Free;
        end;
      end;
end;
```

Whew! That OnCreate handler was complicated, but worthwhile. It sets the glyph for each of the first four buttons to the corresponding icon, as Figure 19-1 shows.

8. Run the program and click each button to hear the corresponding system sound.

To use one of the sounds in a program, just call MessageBeep and pass the constant indicated on the button.

Figure 19-1:
This
program
enables you
to audibly
review the
four dialog
box system
sounds.

Bossing Other Programs Around

If you're a take-charge kind of programmer, why not have your application take charge of launching other applications? Who knows — if the Windows 95 Explorer gets lost in the jungle, *your* program may be able to take over! Even if your ambitions aren't quite so grandiose, knowing how to fire up other programs is useful, and you can do so in three ways.

A quick launch with WinExec

The WinExec function is a bit creaky; it's been around since Windows 3.0. Still, it's adequate for launching programs. Just follow these steps:

1. **Start a fixed-size form project with the caption Launcher.**

2. **Place an edit box on the form, delete its text, and stretch it the entire width of the form.**

3. **Below the edit box, put a push button with the caption Launch, and set its Default property to True; use the following lines for the button's OnClick event handler:**

```
VAR Command : String;
begin
  Command := Edit1.Text + #0;
  IF WinExec(@Command[1], SW_SHOWNORMAL) < 32 THEN
    MessageDlg('Failed to execute ' + Edit1.Text,
      mtError, [mbOK], 0);
end;
```

4. **Run the program and type a command, such as** NOTEPAD.EXE
WIN.INI, **and then press Enter or click the Launch button. Poof!**

Notepad appears with WIN.INI loaded. You can run DOS-based programs as well. WinExec searches the current directory, the Windows
directory, the Windows system directory, the directory containing the
Launcher program, local directories in the PATH, and any mapped
network directories in the PATH, in that order.

Here's a technical note you *can't* skip. I explain in Chapter 14 that, if you
pass string data to Windows API functions, it must be a PChar — a pointer
to an array of characters, with an ASCII zero to signal the end. The code
in the Launcher project creates a PChar *in* the String variable named
Command. First it copies the edit box's text to Command and appends an
ASCII zero, and then the API function passes the expression @Command[1]
to WinExec.

@Command[1] refers to the first character in the string Command, and the @
operator returns the *address* of the variable that follows it. This expression
is a pointer to a zero-terminated array of characters: a PChar! As long as you
have room to tack the #0 character on at the end and the function you're
calling doesn't modify the PChar data you send it, this command is a dandy
way to convert Strings to PChars that work in Delphi 3. You can eliminate
the Command variable altogether and the line that sets its value. Instead of
@Command[1] in the WinExec function call, you'd use PChar(Edit1.Text)

ShellExecute eats WinExecs launch

The ShellExecute function, introduced in Windows 3.1, is WinExec with all
the bells and whistles needed to emulate Program Manager. You can specify
a working directory, automatically load the program associated with data
files, and even auto-print data files. Now *that* is a launcher! Try these steps:

1. **Start a new fixed-size form project and again set its caption to
Launcher.**

2. **Add a column of three labels captioned Command:, Parameters:, and
Working Dir:.**

3. **Place a parallel column of three edit boxes, all with blank Text
properties.**

4. **Dump a push button on the form and set its caption to Launch and its
Default property to True; use the following lines for the button's
OnClick event handler:**

```
VAR Command, Params, WorkDir : String;
begin
  Command := Edit1.Text + #0;
  Params := Edit2.Text + #0;
  WorkDir := Edit3.Text + #0;
  IF ShellExecute(Handle, 'open', @Command[1],
    @Params[1], @WorkDir[1], SW_SHOWNORMAL) < 32 THEN
    MessageDlg('Failed to execute ' + Edit1.Text,
      mtError, [mbOK], 0);
end;
```

5. **Find the uses clause near the top of the program file and add ShellApi to it.**

Fool with this program to get a feel for ShellExecute. Enter NOTEPAD.EXE for the command and C:\DOS for the directory, for example, and Notepad comes up with C:\DOS for its current directory. Enter a bitmap's filename as the command and launch; it automatically comes up in Paintbrush or Paint. If you change open to print in the event handler, the program prints any data file that has a program associated with it!

CreateProcess for control freaks

ShellExecute is decidedly more sophisticated than WinExec, yet it remains fairly understandable. The next step up to the 32-bit CreateProcess function is a quantum leap in complexity. WinExec takes two parameters, ShellExecute takes six, and CreateProcess takes ten, one of which is a record with 18 fields to control the initial appearance of the program! Fortunately for the sanity of programmers everywhere, ignoring many of CreateProcess's parameters is possible by passing NIL as their value.

1. **Start a new fixed-size form project just like the one you used to demonstrate ShellExecute, with three labels captioned Command:, Parameters:, and Working Dir:, three edit boxes in another column, and a button labeled Launch.**

2. **Add a radio group component to the right of the edit boxes, set its caption to Mode and add the three strings Normal, Minimized, and Maximized to its Items list property; finally, set the radio group component's ItemIndex to 0 so that Normal is checked.**

3. **Place a label on the form and set its Alignment property to taRightJustify.**

4. **Add a skinny edit box next to the label; it needs to hold only four characters.**

5. **Place a Windows 95 UpDown component to the right of the edit box.**

6. Select the label, edit box, and UpDown component, press Ctrl+C to copy them to the Clipboard, and then paste them back three times.

7. Set the captions of the four labels to Left:, Top:, Width:, and Height:, and set each UpDown component's Associate property to the adjacent edit box (look at Figure 19-2 to see how the form should appear).

8. Set the form's caption to Launcher32 and give it an OnCreate event handler containing the following lines:

```
UpDown1.Max := Screen.Width;
UpDown2.Max := Screen.Height;
UpDown3.Max := Screen.Width;
UpDown4.Max := Screen.Height;
```

9. Start an OnClick handler for the button, and replace the begin..end pair supplied by Delphi with this imposing chunk of code:

```
CONST Modes : ARRAY[0..2] OF Integer = (SW_SHOWNORMAL,
    SW_SHOWMINIMIZED, SW_SHOWMAXIMIZED);
VAR
  TSI     : TStartupInfo;
  TPI     : TProcessInformation;
  WorkDir : PChar;
  Success : Boolean;
  Mssage  : String;
begin
  IF Edit3.Text = '' THEN WorkDir := NIL
  ELSE WorkDir := StrNew(PChar(Edit3.Text));
  FillChar(TSI, SizeOf(TSI), 0);
  TSI.wShowWindow := Modes[RadioGroup1.ItemIndex];
  TSI.dwFlags := STARTF_USESHOWWINDOW;
  TSI.dwX := StrToIntDef(Edit4.Text, -1);
  TSI.dwY := StrToIntDef(Edit5.Text, -1);
  IF (TSI.dwX > -1) AND (TSI.dwY > -1) THEN
    TSI.dwFlags := TSI.dwFlags OR STARTF_USEPOSITION;
  TSI.dwXSize := StrToIntDef(Edit6.Text, -1);
  TSI.dwYSize := StrToIntDef(Edit7.Text, -1);
  IF (TSI.dwXSize > -1) AND (TSI.dwYSize > -1) THEN
    TSI.dwFlags := TSI.dwFlags OR STARTF_USESIZE;

  Success := CreateProcess(NIL, PChar(Edit1.Text + ' ' +
    Edit2.Text), NIL, NIL, FALSE, NORMAL_PRIORITY_CLASS,
    NIL, WorkDir, TSI, TPI);
  IF WorkDir <> NIL THEN StrDispose(WorkDir);
  IF Success THEN
```

(continued)

(continued)

```
      Mssage := Format('"%s"'#13'Process Handle: %.4x'+
         #13'Thread Handle: %.4x'#13'Process ID: %.8x'#13+
         'Thread ID: %.8x', [Edit1.Text, TPI.hProcess,
         TPI.hThread, TPI.dwProcessID, TPI.dwThreadID])
   ELSE
      Mssage := Format('Failed to execute %s. Error %d',
         [Edit1.Text, GetLastError]);
   MessageDlg(Mssage, mtInformation, [mbOK], 0);
end;
```

Whew! To set up for the big call to CreateProcess, this event handler sets a PChar variable either to a copy of the working directory string or to NIL if no working directory is specified. The event handler initializes a TStartupInfo structure and fills its data fields to select the initial size, state, and position of the program being launched. Then the event handler calls CreateProcess, passing NIL for as many parameters as possible and simple default values for the rest.

If all went well, the event handler displays arcane information about the program that was just launched, as Figure 19-2 shows. Wizards are reputedly able to control you if they know your true name; wizard-level programmers can take control of a program by using this process information. However, in the Launcher32 program, the API function serves simply as decoration. If CreateProcess failed, the program reports that fact and an error code.

Figure 19-2: This program has precisely controlled the size and location of the Notepad it launched.

Lemme Outta Here!

You've seen t-shirts with the motto "$#!+ Happens." Well, the programmer's version says "Programs Crash." Whenever you're developing programs, they *are* going to crash, and they may take a portion of your Windows memory or other resources with them. The only cure is to restart Windows. You also find the occasional DOS game, um, I mean, essential business application that doesn't run under Windows. The ExitWindows function shows you a way out, along with its 16-bit cousin ExitWindowsExec and its 32-bit replacement ExitWindowsEx.

Exit, stage left

Usually, you exit Windows 95 by clicking Start and then choosing the Shut Down command. Here's a little program that not only exits, but also restarts or reboots the system at the touch of a button. Just follow these steps:

1. **Place four buttons across the top of a new form with the captions X, E&xit, &Restart, and Re&boot.**

2. **Reduce their height to the minimum that looks good and set the first button to have the same width as its height.**

3. **Set the remaining three buttons to the same width, just wide enough to show all the captions.**

4. **Set the Tag property of the Exit, Restart, and Reboot buttons to 0, 66, and 67, respectively.**

5. **Pack the buttons so that they touch and shrink the form so that it precisely encloses them.**

6. **Now set the form's BorderStyle property to bsNone.**

7. **Put Close; in the OnClick event handler for the X button.**

8. **Select the other three buttons and enter the following two lines in an OnClick event handler for all three:**

   ```
   WITH Sender AS TButton DO
     ExitWindows(Tag, 0);
   ```

9. **Put these two lines in the OnCreate event handler for the form:**

   ```
   Left := Screen.Width - Width;
   Top := Screen.Height - Height;
   ```

10. **Save the project as SKIDOO.PAS.**

The Skidoo program takes almost no space on-screen, as Figure 19-3 shows, and it stays out of the way in the bottom right corner of the screen. Click one of the three larger buttons to exit Windows, restart Windows, or reboot the whole system. Press the small X button to terminate Skidoo itself. Heck, put SKIDOO.EXE in the Startup submenu of the Windows 95 Start menu!

You may find that the default position for the Skidoo program's window overlaps the taskbar. No problem — just change the second line of the OnCreate event handler to Top := 0;. If you compile this new version, you run into a different problem. No matter what button you press, the system simply offers to log you on as a different user. More sophisticated operating systems create more complex problems!

Fifty ways to leave your windows

Changing the Skidoo program to take advantage of 32-bit API functions is relatively simple. Start by changing ExitWindows to ExitWindowsEx in the OnClick handler for the buttons. Rename the three buttons to &LogOff, &ShutDown, and &Reboot and set their Tag properties to 0, 1, and 2, respectively. That would make for a minimal 32-bit transformation. To really take advantage of the ExitWindowsEx function, however, follow these steps:

1. **Set a new form's BorderStyle property to bsToolWindow and set its caption to a single space.**

2. **Place a speed button in the top left corner of the form.**

3. **Set the speed button's caption to N, and change its font to 16-point Wingdings (yielding a skull and crossbones!).**

4. **Set the form's ClientHeight property to the speed button's height.**

5. **In the form's OnCreate event handler, insert the following lines:**

```
ClientWidth := SpeedButton1.Width;
ShowWindow(Application.Handle, SW_HIDE);
```

The first line shrinks the form's width to fit the speed button, and the second hides the button that would normally appear on the taskbar.

6. **Choose File⇨New Form from the menu bar, and set this form's BorderStyle to bsToolWindow as well.**

7. **Give this form the caption Properties.**

8. **Back in the first form, choose File⇨Use Unit from the menu bar and choose the newly created form.**

9. **Double-click the speed button to start an OnClick event handler and enter the following line:**

```
ExitWindowsEx(Form2.goFlags, 0);
```

10. **Insert an OnMouseUp event handler for the speed button containing the following line:**

```
IF Button = mbRight THEN Form2.ShowModal;
```

Can you guess what it does? If you right-click the skull-button, the second form is displayed. I can show you how to design that form now. Place four radio buttons down the left side of the form, with captions &Shut down, &Power down, &Reboot, and &Log off. Set their Tag properties to 1, 8, 2, and 0, respectively. Add a check box captioned Force and a bitmap button with Kind set to bkOk. Page up into the form definition and find the comment { Public declarations }. Right after it, insert the following line:

```
GoFlags : Integer;
```

In an OnClick event handler shared by all four radio buttons, use this line:

```
goFlags := CheckBox1.Tag OR (Sender AS TRadioButton).Tag;
```

The OnClick handler for the check box needs a few more lines as follows:

```
IF CheckBox1.Checked THEN CheckBox1.Tag := EWX_FORCE
ELSE CheckBox1.Tag := 0;
GoFlags := GoFlags AND (NOT EWX_FORCE);
GoFlags := GoFlags OR CheckBox1.Tag;
```

That does it! Figure 19-4 shows the result. The tiny skull-button window can be placed anywhere on the desktop, and right-clicking the button enables you to control what happens after the button is clicked. (The Properties windows normally never shows.) The Force check box tells the program to shut down even if one or more programs refuse. (Normally one refusal can prevent a shutdown.) And the new Power down option shuts down the system and then turns off its power, but only if the computer supports automated power shut-off.

Figure 19-4:
Click the
skull button
to end your
Windows 95
session.

Where's Windo (ws)?

Most of the time, the Windows directory is C:\WINDOWS, but your programs
don't dare assume that's always right. If you need to locate INI files, for
example, the GetWindowsDirectory function always returns the correct
Windows directory, be it C:\WINDOWS or D:\FENESTRA. For locating DLLs
and other system files, a GetSystemDirectory call is better than hard-coding
C:\WINDOWS\SYSTEM. Follow these steps:

1. **Place two labels on a new form, one below the other, captioned
   Windows Directory and System Directory.**

2. **Place two more labels in a second column.**

3. **Use the following lines for the form's OnCreate event handler:**

```
VAR Buffer : ARRAY[0..255] OF Char;
begin
  GetWindowsDirectory(Buffer, 255);
  Label3.Caption := StrPas(Buffer);
  GetSystemDirectory(Buffer, 255);
  Label4.Caption := StrPas(Buffer);
end;
```

Here you're not passing text *into* the Windows function; rather, you're
supplying it with a buffer into which it can dump text. The buffer is a zero-
based array of characters, which Delphi happily treats as a PChar. The built-
in StrPas function converts the filled buffer's contents into a string. Presto
change-o, you have the Windows and system directories!

Take Your Systems Measurements

You can get the screen's width and height in pixels by using The Delphi
Screen object, but Windows is dying to reveal more through the
GetSystemMetrics function. This function reports on the dimensions of 33
on-screen elements and on whether 6 Windows features are enabled.

Looking up the dozens of constants used by GetSystemMetrics can be a pain, so I use a little program instead. Just follow these steps:

1. **Place a list box on a new fixed-size form and set the form's caption to System Metrics.**

2. **Double-click the list box's Items property to open the string list editor.**

3. **Enter the following 43 strings, 1 per line.**

    (Yes, 43! A tedious process, but you must do it only once.) Here are the system metrics constant names, in order:

```
SM_CXScreen, SM_CYScreen, SM_CXVScroll, SM_CYHScroll,
        SM_CYCaption, SM_CXBorder, SM_CYBorder,
        SM_CXDlgFrame, SM_CYDlgFrame, SM_CYVThumb,
        SM_CXHThumb, SM_CXIcon, SM_CYIcon, SM_CXCursor,
        SM_CYCursor, SM_CYMenu, SM_CXFullScreen,
        SM_CYFullScreen, SM_CYKanjiWindow,
        SM_MousePresent, SM_CYVScroll, SM_CXHScroll,
        SM_Debug, SM_SwapButton, SM_Reserved1,
        SM_Reserved2, SM_Reserved3, SM_Reserved4,
        SM_CXMin, SM_CYMin, SM_CXSize, SM_CYSize,
        SM_CXFrame, SM_CYFrame, SM_CXMinTrack,
        SM_CYMinTrack, SM_CXDoubleClk, SM_CYDoubleClk,
        SM_CXIconSpacing, SM_CYIconSpacing,
        SM_MenuDropAlignment, SM_PenWindows,
        SM_DBCSEnabled
```

Whew! Those were the system metrics constants for Windows 3.1.

Although you can create programs for Windows 3.1 in Delphi 3 and you can create programs for Windows 95 in Delphi 3, you can't create one program that *always* works in both environments.

4. **If you're running under Windows 95 or Windows NT, take a deep breath, wave your fingers vigorously in the air, and then enter 33 more constant names as follows:**

```
SM_CXScreen, SM_CMouseButtons, SM_Secure, SM_CXEdge,
        SM_CYEdge, SM_CXMinSpacing, SM_CYMinSpacing,
        SM_CXSmIcon, SM_CYSmIcon, SM_CYSmCaption,
        SM_CXSmSize, SM_CYSmSize, SM_CXMenuSize,
        SM_CYMenuSize, SM_Arrange, SM_CXMinimized,
        SM_CYMinimized, SM_CXMaxTrack, SM_CYMaxTrack,
        SM_CXMaximized, SM_CYMaximized, SM_Network,
        SM_Reserved5, SM_Reserved6, SM_Reserved7,
        SM_CleanBoot, SM_CXDrag, SM_CYDrag,
        SM_ShowSounds, SM_CXMenuCheck, SM_CYMenuCheck,
        SM_SlowMachine, SM_MidEastEnabled, SM_CMetrics
```

5. **Make the list box wide enough to hold the longest constant name, which is SM_MenuDropAlignment.**

6. **Place a bitmap button below the list box (aligned at the left), set its Kind property to bkHelp, and set Enabled to False.**

7. **Put a label below the list box aligned at the right, set its Alignment property to taRightJustify, and delete its caption.**

8. **Double-click the list box and put the following lines in the resulting OnClick event handler:**

```
BitBtn1.Enabled := True;
Label1.Caption := IntToStr(
  GetSystemMetrics(ListBox1.ItemIndex));
```

9. **Choose Project⇨Options from the menu bar in Delphi 3 and flip to the Application page.**

10. **Click the Browse button next to the Help file line, choose the Delphi WINAPI.HLP file, and then click OK.**

11. **Use the WINAPI.HLP file from the Delphi directory.**

    Alas, the Delphi 3 Help file doesn't devote a separate Help page (as did good old Delphi 1.0) to each system metrics constant.

12. **Now create an OnClick event handler for the Help button, replacing the begin..end pair supplied by Delphi with the following lines:**

```
VAR Buffer : ARRAY [0..255] OF Char;
begin
  WITH ListBox1 DO
    StrPCopy(Buffer, Items[ItemIndex]);
  Application.HelpCommand(HELP_KEY,
    LongInt(@Buffer));
end;
```

13. **Run the program and click various items in the list.**

    The label below the list box displays the current value of the selected item. Better yet, pressing the Help button brings up a description of the particular constant, as Figure 19-5 shows.

Some Windows functions promiscuously accept either a LongInt (a four-byte number) or a PChar (a four-byte pointer). The function called by the Delphi Application.HelpCommand is one such function, so you can convert the String to a PChar by using StrPCopy and then typecast the PChar to a LongInt.

Figure 19-5:
The System
Metrics
program
shows that
the vertical
spacing for
icons on
this system
is 75 pixels.

Free the System Resources!

You can have multimegabytes of RAM free yet still get Out of Memory errors if you're short on *system resources* — system resources that belong to Windows itself are drawn from fixed-size memory blocks totaling just a few hundred kilobytes, and every program needs them. Windows 95 manages system resources very well; you rarely run low. And Windows NT, with its pure 32-bit architecture, *never* runs out. Running programs when system resources are very low (under 10 percent) can yield bizarre results. To check the current percentages, use the class TMemoryStatus, as in the next example:

1. **Place three labels in a column at the left edge of a new fixed-size form and set their captions to G, U, and S.**

2. **Set the form's FormStyle property to fsStayOnTop.**

3. **Set the form's caption to Memory and set its BorderStyle to bsToolWindow.**

4. **Place three gauge components to the right of the three labels, making them quite small from top to bottom, as shown in Figure 19-6.**

5. **Drop a Timer component on the form and put the following lines in the OnTimer event handler:**

```
VAR TMS : TMemoryStatus;
begin
  TMS.dwLength := SizeOf(TMS);
  GlobalMemoryStatus(TMS);
  Gauge1.Progress := TMS.dwMemoryLoad;
  Gauge2.Progress := (100*TMS.dwAvailPhys)
    DIV TMS.dwTotalPhys;
  Gauge3.Progress := (100*TMS.dwAvailPageFile)
    DIV TMS.dwTotalPageFile;
end;
```

That's it! The gauge labeled G shows "memory load" from 0 (meaning the Memory Manager is lying around in its boxer shorts doing nothing) to 100 (meaning the Memory Manager is busier than a past-deadline programmer). The U and S gauges show the percentage of free RAM (actual physical memory) and swap-file memory. You can expect your system's performance to degrade if the percentage of free RAM goes to 0, because swapping data to and from the disk is a lot slower than reading bits from chips.

Figure 19-6:
The
Memory
program
floating
over the
Delphi Code
Editor
shows free
system
resources.

A-Version Therapy

Some programs need to know the Windows or DOS version you're running to avoid calling on a feature that's not *in* that version. Others just want to show off by displaying the version numbers. The Windows 3.1 API function GetVersion gives you both the Windows and DOS version numbers packed into a single LongInt. Each of the LongInt's four bytes represents a major or minor version number, in a peculiar order: Windows major version, Windows minor version, DOS minor version, and DOS major version. Windows 95 reports its version as 3.95, to avoid bothering 16-bit programs that refuse to run unless the major version number is 3.

The 32-bit GetVersionEx function returns slightly different information than its 16-bit predecessor. The DOS version isn't present because DOS itself may not be present. Besides providing the major and minor Windows version numbers, it specifies precisely which 32-bit platform is active (Windows 95, Windows NT, or Win32s under Windows 3.1).

Flag Waving

A program that whips out calculations in seconds on a machine with an 80*x*87 coprocessor may take minutes on a machine without an 80*x*87 coprocessor. It'd be nice to know ahead of time about situations such as this. If you dive into 32-bit programming with Delphi 3, you occasionally hit a submerged rock. The About box form contains a few of these hidden snags. First, the program needs to use the GetVersionEx function (rather than GetVersion). Also use the function GetSystemInfo to obtain system information. Take a look at a Delphi form that reports the kind of processor in your system, the Windows version, the amount of total memory, and the percentage of free system resources. Just follow these steps:

1. **Start a new project with a fixed-size main form and set the form's caption to About *[program name]*.**

2. **Place an image component near the top-left corner of the form, with Width and Height set to 32, and place a bevel component so that a border is around the image.**

3. **Put a label component next to the icon with the caption *[program name]*, Version x.xx and add another label below it with the caption Copyright © 1997 by *[author]*.**

   To enter the copyright symbol in the second label, hold down the Alt key, tap **0 1 6 9** on the numeric keypad, and release Alt. No kidding!

4. **Place four more labels in a column below the copyright label, setting the captions of the last two to Memory: and Memory Load:.**

5. **Place two more labels in a second column, as shown in Figure 19-7.**

6. **Start an OnCreate event handler for the form and replace the begin..end pair supplied by Delphi with the following code:**

```
CONST PlatNames : ARRAY[0..2] OF String =
  ('Win32s', 'Windows 95', 'Windows NT');
VAR
  OVI : TOsVersionInfo;
  SI  : TSystemInfo;
begin
  Image1.Picture.Graphic := Application.Icon;
  OVI.dwOSVersionInfoSize := SizeOf(OVI);
  GetVersionEx(OVI);
  Label3.Caption := Format('%s, version %u.%.2u',
    [PlatNames[OVI.dwPlatformID], OVI.dwMajorVersion,
     OVI.dwMinorVersion]);
  GetSystemInfo(SI);
  CASE SI.dwProcessorType OF
    386 : Label4.Caption := '80386';
    486 : Label4.Caption := '80486';
    586 : Label4.Caption := 'Pentium';
    ELSE Label4.Caption := 'Unknown processor ' +
      IntToStr(SI.dwProcessorType);
  END;
end;
```

7. Create an OnActivate event handler for the form and enter the following code in place of the Delphi-supplied begin..end pair:

```
VAR TMS : TMemoryStatus;
begin
  TMS.dwLength := SizeOf(TMS);
  GlobalMemoryStatus(TMS);
  Label7.Caption := FormatFloat('#,"KB Free"',
    (TMS.dwAvailPhys + TMS.dwAvailPageFile) DIV 1024);
  Label8.Caption := Format('%d%% Load',
      [TMS.dwMemoryLoad]);
end;
```

8. Run the program to make sure that it's working right.

The result should resemble Figure 19-7. Now save it as a template for use in any project that needs an About box. All you need to do is adjust the form's caption and the first two labels to reflect the program's name and copyright information. The About box even grabs the application's icon automatically!

Figure 19-7:
The About box form displays the basic system configuration.

As you can see in Figure 19-7, this About box form is better suited to the 32-bit Windows environment. It reports which Windows platform it's running on and the correct version number. And it reports the processor type and the amount of free memory.

More useful Windows API functions exist, and still more are available that aren't much use. On nights you're having trouble sleeping, try flipping through the Window Software Developers Kit manual to get a feel for the vast and sometimes awkward set of choices.

Chapter 20

Ten Fabulous Function Families

In This Chapter

▶ The most useful built-in Delphi functions

▶ Using random numbers for simulation and visual effects

▶ Checking the capacity and free space on any disk

▶ Using math functions to manage your mortgage and more

▶ Getting a data filename for your program from the command line

*W*indows has hundreds of functions, it's true, but Delphi is no slouch when it comes to built-in functions. I've used quite a few of them in the sample programs already. These built-in Delphi functions can convert variables from one type to another, deal with files and disks, manipulate strings, and even generate random numbers. You don't need to know all of them at once — start with the groups that I discuss in this chapter. To get to know them better, check their dossiers in the Help system.

A Conversion Experience

If you count each function call in the sample programs as a vote, the IntToStr function wins by a landslide. Delphi is touchy about data types; you can't pass a number if a string is expected or vice versa. So before you can display a number as a label's caption or add it to a list, you must process it through IntToStr. Want to impress (or at least confuse) your coworkers? Use the IntToHex function instead of IntToStr. IntToHex turns a number into a hexadecimal string using as many digits as you specify (usually 2, 4, or 8). For example, IntToHex(12648430, 8) yields the string 00C0FFEE. The "00" here is not an exclamation of glee; IntToHex jammed two zeros in at the front because you asked for 8 digits.

Occasionally, I've used StrToInt to go from a string to an integer. That's a little tricky, because passing a string such as four or 3.14159 causes a run-time exception. To handle conversions cleanly, you may want to use StrToIntDef. Pass it a string and a default value; if the string isn't correctly numeric, it returns the default.

```
L := StrToIntDef(Edit1.Text, -1);
```

L gets the numeric value of the edit box's text, or –1 if the text was no good as a number. Delphi has dozens of conversion routines for strings, numbers, and even the date and time. If you need to convert one type of data to another, check the Help system — Delphi probably has a function for it.

Big numbers look better with commas separating every three digits: 2,147,483,648 is easier to read than 2147483648. Surprisingly, the Delphi FormatFloat function inserts those commas for you. Its official purpose is to format floating-point numbers, but it comma-izes LongInts perfectly if you use the following format string:

```
',#'
```

Some Random Thoughts

Suppose that you're writing a screen saver that bounces tennis balls around the screen. If the balls always bounce in the same pattern, they bore you, so you want to vary their bouncing unpredictably. You need a function to generate random numbers, and the aptly-named Random function does the job. Random is two functions in one. Call it with no parameters and it returns a random nonnegative floating-point number less than 1. Pass a whole number from 2 to 65,535, and it returns a random nonnegative whole number that's less than the number you passed. For example, Random(2) returns either 0 or 1.

Now for the exposé — Random, along with its equivalent in every other programming language, is a fraud! The numbers it returns aren't random at all. They're generated by a pseudorandom function inside Delphi. Each number is based on the number before, and the function goes through billions of repetitions before the same number repeats. At the start of any program that uses Random, make one call to the Randomize procedure. This "seeds" the random-number generator based on the exact current time.

You cannot always create a program in Delphi 3 that runs in both Windows 3.1 and Windows 95 environments; sometimes it's an either-or situation. Because you build the next program by using Delphi 3, which runs in Windows 95, just run the next program only in Windows 95. You'll be much happier.

1. **Start a new project and give the form the caption Random-Eyes.**

2. **Set the form's Ctl3D property to False.**

3. **Drop a timer component on the form and put the following lines in its OnTimer event handler:**

```
   VAR X, Y, Delta : LongInt;
begin
  WITH Canvas DO
    BEGIN
      Delta := Random(8) + 3;
      X := Random(ClientWidth-16*Delta) + 4*Delta;
      Y := Random(ClientHeight-8*Delta) + 4*Delta;
      Brush.Color := RGB(Random(256), Random(256),
        Random(256));
      Pen.Width := 3;
      Ellipse(X-4*Delta, Y-4*Delta, X+4*Delta,
        Y+4*Delta);
      Ellipse(X+4*Delta, Y-4*Delta, X+12*Delta,
        Y+4*Delta);
      Brush.Color := clBlack;
      Ellipse(X+2*Delta, Y-Delta, X+4*Delta-2, Y+Delta);
      Ellipse(X+4*Delta+2, Y-Delta, X+6*Delta, Y+Delta);
      MoveTo(X+2*Delta, Y-4*Delta);
      LineTo(X+4*Delta, Y-2*Delta);
      LineTo(X+6*Delta, Y-4*Delta);
    END;
end;
```

This program draws a pair of eyes with size, position, and color that are random. The variable Delta, which determines the size, can take any value from 3 to 10. In general, to get a random number from *A* to *B* inclusive, you use the following line:

```
Random(B-A+1) + A;
```

4. **Run the program several times and you may notice something odd; the "random" pattern of eyes is the same every time.**

   (Whoops! You forgot to Randomize.)

5. **Put this single line in an OnCreate event handler for the form:**

```
Randomize;
```

That does the trick! Unless your system's clock is moribund, each run of the program displays a different pattern of eyes.

The Commando Line-0

Some DOS-based programs don't enable you play until you learn dozens of command-line switches. Windows programs don't hold with that kind of foolishness, but plucking a filename from the command line can be useful. The Delphi ParamCount function returns the number of parameters on the command line, and ParamStr(N) returns the Nth parameter. I grab strings from the command line in the next section.

Here's a nice surprise — ParamStr(0) returns the full path name of the program that's running! If your program needs to locate helper files that reside in its own directory, this can be very handy.

The Secret Life of Files

If the Delphi components can handle the file tasks that you're interested in, use them. If not, well, you have plenty of other choices. Before you tell a component to load data from a file, for example, check with FileExists to make sure that the file exists. You've already seen several functions for slicing and dicing filenames. ExtractFilename, ExtractFilepath, and ExtractFileExt take a filename as their one parameter and return just a portion of it. You can go the other way, too. ExpandFilename takes a filename with no path or a partial path and expands it to a full path name. You can use some of these functions to update the simple editor project that you build in Chapter 5 (and add features to in Chapters 6, 8, and 12).

Load the simple editor project into Delphi and put the following lines in an OnCreate event handler for the form:

```
VAR FileHandle : Integer;
begin
  IF ParamCount < 1 THEN Exit;
  IF NOT FileExists(ParamStr(1)) THEN
    BEGIN
      FileHandle := FileCreate(ParamStr(1));
      IF FileHandle >= 0 THEN
        FileClose(FileHandle)
      ELSE
        BEGIN
          MessageDlg(ParamStr(1) +
            ' is not a valid filename',
            mtError, [mbOK], 0);
          Exit;
        END;
    END;
```

```
  SaveDialog1.Filename := ParamStr(1);
  Memo1.Lines.LoadFromFile(ParamStr(1));
  Memo1.Modified := False;
  OpenDialog1.HistoryList.Add(ParamStr(1));
  Caption := 'My Editor - ' +
    ExtractFilename(ParamStr(1));
end;
```

You convert the simple editor to a rich text editor in Chapter 12. Find the two occurrences of Memo1 in the OnCreate event handler you just wrote and change them to RichEdit1. If the command-line parameter isn't an existing filename, try to create it by using FileCreate. If you succeed, you close the new file; otherwise, you report that the filename is bad and exit. Of course if this program is compiled under Delphi 3, long filename support means more difficulty in coming up with an invalid filename! If all is well, load the file into the editor just as if it had been chosen from the Open File dialog. Open the Windows Explorer and locate the name of the simple editor's EXE file. Try dragging a data file onto the EXE file. It launches and loads the file!

Anytime you write a program that processes data files, give the program the capability to load whatever file is specified on the command line.

Old-timers may be wondering what's become of the FindFirst and FindNext functions. Ever since DOS was a pup, programmers have used these two functions to find files that match a particular specification. Well, they exist in Delphi, too, but it's just so much easier to use a file list box that these functions don't get much exercise! If you do use them in a 32-bit program, you must clean up afterward by calling FindClose.

Disk Must Be the Place

Before your program starts a lengthy task that needs acres of disk space, you better make sure that enough space is available. If your program runs out of space after running for an hour, the user is not going to thank you. The Delphi DiskFree and DiskSize functions take a disk number and return the free space or total capacity in bytes. What's a disk number? Well, 1 means A, 2 means B, 3 means C, and so on. Pass a 0 and the function acts on the current drive. A return value of –1 means the disk number isn't valid.

Follow these steps:

1. **Drop a gauge component near the bottom of a new form with its BorderStyle set to bsDialog and set its Kind property to gkPie.**

2. **Set the gauge's ForeColor property to clFuchsia, BackColor to clBlue, and ShowText to False.**

3. **Place three labels, one below the other, and set their captions to** Used space:, Free space:, **and** Capacity:, **respectively.**

4. **Add two more columns of labels parallel to the first column, select them all, and set their Alignment property to taRightJustify.**

5. **Place a paint box to the left of the first label, set its Color to clBlue, and set its width and height to 14; use the following lines as an OnPaint event handler for the paint box:**

```
VAR R : TRect;
begin
  WITH Sender AS TPaintBox DO
    BEGIN
      R := ClientRect;
      Frame3D(Canvas, R, clDkGray, clWhite, 1);
      Canvas.FillRect(R);
    END;
end;
```

6. **Click the paint box and then press Ctrl+C and Ctrl+V to make a duplicate of it.**

7. **Put the duplicate to the left of the second label and change its Color property to clFuchsia.**

8. **Start an OnCreate event handler for the form and replace the Delphi begin..end pair with the following lines:**

```
VAR Siz : LongInt;
begin
  Siz := DiskSize(3);
  Gauge1.MaxValue := Siz DIV 1024;
  Label6.Caption := FormatFloat(',# "bytes"', Siz);
  Label9.Caption := FormatFloat(',#.# "MB"',
    Siz / 1048576);
  Timer1Timer(Timer1);
end;
```

9. Drop a timer on the form and use the following lines for its OnTimer event handler:

```
VAR Fre, Used : LongInt;
begin
  Fre := DiskFree(3);
  Used := DiskSize(3) - Fre;
  Gauge1.Progress := Fre DIV 1024;
  Label4.Caption := FormatFloat(',# "bytes"', Used);
  Label7.Caption := FormatFloat(',# "MB"',
    Used / 1048576);
  Label5.Caption := FormatFloat(',# "bytes"', Fre);
  Label8.Caption := FormatFloat(',# "MB"',
    Fre / 1048576);
end;
```

The resulting program displays the free space on drive C: both numerically and as a pie slice, with the data updated every second.

The form's layout is modeled after the Windows 95 dialog that displays disk drive properties, but the Windows 95 dialog is static — no updates! Try making a copy of a very large file (perhaps DOOM.WAD) while this program is running and watch the display change!

Casing the Strings Joint

What's the absolute, number-one most popular activity with Strings? No, it's not *cat*'s cradle; it's con*cat*enation. That means gluing one string onto another, such as 'horse' + 'carriage'. The vast majority of sample programs in this book use concatenation in one spot or another. A few of the sample programs have used the substring functions Copy and Pos. Pos returns the position of one string within another or 0 if it's not found. The following example returns 8:

```
Pos('cat', 'communicate')
```

Copy takes the string you pass as its first parameter and returns a chunk of it. The second parameter says where the chunk starts, and the third says how long the chunk is. The following example returns 'lan'.

```
Copy('pusillanimous', 6, 3)
```

You may occasionally find a use for the related functions Insert and Delete. The former inserts one string into another; the latter deletes a chunk.

Several of the string functions have the same name as Delphi component methods. If Delphi objects to the way you're using these functions, stick System and a period in front, such as System.Delete.

Users often enter text higgledy-piggledy, without regard for uppercase or lowercase. You can clean up after them by using UpperCase, LowerCase, AnsiUpperCase, and AnsiLowerCase. The latter two work on "foreign" characters; the former two don't. On the other hand, the latter two are much slower than the former two. To test them, follow these steps:

1. **Place five labels on a new form and set the caption of the first to DÉJA vù.**

   To enter the É, hold Alt, press 0 2 0 1 on the numeric keypad, and release Alt. For the ù, do the same with the numbers 0 2 4 9.

2. **Now put these lines in an OnCreate event handler for the form:**

```
Label2.Caption := UpperCase(Label1.Caption);
Label3.Caption := LowerCase(Label1.Caption);
Label4.Caption := AnsiUpperCase(Label1.Caption);
Label5.Caption := AnsiLowerCase(Label1.Caption);
```

   In the resulting program, the plain UpperCase and LowerCase functions fail to change the É and ù, but they're handled correctly by the ANSI versions.

Delphi also gives you plenty of ways to *compare* strings. CompareStr compares two strings and returns 0 if they're precisely equal. A negative result means that the first string is less than the second; a positive result means the reverse. CompareText does the same, but it compares without regard to case. CompareText('NeUrOtIc','nEuRoTiC') returns 0. Again, for strings containing foreign characters, you use the ANSI versions, AnsiCompareStr and AnsiCompareText. AnsiCompareText('AÑO- NUEVO', 'año nuevo') returns 0, where the non-ANSI version doesn't. Remember, Delphi AnsiString variables can hold immense amounts of text, vastly more than ShortString variables. These four comparison functions chug right along in Delphi 3, comparing strings as large as you care to throw at them.

Delphi 3 also offers handy functions for trimming extraneous characters from strings. TrimRight trims trailing spaces from a string, along with any trailing control characters. TrimLeft does the same for leading spaces and control characters. Total cleanup is handled by Trim, which trims at both ends. Unwanted spaces can be messy if you're converting a user-entered string to a number or treating such a string as a filename. Trim eliminates errors caused by spaces hanging around the start or end of the string (though it can't do anything about unwanted characters in the middle). If you *want* a string with lots of spaces, try the StringOfChar function. Want a string containing 10,000 spaces? StringOfChar(' ', 10000) does the job.

PChar "Pculiarities"

PChars are poison, one hundred percent. Well, almost. You don't need to hassle with most of the PChar functions. A few do have some redeeming social value. Pass a literal string or another PChar to the StrNew function, and it returns a shiny PChar containing a copy of the string. After you finish with the copy, hand it off to StrDispose for destruction.

Never, ever copy a longer string into a string created by StrNew. StrNew allocates just enough memory to hold the string you passed. And never use StrDispose on a string that wasn't created with StrNew.

StrPas is a great function — it takes a PChar and returns a String! If you need to go the other way, StrPCopy does the job, but it's tricky. The function declaration for StrPCopy looks as follows:

```
function StrPCopy(Dest: PChar; Source: String): PChar;
```

The Dest parameter is the destination for the copy, and *your* program must supply it. StrPCopy does not create a PChar the way StrPas creates a String. Almost all the PChar functions work this way — you must to provide any necessary buffers. The function's return value is the PChar you passed into it, which makes some really horrendous nested function calls possible. Even better than StrPCopy is StrPLCopy. StrPLCopy takes one more parameter that specifies the length of the destination PChar. This enables you to avoid the problems that arise if you copy a 256-character string into a 42-character buffer. You get only the first 42 characters of the string, but that's a lot better than having the rest of the characters overwrite unknown locations in memory!

Two other essential PChar functions are StrLCopy and StrLCat. StrLCopy copies one PChar to another, up to a specified maximum length. StrLCat appends one PChar to another, again up to a maximum length. Both functions come in nonlength-limited versions, which you should avoid like the plague. Copying more characters than a PChar can hold is a recipe for disaster!

Just to show PChars *can* be useful; here's a program that displays the DOS environment. Just follow these steps:

1. **Drop a list box on a new form and set the Align property to alClient.**

2. **Replace the begin..end pair of the form's OnCreate event handler with the following lines:**

```
VAR P : PChar;
begin
  P := GetEnvironmentStrings;
  WHILE P[0] <> #0 DO
    BEGIN
      ListBox1.Items.Add(StrPas(P));
      P := StrEnd(P) + 1;
    END;
end;
```

This program calls the Windows 95 API function GetEnvironment-Strings to get a pointer to the environment. As it turns out, the environment is like a bunch of PChars jammed together, with an empty PChar to end it. The WHILE loop in this program adds the current PChar to the list box and then sets it to point one character beyond its end.

New Math

Delphi comes with a whole wad of math functions for doing all the things you hated in high school. I've used Sqr and Sqrt already to get the square and square root of a number. Ln returns the log of a number, and Exp(X) returns the exponential. That's *e* to the *X* power, where *e* is a weird special floating-point constant such as pi. Those awful trig functions are here, too, in the form of Sin, Cos, and ArcTan (sine, cosine, and inverse tangent).

Newer Math

Add the Math unit to the uses clause of a Delphi 3 program and you've got so many functions at your fingertips that you don't know what to do. That is, as long as you have the Developer or Client/Server version; Delphi Desktop doesn't include this marvelous unit. Trig functions, angle conversions, hyperbolic trig functions (hyper-WHAT?), logarithmic and exponential functions are just the beginning. Those who know that standard deviation has nothing to do with the level of weirdness out on the streets can find a whole slew of statistical functions. These functions are hand-crafted (by elves?) to take advantage of special features in the Pentium chip, so they're both speedy and small. And the financial functions enable you to calculate really important stuff, such as the payment on a million-dollar house.

To try that last one, follow these steps:

1. **Place four edit boxes, one below the other along the right side of a new form and put a label below the last one.**

2. **Delete the Text property of the edit boxes and the Caption property of the label.**

3. **Place a column of five labels to the left of the components you already placed, with their Alignment property set to taRightJustify and with the caption shown in Figure 20-1.**

4. **Select the four edit boxes and connect them all to an OnChange event handler in which the following lines replace the Delphi-supplied begin..end pair:**

```
VAR
  PercentDown, PercentInterest,
  TotalCost, MonthlyPayment : Extended;
  MortgageLength            : Integer;
begin
  try
    TotalCost := StrToFloat(Edit1.Text);
    PercentDown := StrToFloat(Edit2.Text) / 100;
    MortgageLength := StrToInt(Edit3.Text) * 12;
    PercentInterest := StrToFloat(Edit4.Text) / 100;
  except
    Exit;
  end;
  MonthlyPayment := -Payment(PercentInterest / 12,
    MortgageLength, TotalCost*(1-PercentDown), 0,
    ptStartOfPeriod);
  Label1.Caption := FloatToStrF(MonthlyPayment,
    ffCurrency, 18, 2);
end;
```

Before you sit down to code a complicated math routine, double-check the Math unit. You don't want to reinvent the wheel!

Dangerous Moves

Delphi has a few extremely powerful functions that are pure poison if you use them incorrectly. You should probably be forced to sign a waiver before you can use them, because the destruction they can wreak if misused is almost beyond belief. On the other hand, they're fast and they're powerful, so what the heck!

The Move procedure is a bulldozer — it pushes a copy of a bunch of bytes from one location to another. You use Move to do things such as take up the slack in an array after you delete an element. But woe betide you if the destination variable isn't big enough. Move pushes the whole block of bytes regardless, and data right after the destination is trashed. FillChar fills a variable with copies of a specified Byte or Char. A command such as the following yields a string of 65 As, if MyString is a ShortString variable:

```
FillChar(MyString, SizeOf(MyString), 'A');
```

Actually all 256 bytes of the string now contain that same character, but the very first byte is the length byte, and *A* corresponds to a 65-character string. FillChar fills as many bytes as you tell it to, blithely ignoring the size of the destination variable. If FillChar overflows, it spews into other data elements of your program.

Never use Move or FillChar on objects — never! You find situations for which these razor-edged power tools are essential or at least way cool. Whenever you use them, triple-check to make sure that the number of bytes to move or fill fit in the destination variable. The SizeOf function returns the size of a variable in bytes — use it! And if something goes wretchedly wrong with your program, make these two functions your prime suspects.

Index

Symbols and Numbers

+ operator with PChar data type, 318
+ (plus) icon in outlines, 181
+ (union), 314, 318
- (minus) icon in outlines, 181
- operator with PChar data type, 318
- (difference), 314, 318
@Command[1] expression, passing to WinExec, 385
& (ampersand)
  in a button caption, 69
  in a component caption, 55
  in menu captions, 111
* (asterisk) as the password character, 76
. mask, creating, 191
.- deleting, 15
*.AVI file mask, adding, 177
*.DLL mask, creating, 191
*.EXE mask, creating, 191
*.ICO mask, creating, 191
*.INI mask, 183
*.MOV file mask, adding, 177
*.QTW file mask, adding, 177
*.RTF mask, adding, 284
*.TXT mask, adding, 213
:= assignment operator, 319
:= symbol, 39
= (equal sign), 39
> in a mask, 159
! in a mask, 159
\ as an item separator, 182
{} (braces), surrounding text, 290
^ (caret), defining pointer types with, 316
0 in a mask, 159
4-byte numbers, 305
32-bit operating systems, 305
80 x 87 math coprocessor, 305
800-by-600 resolution, 16
1,024-by-768 resolution, selecting, 16

• A •

About box
  creating, 116–117
  displaying the basic system configuration, 396–398
Active property
  of the query component, 245
  of the table component, 227
ActiveForm
  adding boxes and buttons to, 355
  creating with an animated page counter, 359–363
  deploying to a Web browser, 356–357
  displaying the current date and time, 357–359, 360
  making an, 354
ActivePage property
  of the notebook component, 161–162
  of the PageControl component, 272
  of the tabbed notebook component, 160
ActiveX components, 353. *See also* OLE
ActiveX forms, 354–355
ActiveX library, 355
ActiveX page
  in the Component palette, 48
  in the New Items dialog box, 354
Add to Custom Colors button in the Color dialog, 29
additional components, locating, 149
Additional page in the Component palette, 47
alias, 222–223
Align buttons, 54
Align horizontal centers button, 54
Align left edges button, 54
Align property, 57, 58
  of the Bevel component, 147, 148
  of list boxes, 81
  of memo boxes, 80

of the notebook and tab set components, 161
of the panel component, 142
Align right edges button, 54
Align tops button, 54
Align vertical centers button, 54
AlignButton property of the UpDown component, 257
Alignment palette, 23, 53–54
Alignment property
  of label components, 74
  of memo boxes, 80
  of a pop-up menu, 120
  of a radio button, 72
AllowAllUp property of speed buttons, 169
AllowGrayed property of check boxes, 74
AllowResize property of the header component, 164
Alt+Spacebar, 31
Alt access key in menus, 111
ampersand (&)
  in a button caption, 69
  in a component caption, 55
  in menu captions, 111
ancestors, 288, 300
AND operator, 317
animated page counter, creating for a Web page, 359–363
AnsiCompareStr function, 406
AnsiCompareText function, 406
AnsiLowerCase function, 406
AnsiString data type, 308–309
  as a pointer, 316
  PChar and, 379
  size of, 313
AnsiString variables, assigning the values of, 377
AnsiUpperCase function, 406
API (Application Program Interface) functions, 381–398
Application object
  controlling the background color of hint boxes, 143
  creating an event handler for, 146
  HintColor property, 143
  HintDelay property, 143

Application page of the Project
    Options dialog box, 13
Apply button, forcing to appear,
    99
applying methods, 345
ArcTan function, 408
arguments, passing to the
    MessageDlg function, 43
arrays, passing as parameters to
    functions, 312
ASCIIZ string, 308
Assignable typed constants
    option, 311
assignment operator (:=), 319
assignments, 319
Associate property of the
    UpDown component, 257
asterisk (*) as the password
    character, 76
audio CDs, playing, 178–180
AutoEdit property
    of the data source component,
        229
    of the database navigator,
        234–235
AutoEnable property of the
    media player component,
    175
AutoMerge property of the main
    menu, 122
AutoOpen property of the media
    player component, 175
AutoPopup property of a pop-up
    menu, 120
AutoRewind property of the
    media player component,
    175
Autosave options in the
    Environment Options
    dialog box, 14
AutoSelect property of edit
    boxes, 76
AutoSize property
    of edit boxes, 77
    of label components, 74

• B •

BackColor property of the gauge
    component, 140
BackgroundColor property of
    the color grid, 137
BackgroundEnabled property of
    the color grid, 137
BackgroundIndex property of
    the color grid, 137

backslash (\) as an item
    separator, 182
backup files, 14–15
bar-type gauge, 140, 141
begin..end pairs, mismatched,
    331
bevel component, 128, 147–148
BevelInner property of the panel
    component, 142, 143
BevelOuter property of the
    panel component, 142, 143
BevelWidth property of the
    panel component, 142, 143
BIOLIFE.DB sample database,
    opening, 238
bitmap button component, 150
bitmap buttons, 166–168
    compared to speed buttons,
        172
bitmap containing four glyphs,
    building, 169–170
bitmap images, displaying with
    transparent areas, 256
Bitmaps filter, creating, 139
BkColor property of the image
    list component, 265
BLOBs (Binary Large OBjects),
    238
bold style, setting in forms, 33
Boolean data type, 304, 306
Boolean evaluation, 11
Boolean operators, 317
BorderIcons property of forms,
    31
BorderStyle property of forms,
    31, 32
BorderWidth property of the
    panel component, 142, 143
Borland Database Engine (BDE),
    221
    accessing database files, 48
bottom-aligned panels for
    components, 58
bound components, 238
braces {}, surrounding text, 290
Break on exception option
    in the Debugging panel, 334
    in the Environment Options
        dialog box, 336
BREAK procedure, 324
Break property of a menu item,
    112, 113
Break statement, 323
Breakpoint list window, 23
breakpoints, 23, 337, 338
    pass count, 338–340

Browse Objects window, 23
browser, 23
Brush property of the shape
    component, 129
bugs, 329
button behavior, default, 69
buttons. *See also* push button
    component
    captions for, 69
    placing the mouse cursor on,
        20
    specifying the appearance of,
        43

• C •

cached updates, 227, 228
calendar, specialized grid for,
    194–196
calendar component, 174
    CalendarDate property, 194
Call stack window, 24, 341
calls, 319
Cancel button, enabling/
    disabling in the WebBrows
    application, 346
Cancel property for a push
    button component, 69
Cancel speed button in the
    WebBrows application,
    344
Canvas property of paint box,
    134
CapsLock key, numeric
    representation in
    Windows, 144
Caption property, 55
    of forms, 27
    of a menu item, 111
    of a push button component,
        69
    of a TabSheet component, 272
captions
    for buttons, 69
    for check boxes, 74
    ellipsis (...) in, 94
    nontext fonts in, 56
Cardinal data type, 305
caret (^)
    defining pointer types with,
        316
    referring to variables, 316
cascading submenus, 114
case, matching in the Find
    dialog, 105
CASE statement, 40, 322

CD Player, creating, 178–180
CDs, playing audio, 178–180
cell data, controlling the editing of, 190
Cells property of a string grid, 189
Center horizontally in a windows button, 54
Center vertically in a windows button, 54
Change Icon dialog, 199
Char data type, 304, 306–307
check boxes, 68, 74
checkable menu items, 112, 113
Checked property
  of a menu item, 112
  of a radio button, 72
child windows, 34
choices, displaying a list of items for, 68
Classes unit, 287
client-aligned panels for components, 58
client/server, moving up to, 251
Client/Server version of Delphi, 10
ClientHeight property of forms, 30
ClientWidth property of forms, 30
code
  commenting out lines of, 290, 334
  editing, 298–299
Code Editor, 17
code module, 300
Col property of the draw grid component, 187
ColCount property of the draw grid component, 186
Collate check box, 103
Color dialog, 29, 90, 100–101, 137
color grid, 137–138
color grid component, 128, 137
Color module in the Display Properties dialog in Windows 95, 28
Color property, 56
  of the Color dialog, 100
  of forms, 27–28
  of label components, 75
  of the paint box component, 134
ColoredButtons property of the media player component, 174

colors
  dithered, 137
  selecting from all possible for Windows, 29
  storage of internal custom, 102
Colors page, syntax highlighting options on, 18
Cols property of a string grid, 189
columns, 227
Columns Editor, 231, 232, 234
Columns property
  of a data-aware grid, 231
  of list boxes, 83, 84
  of a list view, 276
ColWidths property of the draw grid component, 187
combo boxes, 68, 85–86
  DropDownCount property, 85
  Style property, 85
  transforming list boxes into, 51
  in the WebBrows application, 344
command line, returning parameters from, 402
commas, inserting into numbers, 400
comment characters, 290
comment delimiters, 291
commenting out lines of code, 290, 334
comments, 290
common dialog components, 89
common dialogs, 89–90
common events, 60–64.
  See also events
CompareStr function, 406
CompareText function, 406
comparison operators, 317
compatible events, 296
Compile⇨Compile command, 295
compiler, error messages and, 330
compiler directive, 289
compiler error messages, 331
compiler options, setting for safety, 10–14
Compiler page in the Projects Options dialog box, 10–12
compiler switches
  {$I-} for I/O error checking, 379–380

  {$Q+} for overflow checking, 376
  {$R-} for range checking, 373
  {$S+} for stack checking, 374
Complete boolean eval option in the Project Options dialog box, 11
component libraries, extending Delphi with third-party, 12–13
Component palette, 19, 20–21
  ActiveX page, 48
  Additional page, 47
  Data Access page, 48, 221
  Data Controls page, 48, 221
  Dialogs page, 48
  Internet page, 48, 345
  listing of pages, 47–48
  popping all buttons out, 49
  QReport page, 48
  Samples page, 48
  selection arrow, 49
  Standard page, 47, 49
  Standard page on, 49, 67
  System page, 47–48
  Win32 page, 48
  Win 3.1 page, 48
components
  adding identifying labels to, 68
  adjusting the Tab order, 65, 66
  adjusting the width and height of, 52–53
  associating groups of, 68
  associating related, 71
  centering in windows, 53, 54
  changing the Name property of, 294
  cloning, 50–51
  common events for, 60–64
  common properties of, 55–60
  common property list for selected, 55
  controlling the alignment and size of a group of, 57
  data-aware, 238–241
  default events, 61
  descriptive names for, 294
  dimension and location properties, 57
  disabled, 58
  drag-and-drop events for, 61–62
  enforcing conformity of, 54–55
  Help Context, 58
  inserting text descriptions of, 51

(continued)

components *(continued)*
invisible, 58
  keyboard events, 63
  lining up on forms, 53–54
  locating additional, 149
  look-and-feel, 127–128
  moving a single, 49–50
  names for, 60
  nonvisible, 50
  OnClick event, 61
  OnDblClick event, 61
  OnDragDrop event, 61
  OnDragOver event, 61
  OnEnter event, 63
  OnEventDrag event, 62
  OnExit event, 63
  OnMouseDown event, 61
  OnMouseUp event, 61
  OnStartDrag event, 62
  pasting into a group box,
    71–72
  placing, 49–55
  positioning on forms, 64
  resizing a single, 49–50
  selecting multiple, 51–52
  sizing, 52–53
  special events, 64
  system events, 63–64
  tab order, 64–65
  Tab Order property, 59, 64–65
  Z-order for, 65–66
Components list window, 24
components (properties)
  Align property, 57, 58
  Caption property, 55
  Color property, 56
  Ctl3D property, 56–57
  DragCursor property, 59
  DragMode property, 59
  Enabled property, 57
  Font property, 55
  Height property, 57
  Hint property, 58
  Left property, 57
  Name property, 60
  ParentCtl3D property, 56–57
  ParentFont property, 55
  ParentShowHint property, 58
  Popup Menu property, 59
  ShowHint property, 58
  TabOrder property, 59
  TabStop property, 59
  Tag property, 59
  Top property, 57
  True/False ParentColor
    property, 56
  Visible property of, 58

Width property, 57
composers program, building,
  277–280
compound statement, 320
concatenation, 405
condition, 321
conditional breakpoints, 340
conditional statements, 320–322
Confirm/Delete property of the
  database navigator,
  234–235
conformity of components,
  enforcing, 54–55
ConsistentAttributes property
  of a rich text component,
  281
CONST, 311
CONST parameters, 325
constant block, 311
constants, 40, 302, 311
Contents item on the Help file's
  contents page, 116
context-sensitive help, 31, 32
Continue statement, 323
CONTROL.INI
  Custom Colors section,
    100–101
  loading and saving the custom
    colors from, 101–102
Control Panel, color settings in,
  69
Controls unit, 287
conversion functions, 399–400
cooperative multitasking, 150
Copies property of the Print
  dialog, 104
Cos function, 408
Create backup file option in the
  Environment Options
  dialog box, 14–15
CreateProcess function,
  launching programs with,
  386–388
Ctl3D property, 56–57
  of dialog components, 90
  of the Object Inspector
    window, 30
Ctrl+C
  assigning, 116
  copying components, 50–51
Ctrl+F5, 341
Ctrl+F7, 38, 40, 340
Ctrl+F9, 295
Ctrl+V
  assigning, 116
  pasting components, 50–51

Ctrl+X, assigning, 116
Ctrl+Z, assigning, 116
Curly, Larry, Moe event handler,
  377–378
cursor, changing to the no-drag
  (slashed-circle No)
  symbol, 60
Cursor property of forms, 33
CustomColors property of the
  Color dialog, 100–101

• *D* •

Data Access page of the
  Component palette, 48,
  221
data-aware components,
  238–241
data-aware grid, 231
data-aware list box, 241
Data Controls page of the
  Component palette, 48,
  221
data field declarations, 325
data fields in the main form
  object, 325
data files. *See* files
data grid, 229–231, 232
data module, storing nonvisual
  database components, 226
data source component, 229
data types, 222, 302.
  See also type
  choosing, 304
  creating, 309–310
  defining in a type declaration
    block, 287
database component, 251
  TransIsolation property, 251
Database⇨Database Form
  Expert command, 224
Database Designer dialog, 230
database editing form, 225
Database Engine Configuration
  program, establishing
  aliases, 222–223
Database Explorer, developing
  database applications,
  243, 244
Database Form Expert, 224–227
database navigator, 234–235
database navigator component,
  225
database selection form, 250,
  252

database viewer editor,
    building, 235–237
DatabaseName property
    of the query component, 245
    of the table component, 227
databases, 222, 223
    redundancy of, 223
    remote, 251
DataField property of bound
    components, 238
DataSet property of the data
    source component, 229
DataSource property
    of bound components, 238
    in the database navigator, 235
date and time, displaying on a
    Web page, 357–359, 360
date-selection calendar form,
    displaying, 195
DBCtrlGrid component, 243–245
DCU files, generating, 12
debugging, 329
Debugging panel, Break on
    exception option, 334
debugging programs, settings
    for external, 12
decimal numbers
    converting hexadecimal to, 29
    converting to hex, 29
DefAttributes property of the
    rich text component, 281
default button behavior, 69
default drag cursor, 60
default events for components,
    61
default extension, appending, 91
default mouse cursor, 33
Default property of the push
    button component, 69, 70
DefaultColWidth property of the
    draw grid component, 187
DefaultDrawing property of the
    draw grid component, 187
DefaultExt property of the Open
    File dialog, 91
DefaultRowHeight property of
    the draw grid component,
    187
Define Custom Colors button
    in the Color dialog, 29
    disabling, 101
Delphi
    advantages of, 3
    built-in functions, 399–410
    compared to Visual Basic
        (VB), 2

creating your first program,
    21–22
extending with third-party
    component libraries,
    12–13
installing, 9
standard components of,
    67–68
starting, 9
versions of, 10
windows in, 15
Delphi Alignment palette. *See*
    Alignment palette
Delphi Client/Server, 10
Delphi Component palette. *See*
    Component palette
Delphi Desktop, 10
Delphi Developer, 10
Delphi Filter Editor, 92
DELPHI.HLP file, 117
Delphi Main window, 18–21, 23
Delphi object repository, 22,
    146–147
Delphi OLE container. *See* OLE
    container
Delphi SpeedBar buttons, 19–20,
    168
Delphi windows, listing of, 23–24
dependencies, dealing with,
    293–294
descendants, 288, 300
descriptive names for compo-
    nents, 294
Desktop version of Delphi, 10
detail table, 228
details mode for list views, 276
Developer version of Delphi, 10
Device property of the Font
    dialog, 97
DeviceType property of the
    media player component,
    175
dialog components, 90
dialogs, multipage, 159
Dialogs page in the Component
    palette, 48, 89
Dialogs unit, 287
difference (-), 314
digital clock, building, 151–152
dimension and location
    properties for compo-
    nents, 57
Directories/Conditionals page of
    the Project Options dialog
    box, 12–13

directory-browsing form,
    building, 217–220
directory component, 204
directory list box, 209–210
directory outline, getting data
    from a hidden file list box,
    209
directory outline component,
    216–217
Directory property
    of a directory list box, 210
    of the directory outline
        component, 216
    of a file list component, 205
directory-selection dialog,
    creating, 211–213
DirLabel property of a directory
    list box, 210
disabled components, 58
disk, saving embedded objects
    to, 200–202
DiskFree function, 403, 405
DiskSize function, 403, 405
Display grid check box, 50
display modes for list views, 276
Display page, changing the
    Editor font on, 17–18
Display property of the media
    player component, 175
DisplayRect property of the
    media player component,
    175
dithered color, 137
DIV operator, 317
DLLs, locating, 392
Document Source command in
    the WebBrows applica-
    tion, 346
DOS, programming under, 37
DOS environment, displaying,
    407–408
DOS-style filenames, forcing, 92
Down property of speed
    buttons, 169
DownGlyph property of the
    SpinButton component,
    153
drag-and-drop, automating for
    components, 59
drag-and-drop events, for
    components, 61–62
drag cursor, default, 60
DragCursor property of
    components, 59
DragMode property of compo-
    nents, 59

draw grid, events for, 187–189
draw grid component, 173, 186–188
Draw method of image list, 265
drive combo box, 210–211
drive component, 204
Drive property
  of a directory list box, 210
  of the directory outline component, 216
  of the drive combo box, 211
drop-down combo box, 85
drop-down list box, 85, 86
DropDownCount property of combo boxes, 85
Dynamic Link Libraries (DLLs), creating Web server applications as, 48

• E •

edit boxes, 75–79
  border around, 76
  combining with list boxes, 85
  events for, 77–79
  properties of, 76–77
Edit menu, 115–116
Edit⇨Select Size command, 52
Edit⇨Tab Order command, 65
Edit Tab Order dialog., 65, 66
EditMask property for a masked edit box, 158
editor, customizing, 18
editor font, changing on the Display page, 17–18
editor project, enriching, 281–284
EditText property of a masked edit box, 157
ellipsis (...)
  in captions, 94
  in menus, 115
ellipsis button (...)
  in memo boxes, 80
  in the Object Inspector window, 28
e-mail program, 350
embedded objects, saving to disk, 200–202
empty statements, 368
Enabled property, 57
  for a TabSheet component, 272
  of the timer component, 151
EnabledButtons property of the media player component, 174

encapsulation, 288, 300
EndMargin property of the tab set component, 162
enumerated data types, 310
Environment Options command, 14
Environment Options dialog box, 14–15
equal sign (=), 39
error messages, 329–331
error-checking code, turning on/off, 11–12
Evaluate/Modify dialog, 38, 40, 340
event handlers, 17, 37
  connecting to events, 296
  creating for an Application object, 146
  deleting, 295–296
  editing, 298
  parameter lists for, 296–297
  renaming, 298
  Sender parameter, 294–295
  skeletons generated by, 295
  writing, 38
event names, 37
events
  categories of, 37
  for the color grid, 137–138
  common, 60–64
  compatible, 296
  connecting event handlers to, 296
  creating event handlers for, 296
  for the draw grid, 187–189
  for edit boxes, 77–79
  for a file list, 205
  for the Find dialog, 106
  for the Font dialog, 99–100
  for the header component, 165
  for the HeaderControl component, 274
  for hotkey components, 263
  for the image component, 139–140
  for list boxes, 84–85
  for list views, 277
  listing in the Object Inspector window, 37
  for the media player component, 175
  for outline components, 185
  for the PageControl component, 272, 273
  for the push button component, 70–71

for radio buttons, 73
for the rich text component, 281
for scroll bars, 87–88
for the shape component, 129
for a string grid, 190
for TabControl component, 272
for a tree view, 267–268
for the UpDown component, 257–258
Events page on the Object Inspector window, 17, 26, 37, 229
exception handling, 83, 185, 332
exception messages, 334
exceptions, contingency instructions for, 336
Exclusive property of a database component, 228
Execute method, calling for common dialog components, 89–90
ExitWindows function, 389–390
ExitWindowsEx function, 390–392
ExpandFilename function, 402
exploding properties, 28, 30, 36
expression, 317
Exp(X) function, 408
Extended data type, 304, 305
  significant digits in, 370
ExtendedSelect property
  of a file list component, 205
  of list boxes, 83
extending objects, 300
Extra key, 264
ExtractFileExt function, 402
ExtractFilename function, 402
ExtractFilepath function, 402

• F •

F5, 337
F7, 338
F8, 338
F9, 21
fencepost errors, 367–368
fields, 222
  setting properties for, 230
  setting the Visible property of, 231
file common dialog, making, 215
file components, 204
File⇨Delete command in the WebBrows application, 349–350

File dialog, 90
    creating a homemade, 211–213
    customized, 217
File Dialog project, creating,
    205–207
file list boxes, hidden, 207–209
file list component, 204
    events for, 205
    properties of, 204–205,
        206–207
File menu
    creating a template for, 115
    in the WebBrows application,
        349
File⇨New Form command, 35
file-sorting program, writing a
    simple, 82
file variables, 315
FILEDLG project, 205–207
    updating, 210, 211, 213–215
FileEdit property of a file list
    component, 205
FileEditStyle property of the
    Open File dialog, 92
FileExists function, 402
FileList property
    of a directory list box, 210
    of a filter combo box, 213
filename edit box, changing into
    a combo box, 92
Filename property
    of a file list component, 205
    of the media player compo-
        nent, 175
    of the Open File dialog, 91
files
    copying in the WebBrows
        application, 349
    deleting in the WebBrows
        application, 349
    opening in Windows pro-
        grams, 90–94
    opening nonexistent, 93
    sharing, 93
Files of type drop-down list box,
    91, 92
FileType property of a file list
    component, 205, 206–207
FillChar function, 410
filter combo box, 213–215
filter component, 204
Filter Editor, 92
Filter property
    creating a "Files of type"
        listing, 91, 92

of a filter combo box, 213
    of the Open File dialog, 139
Filtered property of a database
    component, 228
FilterIndex property of the Open
    File dialog, 91
filters, 227, 228
finalization error message, 313
financial functions, 408–410
Find common dialog, 105–106
Find dialog, 90
FindClose function, 403
FindComponent method of the
    main form, 133
FindFirst function, 403
FindNext function, 403
FindText property of the Find
    dialog, 105
Fixed-Size Form project,
    selecting, 78
Fixed-Size Form template,
    starting a project using, 87
FixedColor property of the draw
    grid component, 186
FixedCols property of the draw
    grid component, 186
FixedRows property of the draw
    grid component, 186
flat-file database, 223
floating-point calculations, tiny
    errors in, 371
floating-point numbers, 305
floating toolbars, window styles
    for, 32
flyover help, 20, 21
    enabling in the database
        navigator, 235
    status bar Help and, 146
flyover help window, 49–50
FocusControl property
    of label components, 75
    of the SpinButton component,
        153
folders, creating new in the
    WebBrows application,
        350
Font common dialog, 97
    events for, 99–100
    properties of, 97–99
Font property
    of components, 55–56
    of the Font dialog, 98
    of forms, 33–34
    of the tabbed notebook
        component, 160

fonts
    displaying all the characters
        in, 188–189
    nontext, 56
    options affecting the
        availability of, 98–99
FOR..DO loop, 322–323
ForeColor property of the gauge
    component, 140
ForegroundColor property of
    the color grid, 137
ForegroundEnabled property of
    the color grid, 137
ForegroundIndex property of
    the color grid, 137
form components, 25
Form Designer area, 16
form-type object, 325
Form window, 16
FormatFloat function, 400
forms
    adjusting the Tab order of, 65,
        66
    assigning icons to, 34
    BorderIcons property, 31
    BorderStyle property, 31, 32
    brightening with bitmap
        buttons, 166–168
    Caption property, 27
    ClientHeight property, 30
    ClientWidth property, 30
    Color property, 27–28
    Cursor property, 33
    enhancing with data-aware
        components, 238–241
    Font property, 33–34
    FormStyle property, 34–35
    Height property, 30
    HorzScrollBar property, 30
    Icon property, 34
    Left property, 30
    Position property, 32–33
    positioning in the center of
        the screen, 33
    properties of, 30
    setting properties of, 26
    sizing and positioning on the
        screen, 30
    starting with new blank, 34
    Tag property, 34
    Top property, 30
    VertScrollBar property, 30
    Width property, 30
    WindowMenu property, 35
    WindowState property, 33

Forms page of the Project
      Options dialog box, 13, 14
Forms unit, 287
FormStyle property for forms,
      34–35
frames, defining with the Bevel
      component, 147
FTP, (File Transfer Protocol),
      347
FTP application, 347
FullPath method of an item in an
      outline, 182
FUNCTION, 324
function header, 324
functions, 323
   built-in, 399–410
   returning the results of, 372

• G •

gauge component, 128, 140–141
gauges, types of, 140
GDI Windows DLL, 298
Generate DCUs option in the
      Project Options dialog
      box, 12
geometric shape, placing on a
      form, 128
GetEnvironmentStrings
      function, 408
GetSystemInfo function, 397
GetSystemMetrics function,
      392–395
GetVersion function, 396
GetVersionEx function, 396, 397
GetWindowsDirectory function,
      392
global scope, 302
global variables, 302–303
Glyph property
   of bitmap buttons, 166
   of speed buttons, 169
Go speed button
   HTML component of, 345
   in the WebBrows application,
      344
Goto statement, 319
Graphics unit, 287
grid
   changing, 16
   changing the size of, 50
   displaying, 16
   turning off, 50
GridOrdering property of the
      color grid, 137

group boxes, 68, 71–72
   creating, 56
   relationship with radio
      buttons, 73
GroupIndex property
   of menu items, 112, 113, 122
   of speed buttons, 168, 169
groups, forming from menu
      items, 122–123

• H •

Hailstone function, 370
header
   OnSized event, 165
   OnSizing event, 165
header component, 150, 164
HeaderControl component, 256,
      274
Height property
   of components, 57
   of forms, 30
   of the image list component,
      264
Help button, enabling in
      common dialog compo-
      nents, 90
Help files, standardizing access
      to, 116
Help menu, 116–117
HelpContext property
   of components, 58
   of dialog components, 90
hexadecimal numbers
   converting decimal to, 29
   converting to decimal, 29
hexadecimal strings, turning
      numbers into, 399
hidden drive combo box, 210
hidden file list boxes, 207–209
HideSelection property
   of edit boxes, 76
   of the tree view component,
      267
hint boxes, background color of,
      143
Hint property
   of components, 58
   of the shape component, 131
   of speed buttons, 172
HintColor property of the
      Application object, 143
HintDelay property of the
      Application object, 143

hints about code, 331, 332
Hints property of the database
      navigator, 235
HistoryList property of the
      Open File dialog, 92
Horizontal bar gauge, 141
horizontal scroll bar, displaying,
      30
horizontal track bar, 259
HorzScrollBar property of
      forms, 30
hot key (mnemonic access key),
      creating for a component,
      55
hotkey component, 256, 263, 264
HTML, (HyperText Markup
      Language), 48, 343
HTML component in the
      WebBrows application,
      344
HTML folder in the Internet
      folder, 344

• I •

I/O errors, handling, 379–380
Icon Collector program, 190–194
Icon property of forms, 34
icons
   assigning to forms, 34
   in this book, 6
Icons filter, 139
IF statements, 320–321
   nesting, 321
image component, 128, 138
   events for, 139–140
   properties of, 138–139
Image Editor, drawing icons
      with, 34
image list component, 256, 264,
      265
Image Viewer, 139–140
ImageIndex property of tree
      nodes, 267
ImageList Editor, 264
Images property of tree view
      component, 267
implementation section,
      286–287, 289, 300
IN operator, 318
Include TDW debug info option
      in the Project Options
      dialog box, 12
Increment property of the
      SpinEdit component, 154

indexes, 222
IndexName property of a table
    component, 227
inheritance of objects, 288, 300
INI files
    locating, 392
    viewing, 182–185
InitialDir property of the Open
    File dialog, 91
initialization section, 286–287,
    289, 300
Insert Object dialog, building
    into the OLE container,
    198
instance, 288
Integer data type, 305
integer overflow, 376–377
IntegralHeight setting in a list
    box, 83, 84
interface section, 286–287,
    287–288, 300
internal custom colors, storage
    of, 102
Internet, 343
Internet folder, 343
Internet page in the Component
    palette, 48
intersection, 318
Interval property of the timer
    component, 151
IntToHex function, 399
IntToStr function, 399
InvalidateRect API function, 266
InvalidKeys property of the
    hotkey component, 263
invisible components, 58
italic style, setting in forms, 33
ItemHeight property of list
    boxes, 83
ItemIndex property of list
    boxes, 81
Items Editor, displaying, 276
items in a list, reordering, 157
Items property
    of the file list component, 205
    of list boxes, 81
    of a list view, 276
    of the main menu component,
        109
    of tree view component, 267
ItemSeparator property of the
    outline component, 182,
    185

• K •

KERNEL Windows DLL, 298
Key variable, 40
keyboard, manipulating the
    outline component,
    184–185
keyboard events, 63
    forms and, 40–41
Kind property
    of bitmap buttons, 166
    of the gauge component, 140,
        141
    of scroll bars, 86

• L •

L in a mask, 159
label component, 68, 74–75
large icons mode for list views,
    276
LargeChange property of scroll
    bars, 87
LargeImages property, 276–277,
    278
launching programs, 384–388
Layout property of bitmap
    buttons, 166
leaf items in outlines, 181
Left property
    of components, 57
    of forms, 30
left-aligned panels for compo-
    nents, 58
LeftCol property of a draw grid
    component, 187
lines, defining with the Bevel
    component, 147
Lines property
    of memo boxes, 80–81
    of the outline component, 181,
        182
LineSize property of the track
    bar component, 259
LineTo function, 136
Linker page in the Project
    Options dialog box, 12
Links dialog, displaying from
    the OLE container, 200
list, reordering items in, 157
list boxes, 68, 81–85
    combining with edit boxes, 85
    events for, 84–85
    nonvisible sorted, 82

properties of, 81–84
    selecting items in, 83
    transforming into combo
        boxes, 51
list mode for list views, 276
list properties, 36
list view component, 256
list views, 276–277
Ln function, 408
Load Icon button in the Project
    Options dialog box, 13
local variables, 302–303
LOCKS project, 144–145,
    152–153
logic bugs, 329
logic errors, 337
logical operators, 317, 318
long filenames, 92
LongInt data type, 304–305
look-and-feel components,
    127–128
lookup list box, 241–243
looping statements, 322
LowerCase function, 406

• M •

main body of a program, 291,
    299
main form
    FindComponent method, 133
    making nonresizeable, 32
    promoting a new, 13, 14
Main menu, selecting from, 19
main menu component, 109
    AutoMerge property, 122
    Items property, 109
    properties of, 109
main program, 290
Main window, 18–21, 23
Map file option, setting to
        Detailed in the Project
        Options dialog box, 12
Margin property of bitmap
    buttons, 166–167
mask, 157, 158
Mask property
    of a file list component, 205
    of a filter combo box, 213
mask types, predefined, 158
masked edit box, 157–159
masked edit box component,
    150
master/detail forms, 225–226
master/detail relationship, 228

MasterFields, 228
MasterSource, 228
math coprocessor in modern computers, 305
math functions, 408
math operators, 317
Math unit, 408–410
Max property
 of scroll bars, 86
 of the track bar component, 259
 of the UpDown component, 257
MaxLength property of edit boxes, 76
MaxValue property
 of the gauge component, 141
 of the SpinEdit component, 154
MDI Application template, 123
MDI form with three child forms, 35
media player, creating, 177–178, 179
media player component, 173, 174
 events for, 175
 properties of, 174–175
memo box component, 68
memo boxes, 80–81
Memory program, 395–396
menu commands, 19
Menu Designer, 110
 adding templates, 115
menu item components, 110–114
menu items
 checkable, 112, 113
 forming groups of, 122–123
menu layouts, storing as templates, 114–115
menu shortcuts, multicolumn menus and, 114
menu tree, creating, 268–271
menus
 creating new, 110
 merging, 122–124
 multicolumn, 114
 selecting from, 19
 shortcut keys in, 111, 113–114
merging
 menus, 122–124
 multiple-choice, 123–124
 on-again off-again, 123
MessageBeep API function, calling, 382–384

MessageDlg function, 42, 43
Messages unit, 287
Metafiles filter, 139
methods, 325
 applying, 345
 declaring, 326
MIDI files, 177
 compared to WAV files, 177
Min property
 of scroll bars, 86
 of the track bar component, 259
 of the UpDown component, 257
minus (-) icon in outlines, 181
MinValue property
 of the gauge component, 141
 of the SpinEdit component, 154
mnemonic access keys with nontext fonts, 56
MOD operator, 317
modal dialog, 70
ModalResult property for a push button component, 70
Modifiers property of the hotkey component, 263, 264
Mortgage Calculator, 409
mouse cursor
 default, 33
 placing on a button, 20
mouse events
 for components, 61
 forms and, 38–39
Move procedure, 410
MoveTo function, 136
multicolumn menus and menu shortcuts, 114
MultiLine property of the TabControl component, 272
multimedia programming, 174
multipage dialogs, 159
multipage tabbed windows, 12
multiple-choice list box, 81
multiple-choice merging, 123–124
multiple components, selecting, 51–52
Multiple Document Interface (MDI), 34
Multiple Document Interface program, working skeleton of, 123

multiple syntax errors, 331
MultiSelect property
 of a file list component, 205
 of list boxes, 83
MYEDIT.PRJ main project, 96
MyEdit project
 adding a Print dialog to, 104–105
 adding a SpeedBar to, 171–172
 adding find and replace to, 106–108
 building menus for, 117–119

• N •

Name property, 60, 294
named constants, 40
 declaring, 311
 finding out the numeric value of, 38, 40
naming
 components, 60
 programs, 291–292
 variables, 303
needle-type gauge component, 140, 141
nesting IF statements, 321
Network button, suppressing in the Open File dialog, 92
New Form command, 35
New Items dialog box, ActiveX page, 354
nonexistent files, opening, 93
nontext fonts, 56
nonvisible components, 50
nonvisible sorted list boxes, 82
NOT operator, 317
notebook component, 150, 161–163
 connected to a tab set component, 161
null (zero) character, 308
null-terminated string, 308
numbers
 allowing users to tweak up and down, 153
 converting into strings, 399
 floating-point, 305
 inserting commas into, 400
numeric properties, 36
numeric quantities, displaying or adjusting the values of continuous, 68
numeric values of named constants, 38

NumGlyphs property
of bitmap buttons, 166
of speed buttons, 169
NumLock key, numeric
representation in
Windows, 144

• *O* •

OBJ files, generating, 12
object class data type, 288, 300
object definitions, editing, 299
object hierarchy, 23
Object Inspector window, 16–17,
23
Ctl3D property, 30
displaying properties in, 26–27
Events page, 17, 37, 229
Properties page, 16, 17
object properties, 36
Object Properties dialog,
updating and displaying
an embedded OLE object,
198
object repository. *See* Delphi
object repository
objects, 288
extending, 300
inheritance of, 288
passing descendants to
methods, 291
Objects property of a string
grid, 189
OBJREPOS directory, 146–147
off-by-one errors, 367–368
offline data, 245
OLE, (Object Linking and
Embedding), 196. *See also*
ActiveX
OLE container
building a demo of, 197–198
displaying the Links dialog,
200
OLE controls, 174, 353
OLE objects, saving to disk,
200–202
OnActivate event, 42
OnApply event for the Font
dialog, 99
OnCalcFields event handler,
creating, 231
OnChange event, 64
for a calendar component, 194
for the color grid, 137–138
for the directory outline
component, 216–217
for edit boxes, 77

for a file list, 205
for the image list component,
264
for a list view, 277
for scroll bars, 87
for a tree view, 267
OnChange event handler, 64
for edit boxes, 77, 78, 79
for scroll bars, 87
OnChanging event
for a list view, 277
for a tab set, 162
for the TabControl compo-
nent, 272
for a tree view, 267
for the UpDown component,
257
OnClick event, 61
for a file list, 205
for list boxes, 84
for a media player, 175
for the outline component, 185
for the push button component, 70
for a speed button, 171
for a tab set, 162
for the UpDown component,
257
OnClick event handler, 63
creating the framework for,
38–39
for edit boxes, 79
for the Open button, 96
for a radio button, 73
OnClose event, 42
OnCloseQuery event, 42
OnCloseQuery event handler, 42
creating for a form, 119
for memo boxes, 81
OnCollapse method in an
outline component, 185
OnColumnClick event for a list
view, 277
OnCompare event
for a list view, 277
for tree view, 268
OnCompare event handler for a
list view, 279
OnCreate event, 42
OnCreate event handler for
memo boxes, 81
OnDblClick event, 61
for a file list, 205
OnDeactivate event, 42
OnDestroy event, 42
OnDownClick event for the
SpinEdit component, 154

OnDragDrop event, 61
OnDragDrop event handler for
Towers of Hanoi, 132
OnDragOver event, 61
OnDragOver event handler
creating, 62
for Towers of Hanoi, 131, 132,
133
OnDrawCell event for the draw
grid, 187–188
OnDrawCell event handler for
the draw grid, 218
OnDrawItem event for list
boxes, 84
OnDrawItem event handler,
creating for a list box, 85
OnDrawSection event for the
HeaderControl compo-
nent, 274
OnDrawTab event for a tab set,
163
run-time error messages,
332–333
OnEdited event
for a list view, 277
for a tree view, 267
OnEditing event
for a list view, 277
for a tree view, 267
OnEndDrag event, 62
OnEndDrag method, creating, 62
OnEnter event, 63
OnEnter event handler, 64
OnExit event, 63
OnExit event handler, 64
OnExpand method in an outline
component, 185
OnFilterRecord event handler,
228
OnFind event for the Find
dialog, 106
OnGetEditMask event for a
string grid, 190
OnKeyDown event handler, 63
writing, 40
OnKeyPress event, 40
for edit boxes, 77
OnKeyPress event handler
creating, 41
for edit boxes, 77, 78
OnKeyUp event handler, 63
OnMeasureItem event for list
boxes, 84
OnMeasureItem event handler,
creating, 84, 85
OnMeasureTab event for a tab
set, 163

OnMeasureTab event handler
for a tab set, 163–164
OnMouseDown event, 61
for the shape component, 129
OnMouseDown event handler,
63
OnMouseMove event for the
shape component, 129
OnMouseUp event, 61
for the shape component, 129
OnMouseUp event handler, 63
OnPageChanged event for a
notebook component, 162
OnPaint event, 42
OnPaint event handler for a
five-pointed star, 134
OnPaint method of the paint
box component, 134–137
OnPostClick event for a media
player, 175
OnReplace property of the
Replace dialog, 106
OnResize event, 42
OnResize event handler for a
panel component, 144
OnScroll event for scroll bars,
87
OnSectionClick event for the
HeaderControl compo-
nent, 274
OnSectionResize event for the
HeaderControl compo-
nent, 274
OnSectionTrack event for the
HeaderControl compo-
nent, 274
OnSelectionChange event for a
rich text component, 281,
283–284
OnSized event for a header, 165
OnSizing event for a header, 165
OnStartDrag event, 62
OnUpClick event for the
SpinEdit component, 154
open array parameter, 312
Open button, OnClick event
handler for, 96
Open File common dialog, 90, 91
optional elements of, 92–94
properties of, 90–92
operands, 317
operators, 317
options, choosing between, 68
Options⇨Project command, 11

Options property
of the Color dialog, 101
of a data grid, 229
of dialog components, 90
of the draw grid component,
187
of the Font dialog, 98–99
of the Open File dialog, 92
of the outline component, 182
of the Print dialog, 104
of a string grid, 189
OR operator, 317
order by SQL keyword, 248
ordinal types, 310, 314
Orientation property
of the track bar component,
259
of the UpDown component,
256
original data, 245
Out of Memory errors, 395
outline component, 173, 181,
216
events for, 185
manipulating with the
keyboard, 184–185
properties of, 181–182, 185
OutlineStyle property of the
outline component, 181
Output directory line on the
Directories/Conditionals
page, 13
overflow errors, checking for,
376–377

• P •

p-code, 3
PageControl component, 256,
272
ActivePage property, 272
events for, 272, 273
PageIndex property
of the notebook component,
161, 162
of the tabbed notebook
component, 160
Pages property
of the notebook component,
161, 163
of the tabbed notebook
component, 159
Pages radio button of the Print
dialog, 104
PageSize property of the track
bar component, 260

paint box, Canvas property, 134
paint box component, 128,
133–137
Color property, 134
palettes, window styles for, 32
panel component, 128, 142
adjusting the inner and outer
bevels of, 143
events for, 144–145
properties of, 142–143
panels, 142–143
Panels Editor dialog box for
status bars, 260, 261
Panels property of the status
bar component, 260, 261
Paragraph property of a rich
text component, 281
ParamCount function, 402
parameter lists for event
handlers, 296–297
parameters
in functions, 324
passing to the MessageDlg
function, 43
ParamStr function, 402
parent MDI form, 34
ParentCtl3D property, 56–57
ParentFont property, 55
of the tabbed notebook
component, 160
parenthesis-asterisk pairs,
surrounding text, 290
ParentShowHint property, 58
Pascal, programming Web pages
in, 353
pass count breakpoints, 338–340
password-entry dialog, building,
78–79
PasswordChar property of edit
boxes, 76
Pause speed button, 337
PChar data type, 304, 308, 316
+ and - operators with, 318
AnsiString and, 379
declaring, 308
PChar functions, 407–408
PChar variables, treating like
strings, 377–379
Pen property of the shape
component, 128
Picture property of the image
component, 138–139
PictureClosed property of the
outline component, 182
PictureLeaf property of the
outline component, 182

PictureMinus property of the outline component, 182
PictureOpen property of the outline component, 182
PicturePlus property of the outline component, 182
pie-type gauge component, 140, 141
PlainText property of the rich text component, 281
plus (+) icon in outlines, 181
plus sign (+) before exploding properties, 27, 28, 31
pointers, 315–316
   protection from, 342
polymorphism, 291, 300
POP (Post Office Protocol), 350
pop-up menus, 119–122
   creating, 120
   designing, 120
   displaying, 59
PopupMenu property, 59
   of the gauge component, 141
   of a pop-up menu, 121
   of visible components, 119
Position property
   of forms, 32–33
   of scroll bars, 86
   of the track bar component, 259
   of the UpDown component, 257
predefined mask types, 158
preferences, setting for safety, 14–15
Preferences page, displaying, 14
primary index, 222, 226
Print common dialog, 103–105
Print Range group box in the Print dialog, 104
Print Setup common dialog, 102–103
Print to file check box in the Print dialog, 104
Printer dialog, 90
PrintRange property of the Print dialog, 104
private section, 288
proactive exception handler, 336
PROCEDURE, 324
procedure call, 319
procedure header, 324
program file, 300
program window, moving around on the screen with arrow keys, 40

programming
   key to understanding, 327–328
   multimedia, 174
   self-referential, 3
   summary of the basics, 299–300
programs
   activating features in, 68
   blueprints for, 25–26
   creating Windows help systems for, 58
   creating your first, 21–22
   dissecting empty, 285–292
   launching with CreateProcess, 386–388
   launching with ShellExecute, 385–386
   launching with WinExec, 384–385
   main body of, 291
   naming, 291–292
   specifying attributes for final compiled, 13
   suspending, 337
   writing bug-repellent, 342
progress bar, 258
progress bar component, 256, 259
Progress property of the gauge component, 141
Project command, 11
Project Manager window, 23
Project Options dialog box
   Applications page, 13
   Compiler page, 10–12
   Directories/Conditionals page, 12–13
   displaying, 11
   Forms page, 13, 14
   Linker page, 12
   pages in, 12
Project Source command, 285
Project Source window, 23
Project⇨Web Deploy command, 356
Project1, 285, 290
properties, 26
   changing visible, 27–30
   displaying in the Object Inspector window, 26–27, 28
   of the draw grid component, 186–187
   of edit boxes, 76–77
   of the file list component, 204–205

of the Find common dialog, 105–106
of the header component, 164
of the image component, 138–139
of list boxes, 81–84
of a list view, 276–277
of the outline component, 181–182
of properties, 281
of the push button component, 69–70
of radio buttons, 72–73
of the rich text component, 281
of scroll bars, 86–88
setting for the fields of a table, 230
of a string grid, 189
of the timer component, 151
of the tree view component, 267
types of, 36
of the UpDown component, 256–257
Properties page on the Object Inspector window, 16, 17, 26–27
public section, 288
pulled-down value lists, 28
push button component, 68, 69–71
PWideChar data type, 309

• **Q** •
QReport page in the Component palette, 48
query, 222
query component, 245–248

• **R** •
radio buttons, 68, 72–73
   events for, 73
   menu items acting like, 112
   properties of, 72–73
   relationship with group boxes, 73
   speed buttons acting like, 170
RadioGroup component, 73
RadioItem property of a menu item, 112
rainbow, creating, 134–135
Random function, 400–401

Randomize procedure, calling, 400–401
Range checking compiler option, turning on, 372–374
range errors, checking for, 372–374
Range subproperty, 30
read-only file viewing, enabling, 92, 93
ReadOnly property of edit boxes, 76
Record type declaration, 313
records, 222
recursion, 375
redundancy of databases, 223
remote database, 251
remote tables, transaction processing for, 251
REPEAT..UNTIL loops, 322, 323
   off-by-one problem in, 367–368
Replace dialog, 90, 106–108
ReplaceText property of the Replace dialog, 106
report component, 248–249
ReportSmith, activating, 248–249
ReportSmith Runtime, running, 249
repository. *See* Delphi object repository
RequestLive property of the query component, 245
resource file, 291
Result variable, using in functions, 372
ResultSetLive property of the query component, 245
rich text component, 256, 280–281
   events for, 281
   OnSelectionChange event, 281, 283–284
   properties of, 281
right-aligned panels, 58
root node, making visible in a tree view, 267
Row property of the draw grid component, 187
RowCount property of the draw grid component, 186
RowHeights property of the draw grid component, 187
rows, 227
Rows property of a string grid, 189

ruler, drawing across the top of a form, 135–137
Run⇨Add Watch command, 341
Run button on the SpeedBar, 21
Run method of a report component, 249
Run⇨Program Pause command, 337
Run⇨Run command, 21
Run⇨Step Over command, 338
run-time errors, 329
run-time-only properties of the media player component, 175
Run⇨Trace Into command, 338
Runtime errors options, turning on/off, 11–12

• *S* •

safety net, creating with options, 10
Samples page in the Component palette, 48
Save File dialog, 94
Save Literal Characters check box, 158
scope of variables, 302
screen elements, options affecting, 98
scroll bar component, 68
scroll bars, 86
   events for, 87–88
   modifying, 148
   properties of, 86–88
   sample program, 87–88
scroll box component, 128
ScrollBars property of memo boxes, 80
ScrollLock key, numeric representation in Windows, 144
secondary form, making nonresizeable, 32
secondary index, 222
Sections property
   of the header component, 164
   of a HeaderControl component, 274
SectionWidth property of the header component, 164
SelAttributes property of the rich text component, 281
select command
   formatting SQL, 247
   where clause with, 247–248

Select Size command, 52
SelectColor property of the tab set component, 162
Selected property
   of the file list component, 205
   of list boxes, 83
SelectedIndex property of tree nodes, 267
selection arrow in the Component palette, 49
SelEnd property of the track bar component, 259
self-referential programming, 3
SelStart property of the track bar component, 259
semicolons
   ending statements, 319
   spurious, 368–370
Sender parameter of event handlers, 294–295
separator line, inserting in menus, 110
session component, 249
set properties, 36
set type, 312, 313–314
SetPolyFillMode function, 134
SetTick method, 259
SETUP program, 9
shape component, 128
   events for, 129
   properties of, 128–129, 131
Shape property
   of the Bevel component, 147, 148
   of the shape component, 128
ShellExecute function, launching programs with, 385–386
shift-lock program, synchronizing with the keyboard, 152
short-circuit Boolean evaluation, 11
shortcut keys, 19
   assigning to pop-up menus, 120
   in menus, 111, 113–114
ShortCut property
   of a menu item, 111
   of a pop-up menu, 120
ShortString data type, 307
Show Hints box, 331, 332
Show Warnings box, 331, 332
ShowAccelChar property of label components, 74
ShowButtons property of tree view component, 267

ShowGlyphs property of a file list component, 204–205
ShowHint property, 58
  of the database navigator, 235
  of the panel component, 143
ShowLines property of a tree view component, 267
ShowRoot property of a tree view component, 267
significant digits, 305, 370
simple combo box, 85
simple editor project, enriching, 281–284
simple statement, 319
SimplePanel property of the status bar component, 260
SimpleText property of the status bar component, 260
Simpmail application, sending e-mail, 351
Simpmail Delphi 3 project, 350
Sin function, 408
Single Document Interface, 15
single-selection list box, 81
Size dialog, 52–53
SizeGrip property of the status bar component, 260
skeletons for event handlers, 295
Skidoo program, 389–390
small icons mode for list views, 276
SmallChange property of scroll bars, 87
SmallImages property, 276–277, 278
SMTP (Simple Mail Transfer Protocol), 350
Snap to grid check box, 50
Sorted property of list boxes, 82
sound player, creating a general-purpose, 175–177
sounds, adding to message boxes, 382–384
Space equally, horizontally button, 54
Space equally, vertically button, 54
Spacing property of bitmap buttons, 166, 167
special events for components, 64
speed button component, 150
speed buttons
  acting like radio buttons, 170
  compared to bitmap buttons, 172

events for, 171–172
properties of, 168–170, 172
SpeedBar
  adding to a simple editor, 171–172
  Run button on, 21
SpeedBar buttons, 19–20, 168
spin buttons, 255
  creating, 156–157
  making bigger, 154–156
spin edit boxes, 153–154
SpinButton component, 150, 153
SpinEdit component, 150, 153
  events for, 154
  properties of, 154
  replacing, 258
SQL, (Structured Query Language), 222
SQL property of the query component, 245
SQL scratch pad, building, 246
SQL statements, examples of, 246–248, 249
SQLPAD program, 246–247
Sqr function, 408
Sqrt function, 408
stack, 374
Stack checking check box, 374, 375
stack function calls, 374
stack overflow error message, 334
stack overflows, Windows 95 and, 375
Stack size setting on the Linker page, 375
standard components, 67
  problems solved by, 68
Standard page on the Component palette, 47, 49, 67
star, creating a five-pointed, 134
Start⇨Programs command in Windows 95, 9
StartMargin property of the tab set component, 162
state images in a tree view, 271
State property of check boxes, 74
StateImages property
  of an image list, 276–277, 278
  of a tree view component, 267
StateIndex property of tree nodes, 267
statements, 319
status bar, 258, 260
status bar component, 145–146,

256
Panels property, 260, 261
SimplePanel property, 260
SimpleText property, 260
SizeGrip property, 260
status bar Help, flyover help and, 146
status line at the bottom of a form, 145–146
status line form, saving as a template, 146–147
StatusBar Panels Editor, 260, 261
StayOnTop style, 35
StdCtrls unit, 293
Step command, displaying a video's first frame with, 178
Step Over command, 338
Step Over speed button, 338
StrDispose function, 407
Stretch property of the image component, 139
strikeout style, setting in forms, 33
String data type, 304, 307
string grid, 189
  events for, 190
  properties of, 189
string grid component, 174, 186
string-list properties, 36
String variables, assigning the values of, 377
StringOfChar function, 406
strings
  comparing, 406
  converting into integers, 399–400
  trimming extraneous characters from, 406
StrLCat function, 407
StrLCopy function, 407
StrNew function, 407
StrPas function, 392, 407
StrPCopy function, 407
StrToIntDef function, 399–400
structured data types, 312
Style property
  of the Bevel component, 147, 148
  of bitmap buttons, 167
  of a combo box, 85
  of list boxes, 82, 83
  of the tab set component, 162
Style subproperty of the Font property, 33

submenu items, defining
    shortcut keys for, 111
submenu structures, moving
    around, 110
submenus, cascading, 114
subpanels, setting up in status
    bars, 260
Succ built-in function, 39
syntax errors, multiple, 331
syntax highlighting options on
    the Colors page, 18
system configuration,
    displaying, 396–398
system events, 63–64
    forms and, 41–43
system files, locating, 392
System Metrics program,
    392–395
System page in the Component
    palette, 47–48
system resources, checking,
    395–396
SysUtils unit, 287, 312

• T •

Tab order, 64–65
Tab Order command, 65
tab set component, 150, 161–163
    connected to a notebook
        component, 161
tabbed notebook component,
    150, 159–161
tabbed windows, multipage, 12
TabControl component, 256, 272
TabFont property of the tabbed
    notebook component, 160
TabIndex property
    of the tab set component, 161
    of the TabControl component,
        272
table component, 227
table data, displaying in a
    grid-style view, 229–231,
    232
table selection form, 250, 252
TableName property of a table
    component, 227
tables, 222, 227
    transaction processing for
        remote, 251
TabOrder property, 59, 64–65
Tabs property
    of the tab set component, 161
    of the TabControl component,
        272
TabSheet component, 272

TabStop property, 59
TabVisible property for a
    TabSheet component, 272
Tag property, 59
    of forms, 34
templates, 22
    storing menu layouts as,
        114–115
text, searching for, 105–106
text editor, building a simple,
    94–97
text length in edit boxes, 76
text-only gauge, 140, 141
Text property of edit boxes, 76
TextFile file type, 315
TextOut function, 136
Thousands property of the
    UpDown component, 257
Thread Status window, 24
tick marks, setting additional in
    track bars, 259
TickMarks property of the track
    bar component, 259
TickStyle property of the track
    bar component, 259
TimeFormat property of the
    media player component,
    175
timer component, 150, 151
timers inside Windows, 151
Title property of the Open File
    common dialog, 90–91
TitleFont property of a data
    grid, 229
TMemoryStatus class, 395
Tools⇨Environment Options
    command, 14
Tools⇨Image Editor command,
    34
Tools⇨Options⇨Environment
    command, 334
Top property, 57
    of forms, 30
TopRow property of a draw grid
    component, 187
Towers of Hanoi puzzle
    program, 129–133
Trace Into command, 338
Trace Into speed button, 338
track bar, 258
track bar component, 256,
    259–260
track bars, highlighting ranges
    on, 259–260
TrackLength property of the
    media player component,
    175

TrackPosition property of the
    media player component,
    175
Tracks property of the media
    player component, 175
TransIsolation property of the
    database component, 251
Transparent color combo box,
    265
transparent-drawing feature of
    image list, 265–266
Transparent property of label
    components, 75
tree nodes, properties of, 267
tree of lines in outlines, 181
tree view component, 256, 266
    events for, 267–268
    properties of, 267
Trim function, 406
TrimLeft function, 406
TrimRight function, 406
True/False ParentColor
    property, 56
True/False properties, 36
TrueType fonts, 98
truth table, 317–318
try..except exception handling,
    336
try..finally exception handling,
    336–337
TTreeNodes objects, 267
type, 304; data types
type declaration block, 287, 300,
    304
typecasting, 310–311, 314–315
typed constant, 311
typed file, 315

• U •

underline style, setting in forms,
    33
Unicode characters in
    PWideChar, 309
Unicode standard, 306
union (+), 314, 318
unit keyword, 286
units, 286, 300
    deleting from the uses clause,
        293
    parts of, 286
Unit1, 285, 286, 291
universal No symbol, changing
    the cursor to, 59, 60
unknown identifier error
    message, 293, 294, 330

UnselectColor property of the tab set component, 162
untyped file, 315
UpCase function, 41
UpDown component, 255, 256
  combining with an edit box, 258
  events for, 257–258
  properties of, 256–257
UpGlyph property of the SpinButton component, 153
UpperCase function, 406
USER Windows DLL, 298
uses clause, 287, 300
  adding units to, 298–299
  deleting units from, 293

• V •

value lists, 28
Value property of the SpinEdit component, 154
var, 288, 302
VAR parameters, 324–325
variable declaration block, 288, 300
variables, 288, 302
  assigning to a function's return value, 372
  declaring, 302
  examining, 340
  naming, 303
  scoping, 302
vertical scroll bar, displaying, 30
vertical track bar, 259
VertScrollBar property of forms, 30
View⇨Call Stack command, 341
View⇨Object Inspector command, 26
View⇨Project Source command, 285
ViewStyle property of a list view, 276
Virtual Key (VK) left arrow, 40
Visible property
  of components, 58
  setting for a field, 231
VisibleButtons property
  of the database navigator, 234–235
  of the media player component, 174

Visual Basic (VB)
  compared to Delphi, 2
  limitations of, 2–3
visual inheritance, 26

• W •

WantReturns property of memo boxes, 80
WantTabs property of memo boxes, 80
warnings about code, 331, 332
Watch List window, 24
Watch window, variables in, 341
WAV files, 177
  compared to MIDI files, 177
Web, 343
Web browser, deploying an ActiveForm to, 356–357
Web Deploy command, 356
Web pages
  creating with an animated page counter, 359–363
  programming in Pascal, 353
Web server applications, creating as Dynamic Link Libraries (DLLs), 48
WebBrows application, 344
where clause with the SQL select command, 247–248
WHILE..DO loop, 322, 323, 324
WideChar data type, 306
Width property, 57
  of forms, 30
  of the image list component, 264
Win32 page in the Component palette, 48
Win 3.1 page in the Component palette, 48
Window List window, 24
WindowMenu property of forms, 35
windows, 15
  centering components in, 53, 54
  tabbed multipage, 12
Windows 3.1 crashes, 150
Windows 95
  bars, 258–262
  Color dialog, 101
  components, 255, 256
  crashes, 14
  exiting, 389–392
  progress bar component, 259
  stack overflows and, 375

status bar, 260
track bar component, 259–260
Windows
  timers inside, 151
  versions of, 396
Windows colors, selecting from all possible, 29
Windows Control Panel, color settings in, 69
Windows directory, locating, 392
Windows DLLs, 298
Windows fonts, choosing from, 97–100
Windows help systems, creating for programs, 58
Windows libraries, 298
Windows Multiple Document Interface. See Multiple Document Interface (MDI)
Windows unit, 287
WindowState property of forms, 33
WinExec function, 384–385
Wingdings font, 56
  displaying all the characters in, 188–189
  pictographs from, 143
WITH Sender As TLabel DO expression, 62
WordWrap property of label components, 75
WordWrap True/False property of memo boxes, 80
Wrap property of the UpDown component, 257

• X •

X dimension, 65
XOR operator, 317

• Y •

Y dimension, 65

• Z •

Z dimension, 65
Z-order for components, 65–66
zero-delimited string, 308